Economic Growth and Development

Economic Growth and Development

Nathan Saunders

STATES
ACADEMIC PRESS
www.statesacademicpress.com

Economic Growth and Development
Nathan Saunders
ISBN: 978-1-63989-164-1 (Hardback)

Published by States Academic Press,
109 South 5th Street,
Brooklyn, NY 11249, USA

Cataloging-in-Publication Data

Economic growth and development / Nathan Saunders.
p. cm.
Includes bibliographical references and index.
ISBN 978-1-63989-164-1
1. Economic development. 2. Development economics. 3. Economic policy. 4. Economics. I. Saunders, Nathan.
HD75 .E26 2022
338.9--dc23

For more information regarding States Academic Press and its products, please visit the publisher's website www.statesacademicpress.com

Table of Contents

	Preface	**VII**
Chapter 1	**Introduction to Economic Growth and Development**	**1**
	a. Keynesian Theory	7
	b. Labour and Technology in Growth Models	15
	c. Harrod Domar Model	21
Chapter 2	**Neo-Classical Growth Models**	**27**
	a. Production Function	27
	b. Uzawa Two Sector Growth Model	40
	c. Uzawa Steady State Growth Theorem	47
	d. Golden Rate	49
	e. Solow Growth Model	56
	f. AK Model	72
	g. Nelson-Phelps Model	77
Chapter 3	**Theories of Development**	**83**
	a. Adam Smith's Theory of Development	83
	b. Human Capital	90
	c. Marxian Theory of Development	96
	d. Ricardian Theory of Development	109
	e. Schumpeter's Capitalist Development	114
	f. Malthusian Theory of Economic Development	124
	g. J.S Mill's Theory of Development	127
Chapter 4	**Dual Economy Models**	**130**
	a. Role of State	130
	b. Balanced and Unbalanced Growth	133
	c. Leibenstein Critical Minimum Effort Theory	139
	d. Theory of Dualism	143
	e. Big Push Theory	147
	f. Lewis Model of Unlimited Labour Supply	153
	g. Ranis and Fei Model	158
	h. Harris Todaro Migration Model	163
	i. Low Level of Equilibrium Trap	165
Chapter 5	**Planning and Governance**	**169**
	a. Trade in Developing World	169
	b. Agriculture and Globalisation	175
	c. Prebisch and Singer: Theory of International Trade	187
	d. WTO and Developing Countries	194
	e. Smart Cities	202
	f. Dual Gap Analysis	207
	g. Payments and Tariff Protection	211

h. Project Evaluation and UNIDO Guidelines 215
i. Static and Dynamic Gains from Trade 221
j. Staple Theory 230

Permissions

Index

Preface

The increase in the market value of various goods produced and services offered by an economy over a period of time is known as economic growth. It is measured in terms of an increase or decrease in the GDP or market productivity. Economic development is concerned with different aspects of the society such as employment, education, health, social exclusion, environmental sustainability and safety. Some of the important factors which affect the economic growth of a country are natural resources, capital accumulation, population and technological progress. The aspects of economic development are studied under the subject of development economics. The key areas of research under this subject are geography and development, and economic development and ethnicity. Most of the topics introduced in this book cover new techniques and applications of economics of growth and development. It picks up individual branches and explains their need and contribution in the context of a growing economy. This book attempts to assist those with a goal of delving into the field of economics of growth and development.

A detailed account of the significant topics covered in this book is provided below:

Chapter 1- Economic growth refers to the increase which is observed in the national output. The improvement in the living standards and quality of life falls under the umbrella of economic development. This is an introductory chapter which will introduce briefly all the significant aspects of economic growth and development such as labour and technology in growth models and Harrod Domar model.

Chapter 2- The neo-classical growth theory explains how a stable economic growth rate results from a combination of three factors, labor, capital and technology. Some of the neo-classical growth models are Uzawa two sector growth model, Uzawa steady state growth theorem, golden rate and Solow growth model. This chapter discusses in detail these neo-classical growth models.

Chapter 3- Theories which deal with how desirable change in the society can be achieved are termed as theories of development. A few major theories studied within this field are Adam Smith's theory of development, Marxian theory of development, Ricardian theory of development, Schumpeter's capitalist development and Malthusian theory of economic development. All the diverse theories of development have been carefully analyzed in this chapter.

Chapter 4- The existence of two distinct economic sectors within one country, which have different levels of development, patterns of demand and technology, is termed as dual economy. A few models studied in relation to dual economy are vicious circle of poverty, balanced and unbalanced growth and Leibenstein critical minimum effort theory. The diverse facets of these theories have been thoroughly discussed in this chapter.

Chapter 5- Planning and governance have a significant impact on growth and development of an economy. Some of the major areas of study related to planning and governance with respect to economic growth and development are trade in developing world, role of MNC's in developing countries and dual gap analysis. The topics elaborated in this chapter will help in gaining a better perspective about these aspects of planning and governance.

I would like to make a special mention of my publisher who considered me worthy of this opportunity and also supported me throughout the process. I would also like to thank the editing team at the back-end who extended their help whenever required.

Nathan Saunders

1

Introduction to Economic Growth and Development

Economic growth refers to the increase which is observed in the national output. The improvement in the living standards and quality of life falls under the umbrella of economic development. This is an introductory chapter which will introduce briefly all the significant aspects of economic growth and development such as labour and technology in growth models and Harrod Domer model.

Economic development can be referred as the quantitative and qualitative changes in the economy. Arthur Lewis defined economic development as the enlargement of the range of people choices. Economic development focuses on the spectrum of spheres ranging from health, education, employment, safety, environmental sustainability, social exclusion, gender empowerment, infrastructure, and other activities whereas economic growth measured in terms of rise in GDP or market productivity.

The study of economic development was borne out of an extension to traditional economics that focused entirely on national product, or the aggregate output of goods and services, the latter known as economic growth. Economic development mainly concerned in expansion of people's entitlements and their corresponding capabilities, morbidity, nourishment, literacy, education, and other socio-economic indicators.

Economic growth, that is, more income is only one of the things desired by poor people. Adequate nutrition, safe water, better medical services, more and better schooling for their children, cheap transport, adequate shelter, continuing employment and secure livelihood, and productive remunerative satisfying job do not show up in higher income per head. There are even other non-material benefits that are often more highly valued by poor people than material benefits but they do not reflect in higher income figure. For instances, freedom to choose, movement, speech, safe working condition, expressing cultural, regional, linguistic and religious identity, empowerment are some factors often more important than income.

It is quite often observed in the many parts of world that economic growth can be rapid without the improvement in the quality of life. In other words, per capita increase in GDP only benefits a small section of minority population and rest of the vast majority of population deprived from the fruits of increased GDP. It led to concentration of wealth in few hands, stark inequality, existence of dual economy where one sect enjoyed the increased production of goods and services and remaining large section of population starving and yet to receive any benefits of higher GDP.

Economic growth set the prerequisite condition for economic development. The economic growth accompanied by proper distribution of resources across the population, building institutional mechanisms which ensure qualitative change in the lives of people, and environmental sustainability guaranteed the economic development. It has been observed that there is positive correlation between incomes per head and indicators of human development. It does not refer that higher income led higher development since many countries have achieved high human development at low level of income. This correlation depend on how additional income from growth being used for public education, health, and employment opportunities. Economic is indeed important, not for itself, but for what it allows a country to do with the resources that generated, expanding both individual incomes and the public revenue that can be used to meet the social commitment. Initial endowments like distribution of assets are also important factor in determining economic development. If land are fairly distributed among the population and education is accessible for masses, then the benefits of economic growth can easily percolate down to the end of the population.

Economic growth is quite often considered to be an essential part of development. But growth (known as continuing increase of the quantity of goods and services produced and consumed over time) is simply the inter-temporal dimension of any policy objective, although it has been wrongly monopolized by production and consumption, it should apply to poverty to poverty reduction, employment, investment, a more equitable income distribution, environment protection, leisure and, of course, also to income. But once you specify for income, consumption and production, the 'What?' 'To whom?' 'By whom?' 'For what?' and 'When?' growth becomes the incidental result, not the objective, of a sensible economic policy. Growth is too unspecified, abstract, aggregate and unbounded to be a sensible objective of policy. It also implies an infinite horizon, without the limits to increases in income. What matters is the composition of national income, to what uses it is put, its distribution among beneficiaries, now and for future generations; and with how much efforts and in what conditions it is produced. If and only if the extra resources resulting from growth go largely to the poor, and if they are spent on public health and education, will a contribution to human development result.

In measuring economic growth, the national income is a quite inadequate measure of human development for several reasons. It counts only goods and services that are exchanged for money, leaving out of account the large amount of work done inside family, mainly by women, and work done voluntarily for children or older people or in communities. Public services are counted at their cost, so that doubling the wages of all public services appears to double their contribution to welfare or development. National income accounting does not distinguish between goods and regrettable necessities, like military expenditure or anti-crime expenditure, products needed to combat 'bads'. Addictive eating and drinking is counted twice, when the food and the alcohol are consumed, and when large sums are spent on diet industry and on cures for alcoholism. Much of what is now counted as economic growth is really either combating evils, and fixing the blunders and social decay from the past, or borrowing resources from the future, or shifting functions from community and household to the market.

One more dimension that untouched in discussion of economic growth is related to gender issues. In events where women are provided opportunity to choose the size of their family it has been found that without adverse economic and social consequences, smaller families are indeed chosen. With human development through expanding education, especially for women and girls, the reduction in infant mortality, improved medical facilities led to significant fall in fertility rate among women. There are strong evidences which show that more surviving children also led to reduction in population growth by evading uncertainties in family. Human development is a powerful tool to curb the population growth, and reduced population growth open up the news ways of economic advancement.

Economists have suggested the division of all countries into three groups: low, medium, and high level of human development. For countries with low level of human development the basic human development Index can be used to rank their performance. For countries with medium value of human development They also add one supplementary indicator to each of the three basic variables, life expectancy, literacy, and log of GDP per head. In the longevity category they add infant and child mortality (under five); in the education category they add the secondary school enrollment; and income category they add the incidence of income poverty in the country.

Factor Affecting Economic Growth

Natural Resources

The principal factor determining economic growth of a country is the natural resources. A country suffering from non-availability of natural resources would not be able develop rapidly. Having said this, it is also a recognized fact that presence of abundant resources does not guarantee the economic growth; it must be accompanied by proper exploitation of these resources. If the existing resources are not properly utilized or exploited, the country would not be able to develop. One of the main factors which ensure the utilization of resources is technological advancement. Therefore, natural resources can be put in right place to augment economic growth through introducing improved technology. As pointed out by economist that the value of resource depend upon its usefulness, and the usefulness of resource mainly depend on accommodating and updating the technology which can be used a means to define its usefulness.

It is often said that economic growth could be achieved even when an economy is inadequate in natural resources. On such country is Japan which even deficient in natural resource but one of the developed countries of the world because it has been succeeded in forming human capital and discover new used of its limited resources. A country which considered poor in resources in one point of time may considered rich in resources after passage of time, not because of new avenues of resources are discovered but equally because creating new resources and using limited resources most efficient way. Moreover, by importing those resources from other countries, it has been able to overcome the inadequacy of natural resources through using the superior technology, efficient management skills.

Thus for economic growth mere presence of abundant resources are not enough. What is essential is their proper exploitation through improved technology and efficient management skills so there would be little wastage of scarce resources.

Capital Accumulation

The second most important factor in economic growth is capital accumulation. Capital means stock of physical reproducible factor of production. When the capital stock grows over period of time, this is defined as capital accumulation. The process of capital accumulation is cumulative and self-sustaining provided three inter-related stages preceded:

- The existence of continuous rise in saving.

- To us these saving for investment in capital goods.
- Intermediaries to mobilize saving and divert them for investment.

One of the prominent reason of lower growth in underdeveloped countries is lower saving, equally opposite in developed countries higher saving ensure the capital formation and sustain continuous growth. Due to low propensity to save in least developed countries, voluntary saving are not sufficient to ensure desired growth. Due to low level of income poor countries are close to subsistence level of consumption which led to low level of saving. In such circumstances possibility to raise saving are dismal, and economic growth would rely on other sources of capital accumulation, like external loans, grants or aid.

Capital formation is the key component of economic growth. On the one hand it ensure effective demand, and other hand, it creates productive efficiency for future production. Higher investment in capital goods and consumer goods industries creates employment opportunities which led to higher consumption reflects in effective demand. On the other hand new avenues for capital goods open up the ways for productive efficiency in production. The processes of capital accumulation reflect in higher national output, essential to meet the demand of increasing population.

Technological Progress

Technological changes are count as the most important factor in the process of economic growth. They are mostly referring as the change in mode of production through new technique emerges out from research or innovation. Changes in technology lead to increase in productivity of labour, capital and other factors used in production. Schumpeter regards innovation as most important technological factor in economic growth. Modern economic growth theories even assume that without technical progress, a country cannot sustain the growth in per capita income indefinitely. Due to low technological progress in least developed countries they are not able to break the vicious circle of underdevelopment. Developed countries are succeeded in continuous adaptation of new technology due to higher spending in research and development activities.

Population

Population growth is also another important factor which affects the economic growth. There are evidences which shows that population growth systematically change with the overall development of a society. The changes in population growth along with development process normally are known as demographic transition. The idea is very simple, when the population growth is high, economy has to put more effort for achieving higher growth since higher population pull down the per capita income growth and vice versa. A strong family planning targets or the provision of incentive to have less children, spread of education can pull down the population growth and permit long-run growth.

Marketable Surplus of Agriculture

Increase in agricultural production accompanied by a rise in productivity is important from the point of view of the development of a country. But what is more important is that the marketable surplus of agriculture increases. The term 'marketable surplus' refers to the excess of output in the agricultural sector over and above what is required to allow the rural population to subsist.

The importance of the marketable surplus in a developing economy emanates from the fact that the urban industrial population subsists on it. With the development of an economy, the ratio of the urban population increases and increasing demands are made on agriculture for food grains. These demands must be met adequately; otherwise the consequent scarcity of food in urban areas will arrest growth.

In case a country fails to produce a sufficient marketable surplus, it will be left with no choice except to import food grains which may cause a balance of payments problem. If some country wants to step-up the tempo of industrialization, it must not allow its agriculture to lag behind. The supply of the farm products particularly food grains, must increase, as the setting-up of industries in cities attracts a steady flow of population from the countryside.

Conditions in Foreign Trade

The classical theory of trade has been used by economists for a long time to argue that trade between nations is always beneficial to them. The theory suggests that the presently less developed countries should specialize in production of primary products as they have comparative cost advantage in their production. The developed countries, on the contrary, have a comparative cost advantage in manufactures including machines and equipment and should accordingly specialize in them. In the recent years, a powerful school has emerged under the leadership of Raul Prebisch which questions the merits of unrestricted trade between developed and under-developed countries on both theoretical and empirical grounds.

Foreign trade has proved to be beneficial to countries which have been able to set-up industries in a relatively short period. These countries sooner or later captured international markets for their industrial products. Therefore, a developing country should not only try to become self-reliant in capital equipment as well as other industrial products as early as possible, but it should also attempt to push the development of its industries to such a high level that in course of time manufactured goods replace the primary products as the country's principal exports. In countries like India the macro-economic interconnections are crucial and the solutions of the problems of these economies cannot be found merely through the foreign trade sector or simple recipes associated with it.

Economic System

The economic system and the historical setting of a country also decide the development prospects to a great extent. There was a time when a country could have a laissez faire economy and yet face no difficulty in making economic progress. In today's entirely different world situation, a country would find it difficult to grow along the England's path of development.

The third world countries of the present times will have to find their own path of development. They cannot hope to make much progress by adopting a laissez faire economy. Further, these countries cannot raise necessary resources required for development either through colonial exploitation or by foreign trade. They now have only two choices before them:

- They can follow a capitalist path of development which will require an efficient market system supported by a rational interventionist role of the State.

- The other course open to them is that of economic planning.

The latest experiments in economic planning in China have shown impressive results. Therefore, from the failure of economic planning in the former Soviet Union and the erstwhile East European socialist countries it would be wrong to conclude that a planned economy has built-in inefficiencies which are bound to arrest economic growth.

Non-Economic Factors in Economic Development

From the available historical evidence, it is now obvious that non- economic factors are as much important in development as economic factors. Here we attempt to explain how they exercise influence on the process of economic development.

- Human Resources: Human resources are an important factor in economic development. Man provides labour power for production and if in a country labour is efficient and skilled, its capacity to contribute to growth will decidedly be high. The productivity of illiterate, unskilled, disease ridden and superstitious people is generally low and they do not provide any hope to developmental work in a country. But in case human resources remain either unutilized or the manpower management remains defective, the same people who could have made a positive contribution to growth activity prove to be a burden on the economy.
- Technical Know-How and General Education: It has never been, doubted that the level of technical know-how has a direct bearing on the pace of development. As the scientific and technological knowledge advances, man discovers more and more sophisticated techniques of production which steadily raise the productivity levels. Schumpeter was deeply impressed by the innovations done by the entrepreneurs, and he attributed much of the capitalist development to this role of the entrepreneurial class. Since technology has now become highly sophisticated, still greater attention has to be given to Research and Development for further advancement. Under assumptions of a linear homogeneous production function and a neutral technical change which does not affect the rate of substitution between capital and labour, Robert M. Solow has observed that the contribution of education to the increase in output per man hour in the United States between 1909 and 1949 was more than that of any other factor.
- Political Freedom: Looking to the world history of modern times one learns that the processes of development and underdevelopment are interlinked and it is wrong to view them in isolation. We all know that the under-development of India, Pakistan, Bangladesh, Sri Lanka, Malaysia, Kenya and a few other countries, which were in the past British colonies, was linked with the development of England. England recklessly exploited them and appropriated a large portion of their economic surplus.
- Social Organisation: Mass participation in development programs is a pre-condition for accelerating the growth process. However, people show interest in the development activity only when they feel that the fruits of growth will be fairly distributed. Experiences from a number of countries suggest that whenever the defective social organisation allows some elite groups to appropriate the benefits of growth, the general mass of people develop apathy towards State's development programs. Under the circumstances, it is futile to hope that masses will participate in the development projects undertaken by the State. Growth

of monopolies in industries and concentration of economic power in the modern sector is now an undisputed fact. Furthermore, the new agricultural strategy has given rise to a class of rich peasantry creating widespread disparities in the countryside.

- Corruption: Corruption is rampant in developing countries at various levels and it operates as a negative factor in their growth process. Until and unless these countries root-out corruption in their administrative system, it is most natural that the capitalists, traders and other powerful economic classes will continue to exploit national resources in their personal interests. The regulatory system is also often misused and the licenses are not always granted on merit. The art of tax evasion has been perfected in the less developed countries by certain sections of the society and often taxes are evaded with the connivance of the government officials.
- Desire to Develop: Development activity is not a mechanical process. The pace of economic growth in any country depends to a great extent on people's desire to develop. If in some country level of consciousness is low and the general mass of people has accepted poverty as its fate, then there will be little hope for development. According to Richard T. Gill, "The point is that economic development is not a mechanical process; it is not a simple adding- up of assorted factors. Ultimately, it is a human enterprise. And like all human enterprises, its outcome will depend finally on the skill, quality and attitudes of the men who undertake".

Keynesian Theory

Origin of Keynesian Theory

During the Great Depression of the 1930s, existing economic theory was unable either to explain the causes of the severe worldwide economic collapse or to provide an adequate public policy solution to jump-start production and employment. British economist John Maynard Keynes spearheaded a revolution in economic thinking that overturned the then prevailing idea that free markets would automatically provide full employment that is, that everyone who wanted a job would have one as long as workers were flexible in their wage demands. The main plank of Keynes's theory, which has come to bear his name, is the assertion that aggregate demand measured as the sum of spending by households, businesses, and the government is the most important driving force in an economy. Keynes further asserted that free markets have no self-balancing mechanisms that lead to full employment. Keynesian economists justify government intervention through public policies that aim to achieve full employment and price stability.

The Revolutionary Idea

Keynes argued that inadequate overall demand could lead to prolonged periods of high unemployment. An economy's output of goods and services is the sum of four components: consumption, investment, government purchases, and net exports (the difference between what a country sells to and buys from foreign countries). Any increase in demand has to come from one of these four components. But during a recession, strong forces often dampen demand as spending goes down. For example, during economic downturns uncertainty often erodes consumer confidence, causing them to reduce their spending, especially on discretionary purchases like a house or a car. This reduction in spending by consumers can result in less investment spending by businesses, as firms respond to weakened demand for their products. This puts the task of increasing output on the shoulders of the government. According to Keynesian economics, state intervention is necessary to moderate the booms and busts in economic activity, otherwise known as the business cycle. There are three principal tenets in the Keynesian description of how the economy works:

- Aggregate demand is influenced by many economic decisions—public and private. Private sector decisions can sometimes lead to adverse macroeconomic outcomes, such as reduction in consumer spending during a recession. These market failures sometimes call for active policies by the government, such as a fiscal stimulus package (explained below). Therefore, Keynesian economics supports a mixed economy guided mainly by the private sector but partly operated by the government.

- Prices, and especially wages, respond slowly to changes in supply and demand, resulting in periodic shortages and surpluses, especially of labor.

- Changes in aggregate demand, whether anticipated or unanticipated, have their greatest short-run effect on real output and employment, not on prices. Keynesians believe that, because prices are somewhat rigid, fluctuations in any component of spending consumption, investment, or government expenditures cause output to change. If government spending increases, for example and all other spending components remain constant, then output will increase. Keynesian models of economic activity also include a multiplier effect; that is, output changes by some multiple of the increase or decrease in spending that caused the change. If the fiscal multiplier is greater than one, then a one dollar increase in government spending would result in an increase in output greater than one dollar.

Stabilizing the Economy

No policy prescriptions follow from these three tenets alone. What distinguishes Keynesians from other economists is their belief in activist policies to reduce the amplitude of the business cycle, which they rank among the most important of all economic problems. Rather than seeing unbalanced government budgets as wrong, Keynes advocated so-called countercyclical fiscal policies that act against the direction of the business cycle. For example, Keynesian economists would advocate deficit spending on labor-intensive infrastructure projects to stimulate employment and stabilize wages during economic downturns. They would raise taxes to cool the economy and prevent inflation when there is abundant demand-side growth. Monetary policy could also be used to stimulate the economy—for example, by reducing interest rates to encourage investment. The exception occurs during a liquidity trap, when increases in the money stock fail to lower interest rates and, therefore, do not boost output and employment.

Keynes argued that governments should solve problems in the short run rather than wait for market forces to fix things over the long run, because, as he wrote, "In the long run, we are all dead." This does not mean that Keynesians advocate adjusting policies every few months to keep the economy at full employment. In fact, they believe that governments cannot know enough to fine-tune successfully.

Keynesianism Evolves

Even though his ideas were widely accepted while Keynes was alive, they were also scrutinized and contested by several contemporary thinkers. Particularly noteworthy were his arguments with the Austrian School of Economics, whose adherents believed that recessions and booms are a part of the natural order and that government intervention only worsens the recovery process. Keynesian economics dominated economic theory and policy after World War II until the 1970s, when many advanced economies suffered both inflation and slow growth, a condition dubbed "stagflation." Keynesian theory's popularity waned then because it had no appropriate policy response for stagflation. Monetarist economists doubted the ability of governments to regulate the business cycle with fiscal policy and argued that judicious use of monetary policy (essentially controlling the supply of money to affect interest rates) could alleviate the crisis. Members of the monetarist school also maintained that money can.

Concepts of Keynesian Theory

Keynes wrote the General Theory following a meticulous plan. The clean structure of the volume makes it easier to understand Keynes' model and the postulated relationships between dependent and independent variables. The manuscript is organized in six books:

- Book I - Introduction: These three chapters focus on the problem of unemployment, criticize the classical economists, and give an overview of the system to be developed.
- Book II - Definitions and Ideas: This is a methodological section justifying the choice of units and the definitions of economic terms such as income, savings, and investment.
- Book III - The Propensity to Consume: This is a core chapter where the principle of effective demand is thoroughly explained, and the investment multiplier is introduced.
- Book IV - The Inducement to Invest: Here investment is described as determined by expectations and the rate of interest. The quantity of money and liquidity preference, in turn, determines the interest rate. The General Theory is hence complete.
- Book V - Money-Wages and Prices: This is a kind of complementary section bringing the employment function, prices and wages into a functional relationship.
- Book VI - Short Notes Suggested by the General Theory: The chapter about the trade cycle in this section illustrates the full dynamics of the Keynesian model.

Paul Krugman has said that the GT is like a meal, with an appetizer at the beginning (Book I) and dessert at the end (Book VI). The main course is contained in the Books II, III, and IV. Book V is more of a complement, to make the theory air-tight against classical explanations of unemployment based on the level of money-wages and prices.

The Principle of Effective Demand

The main idea introduced in Book I is the principle of effective demand. Classical theorists assume that all production generates its own demand (Say's Law). They equate production with income, and all income is used for acquiring all produced goods, supply and demand move in parallel until full employment is achieved. Keynes, however, makes a difference between production/supply, and demand the aggregate supply function is the total price of goods produced by employing N persons. The aggregate demand is that demand for goods caused by employing also N persons. Both curves are not the same the point where they meet is called the effective demand. "This is the substance of the General Theory".

Keynes explains why he will refer to output in terms of aggregate prices. Since there are many different industries, referring to physical output makes aggregation tricky or impossible. Employment is an independent variable and skilled labor can be handled as a multiple of unskilled labor. "I propose, therefore, to make use of only two fundamental units of quantity, namely quantities of money-value and quantities of employment". In Input-Output-Analysis we would represent the economy today by a matrix with n sectors (n rows and n columns) which describes the flow of physical products from one sector to the other. Multiplying this matrix with the vector of unitary prices for the n sectors, we can compute the total supply of each sector, and the sum of the supply of all sectors would produce the aggregate supply for the economy. However, Input-Output- Analysis was still in its infancy and its methods are missing in the General Theory.

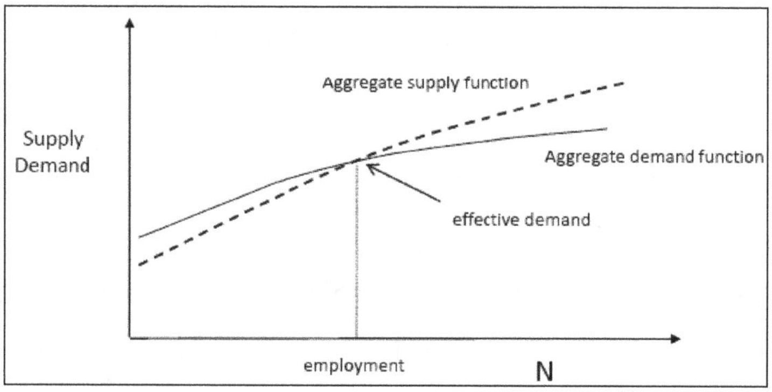

The effective demand is the crossing point of aggregate supply and aggregate demand.

The message to be developed in Books III and IV is that the effective demand can be too low so that full employment is not achieved. In figure, at low employment, there is more demand than supply (households have to spend their savings because the total wages are too low). Full employment requires a level of aggregate demand which is not available. Supply and demand meet therefore at an intermediate point, the effective demand. Aggregate demand can be too low due to insufficient consumption or insufficient investment, or both, the next problem to be explained.

The Propensity to Consume

Aggregate demand is composed of demand C for consumption and demand I for investment goods. Both are governed by different rules. In Keynes' opinion not all income Y transforms automatically into demand C+I for finished goods. The more income Y a person obtains the less proportion he or she spends in direct consumption C of goods. The consumption function bends down at higher levels of aggregate income.

In many appraisals of the Keynesian model, it is assumed that consumption is a linear function of income Y of the form $C = C_0 + cY$, where C_0 is a constant and c is the fraction of income devoted to consumption. In the General Theory there is no diagram of this function, and clear indications that Keynes did not consider consumption to be a linear function of income. He states clearly that "these reasons will lead, as a rule, to a greater proportion of income being saved as real income increases". That is, the constant c is lower, the higher Y is.

The factors determining the level of consumption are objective and subjective. Objective factors are, for example, wage changes, changes in net income, time discounting (that is, if it is better to buy something now or later), as well as future income expectations. Reduce to precaution, foresight, calculation, improvement, independence, enterprise, pride and avarice, as well as their opposites such as enjoyment, shortsightedness, generosity, miscalculation, ostentation, and extravagance.

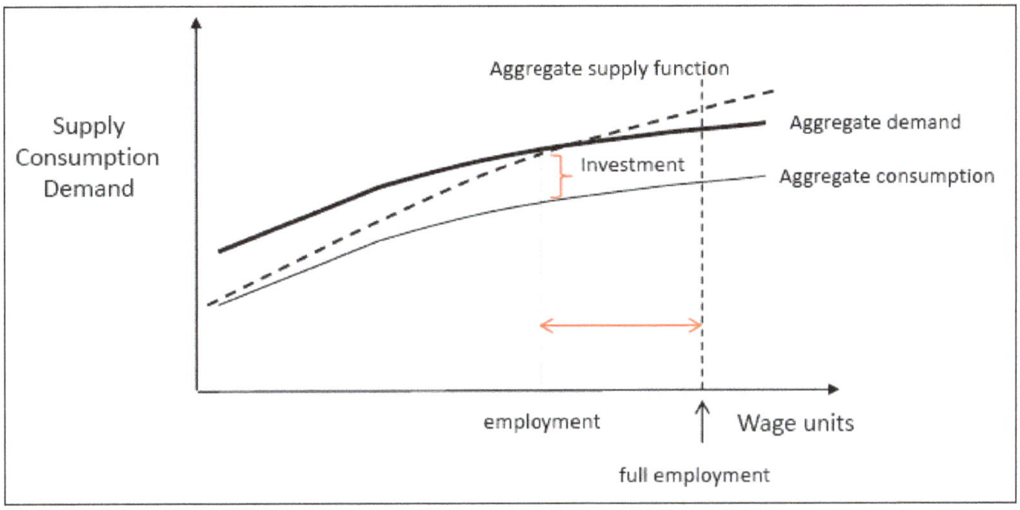

Aggregate demand and aggregate supply do not necessarily cross at full employment level.

Figure shows a hypothetical consumption function and a fixed level of investment I. Notice that the horizontal axis is now expressed in terms of wage units, so that the more employment we have, the more wages are paid. The horizontal axis provides us with a variable which can measure how much income is in the hands of society. The effect of a fixed investment I is to displace the consumption function up, producing an aggregate demand which intersects the aggregate supply function. In this example, equilibrium has been found at less than full employment. The later could only be achieved increasing the investment I, or raising the consumption function. Keynes considers the consumption function rather stable, so that filling the employment gap can only be done by increasing the investment.

Keynes considers thus the special concave form of the consumption function as a given, "The fundamental psychological law, upon which we are entitled to depend with great confidence both a priori from our knowledge of human nature and from the detailed facts of experience, is that men are disposed, as a rule and on the average, to increase their consumption as their income increases, but not by as much as the increase in their income.

Investment and the Multiplier

In conditions where full employment has not been reached, a higher level of investment can fill the gap between the consumption and the supply function. In figure now the horizontal axis represents spendable income and the vertical axis total demand. If income equals demand, the economy is in equilibrium (that is, all points in the 45 degree diagonal represent possible levels of equilibrium for different total incomes). Figure shows that increasing investment from I_1 to I_2 displaces aggregate demand from $C+I_1$ to $C+I_2$ so that a new equilibrium, at a higher level of income and employment, can be achieved. The interesting point here is that the increase ΔY in total income is higher than the increase ΔI of the investment. The red line shows the path to a new equilibrium: the higher investment leads to more demand and thus higher income. Higher income translates into higher consumption at the increased investment level. This leads again to higher income an so on, up to the new point where aggregate supply and demand are in equilibrium again. The income increase is a multiple of the increase in investment. Enter the multiplier.

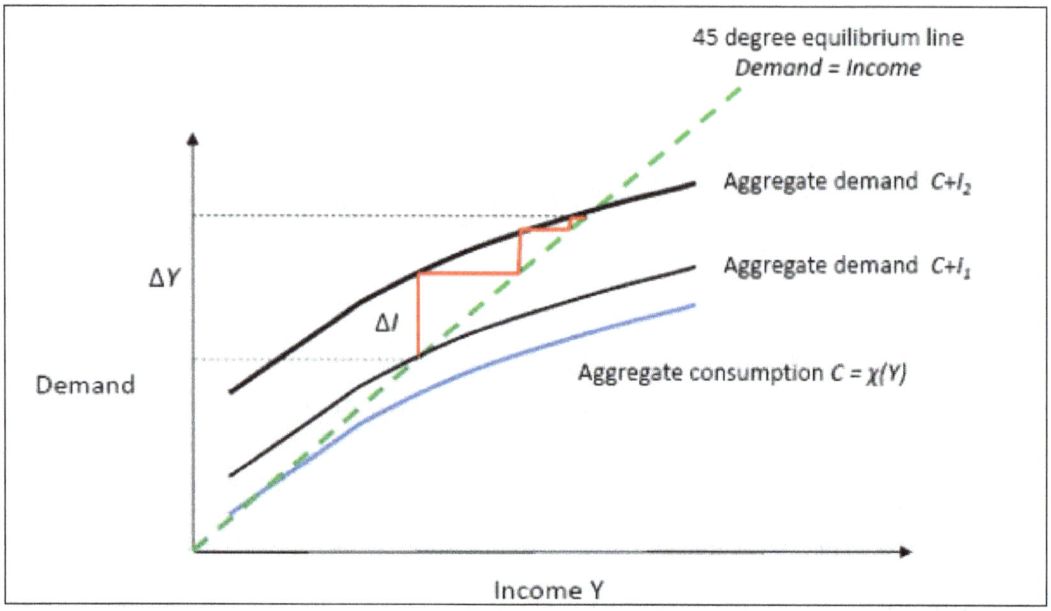

An increase $\Delta I = I_2 - I_1$ in investment produces an even higher increase ΔY in income.

The derivation of an expression for the multiplier is easy. The variables are income Y, consumption C and investment I. We know that $Y = C + I$ and assuming that consumption is a fraction c of Y we get $Y = cY + I$. Considering increments we obtain:

$$\Delta Y = c\Delta Y + \Delta I$$

and therefore,

$$\Delta Y = \frac{\Delta I}{1-c} = k\Delta I$$

The number k is called the "investment multiplier" or alternatively the "income multiplier". Since is lower than 1, the multiplier is higher than 1. Given Keynes "fundamental psychological law" the multiplier has to be always larger than 1.

This derivation is valid for small increments of the investment. For larger increments the assumption that c is constant does not hold and a more complex expression would have to be derived. The investment multiplier is thus a wonderful thing, most of all when society has reached a level of income with a low propensity to consume. If the private sector is not investing enough, the state can take the initiative and increase the level of investment. The effects spill over to all sectors of society.

Investment and the Interest Rate

Keynes rejects the classical theory according to which, the interest rate is determined by the equilibrium between supply and demand of loanable funds. In Keynes' model the interest rate is determined by the money supply and the curve of liquidity preference. Whatever the interest rate, for each amount of investment first the most productive capital goods will be bought, and then the less productive ones. The "schedule of the marginal efficiency of capital" is a decreasing function which relates total investment I to interest rate r. When the interest rate is high, only a few investment opportunities are profitable. When the interest rate is low, more money can be invested since more options are available.

The schedule of marginal efficiency is in part psychological, since it is determined by the expected future rewards of an investment. That is, economic pessimism can decrease investment for a given interest rate. Economic optimism can raise investment without any change of the interest rate. This is illustrated in figure where the different expected schedules for the marginal efficiency of capital displace upwards with increasing optimism. Given these expectations and the interest rate, the level of investment gets determined.

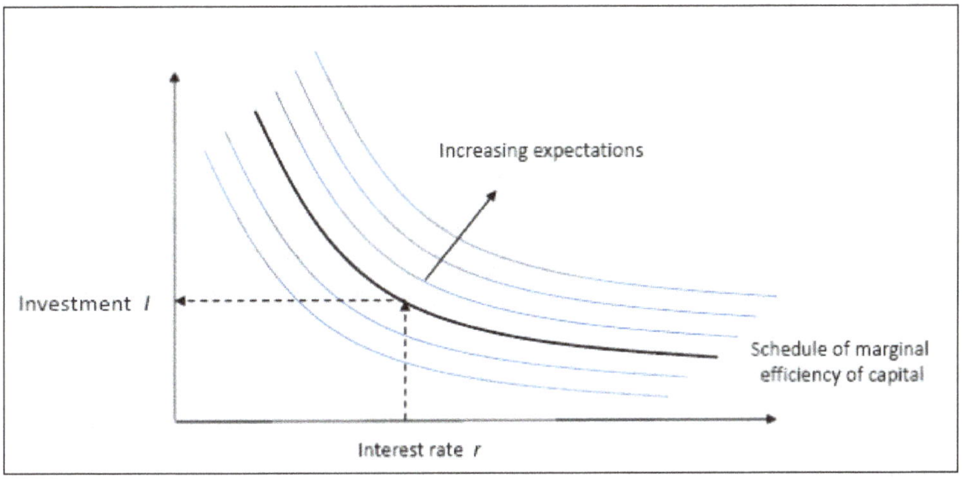

The expected schedule of the marginal efficiency of capital and the interest rate r determine the investment I.

However, investors can err on the side of caution if their expectations are too low. Here the state can intervene and give a little nudge to the economy.

The Money Supply, Liquidity Preference and the Interest Rate

For Keynes, the interest rate is what investors are ready to pay someone for his "liquidity". There are many reasons why a person would prefer to keep money unused, for future use, in consumption or investment, or as a precaution against unforeseen events. There can also be speculative motives. Keynes calls the cash held for future transactions or precaution M_1 and the cash held for speculative motive M_2, then:

$$M = M_1 + M_2 = L_1(Y) + L_2(r)$$

Where L_1 is a function of Y and the speculative liquidity preference is a function of the interest rate r.

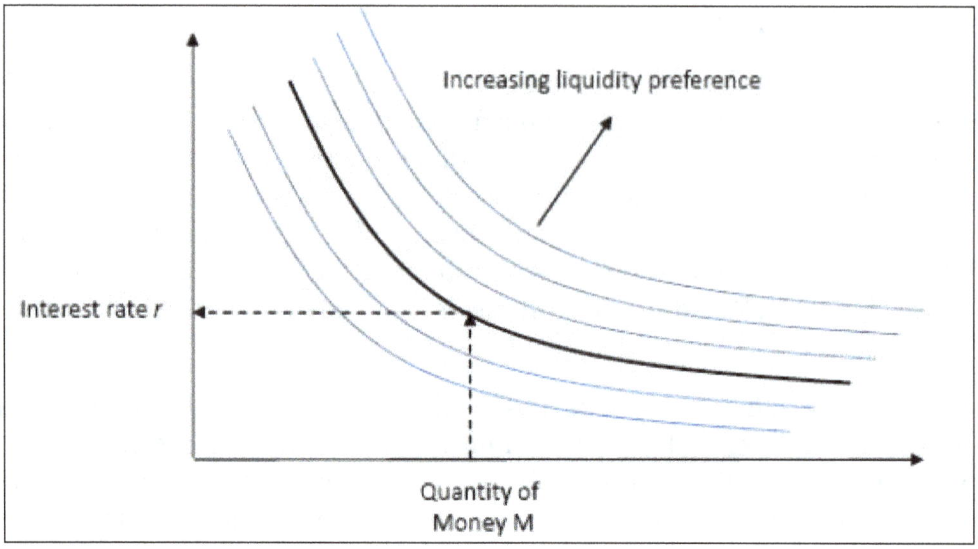

The current liquidity preference curve and the money supply determine the interest rate r.

Figure shows the way that the curve of liquidity preference determines the rate of interest. The various curves denote different levels of income and different psychological levels of liquidity preference (for example during a crisis). But in general, the more money that is available, the lower the rate of interest, and vice versa. Therefore, given a certain liquidity preference and a certain quantity of money, the rate of interest is fixed as shown in the figure. Keynes points out, "Liquidity-preference is a potentiality or functional tendency, which fixes the quantity of money which the public will hold when the rate of interest is given; so that if r is the rate of interest, M the quantity of money and L the function of liquidity-preference, we have. This is where, and how, the quantity of money enters into the economic scheme".

Keynes Economic Machine

The four figures above capture the essentials of Keynes' General Theory, Keynes proceeds to summarize the variables:

- The independent variables are propensity to consume, the schedule of the marginal efficiency of capital, and the rate of interest (they are capable of further analysis).
- The dependent variables are the volume of employment and the national income.

And Krugman's own summary is in the form of bullet points:

- Economies can and often do suffer from an overall lack of demand, which leads to involuntary unemployment.
- The economy's automatic tendency to correct shortfalls in demand, if it exists at all, operates slowly and painfully.
- Government policies to increase demand, by contrast, can reduce unemployment quickly.
- Sometimes increasing the money supply won't be enough to persuade the private sector to spend more, and government spending must step into the breach".

Labour and Technology in Growth Models

The history of development or growth economics can be said to begin with the popularization of the ideas which defined the school of economic thought known as mercantilism. The original theory of mercantilism, which, as the name suggests was economics written for, and by, merchant capital, has most likely been rescued from a place in the footnotes of the history of economic ideas by resurgence in the roster of proponents of economic nationalism and neo-mercantilism.

Mercantilism was the belief that a nation's prosperity was gleaned from its stores of bullion (gold, silver and other precious commodities), standing in as it were for a modern conception of capital. In order to ensure a steady improvement of the nation's material well-being, it was considered vital to secure an ever-increasing stock of bullion through the maintenance of a highly positive trade balance of exports over imports, and/or through acquisitions of colonial dependencies from which bullion could be extracted without the need for a fair compensation. This idea that economic development was essentially a zerosum game for the nation-states involved, and the recipe for success that the conception called for, have come to be crystallized in the adage "beggar thy neighbor".

The literature on development or growth theory after the Second World War has borrowed heavily from the Harrodian framework. The Harrod-Domar model of growth, named after Roy Harrod and Evsey Domar , is an early and very influential post keynesian model of economic growth. This section relies on Harrod's original explication of the framework. The Harrod-Domar model explains a nation's growth rate in terms of a dynamic between three factors – the savings rate, the level of capital productivity at the margin, and rate of capital decay or depreciation. Harrod talks about three different kinds of growth rates in the economy. These are the warranted rate of growth, the actual rate of growth and lastly, the natural rate of growth. The warranted rate of growth was one where each capitalist's ex-ante investment plans are fully realized ex-post, that is, "The warranted rate of growth is taken to be that rate of growth which, if it occurs, will leave all parties satisfied that they have produced neither more nor less than the right amount. Or, to state the matter otherwise, it will put them into a frame of mind which will cause them to give such orders as will maintain the same rate of growth.

A close conceptual parallel to what Harrod may have had in mind with the warranted rate of growth is the Nash equilibrium solution concept in the field of Game Theory applied to the field of investment demand, the warranted rate of growth is that rate of growth at which all investment demand and investment supply decisions are Nash. This warranted rate of growth, except under exceptional conditions, would most likely diverge from the actual rate of growth observed for some given period, for "random and seasonal causes". The third, the natural rate of growth, is the growth rate of the economy in 'efficiency units'. It represents the maximal rate of growth of national income given the constraints of population size, state of technology and the 'leisure preference schedule' the supply of wage labor, assuming there is full employment of capital and labor resources.

Harrod, in his 1939 article, lays down the three axiomatic propositions his model builds on, essentially meant to be a dynamic model of business cycles in a mature capitalist economy, as, firstly, that the most important determinant of a nation's supply of savings is it's level of income; secondly, the demand for savings is determined the rate of increase of national income; and thirdly, that demand equals supply. For Harrod, dynamic theory did not imply a model which is dynamic only in so far as it presents a series of static 'equilibrium' snapshots of the economy for any given time (which Harrod felt was the sum outcome of lagged theories of growth, which also purport to be dynamic theories). Properly, for Harrod, dynamic theory was one employing propositions involving the rate of national income growth as an unknown variable. He reports his model as one that 'marries the accelerator principle with the multiplier.

Harrod's model is infamous in economics for its supposedly dismal outlook for stable economic progress. In Harrod's framework, deviations of the actual rate from the warranted rate of growth, in either direction, are explosive, so that a mismatch of actual rate of growth vis-à-vis the warranted rate pulls the economy further and further away from equilibrium between the two. Furthermore, there is no inherent mechanism in the model to ensure the coincidence of the warranted rate of growth with the natural rate of growth, despite the fact those dislocations between the two. A 'proper' or full employment warranted rate of growth above the natural rate (which acts as a ceiling to the actual rate of growth) would imply that an economy would permanently abide a chronic tendency to depression. The tensions between the warranted rate of growth and firstly, the actual rate of growth, and, secondly, the natural rate of growth, have come to be known as the 'two knife-edges' in the Harrod- Domar model.

Historically, the next major advance in development theory in economics came with the first balanced growth doctrine, attributed to the Krakow-born, Austrain-school economist Paul Rosenstein-Rodan, who, in his 1943 article "Problems of Industrialisation of Eastern and South-Eastern Europe", first promulgated the Big Push Model of economic growth. The Big Push doctrine argues for the implementation of generalized large scale investment programmes aimed at industrializing underdeveloped nations with surplus workforces engaged in a traditional or pre-modern primary sector. The rationale for the Big Push revolves around three indivisibilities - that of production (with respect to input-, process-, or output-indivisibility), complementarity of consumption/demand and indivisibility of savings supply. These fundamental indivisibilities give rise to external economies which must be addressed and exploited by any strategy of growth if it is to be successful. Successfully exploiting the eternal economies caused by the various indivisibilities can allow a developing nation to find increasing returns to factor, and economies of scale in the long run.

Among other models recognized in the classical development literature as pioneering the balanced growth doctrine, RagnarNurkse's model of balanced growth, with its reference to Smith's theory of the division of labor, emphasized that the inducement to invest in an underdeveloped economy is limited by the size of the home market. Nurkse employed the concept of circular cumulative causation introduced by Myrdal in 1956, and spoke of a vicious circle of poverty endemic to underdeveloped nations. Similar to the idea of the Big Push, Nurkse's growth strategy involved a large scale investment impetus covering equitably the major sectors of the economy, the investment designed with a mind to exploiting linkages between industries and complementarities of demand in order that the size of the domestic market expands. Since the small size of the domestic market was seen as a general cause of underdevelopment, an expansion of the home market was taken to clear the way for economic growth.

Myrdal and Nurkse's circular causation hypothesis discussed how interactions among institutions or industries that are tied through forward and backward linkages, could form self-reinforcing causation loops which incorporated feedback. A famous, albeit negative example of a causation loop with feedback is known as the vicious circle (or cycle) of poverty. The logic of the argument for a so called poverty-trap, begins with the existence of low real wages or per capita incomes (a defining feature of an underdeveloped nation). A low level of real per capita income implies a weak effective demand or low level of purchasing power, which reduces the inducement for capital accumulation in commodity and capital goods production, engendering a low rate of investment for the economy. Low investment levels imply a low level of productivity, which feeds back into the cycle to cause the perpetuation of a low level of income, completing the circle of cumulative causation. Interest in this concept has been profitably employed throughout the time since, most recently, a vicious cycles governing the pricing of sub-prime housing loan derivatives has been identified in the literature as a leading cause of the financial crisis of 2007-2010. As with most theorizing in development economics, the doctrine of unbalanced growth was soon confronted with its counterpoint in Albert Otto Hirschman 's strategy of unbalanced growth, which counted Hans Singer among its proponents. Criticizing the doctrine of the Big Push, Hirschman argued that the underdeveloped countries that were being advised to undertake massive social and technical investment programmers were precisely the countries that could scarcely afford this policy prescription. Unless the plan was to fund this big push with foreign capital, loans or through deficit financing, a better plan would be a more compact investment policy focused on investment and promotion of key industries with strong forwards and backward linkages'.

Quite apart from the debate concerning balanced or unbalanced growth strategies, the 1950s saw the rise in development theory of two highly influential insights into the nature of economic growth, which has come to be known as structuralism development theory. Early structuralism is defined by the work of the Argentine Raul Prebisch. The St. Lucian Arthur Lewis is also considered by many to be a structuralism, though, unlike Prebisch, he was equally a neoclassical. The structuralisms are so named due to their discovery that the factors causing underdevelopment may inhere not in any paucity or lack of resources for capital accumulation, the theme largely of all development theory that preceded it, but in the very arrangement of the economic order between different sectors of production nationally, and between sectors internationally.

Lewis' dual sector model of growth is original in the literature on technological dualism in economic development. The theory begins with the assumption that the under developing economy is subject to zero marginal productivity in agriculture, due to the existence of significant surplus labor in the primary sector. On the side of production, entrepreneurs in the manufacturing sector charge a fixed markup over their costs, and manufacturing offers workers a higher fixed wage rate compared to agricultural wages.

The source of growth in Lewis's model stems from the movement of surplus labor away from its low marginal product use in agriculture towards its 'fructification' in the capital intensive industrial sector. In 1956, Robert Solow of Harvard, simultaneously and independently with Trevor Swan, put forth a critique of the Harrodian model of the economy, exemplified in their neoclassical long-run growth model, which was a Harrodian economy with endogenous labor and flexible substitution between labor and capital. They had noted that the dismal results of the twin knife-edges emerged only due to very restrictive assumptions governing the nature of technical substitution between factors of production, and the reliance on the capital stock as being the only factor determining output.

The neoclassical growth model also introduced the new term for productivity growth. This new term was meant to capture improvements in productivity not due to capital deepening, but due to generalized increases in productivity due to technological advancement in the production function. The model employs a neoclassical aggregate production function obeying the Inada-Uzawa conditions, which are a class of production functions displays an elasticity of substitution that is asymptotically one. With near perfect substitution possible between the two factors of production, such aggregate production functions ensure a stable economic growth path exists for the system. Among this class of production functions, the Solowian aggregate function is asymptotically Cobb-Douglas, with constant returns to scale. The Solow-Swan formulation skirts entirely the issue of the first of Harrod's knife-edges by assuming away the question of the equivalence of savings and investment. Of the second knife edge, it is able to show that in the long run it is most likely for an economy to converge to a balanced growth equilibrium, with the rate of expanse of income being equal to the rate of technological progress at that point. The short run implications of the model are primarily that growth is determined by the change in the capital investment (deriving from a change in the savings rate), rate of increase of the labor force, and the economy-wide depreciation rate.

The essential implication of the model for developing economies was that, given time and enough technical progress, the poorer countries of the world were sure to catch up with the old guard of the First World. This derives from a result in the model predicting that in a world of open market economies and global financial capital, investment will flow from rich countries to poor countries, until capital per worker and income per worker equalize across countries. Its promise of balanced growth equilibrium along with full employment must have been music to the ears of development advisors disappointed by the lack of easy answers in the stark harrodian framework.

The 1956 Solow-Swan model of growth became renowned for its mathematical elegance and smoothness, and decidedly positive outlook on the prospects of long run, stable economic development. It became the new focus of development theorizing and effectively relegated debates relating to the pre-war Harrod-Domar model to heterodox circles.

The Production Function

These days, a standard growth theory will usually be modeled as a macro economy exhibiting a particular relationship between the level of product or output on the one hand, and the amount of inputs used in the production of this output (usually modeled as a vector of inputs), on the other. These inputs in the production process are also sometimes called the factors of production. This mathematical relationship between factors and output, perfectly general in scope, if unique for every mapping from the set of input vectors to the set of outputs, is called the production function of the economy.

The production function specifies through a mathematical rule what level of output we should16 obtain when we employ a certain set of inputs such as raw material, labor power, machinery and land, etc. in a specific amount, and in a given manner as dictated by technology or know-how. In recent times the production function has come to encompass both the broadest rules which we believe govern the working of the economic system, as well as many of the specific minutiae of a particular system whose unique features we may wish to capture or account for. In its turn, this has meant that modern production functions can be sometimes assume forms that are elegant and tractable, formulae often an inch or so in length, while at other times and for other purposes, production functions are written down which can look enormously complex and forbidding. A student of growth theory today will soon discover that a wide variety of production functions populate the literature (some differ phenotypically while others differ genotypically) and that each production function, howsoever mundane or novel, aims at generating a simplified mock-up or simulation of the real economy under analysis.

A simple production function may suffice in providing a representation of reality which captures the outlines and broad contours of the real economic system, but a more mathematically complex form may be required to understand economies with 'color' or 'flavor', or 'atypical' economies exhibiting anomalous behavior. Also, since production functions are merely mathematical models of theories, as the theories of growth themselves become richer in substance, the production functions that can be employed to operationalize them also become more complex.

What is beyond doubt is that, despite strong reservations from certain heterodox economic schools which question the validity of mathematical formalism in economics, the concept of the production function is now a cornerstone concept in modern producer theory, macroeconomics and the theory of growth and development. Many of the historically relevant debates in growth theory have often boiled down to differences in opinion and interpretation concerning the mathematical form and even the very meaning of the production function a point we will revisit when we examine the intellectual legacy of the Harrod Solow controversy. Some of these debates may appear trivial to a mathematician whose concern is with the formal 'purity' and elegance of the function. But to the student of economic growth, it is one of the fundamental problems to identify which production function is best suited to describe a particular economy or to most closely approximate the actual empirical record.

Production and Productive Activity

And yet, important as the problem of adequately specifying the production function is, for the moment it is a secondary concern. As a propaeduetic, let us firstly ask ourselves a question which is very simplistic, and indeed to some ears it will sound naïve - Why does a society undertake production of any sort in the first place? Indeed, the straight answer is that the basic purpose of all productive activity is consumption- the generation of valuable goods and services whose value lies precisely in the fact that their utilization yields to the user a certain quantum of well-being or a limited satisfaction of some wants and needs. The degree to which such needs are satisfied for an average individual in an economy is a measure of the success of the production process in simple terms, production processes which create more well-being for a greater number of people are more successful and more accomplished, and countries that adopt such production techniques are richer and more prosperous than those that do not. In the framework we will adopt for the remainder of this chapter, the assumption is that more real output equals more welfare for a nation or community. This is to say we assume that production processes and activities that increase well-being do so by generating more output. This is the classical assumption of the equivalence between economic growth and development.

This is so since production activity and well-being are associated in two ways. Firstly, when there is an improvement in the quality-to-price ratio of commodities, it becomes cheaper for consumers to afford a certain level of well-being or utility, and hence production improvements of a qualitative nature raise the average level of well-being. Well-being is also thought to increase when the level of income rises, since, even assuming that the qualitative aspects of products does not change, a larger real income implies that people can consume more and derive a greater quantum of utility from this higher level of consumption. Most modern measures of economic well-being account only for the effects of income increments, since the gains from quality-price ratio improvements is still very difficult to measure using currently collected production data. Economic growth (as measured by the GDP), recognized by Adam Smith in his post-mercantilist world as the most crucial of all elements anchoring a nation's ambitions, is thus closely related to the growth of well-being increases in the productive capabilities of a nation enlarges the corpus of goods and services available for trade, raising in turn the level of well-being that people may derive from the consumption of more goods and services.

Productive activity itself may take many forms, depending on who is undertaking the process of production, why and for whom. Three major streams of productive activity distinguished in such a manner may be typified as follows:

- Production for the household.
- Production for the market.
- Production for the public economy.

To elaborate the first of these, consider a productive activity which may occur within the domain of the household, where (broadly defined) goods and services such as clean habitation, physical security and comfort, and home-cooked meals are produced by various members of a household for their own consumption. Since goods and services produced in the household are generally non-traded, they are excluded from consideration as economic production, though undoubtedly valuable and useful in themselves. Thus, despite their intrinsic value, items of household production do not have an associated economic price, since they are produced for direct consumption by the household and not for sale. No incomes are generated since no money has changed hands, though value, and output, of course has been created. This is very different from the case of those goods and services which are produced for sale in a market. Such goods are produced in order that they may be traded for other goods and services, and hence production for the market is properly considered to be economic production. Often, a further simplifying assumption is imposed on this type of production – production for the market is considered to be production in pursuit of profit, or the amount of a producer's revenues net of her costs.

The third category concerns the production of what are known as public goods, goods that are non-rivalrous and non-excludable in use, typical examples of which are street lighting, knowledge or national security. Public goods ought to be provided to citizens by their respective governments (free markets generally fail to ensure optimal supply and allocation of such goods) and though these goods are not always produced for the purpose of trade, they are considered to be items of economic production, and, as such, find themselves counted in measures of economic production such as the GDP or GNP. Of all three however, it is clearly the realm of production for the market which stands as the single most important domain of productive activity production for the market is considered to be the principal engine or primus motor of the generation of economic growth and therefore well-being in society.

This is so since market production has a dual role in the modern economy, it not only provides consumers commodities with intrinsic usefulness, but also plays the role of creation and distribution of incomes since all public and household production is ultimately financed by incomes generated in market production the only sphere of production in which money must necessarily change hands in a monetized economy. Therefore productive activity which is economic or market-driven is what generates output, and therefore incomes, and is the source of economic growth, which itself is nothing but the rate of change of the level of national income. We have positive economic growth whenever our national income (as measured by GDP or NNP) is higher today than it was, say, a year ago. This must mean that market-oriented productive activity either improved in quality or quantity terms over the period of the last one year output in the market sector must have exceeded the level set the year before. This is exactly what any general production function tries to show that by increasing the quality or quantity of inputs; national output (and therefore, national income) increases.

Harrod Domar Model

This model of growth was developed by two different economists, each working independently of the other, but almost con-currently. These two economists were R.F. Harrod and E.D. Domar. Harrod, of course, published his theory earlier than Domar. Harrod's book Towards a Dynamic Economics was published in 1948, while Domar's book Essays in the theory of Economic Growth was published in New York in 1957. Harrod Model and Domar Model may differ in details, but the ideas contained in both of the models are so similar that the two models have got integrated and more generally are presented as a single united model, known as the Harrod-Domar Model (HDM).

HDM integrated the classical and Keynesian analysis of economic growth. In the HDM, capital accumulation plays a crucial role in the process of economic growth. Both the classical economists and the Keynesians had recognised the critical role of capital accumulation in the process of economic growth. But the classical economists considered only the capacity of the capital accumulation, and, believing that supply created its own demand, did not pay attention to the demand side. Keynesians, on the other hand, erred in the opposite direction. Concerned primarily with the shortperiod, they considered only the adequacy of demand and neglected the problem of increase in capacity through investment in the long run. HDM considered both the sides of the investment process.

Essence of the Model

Starting from a full employment equilibrium level of income, the HDM postulated that continuous maintenance of this equilibrium required that the volume of spending generated by investment must be sufficient to absorb the increased output resulting from investment. Given the marginal propensity to save, the more the capital is accumulated and the larger the initial national income. The larger must be the absolute volume of net investment, maintenance of full employment, therefore, required an ever-expanding amount of net investment. This, in turn, required a continuous growth in real national income. Capital accumulation and growth of income must go side by side. An increase in capital expands the productive capacity of the economy. If it is not accompanied by an increase in income, any of the following things may happen:

- The new capital may remain untitled.

- The new capital may replace old capital depriving the latter of its labour and/or markets.
- The new capital may be substituted for labour (and possibly other factors).

Thus, increase in capital unaccompanied by an increase in income would result into unemployment of capital and /or labour. Excessive capital accumulation may result into overproduction and consequently into a fall in investment leading to depression.

Assumption of the Model

The HDM is based on the following assumption:

- An initial full-employment level of income exists.
- There is no government interference in the functioning of the economy.
- The exogenous factors do not influence the growth variables, i.e., it is a closed economy model.
- There are no lags in adjustment, i.e., the economic variables like savings, investment, income, expenditure adjust them in the same period. Any change in saving brings about the corresponding change in investment in the same period.
- The average propensity to save(S/Y) and marginal propensity to save ($\Delta S/\Delta Y$) are equal to each other, i.e. the absolute change in saving is equal to the relative change in saving.
- Propensity to save and "capital coefficient"(capital-output ratio) are constant. The law of constant returns operated because of the fixity of capital-out ratio.
- Income, investment and savings are all defined in the net sense. It implies that these variables exclude depreciation.
- Saving and investment are equal in ex-ante and ex-post sense, i.e., accounting and functional equality between saving and investment the equality can be expressed as:

  $$S_o = I_o \text{ (accounting equality)}$$
  $$S_e = I_e \text{ (functional equality)}$$

S_0 and I_0 are observed saving and investment. S_e and I_e are expected saving and investment. All these assumptions are not necessary for the final solution of the problem; nevertheless, they serve the purpose of simplifying the analysis.

The Harrod Model

R.F. Harrod tries show in his model how steady (i.e., equilibrium) growth may occur in an economy. Once the steady growth is interrupted and the economy falls into disequilibrium, cumulative forces tend to perpetuate this divergence thereby leading to either secular definition or secular inflation. In other words, Harrod's growth model concentrated largely on the following question:

- How can steady growth-rate be achieved with fixed capital-output ratio (capital coefficient) and fixed saving-income ratio (propensity to save)?

- How can the steady growth-rate be maintained or what are the conditions for maintaining the stable growth?
- How do natural factors put a ceiling on the growth-rate of the economy?

Statement of the Model

The Harrod model is based on three growth rates. One, there is the actual growth rate denoted by G. It is determined by the saving ratio and the capital-output ratio. It shows short-run cyclical variation in the rate of growth. Two, there is the warranted growth rate denoted by G_w. It is the full capacity growth rate of income in an economy. Three, there is the natural growth rate denoted by G_n. This is regarded as 'the welfare optimum'. It may also be called the potential or the full employment rate of growth.

- Actual Growth Rate (G): The first fundamental equation in the HM is as follows:

  $GC = s$

  Where, G = actual rate of growth (or $\Delta Y/Y$)

  C = the marginal capital output ratio[or $(I/\Delta Y)$]

  s = saving income ratio [or (S/Y)]

The GC = s explains the simple truth that savings and investment are equal to each other in terms of ratio. Substituting the values of G,C and s in GC = s explains this phenomenon:

$$GC = s$$

Substituting the values, we get,

$$(\Delta Y / Y)\times(I / \Delta Y) = S / Y$$

$$\frac{\Delta Y}{Y}\times\frac{I}{\Delta Y}=\frac{S}{Y}$$

$$\frac{I}{Y}=\frac{S}{Y}$$

$$I = S$$

The equality between saving and investment (export sense) is thus a necessary condition for achieving steady growth. It is also called the dynamic equilibrium.

- Warranted Growth Rate (G_w): It is the full capacity growth rate of income in an economy. It is also known as 'full employment growth rate' or 'potential growth rate'. The equation for warranted growth can be stated as follows:

  $G_w C_r = s$

  where,

  G_w = warranted growth rate.

Cr = amount of capital required to maintain the warranted growth rate.

s = saving-income ratio.

$G_w C_r = s$

States that if the economy is to advance at the steady rate of Gw that will fully utilise its capacity, income must grow at the rate of s/C_r per year, i.e., $G_w = s/C_r$.

If income grows at the warranted rate, the capital stock of the economy will be fully utilised; the entrepreneurs will be willing to continue to invest the amount of saving generated at full potential income. G_w is therefore, a self-sustaining rate of growth and if the economy continues to grow at this rate, it will follow the equilibrium path shown in figure below:

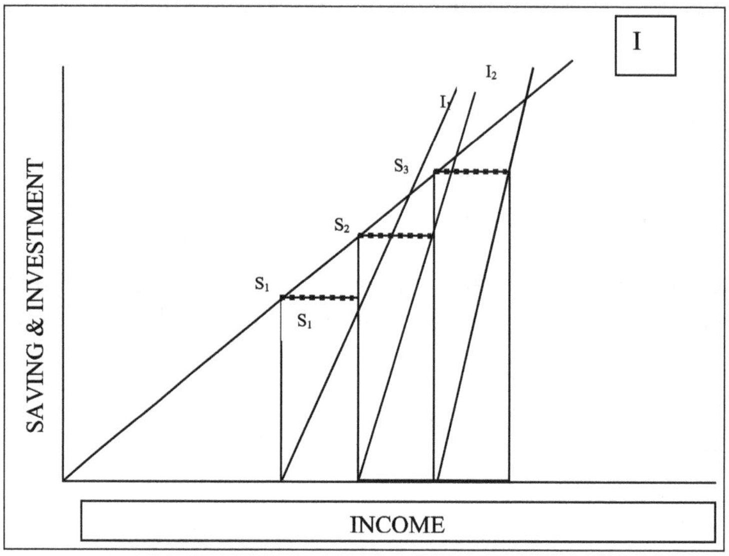

In figure, income is measured along the horizontal axis, and saving and investment are measured along the vertical axis. It would be seen that the change in income from Y_1 toY_2 induced investment would be to equal savings S_1 at $A(Y_2)$. This investment, in turn, raised income to Y_3 and Y_3 induced I_2 to equal S_2 at $B(Y_3)$. I_2 in turn raised income to Y_4 and Y_4 induced I_3 to equal S_3 at $C(Y_4$ income). In this way, the economy moves on the growth path.

The point of intersection of the investment line and the line running parallel to the Y axis indicated the required investment that is forthcoming. The greater proportion of savings, the greater must be the rate of increase in output to induce sufficient investment to maintain equilibrium if we assume no change in the investment co-efficient. The warranted growth rate equation in the model implies that actual investment (ex-post investment) must be equal to expected investment (ex-ante investment), if an economy is to achieve stable growth. In such a situation, the following equalities will obtain:

$G = G_w$, and

$C = C_r$

The economy would be in equilibrium. If these equalities do not obtain, the economy will be pushed into a state of disequilibrium if either of the following situations obtain.

1. $G > G_w$ or $C < C_t$
2. $G < G_w$ or $C > C_t$

- State if disequilibrium when $G > G_w$: Under this situation, growth rate of income is higher than the growth rate of output. It means that the demand for output (because of higher lever of income) would exceed the supply of output (because of lower level of output). The economy would experience inflation. Stated another way, if $C<C_r$, the actual amount of capital falls short of the required amount of capital. This will lead to the deficiency of capital. This, in turn, would adversely affect the goods to be produced. Fall in output would affect the goods to be produced. Fall in output would affect the goods to be produced. Fall in output would result in scarcity of goods, and hence inflation. Either of the two ways lead to inflation. And growth under inflationary situation is not stable.
- State of disequilibrium when $G < G_w$: In this situation, the growth rate of income is less than the growth rate of output. There would be more goods for sale but the income would be insufficient to purchase these goods. There would be deficiency of demand and the economy would face the problem of over production. Similarly, when $C>C_r$, actual amount of capital would be larger than the required amount of capital for investment. The larger amount of capital available for investment. The larger amount of capital available for investment would lower the marginal efficiency of capital in the long-period. Secular decline in the marginal efficiency of capital would lead to depression and unemployment. Economic growth under the situation of depression cannot be stable.

  Harrod stated that once g departs from G_w, it will further depart away from equilibrium. He wrote, "Around that line of advance which it adhered to would alone give satisfaction, centrifugal forced are at work, causing the system to depart further and further form the required line of advance." Thus, equilibrium between G and G_w is a knife-edge equilibrium. It follows that one of the major tasks of public policy is to bring G and G_w together in order to maintain long-run stability. For this purpose, Harrod introduces his third concept of natural rate of growth.
- Natural Growth-rate (G_n): It is the maximum growth rate that an economy can achieve with its available natural resources. The equation for the natural growth rate can be state as follows:

  $G_n\ C_r\ = \text{or} \neq s$

It stated that the natural growth rate is determined by macro variables like population, technology, natural resources and capital equipment. These factors, place a ceiling beyond which expansion of output is not possible.

Interaction between G, G_w and G_n

Comparing G_w and G_n, it may be concluded that G_n may or may not be equal to G_w. In case G_n

happen to be equal to G_w, the condition of steady growth would prevail. But such a possibility is remote one because a variety of factors (influencing G_n and G_w) come into play and make balance between these two growth-rated difficult. There exists a greater probability of inequality between G_n and G_w. It may take two terms:

a) $G_w > G_n$

b) $G_n > G_w$

- $G_w > G_n$: It G_w exceeds G_n, G would lie below G_n for most of the time.

  In this situation, there would be a tendency for cumulative recession. A downward trend would set in, resulting in unemployment and depression. However, downward trend cannot continue indefinitely. The reason is that lower limit to depression is set by the minimum consumption level. The consumption cannot fall below a minimum level. The minimum consumption requirements can be made possible by reducing the working capital. The entrepreneurs may not reduce fixed capital in the hope that future might entail bright prospects for investment. These two factors would gradually set the wheels of recovery in motion. The economy would experience upward trend.

- $G_n > G_w$: In this situation, G would also exceed G_w for most of the time.

  There would be a tendency for cumulative boom and full employment. Such a situation will create inflationary trend. To check this trend, savings should be encouraged, as these would ensure a high level of employment without inflationary pressures.

Assumptions of the Model

The HM is based on the following assumptions:

- The level of ex-ante aggregate saving is a constant proportion of aggregate income. It means propensity to save is assumed to be constant.
- Technical progress has been assumed to be labour augmenting or 'neutral'. This implies that neutral technical progress is the basis of the model.
- The requirements of capital and labour per unit of output are constant, i.e., capital-output and labour-output ratios are assumed constant.
- Constant returned to scale operate. This implies that output increased at a constant rate.

References

- Factors-that-influence-the-economic-development-of-a-country-5942: yourarticlelibrary.com, Retrieved 04, April 2020
- What-Is-Keynesian-Economics: imf.org, Retrieved 19, January 2020
- The-Keynesian-Model-in-the-General-Theory-A-Tutorial: arxiv.org, Retrieved 25, July 2020

2

Neo-Classical Growth Models

The neo-classical growth theory explains how a stable economic growth rate results from a combination of three factors, labor, capital and technology. Some of the neo-classical growth models are Uzawa two sector growth model, Uzawa steady state growth theorem, golden rate and Solow growth model. This chapter discusses in detail these neo-classical growth models.

Production Function

The production function of a firm is a relationship between inputs used and output produced by the firm. For various quantities of inputs used, it gives the maximum quantity of output that can be produced. Consider a manufacturer who produces shoes. She employs two workers – worker 1 and worker 2, two machines – machine 1 and machine 2, and 10 kilograms of raw materials. Worker 1 is good in operating machine 1 and worker 2 is good in operating machine 2. If worker 1 uses machine 1 and worker 2 uses machine 2, then with 10 kilograms of raw materials, they can produce 10 pairs of shoes. However, if worker 1 uses machine 2 and worker 2 uses machine 1, which they are not good at operating, with the same 10 kilograms of raw materials, they will end up producing only 8 pairs of shoes. So with efficient use of inputs, 10 pairs of shoes can be produced whereas an inefficient use results in production of 8 pairs of shoes. Production function considers only the efficient use of inputs. It says that worker 1, worker 2, machine 1, machine 2 and 10 kilograms of raw materials together can produce 10 pairs of shoes which is the maximum possible output for this input combination.

A production function is defined for a given technology. It is the technological knowledge that determines the maximum levels of output that can be produced using different combinations of inputs. If the technology improves, the maximum levels of output obtainable for different input combinations increase. We then have a new production function. The inputs that a firm uses in the production process are called factors of production. In order to produce output, a firm may require any number of different inputs. However, for the time being, here we consider a firm that produces output using only two factors of production, factor 1 and factor 2. Our production function, therefore, tells us what maximum quantity of output can be produced by using different combinations of these two factors. We may write the production function as: $q = f(x_1, x_2)$. It says that by using x_1 amount of factor 1 and x_2 amount of factor 2, we can at most produce q amount of the commodity.

Factor		X_2						
0		1	2	3	4	5	6	
	0	0	0	0	0	0	0	0
	1	0	1	3	7	10	12	13
X_1	2	0	3	10	18	24	29	33

	3	0	7	18	30	40	46	50
	4	0	10	24	40	50	56	57
	5	0	12	29	46	56	58	59
	6	0	13	33	50	57	59	60

A numerical example of production function is given in table. The left column shows the amount of factor 1 and the top row shows the amount of factor 2. As we move to the right along any row, factor 2 increases and as we move down along any column, factor 1 increases. For different values of the two factors, the table shows the corresponding output levels. For example, with 1 unit of factor 1 and 1 unit of factor 2, the firm can produce at most 1 unit of output; with 2 units of factor 1 and 2 units of factor 2, it can produce at most 10 units of output; with 3 units of factor 1 and 2 units of factor 2, it can produce at most 18 units of output and so on.

Isoquant

Consider a production function with two inputs factor 1 and factor 2. An isoquant is the set of all possible combinations of the two inputs that yield the same maximum possible level of output. Each isoquant represents a particular level of output and is labeled with that amount of output.

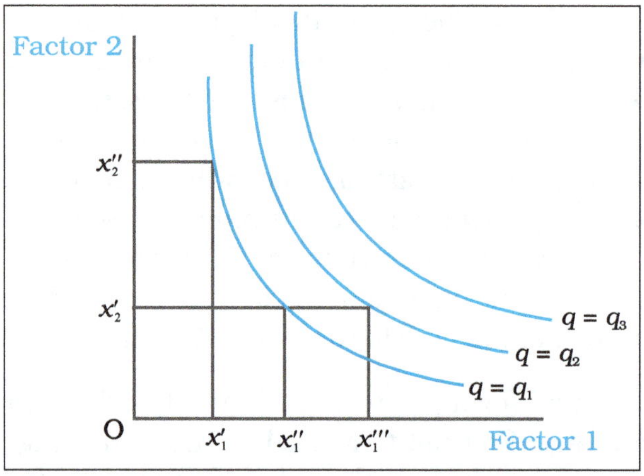

In the diagram, we have three isoquants for the three output levels, namely $q = q_1$, $q = q_2$ and $q = q_3$ in the inputs plane. Two input combinations (x'_1, x''_2) and (x''_1, x'_2) give us the same level of output q1 . If we fix factor 2 at x'_2 and increase factor 1 to x'''_1, output increases and we reach a higher isoquant, $q = q_2$. When marginal products are positive, with greater amount of one input, the same level of output can be produced by using lesser amount of the other. Therefore, isoquants are negatively sloped.

The Short Run and the Long Run

In the short run, a firm cannot vary all the inputs. One of the factors, factor 1 or factor 2, cannot be varied, and therefore, remain fixed in the short run. In order to vary the output level, the firm can vary only the other factor. The factor that remains fixed is called the fixed input whereas the other factor which the firm can vary is called the variable input. Consider the example represented through table. Suppose, in the short run, factor 2 remains fixed at 5 units. Then the corresponding column shows the different levels of output that the firm may produce using different quantities of factor 1 in the short run.

In the long run, all factors of production can be varied. A firm in order to produce different levels of output in the long run may vary both the inputs simultaneously. So, in the long run, there is no fixed input. For any particular production process, long run generally refers to a longer time period than the short run. For different production processes, the long run periods may be different. It is not advisable to define short run and long run in terms of say, days, months or years. We define a period as long run or short run simply by looking at whether all the inputs can be varied or not.

Total Product, Average Product and Marginal Product

- Total Product: Suppose we vary a single input and keep all other inputs constant. Then for different levels of employment of that input, we get different levels of output from the production function. This relationship between the variable input and output, keeping all other inputs constant, is often referred to as Total Product (TP) of the variable input.

  In our production function, if we keep factor 2 constant, say, at the value $\overline{x_2}$ and vary factor 1, then for each value of x_1, we get a value of q for that particular $\overline{x_2}$. We write it in the following way:

  $$q = f(x_1 : \bar{x}_2)$$

  This is the total product function of factor 1. Let us again look at Table. Suppose factor 2 is fixed at 4 units. Now in the Table, we look at the column where factor 2 takes the value 4. As we move down along the column, we get the output values for different values of factor 1. This is the total product of factor 1 schedule with $x_2 = 4$. At $x_1 = 0$, the TP is 0, at $x_1 = 1$, TP is 10 units of output, at $x_1 = 2$, TP is 24 units of output and so on. This is also sometimes called total return to or total physical product of the variable input. Once we have defined total product, it will be useful to define the concepts of average product (AP) and marginal product (MP). They are useful in order to describe the contribution of the variable input to the production process.

- Average Product: Average product is defined as the output per unit of variable input. We calculate it as:

  $$AP_1 = \frac{TP}{X_1} = \frac{f(x_1 : \bar{x}_2)}{x_1}$$

  Table gives us a numerical example of average product of factor 1. In table, we have already seen the total product of factor 1 for $x_2 = 4$. In table we reproduce the total product schedule and extend the table to show the corresponding values of average product and marginal product. The first column shows the amount of factor 1 and in the fourth column we get the corresponding average product value. It shows that at 1 unit of factor 1, AP_1 is 10 units of output, at 2 units of factor 1, AP_1 is 12 units of output and so on.

- Marginal Product: Marginal product of an input is defined as the change in output per unit of change in the input when all other inputs are held constant. When factor 2 is held constant, the marginal product of factor 1 is:

$$MP_1 = \frac{\text{change in output}}{\text{change in input}}$$

$$= \frac{\Delta q}{\Delta x_1}$$

where Δ represents the change of the variable.

If the input changes by discrete units, the marginal product can be defined in the following way. Suppose, factor 2 is fixed at $\bar{x}_2$ .With $\bar{x}_2$ amount of factor 2, let, according to the total product curve, x_1 units of factor 1 produce 20 units of the output and $x_1 - 1$ units of factor 1 produce 15 units of the output. We say that the marginal product of the x_1 th unit of factor 1 is:

$$MP_1 = f(x_1;\bar{x}_2) - f(x_1 - 1;\bar{x}_2) = (\text{TP at } x_1 \text{ units}) - (\text{TP at } x_1 - 1 \text{ unit})$$

$$= (20 - 15) \text{ units of output} = 5 \text{ units of output}$$

Since inputs cannot take negative values, marginal product is undefined at zero level of input employment. Marginal products are additions to total product. For any level of employment of an input, the sum of marginal products of every unit of that input up to that level gives the total product of that input at that employment level. So, total product is the sum of marginal products.

Average product of an input at any level of employment is the average of all marginal products up to that level. Average and marginal products are often referred to as average and marginal returns, respectively, to the variable input. In the example represented through Table, if we keep factor 2 constant say, at 4 units, we get a total product schedule. From the total product, we then derive the marginal product and average product of factor 1. The third column of table shows that at zero unit of factor 1, MP_1 is undefined. At $x_1 = 1$, Mp_1 is 10 units of output, at $x_1 = 2$, MP_1 is 14 units of output and so on.

Factor 1	TP	MP_1	AP_1
0	0	-	-
1	10	10	10
2	24	14	12
3	40	16	13.33
4	50	10	12.5
5	56	6	11.2
6	57	1	9.5

The Law of Diminishing Marginal Product and the Law of Variable Proportions

The law of diminishing marginal product says that if we keep increasing the employment of an input, with other inputs fixed, eventually a point will be reached after which the resulting addition to output (i.e., marginal product of that input) will start falling. A somewhat related concept with the law of diminishing marginal product is the law of variable proportions. It says that the marginal product of a factor input initially rises with its employment level. But after reaching a certain level of employment, it starts falling. The reason behind the law of diminishing returns or the law of variable proportion is the following. As we hold one factor input fixed and keep increasing the other, the factor proportions change. Initially, as we increase the amount of the variable input, the factor proportions become more and more suitable for the production and marginal product increases. But after a certain level of employment, the production process becomes too crowded with the variable input and the factor proportions become less and less suitable for the production. It is from this point that the marginal product of the variable input starts falling. Let us look at table again. With factor 2 fixed at 4 units, the table shows us the TP, MP_1 and AP_1 for different values of factor 1. We see that up to the employment level of 3 units of factor 1, its marginal product increases. Then it starts falling.

Shapes of Total Product, Marginal Product and Average Product Curves

An increase in the amount of one of the inputs keeping all other inputs constant generally results in an increase in output. Table shows how the total product changes as the amount of factor 1 increase. The total product curve in the input-output plane is a positively sloped curve. Figure shows the shape of the total product curve for a typical firm. We measure units of factor 1 along the horizontal axis and output along the vertical axis. With x_1 units of factor 1, the firm can at most produce q_1 units of outputs. According to the law of variable proportions, the marginal product of an input initially rises and then after a certain level of employment, it starts falling. The MP curve in the input-output plane, therefore, looks like an inverse 'U'-shaped curve. Let us now see what the AP curve looks like. For the first unit of the variable input, one can easily check that the MP and the AP are same. Now as we increase the amount of input, the MP rises. AP being the average of marginal products, also rises, but rises less than MP. Then, after a point, the MP starts falling. However, as long as the value of MP remains higher than the value of the prevailing AP, the latter continues to rise. Once MP has fallen sufficiently, its value becomes less than the prevailing AP and the latter also starts falling. So AP curve is also inverse 'U'-shaped.

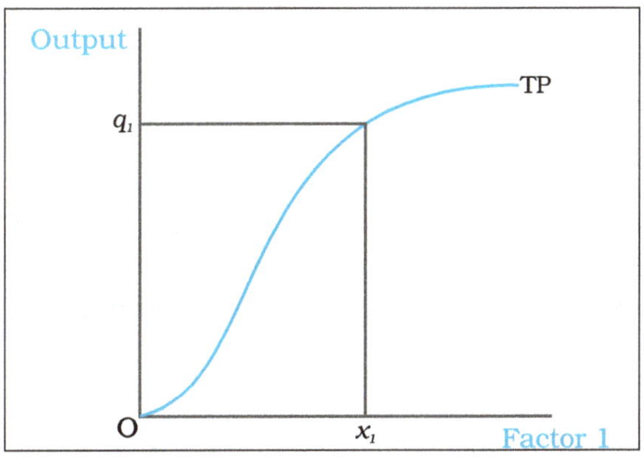

Total Product: This is a total product curve for factor 1. When all other inputs are held constant, it shows the different output levels obtainable from different amounts of factor 1.

As long as the AP increases, it must be the case that MP is greater than AP. Otherwise, AP cannot rise. Similarly, when AP falls, MP has to be less than AP. It, therefore, follows that MP curve cuts AP curve from above at its maximum.

Figure shows the shapes of AP and MP curves for a typical firm. The AP of factor 1 is maximum at x_1. To the left of x_1, AP is rising and MP is greater than AP. To the right of x_1, AP is falling and MP is less than AP.

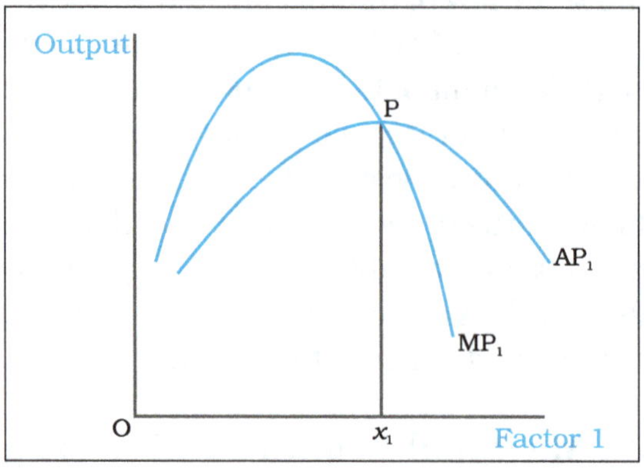

Average and Marginal Product: These are average and marginal product curves of factor 1.

Returns to Scale

Now we shall see what happens when all inputs vary simultaneously.

- Constant returns to scale (CRS) is a property of production function that holds when a proportional increase in all inputs results in an increase in output by the same proportion.
- Increasing returns to scale (IRS) holds when a proportional increase in all inputs results in an increase in output by more than the proportion.
- Decreasing returns to scale (DRS) holds when a proportional increase in all inputs results in an increase in output by less than the proportion. For example, suppose in a production process, all inputs get doubled. As a result, if the output gets doubled, the production function exhibits CRS. If output is less than doubled, the DRS holds, and if it is more than doubled, the IRS holds

Consider a production function,

$$q = f(x_1, x_2)$$

Where the firm produces q amount of output using x_1 amount of factor 1 and x_2 amount of factor 2. Now suppose the firm decides to increase the employment level of both the factors t ($t > 1$) times. Mathematically, we can say that the production function exhibits constant returns to scale if we have,

$$f(tx_1, tx_2) = t.f(x_1, x_2)$$

i.e. the new output level $f(tx_1, tx_2)$ is exactly t times the previous output level $f(x_1, x_2)$.

Similarly, the production function exhibits increasing returns to scale if,

$$f(tx_1, tx_2) > t.f(x_1, x_2)$$

It exhibits decreasing returns to scale if,

$$f(tx_1, tx_2) < t.f(x_1, x_2)$$

Costs

In order to produce output, the firm needs to employ inputs. But a given level of output, typically, can be produced in many ways. There can be more than one input combinations with which a firm can produce a desired level of output. In Table, we can see that 50 units of output can be produced by three different input combinations ($x_1 = 6, x_2 = 3$), ($x_1 = 4, x_2 = 4$) and ($x_1 = 3, x_2 = 6$). The question is which input combination will the firm choose? With the input prices given, it will choose that combination of inputs which is least expensive. So, for every level of output, the firm chooses the least cost input combination. This output-cost relationship is the cost function of the firm.

Cobb-Douglas Production Function

Consider a production function,

$$q = x_1^{\alpha} x_2^{\beta}$$

Where α and β are constants. The firm produces q amount of output using x_1 amount of factor 1 and x_2 amount of factor 2. This is called a Cobb-Douglas production function.

Suppose with $x_1 = \bar{x}_1$ and $x_2 = \bar{x}_2$, we have q_0 units of output, i.e.

$$q_0 = x_1^{\alpha} x_2^{\beta}$$

If we increase both the inputs t (t > 1) times, we get the new output,

$$q_1 = (t\bar{x}_1)^{\alpha} (t\bar{x}_2)^{\beta}$$

$$= t^{\alpha+\beta} \bar{x}_1^{\alpha} \bar{x}_2^{\beta}$$

When $\alpha + \beta = 1$, we have $q1 = tq_0$. That is, the output increases t times. So the production function exhibits CRS. Similarly, when $\alpha + \beta > 1$, the production function exhibits IRS. When $\alpha + \beta < 1$ the production function exhibits DRS.

Short Run Costs

In the short run, some of the factors of production cannot be varied, and therefore, remain fixed. The cost that a firm incurs to employ these fixed inputs is called the total fixed cost (TFC). Whatever amount of output the firm produces, this cost remains fixed for the firm. To produce any required level of output, the firm, in the short run, can adjust only variable inputs. Accordingly, the cost that a firm incurs to employ these variable inputs is called the total variable cost (TVC). Adding the fixed and the variable costs, we get the total cost (TC) of a firm,

$$TC = TVC + TFC$$

In order to increase the production of output, the firm needs to employ more of the variable inputs. As a result, total variable cost and total cost will increase. Therefore, as output increases, total variable cost and total cost increase. In Table, we have an example of cost function of a typical firm. The first column shows different levels of output. For all levels of output, the total fixed cost is $20. Total variable cost increases as output increases. With output zero, TVC is zero. For 1 unit of output, TVC is $10; for 2 units of output, TVC is $18 and so on. In the fourth column, we obtain the total cost (TC) as the sum of the corresponding values in second column (TFC) and third column (TVC). At zero level of output, TC is just the fixed cost, and hence, equal to $20. For 1 unit of output, total cost is $30; for 2 units of output, the TC is $38 and so on. The short run average cost (SAC) incurred by the firm is defined as the total cost per unit of output. We calculate it as:

$$SAC = \frac{TC}{q}$$

In Table, we get the SAC-column by dividing the values of the fourth column by the corresponding values of the first column. At zero output, SAC is undefined. For the first unit, SAC is $30; for 2 units of output, SAC is $19 and so on. Similarly, the average variable cost (AVC) is defined as the total variable cost per unit of output. We calculate it as:

$$AVC = \frac{TVC}{q}$$

Also, average fixed cost (AFC) is,

$$AFC = \frac{TFC}{q}$$

Clearly,

$$SAC = AVC + AFC$$

In Table, we get the AFC-column by dividing the values of the second column by the corresponding values of the first column. Similarly, we get the AVC-column by dividing the values of the third column by the corresponding values of the first column. At zero level of output, both AFC and AVC are undefined. For the first unit of output, AFC is $20 and AVC is $10. Adding them, we get the SAC equal to $30. The short run marginal cost (SMC) is defined as the change in total cost per unit of change in output.

$$SMC = \frac{\text{change in total cost}}{\text{change in output}} = \frac{\Delta TC}{\Delta q}$$

Where, Δ represents the change of the variable.

If output changes in discrete units, we may define the marginal cost in the following way. Let the cost of production for q_1 units and $q_1 - 1$ units of output be $20 and $15 respectively. Then the marginal cost that the firm incurs for producing q_1 th unit of output is,

$$MC = (TC \text{ at } q_1) - (TC \text{ at } q_1 - 1)$$

$$= \$20 - \$15 = \$5$$

Just like the case of marginal product, marginal cost also is undefined at zero level of output. It is important to note here that in the short run, fixed cost cannot be changed. When we change the level of output, whatever change occurs to total cost is entirely due to the change in total variable cost. So in the short run, marginal cost is the increase in TVC due to increase in production of one extra unit of output. For any level of output, the sum of marginal costs up to that level gives us the total variable cost at that level. One may wish to check this from the example represented through Table. Average variable cost at some level of output is therefore, the average of all marginal costs up to that level. We see that when the output is zero, SMC is undefined. For the first unit of output, SMC is $10; for the second unit, the SMC is $ 8 and so on.

Output (Units)	TFC $	TVC $	TC $	AFC $	AVC $	SAC $	SMC $
0	20	0	20	-	-	-	-
1	20	10	30	20	10	30	10
2	20	18	38	10	9	19	8
3	20	24	44	6.67	8	14.67	6
4	20	29	49	5	7.25	12.25	5
5	20	33	53	4	6.6	10.6	4
6	20	39	59	3.33	6.5	9.83	6
7	20	47	67	2.86	6.7	9.57	8
8	20	60	80	2.5	7.5	10	13
9	20	75	95	2.22	8.33	10.55	15
10	20	95	115	2	9.5	11.5	20

Shapes of the Short Run Cost Curves

Now let us see what these short run cost curves look like in the output cost plane. In order to increase the production of output the firm needs to employ more of the variable inputs. This results in increase in total variable cost and hence, an increase in total cost. Therefore, as output increases, total variable cost and total cost increase. Total fixed cost, however, is independent of the amount of output produced and remains constant for all levels of production.

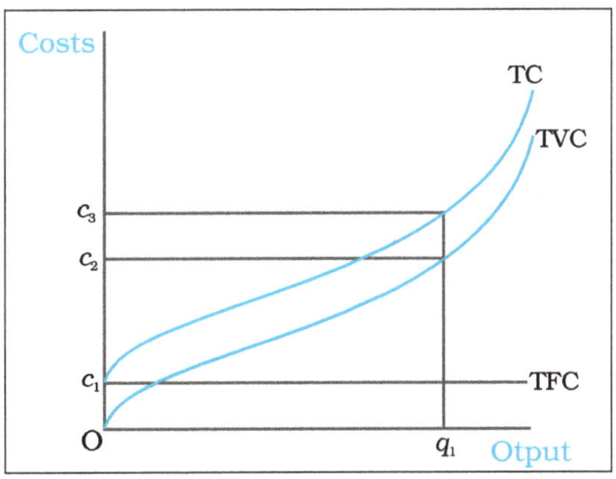

Figure illustrates the shapes of total fixed cost, total variable cost and total cost curves for a typical firm. TFC is a constant which takes the value c_1 and does not change with the change in output. It is, therefore, a horizontal straight line cutting the cost axis at the point c_1. At q_1, TVC is c_2 and TC is c_3.

AFC is the ratio of TFC to q. TFC is a constant. Therefore, as q increases, AFC decreases. When output is very close to zero, AFC is arbitrarily large, and as output moves towards infinity, AFC moves towards zero. AFC curve is, in fact, a rectangular hyperbola. If we multiply any value q of output with its corresponding AFC, we always get a constant, namely TFC.

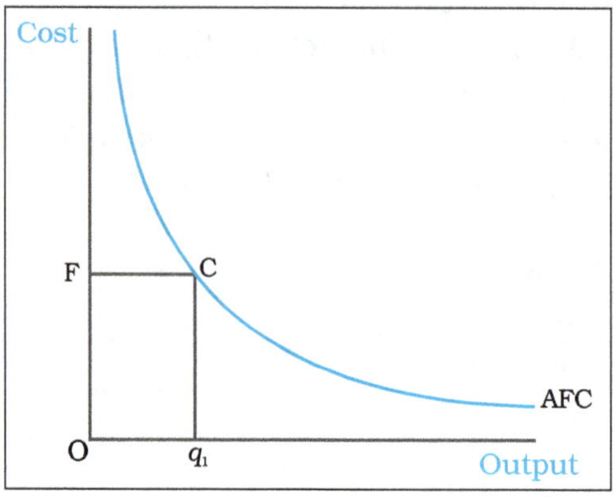

Figure shows the shape of average fixed cost curve for a typical firm. We measure output along the horizontal axis and AFC along the vertical axis. At q_1 level of output, we get the corresponding average fixed cost at F. The TFC can be calculated as:

TFC = AFC × quantity = OF × Oq_1 = the area of the rectangle $OFCq_1$

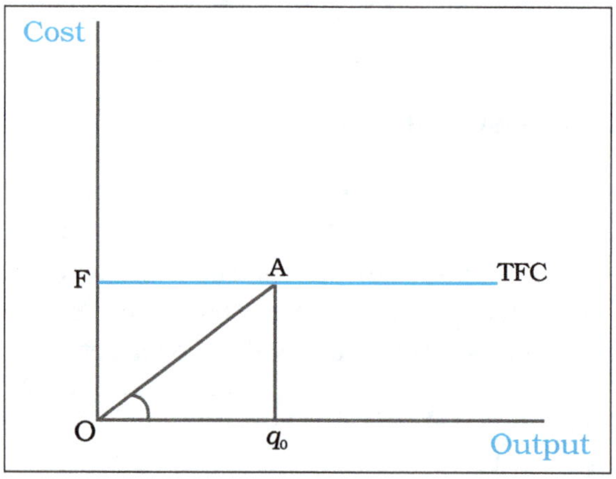

We can also calculate AFC from TFC curve. In figure, the horizontal straight line cutting the vertical axis at F is the TFC curve. At q_0 level of output, total fixed cost is equal to OF. At q_0, the corresponding point on the TFC curve is A. Let the angle $\angle AOq_0$ be θ. The AFC at q_0 is:

$$AFC = \frac{TFC}{quantity}$$

$$= \frac{Aq_0}{Oq_0} = \tan\theta$$

Let us now look at the SMC curve. Marginal cost is the additional cost that a firm incurs to produce one extra unit of output. According to the law of variable proportions, initially, the marginal product of a factor increases as employment increases, and then after a certain point, it decreases. This means initially to produce every next unit of output, the requirement of the factor becomes less and less, and then after a certain point, it becomes greater and greater. As a result, with the factor price given, initially the SMC falls, and then after a certain point, it rises. SMC curve is, therefore, 'U'-shaped.

At zero level of output, SMC is undefined. When output is discrete, the TVC at a particular level of output is the sum of all marginal costs up to that level. When output is perfectly divisible, the TVC at a particular level of output is given by the area under the SMC curve up to that level. Now, what does the AVC curve look like? For the first unit of output, it is easy to check that SMC and AVC are the same. So both SMC and AVC curves start from the same point. Then, as output increases, SMC falls. AVC being the average of marginal costs, also falls, but falls less than SMC. Then, after a point, SMC starts rising. AVC, however, continues to fall as long as the value of SMC remains less than the prevailing value of AVC. Once the SMC has risen sufficiently, its value becomes greater than the value of AVC. The AVC then starts rising. The AVC curve is therefore 'U'-shaped. As long as AVC is falling, SMC must be less than the AVC and as AVC, rises, SMC must be greater than the AVC. So the SMC curve cuts the AVC curve from below at the minimum point of AVC.

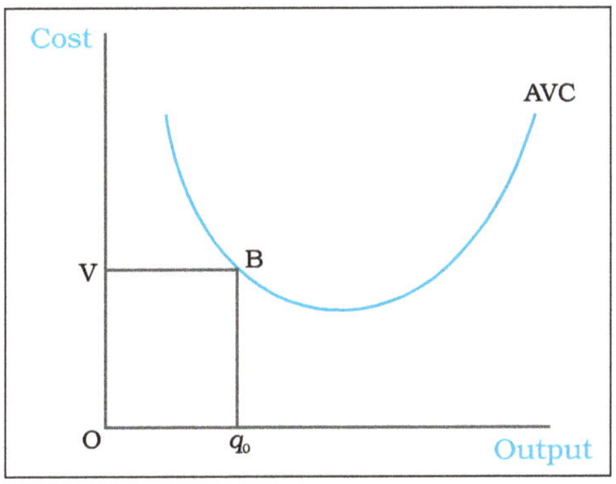

In figure we measure output along the horizontal axis and AVC along the vertical axis. At q_0 level of output, AVC is equal to OV. The total variable cost at q_0 is,

$$TVC = AVC \times quantity = OV \times Oq_0 = \text{the area of the rectangle } OVBq_0$$

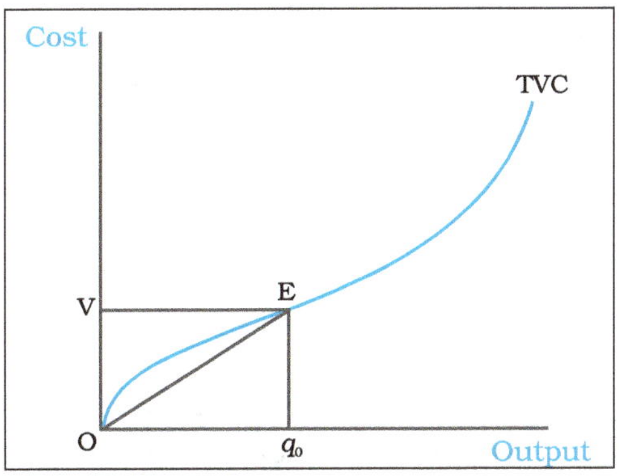

In figure, we measure output along the horizontal axis and TVC along the vertical axis. At q_0 level of output, OV is the total variable cost. Let the angle $\angle Eoq_0$ be equal to θ. Then, at q_0, the AVC can be calculated as,

$$AVC = \frac{TVC}{output} TVC$$

$$= \frac{Eq_o}{Oq_o} = \tan\theta$$

Let us now look at SAC. SAC is the sum of AVC and AFC. Initially, both AVC and AFC decrease as output increases. Therefore, SAC initially falls. After a certain level of output production, AVC starts rising. Now AVC and AFC are moving in opposite direction. Here, initially the fall in AFC is greater than the rise in AVC and SAC is still falling. But, after a certain level of production, rise in AVC overrides the fall in AFC. From this point onwards, SAC is rising. SAC curve is therefore 'U'-shaped. It lies above the AVC curve with the vertical difference being equal to the value of AFC. The minimum point of SAC curve lies to the right of the minimum point of AVC curve.

Similar to the case of AVC and SMC, here too as long as SAC is falling, SMC is less than the SAC and when SAC is rising, SMC is greater than the SAC. SMC curve cuts the SAC curve from below at the minimum point of SAC.

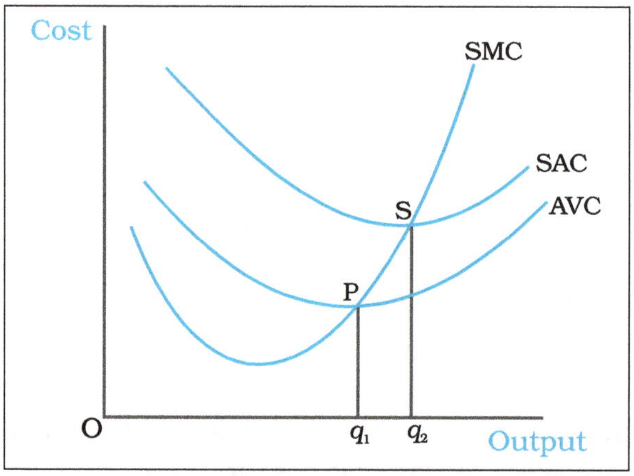

Figure shows the shapes of short run marginal cost, average variable cost and short run average cost curves for a typical firm. AVC reaches its minimum at q1 units of output. To the left of q_1, AVC is falling and SMC is less than AVC. To the right of q_1, AVC is rising and SMC is greater than AVC. SMC curve cuts the AVC curve at 'P' which is the minimum point of AVC curve. The minimum point of SAC curve is 'S' which corresponds to the output q_2. It is the intersection point between SMC and SAC curves. To the left of q_2, SAC is falling and SMC is less than SAC. To the right of q_2, SAC is rising and SMC is greater than SAC.

Long Run Costs

In the long run, all inputs are variable. The total cost and the total variable cost therefore, coincide in the long run. Long run average cost (LRAC) is defined as cost per unit of output, i.e.

$$LRAC = \frac{TC}{q}$$

Long run marginal cost (LRMC) is the change in total cost per unit of change in output. When output changes in discrete units, then, if we increase production from $q_1 - 1$ to q_1 units of output, the marginal cost of producing q_1 th unit will be measured as:

$$LRMC = (TC \text{ at } q_1 \text{units}) - (TC \text{ at } q_1 - 1 \text{ units})$$

Just like the short run, in the long run, the sum of all marginal costs up to some output level gives us the total cost at that level.

Shapes of the Long Run Cost Curves

IRS implies that if we increase all the inputs by a certain proportion, output increases by more than that proportion. In other words, to increase output by a certain proportion, inputs need to be increased by less than that proportion. With the input prices given, cost also increases by a lesser proportion. For example, suppose we want to double the output. To do that, inputs need to be increased by less than double. The cost that the firm incurs to hire those inputs therefore also needs to be increased by less than double. What is happening to the average cost here? It must be the case that as long as IRS operates, average cost falls as the firm increases output. DRS implies that if we want to increase the output by a certain proportion, inputs need to be increased by more than that proportion. As a result, cost also increases by more than that proportion. So, as long as DRS operates, the average cost must be rising as the firm increases output. CRS implies a proportional increase in inputs resulting in a proportional increase in output. So the average cost remains constant as long as CRS operates. It is argued that in a typical firm IRS is observed at the initial level of production. This is then followed by the CRS and then by the DRS. Accordingly, the LRAC curve is a 'U'-shaped curve. Its downward sloping part corresponds to IRS and upward rising part corresponds to DRS. At the minimum point of the LRAC curve, CRS is observed.

Let us check how the LRMC curve looks like. For the first unit of output, both LRMC and LRAC are the same. Then, as output increases, LRAC initially falls, and then, after a certain point, it rises. As long as average cost is falling, marginal cost must be less than the average cost. When the average cost is rising, marginal cost must be greater than the average cost. LRMC curve is therefore a 'U'-shaped curve. It cuts the LRAC curve from below at the minimum point of the LRAC.

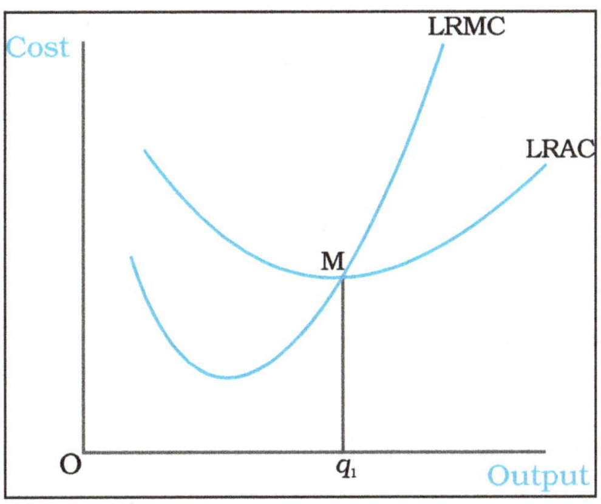

Figure shows the shapes of the long run marginal cost and the long run average cost curves for a typical firm. LRAC reaches its minimum at q_1. To the left of q_1, LRAC is falling and LRMC is less than the LRAC curve. To the right of q_1, LRAC is rising and LRMC is higher than LRAC.

Uzawa Two Sector Growth Model

The two-sector model of economic growth given by Uzawa is basically a neo-classical model. This model states that every sector in the economy employs fixed co-efficient of the factors and there is initial stage of static equilibrium in the economy. The central result of the Uzawa two-sector growth model is that the uniqueness of factor market ("momentary") equilibrium and the stability of the steady-state growth path depends crucially on the relative factor-intensities of the two sectors and attendant savings hypotheses. The most celebrated result is that we are only assured stability if the consumer goods sector is more capital-intensive than the investment goods sector. In Uzawa's model there are two productive inputs the labour and capital which are substitutable to each other and freely transferable from one sector to the other. Thus, Uzawa introduced a two-sector and two-factor model in the neo-classical framework.

Assumptions

Let us look at a few assumptions of this model. This model is based upon following assumptions:

- There are two productive inputs-labour and capital which can be substituted for each other.
- The factors are perfectly mobile across all sectors of the economy.
- The capital depreciates at a constant rate.
- The supply of labour is fixed at any point of time. The size of the labour force is exogenously determined.
- At any point of time, the supply of capital is determined by its existing stock.
- All the wages are spent on consumer goods and all the profits are reinvested.

The Basic Model

In a two-sector economy, two produced goods are consumer goods and the capital goods, produced by using both labour and capital. Thus, this model assumes two inputs and two outputs. Moreover, one of the two outputs i.e. capital goods is also an input. Thus, introduction of two-sectors in the neo-classical framework raised a number of special problems for the possibility of steady growth and its stability. The basic set up of Uzawa Model is given below:

- The Consumer Goods Sector: The production function of the consumer goods is $Y_c = F_c(K_c, L_c)$, Where, Yc = output of consumer good; Lc = labour used in consumer good sector; Kc = capital used in consumer good sector; Fc(ï½·) is the consumer goods industry production function.
- The Capital Goods Sector: The production function of the capital goods is $Y_i = F_i(K_i, L_i)$. Where, Y_i = output of investment good; L_i = labour used in investment good sector; and Ki = capital used in investment good sector; Fi(ï½·) the investment goods industry production function.

Both production functions $F_c(\text{ï}^{1/2}\cdot)$ and $F_i(\text{ï}^{1/2}\cdot)$ are Neoclassical, in the sense of exhibiting constant returns to scale, continuous technical substitution, diminishing marginal productivities to the factors, etc.

- Total Output of two sectors: $Y = Y_c + pY_i$, Y = total output of economy; p = price of investment good (in terms of consumer good).
- Total Demand for Labour and Capital in two sectors:
    - L = total supply of labour $L_c + L_i = L$
    - K = total supply of capital $K_c + K_i = K$

Since, $L_c + L_i$ are total demand for labour and $K_c + K_i$ are total demand for capital, above two equations show equilibrium in the labour and capital markets. In the labour market, the wages are just equal to the marginal product of labour and are expressed as:

w = return to labour (wages)

$$w = dY_c / dL_c = p\text{ï}^{1/2} \cdot (dY_i / dL_i)$$

While in capital market, the rate of return is just equal to the marginal product of capital:

r = return to capital (profit/interest)

$$r = dY_c / dK_c = p\text{ï}^{1/2} \cdot (dY_i / dK_i)$$

Further, labour supply is assumed to grow exogenously at the exponential rate n, thus the growth rate of labour is $gL = (dL/dt)/L = n$ where 'n' is the natural rate of growth of population.

Finally, as the investment goods industry produces all the new capital goods in the economy, then, ignoring depreciation, we can define the change in the total stock of capital as that sector's output, i.e. dK/dt = Yi, so growth rate of capital is $gK = (dK/dt)/K = Y_i / K$ each sector of the economy will have its own optimal capital and labour ratio which will be Kc/Lc for the consumer goods industry and Ki/Li for the capital goods industry. Under the conditions of full employment, the overall capital-labour ratio for the economy will be:

$$\frac{K}{L} = \frac{K_c + K_i}{L_c + L_i} = \frac{K_c}{L_c + L_i} + \frac{K_i}{L_c + L_i}$$

$$\frac{K}{L} = \frac{K_c + K_i}{L_c + L_i} = \frac{L_c}{L_c + L_i} \cdot \frac{K_c}{L_c} + \frac{L_i}{L_c + L_i} \cdot \frac{K_i}{L_i}$$

$$= \frac{L_c}{L_c + L_i} \cdot \frac{K_c}{L_c} + \left(1 - \frac{L_c}{L_c + L_i}\right) \frac{K_i}{L_i}$$

This shows that the capital labour ratio in the economy is the weighted average of the capital labour ratio of two sectors of the economy. Uzawa further states that the allocation of labour and capital in each sector of the economy would depend upon the relative factor price ratios i.e. w/r which further determine the ratio of prices of two commodities i.e. consumer goods and that of the capital goods i.e. P_c/P_i. Both industries male optimal adjustments and these yield unit costs; competition that sets the price ratio P_c/P_i for the two commodities equal to the ratio of unit costs. Thus, any w/r determines an equilibrium P_c/P_i.

The Conditions for Stability

In the two-sector model by Uzawa, for stable equilibrium of the economy, with given wage-profit ratio (w/r) and capital-labour ratio (K/L) and given the outputs Y_c and Y_i, the following conditions must be met:

$$\frac{wL}{rK} = \frac{P_c Y_c}{P_i Y_i}$$

This stability proposition further state that even in the growing economy, the capital labour ratio remains constant. This is possible only if the growth of capital is just equal to the growth of labour force. The labour supply grows geometrically at rate $\lambda$and is defined as $\Delta L/L = \lambda$. In order to find the growth of capital stock, we must calculate ΔK which is given as under:

$$\Delta K = r.(K/P_i) - \mu.K$$

The stability proposition states that under conditions of equilibrium the rate of change in capital labour ratio ($k = K/L$) should be zero i.e.

$\Delta k/k = (\Delta K/K) - (\Delta L/L) =$ (change in capital labour ratio in capital goods sector) $- \lambda - \mu = 0$

$$\text{i.e. } f'(k_i) - \lambda - \mu = 0$$

$$\text{or } f'(k_i) - (\lambda + \mu) = 0$$

Here, the marginal product function i.e. $f'(k_i)$is a decreasing function of k_i and as k_i increases, f'(-k_i)falls and ultimately, it becomes equal to $\lambda + \mu$.

Finally, another important condition of stability, which is related with above two conditions is that the consumption goods sector is more capital intensive than the capital goods sector. With these conditions in view, we can analyses the working of this model through diagrams.

Diagrammatic Explanation

The stable equilibrium in the economy depends upon the relationship between the factor intensities of the two sectors. The factor intensities in the two sectors can be understood with help of the following figure. In figure, we have taken intensive production functions of the two sectors of the economy. Here, intensive production functions are the same production functions as already defined in the basic model but are expressed in per capita or per labour unit terms e.g. in intensive production function, following notations are used:

$$y_c = Y_c/L;\ \lambda_c = L_c/L;\ k_c = K_c/L_c;\ f_c(k_c) = F_c(K_c, L_c)/L_c;\ y_i = Y_i/L;\ \lambda_i = L_i/L;$$

$$k_i = K_i / L_i;\ f_i(k_i) = F_i(K_i, L_i)/L_i;\ y = Y/L;\ k = K/L$$

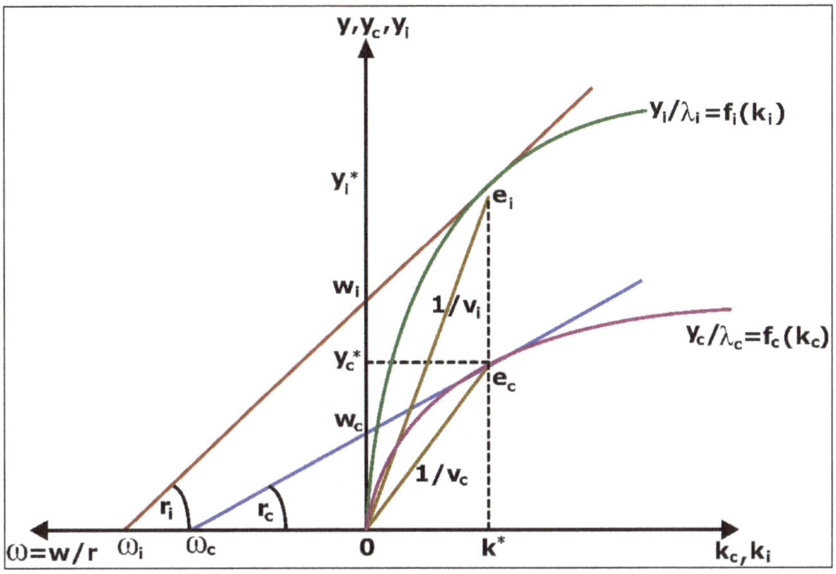

Two-Sector Model (for given k*).

In this figure y_c and y_i are the production functions of the consumer goods and capital goods sector, respectively. On X-axis, on the right side, we take capital labour ratio i.e. k =K/L and on the left side, we have taken wage-interest ratio or factor price ratio, represented as ω = w/r while the Y-axis show the per capita out of the economy as a whole (y); per capita output in capital goods sector (y_i) and in consumer goods sector (y_c). Let us begin with a given capital-labour ratio, k*. Suppose we wish to specialize completely in the production of consumer goods, i.e. suppose $y_i = 0$ so that $y = y_c = y_c/\lambda_c$, where $\lambda_c = 1$ (all labour allocated to consumer goods sector) and $k_c = k^*$ (so all capital allocated to consumer goods sector). We see immediately that our entire economy is governed by the intensive production function f c(k_c). So, with k*, we produce y_c^* as our aggregate output. The slope of the ray tangent to the production function is fc' (= rc), the marginal product of capital, the point where that ray intersects the vertical axis, (= w_c), the marginal product of labour. Most importantly, the point where the tangent ray intersects the horizontal axis is ωc = w_c/r_c, the ratio of marginal products. If we specialize in producing consumer goods, then the ratio ωc can be seen as the resulting equilibrium factor price ratio, i.e. the factor prices that clear the capital and labour markets, where the initial supply of capital and labour is captured by the given capital-labour ratio k*.

On the other hand, if we specialize completely in investment goods production, $y_c = 0$, and so y = pï½·y_i = pï½·y_i/λ_i as $\lambda_i = 1$ (all labor to investment goods production) and $k_i = k^*$ (all capital to investment goods). Thus, aggregate per capita output is governed by the intensive production function $f_i(k_i)$ depicted in figure. With the given k*, notice, we will produce y = pï½·y_i^* which (although this depends on p) seems to be more than y_c^*. This should alert us to the fact that the investment goods industry is less capital-intensive than the consumer goods industry.

Through this figure, we can also observe the relative factor price intensities which are measured as the slope of a ray from the origin to the relevant point on an intensive production which is 1/v, the reciprocal of the capital-output ratio, v. Thus, letting v_c and v_i denote the capital-output ratios in the consumer goods and investment goods industries respectively, we can see in figure by the rays connecting 0 to e_c and e_i, that $1/v_i > 1/v_c$, so that $v_c > v_i$, in other words, you need more capital per unit of output in the consumer goods industry than in the investment goods industry. Relatively speaking, consumer goods are capital-intensive and investment goods are labour-intensive. Of course, we could have drawn this differently so that the factor-intensities were reversed.

We can further observe in the figure that a tangent line with slope intersects the horizontal axis at $\omega_i = w_i/r_i$, the equilibrium factor price ratio. We can easily notice that $\omega_i > \omega_c$, which is another indication that the consumer goods industry is relatively capital-intensive. Specifically, note that relative factor shares can be denoted $k/\omega = rK/wL$. The higher this k/ω ratio, the greater the capital-intensity. In terms of figure holding $k = k^*$ constant, we see that as $\omega_i > \omega_c$, then $k^*/\omega_i < k^*/\omega_c$, indicating, once again, that the investment goods sector is relatively capital intensive.

Thus, for a given k, the resulting equilibrium factor-price ratio will depend on the allocation of two factors between the two sectors of the economy. Specifically, if all the factors are allocated to the consumer goods sector, the equilibrium will be ω_c; and on the other hand if all factors are allocated to the investment goods sector, the equilibrium will be ω_i. The assumption of strict concavity of production functions guarantees this uniqueness. If we do not know the sectoral composition of output, we cannot determine what the actual equilibrium factor-price ratio ω is: it can range from a minimum of ω_c (complete specialization in consumer goods) to a maximum of ω_i (complete specialization in investment goods), i.e. for a given k,

$$\omega \min ||\leq \omega ||\leq \omega \max$$

Where, $\omega_{min} = \omega_c$ and $\omega_{max} = \omega_i$.

Similarly, we can also find a solution with given value of ω i.e. the factor price ratio. This can be observed from figure. In this figure the given factor-price ratio ω^* will set a point on the horizontal axis from which emanate two rays, one with slope r_c and another with slope r_i, corresponding to the marginal products of capital for the consumer goods and investment goods industries. These rays form tangencies with the intensive production functions of both the consumer goods and capital goods industries at points e_c and e_i respectively, which translate into resulting capital-labour ratios k_c and k_i. Thus, this indicates the relationships $k_c(\omega)$ and $k_i(\omega)$ such that $k_c > k_i$, which is another indicator of the relative factor intensity of the sectors and we can also notice that $k_c/\omega^* > k_i/\omega^*$.

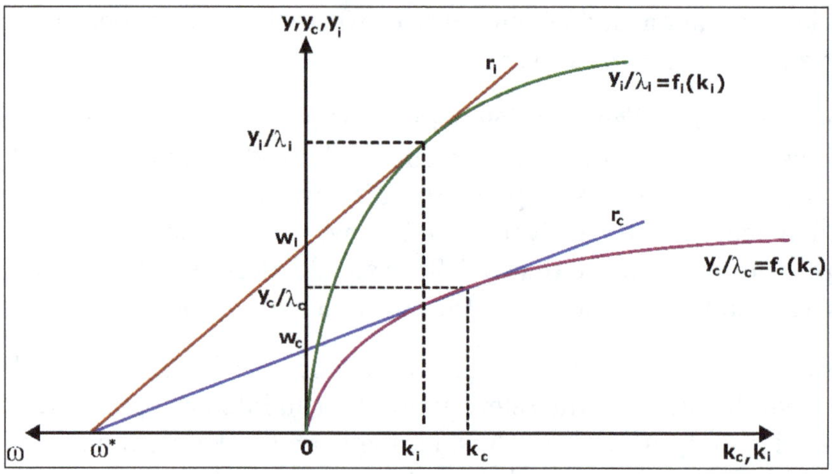

Two Sector Model (for given ω *).

We can also notice in figure that although the factor-price ratio is the same for both sectors, so $\omega^* = r_i/w_i = r_c/w_c$, we have it that $r_i \neq r_c$ and $w_i \neq w_c$, so it seems that the rates of return to capital and wages are not equal across sectors. But we must also keep in mind the price of investment goods, p. specifically, p will be such that pï½·$r_i = r_c$ and pï½·$w_i = w_c$. Finally, that the amount that will be produced when factor prices are ω^* can be determined from y_c/λ c and y_i/λ_i on the vertical axes. Since, both industries have positive output per capita (y_c, y_i > o), so we are not specializing exclusively in either of them. Both sectors are allowed to operate and the particular amounts they produce will be dictated by the equilibrium factor price ratio i.e. ω^*.

The feasible solutions in each of the cases mentioned above that is in case of given k* and ω^* and then varying their levels can be observed from the figure. It should be noticed that varying the given k, these upper and lower boundaries for equilibrium factor prices will vary. If we observe the figure, we can say if k is increased above k*, then both ω_c and ω_i will increase. We depict the resulting boundaries in figure as the upward-sloping curves ω_c(k) and ω_i(k). We draw them as straight lines, but this is not necessarily the case. The only things that are posited are:

- That the relationship between k and ω_c and ω_i is unique and monotonically increasing (by assumptions of strict concavity and constant returns to scale for the production function).
- That the investment goods boundary ω_i(k) will always lies above the consumer goods boundary ω_c(k) (from the assumption that consumer goods industry is more capital intensive than the investment goods industry). Naturally, if we change the assumption of factor-intensity, so that investment goods are more capital-intensive than consumer goods, then ω_c(k) would lie everywhere above ω_i(k).

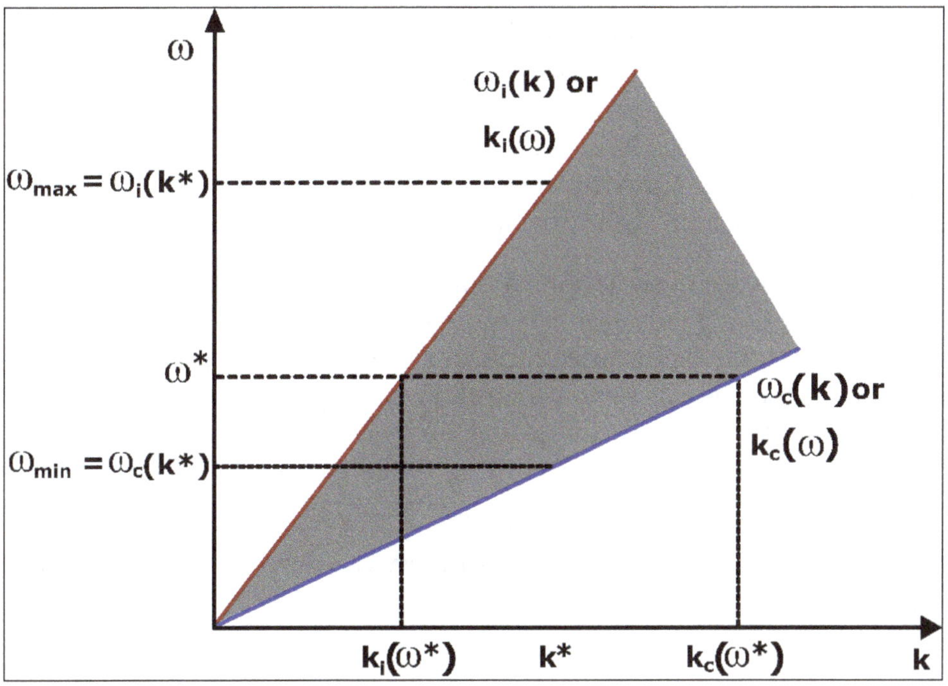

Factor Prices and Quantities.

Now, we can easily have a look at the locus of factor market equilibrium in figure.

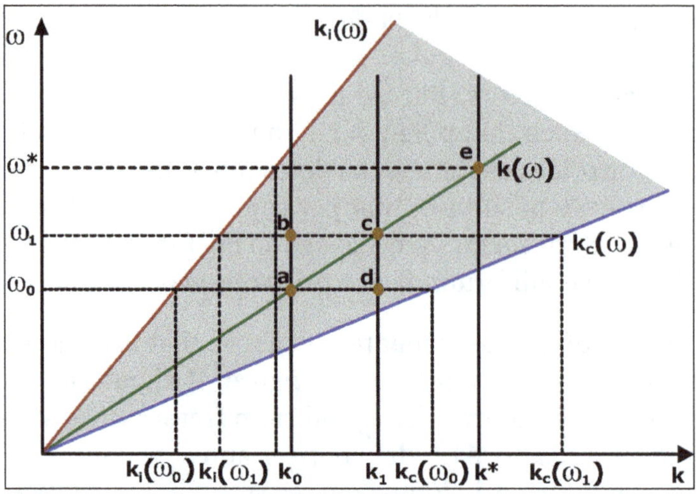

Factor Market Equilibrium Locus.

In figure, suppose we are given an initial aggregate capital-labor ratio k_0. As we say nothing about allocation between sectors, then there is a whole range of equilibrium factor prices ω which are consistent with that allocation (within some maximum/minimum range). Picking one of these factor price ratios which will then determine a sectoral allocation of $k_c(\omega)$ and $k_i(\omega)$. But this may not be necessarily market-clearing, i.e. it may be that $\lambda_c k_c(\omega) + \lambda_i k_i(\omega) \neq k_0$, so that our demands for factors are not equal to our initial supplies of the factor, which implies that the factor price ratio we have chosen is not appropriate. So, for the initial k_0, we must search for a market-clearing factor price ratio that makes demands equal to supplies. The line k(ω) in figure maps out the locus of equilibrium factor prices for every aggregate capital-labor ratio. The fact that this is upward-sloping everywhere and lies between the boundaries is important. Suppose we begin at k_0. The locus k(ω) tells us that ω_0 is the market-clearing factor price ratio. Thus, the corresponding sectoral allocations $k_c(\omega_0)$ and $k_i(\omega_0)$ are equilibrium allocations, i.e. $\lambda_c k_c(\omega_0) + \lambda_i k_i(\omega_0) = k_0$. In contrast, for initial capital stock k_0, the wage-profit ratio ω 1 is not market clearing, so $\lambda_c k_c(\omega_1) + \lambda_i k_i(\omega_1) \neq k_0$. However, for initial capital stock k_1, ω_1 is the market clearing wage-profit ratio (i.e. $\lambda_c k_c(\omega_1) + \lambda_i k_i(\omega_1) = k_1$). So positions a and c represent factor market equilibrium, while positions such as b and d are factor market disequilibrium. The curve k(ω) is merely the locus of equilibrium positions.

Thus, this model also proposes the solutions if both the ω* and k* can be varied but in each case we find that the consumption goods sector is more capital intensive than the investment sector. We have observed that for any factor price ratio, since consumption goods sector is more capital intensive than the investment goods sector, then $rK_c/wL_c > rK_i/wL_i$. Under constant returns to scale and perfect competition, it is generally the case that when the factor price ratio i.e. w/r increases, the price ratio P_c/P_i will increase or rise according to the share of wages in the consumer goods sector being greater or smaller than that of the investment good sector. Accordingly, this model states that as P_c/P_i falls, w/r rises and vice versa. Also, we can derive from the equation, $\frac{wL}{rK} = \frac{P_c Y_c}{P_i Y_i}$ that $K/L = (w/r)\ (P_i.Y_i / P_c.Y_c)$.

An increase in w/r raises P_i/P_c, then K/L must rise unless Y_i/Y_c falls. But if Y_i/Y_c falls there is a shift of output in favour of consumer goods which are more capital intensive commodities leading to a rise in overall K/L. Thus, k_i and k must move together under the stability proposition. However, the stability condition of the consumer goods sector being more capital intensive than the investment goods sector is a sufficient condition for stability but not necessary as the stability may also occur even if this condition is violated. Uzawa states that in Cobb-Douglas type production function with elasticities α_i and 1-α_i for K_i and L_i and αc and 1-α_c for K_c and L_c, under full employment, the equation for demand and supply for investment goods is rK = $\alpha_i.P_i.Y_i + \alpha_c.P_c.Y_c$ But we also know that rK = P_iY_i. Therefore, we can easily note that,

$$P_iY_i = \alpha_i.P_i.Y_i + \alpha_c.P_c.Y_c$$

$$P_iY_i - \alpha_i.P_i.Y_i = \alpha_c.P_c.Y_c$$

$$(1-\alpha_i).P_iY_i = \alpha_c.P_c.Y_c$$

$$P_iY_i / P_c.Y_c = \alpha_c / (1-\alpha_i)$$

But, we have also seen that $\frac{wL}{rK} = \frac{P_cY_c}{P_iY_i}$ i.e. $P_iY_i / P_c.Y_c = rK / wL$.

Therefore, $rK / wL = \alpha_c / (1-\alpha_i)$.

Since, the elasticities in each sector of the economy are constant, the right hand side of this equation will also be constant showing that rK/wL will always remain constant. Hence, whenever r/w falls (so k_i rises), K/L must rise. This implies that k_c and k_i move together and stability occurs regardless of which sector is more capital intensive. However, one strong assumption regarding the stability of the system is that it occurs only if all the wages are spent on consumption and all the profits on investment goods. Robert Solow and Frank Hahn severely criticised these basic assumptions of Uzawa's model for stable growth. Solow states that its weak an assumption for such as important result for stable equilibrium growth path. Frank Hahn went further and called the assumptions regarding capital intensity and savings as 'terrible assumption', which probably never or rarely hold true in the real world. It is thus reasonable to conclude from this exercise that, if anything, these models have taught us that the real world is a bit more complicated than one-sector models let on. Rather than the smooth convergence to a single steady state path we find in the Uzawa two-sector model indicates that we ought to expect a good amount of indeterminacy, instability and cyclical behaviour in growth paths.

Uzawa Steady State Growth Theorem

The steady-state growth theorem applies to the one-sector neoclassical growth model. We begin by defining the model precisely and then defining a balanced growth path. A neoclassical growth model is given by the following economic environment:

$$Y_t = F(K_t, L_t; t),$$

$$\dot{K}_t = Y_t - C_t - \delta K_t, \; K_0 > 0, \; \delta \geq 0$$

And, $L_t = L_0 e^{nt}$, $L_0 > 0$, $n \geq 0$.

The production function F satisfies the standard neoclassical properties: constant returns to scale in K and L, positive and diminishing marginal products of K and L, and the Inada conditions that the marginal product of a factor input goes to zero as that input goes to infinity and goes to infinity as the input goes to zero. A balanced growth path in the neoclassical growth model is defined as a situation in which all quantities grow at constant exponential rates (possibly zero) forever. We follow the usual convention of also referring to this as a steady state. Finally, we will define $F_K K/Y$ to be the capital share and $F_L L/Y$ to be the labor share. As usual, the two factor shares sum to a value of unity, by Euler's theorem. We follow standard notation in denoting $y \equiv Y/L$ and $k \equiv K/L$, and we will use an asterisk superscript to denote a variable along the steady-state path.

With these definitions, we can now present the Steady-State Growth Theorem:

Theorem: If a neoclassical growth model possesses a steady state with constant, nonzero factor shares and $\dot{y}^*_t/y^*_t = g > 0$, then it must be possible along the steady state path to write the production function as $Y^*_t = G(K^*_t, A_t L_t)$, where $\dot{A}_t/A_t = g$ and where G is a neoclassical production function. As is well-known, in the case of Cobb-Douglas production, capital- and labor-augmenting technical changes are equivalent. One sometimes sees the theorem interpreted as saying that technical change must be labor augmenting or the production function must be Cobb-Douglas. This is equivalent to the statement of the theorem as given.

Proving the Theorem

This proof largely follows Uzawa in spirit. The main innovation in the proof is in writing the key differential equation below in terms of the elasticity of output with respect to the capital-output ratio. This produces a familiar equation in a way that Uzawa's consideration of the marginal product of capital does not. The capital-output ratio is a key variable throughout the proof, so we define $x \equiv K/Y$. We also make the standard definition $f(k;t) \equiv F(k, 1;t)$. The proof now follows:

1. The first step of the proof is to rewrite the production function in terms of the capital-output ratio: $y_t = \phi(x_t;_t)$. Intuitively, this step is readily understood by drawing the production function in (k, y) space: for each ray through the origin that is for each capital-output ratio there is a unique level of output per worker on that ray.

2. Next, we note that the elasticity of y_t with respect to x_t satisfies a familiar property:

$$\frac{\partial \log y_t}{\partial \log x_t} = \frac{\alpha(x_t;t)}{1-\alpha(x_t;t)}$$

where $\alpha(x_t;t) \equiv f_k k_t/yt$ is the capital share. This equation says that the elasticity of output with respect to the capital-output ratio is equal to the ratio of the capital and labor shares. Such an equation is well-known in the case of Cobb-Douglas production.

3. Now comes the key step of the proof. From this point on, we assume the economy is on a balanced growth path. Because the capital share is constant in steady state, the right side of equation is invariant over time. Then, since $y_t = \varphi(x_t;t)$, we can write this equation as:

$$\frac{\partial \log \phi(x^*;t)}{\partial \log x^*} = \frac{\alpha(x^*)}{1-\alpha(x^*)}$$

Where, we use an asterisk to indicate a quantity along a balanced growth path. Because the right-hand side of this equation does not depend on time, this partial differential equation can be solved to yield.

$$\log\phi\left(x^*;t\right)=a(t)+\int\frac{\alpha\left(x^*\right)}{1-\alpha\left(x^*\right)}\frac{dx^*}{x^*}$$

for some function a(t). And therefore, $y_t^*=\phi\left(x^*;t\right)=A(t)\psi\left(x^*\right)$

Where,

$$A(t)\ \equiv\ \exp(a(t))>0 \text{ and } \psi\left(x^*\right)\ \equiv\exp\left(\int\frac{\alpha\left(x^*\right)}{1-\alpha\left(x^*\right)}\right)$$

This is the crucial result. We've shown that the effects of t and x ∗ can be separated. This implies, for example, the familiar result that $y_t^*/A_t=\psi(x^*)$ is constant along a balanced growth path, where At ≡ A(t). Since y_t^* grows at rate g by assumption, it must therefore be the case that $A_t/A_t=g$ as well.

4. To conclude the proof, note that $k_t=x_t y_t$, so that

$$\frac{k_t^*}{A_t}=\frac{y_t^*}{A_t}\psi^{-1}\left(\frac{y_t^*}{A_t}\right)\equiv\tilde{G}^{-1}\left(\frac{y_t^*}{A_t}\right)$$

Inverting, we have,

$$\left(\frac{y_t^*}{A_t}\right)\equiv\tilde{G}\left(\frac{k_t^*}{A_t}\right)$$

And therefore,

$$Y_t^*=A_tL_t\tilde{G}\left(\frac{k_t^*}{A_tL_t}\right)\equiv G\left(K_t^*\ ,\ A_tL_t\right).$$

And this proves the key result: technical change is labor augmenting along the balanced growth path. Finally, since $Y_t^*=F\left(K_t^*,L_t;t\right)=G(K_t^*,A_tL_t)$, it must be the case that G satisfies the standard neoclassical properties as well.

Golden Rate

Let us first consider the equation which describes the capital dynamic. We know that the change in the level of capital over a period is given by:

$$\dot{K}(t)=I(t)-\delta K(t)=s\cdot F\left[L(t),K(t),T(t)\right]-\delta K(t)$$

In order to transform this equation into the intensive from which is more intuitively appealing, we divide both sides of the equation by the stock of labor, L, yielding,

$$\frac{\dot{K}}{L} = s \cdot f(k) - \delta k$$

We make one further substitution to arrive at an equation which is completely in per capita form. The derivative of per-capita capital availability, k = K/L, with respect to time is given by:

$$\dot{k}(t) = \frac{d(K/L)}{dt} = \frac{\dot{K}}{L} - nk$$

Rearranging the terms gives us the value of K/L in per-capita terms. Substituting this value into the relevant equation, we get the per-capita or intensive form describing the capital stock dynamic:

$$\dot{k} = s \cdot f(k) - (n + \delta) \cdot k$$

The non-linear equation written above is the intensive form fundamental differential equation of the Solow-Swan neoclassical growth model. Since we have manipulated L stock out of the picture, the fundamental equation in intensive form depends only on the k variable. The term $(n + \delta)$ can be considered to be the effective depreciation rate for k (= K/L), the capital-labor ratio or per-capita capital intensity. Note that under the governing assumptions, this is a constant and exogenously determined rate.

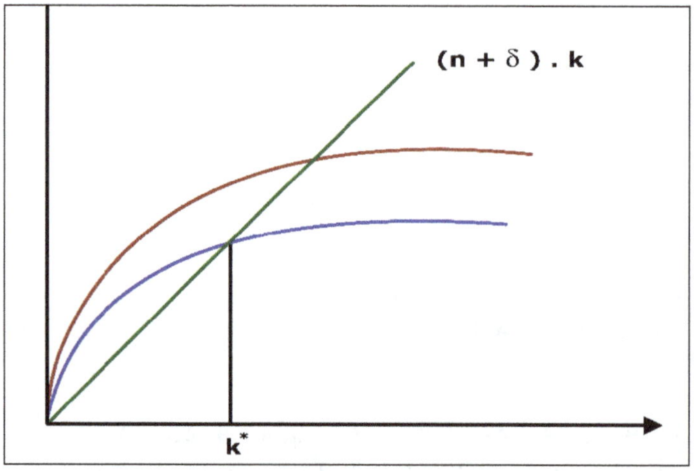

In order to visualize this fundamental dynamic equation, consider the figure given below. Of the three curves on the graph, the topmost represents the production function in intensive from, f. The straight line shooting upwards and out from the origin represents the locus of effective depreciation, $(n + \delta) \cdot k$. The bottom curve represents the per-capital savings out of income at the exogenously determined rate, s. Let us see how the major neoclassical properties are reflected in the shape of the curves drawn above. Firstly, both the per-capita output curve and the per-capita savings curve start from the origin due to the property of essentiality (F(0,0) or f(0) = 0). Secondly, since the k factor must exhibit positive but diminishing marginal returns, both curves must have a positive but declining slope, so that the curves rise as k increases, but get flatter as they do. The Inada-Uzawa conditions imply that both curves have a slope approaching infinity when k= 0, and a slope approaching zero as k goes to infinity - meaning that the curves are vertical at the point where k= 0, and eventually become flat as k becomes very large.

The Solow-Swan model: The lowest curve represents gross investment, $s \cdot f(k)$ a constant fraction s of percapita income, $y = f(k)$. The straight line from the origin is the line of effective depreciation, $(n+\delta) \cdot k$. The steady state is defined as the point where the gross savings curve intersects the effective depreciation line this is the point k in the figure.

Now, a cursory glance at the figure drawn above will convince you that and this is due to the particular assumptions of the neoclassical production function- the straight line effective depreciation curve and the per-capita savings curve intersect only once right of the origin. Thus, the non-trivial solution of the dynamic differential equation of the Solow-Swan model is found at the point where the effective depreciation curve is crossed by the $s \cdot f(k)$ curve. This point is called the long-term or steady-state solution of the economy. Let us denote the unique k at which this happens as k*. The steady state is a kind of balanced growth equilibrium. Balanced growth equilibrium is one where all the variables involved grow at the same rate. Thus, if one declares that with a growth rate of output of 10% the economy has achieved balanced growth, then it must be that capital stock, labor stock, and even technology, if not exogenously fixed, are growing at a rate of 10% over time. If this constant and common rate of growth were taken to be zero, then the balanced growth equilibrium is also called a steady state. The steady state condition for the intensive form of the fundamental equation is thus the condition that $\dot{k} = 0$ or that the time derivative of the per-capita capital intensity become zero. It is not difficult to find the closed-form formula for this condition:

$$s \cdot f\left(k^*\right) = (n+\delta).k^*$$

In the steady state, all per-capita quantities involved experience a zero rate of growth. Since k is constant at k^*, the per-capita consumption and per-capita output also become constant at , the per-capita consumption and per-capita output also become constant at $c^* = (1-s)f\left(k^*\right)$ and $y^* = f\left(k^*\right)$ respectively. Though the per-capita variables do not change over time in the steady state, the non-intensive form variables the Y, C, K (and, of course, L) variables grow over time at the rate dictated by population – n.

Effect of One-Time Parametric Shocks

A one-time shock or parametric shift in any of the constant factors, say, in the exogenously given level of technology, T (or A in the Cobb-Douglas), does not alter the steady state rate of growth of per-capita variables in the system, but affects the levels of per-capita variables. An increase in T for instance, will cause the production function to jump or shift up. An increase in the rate of savings out of income, s, will cause the $s \cdot f\left(k^*\right)$ curve to move up, and closer to the $f(k)$ curve-leading to an increase in the value of k^*. An increase in n or δ will increase the slope of the effective depreciation line, reducing the value of k^*.

Employing such parametric shifts in order to mimic or simulate events and features of the real economy can offer useful insight if done judiciously. For instance, one could introduce to the bare model a technological shock (in the form of a higher value for the T parameter), hoping to account for some real event such as the spread of cheap computing technologies or the internet. Such an shock would cause the $f(k)$ and $s \cdot f(k^*)$ curves to shift upwards, leading to an increase in the steady state value (level) of k^*.

Simple comparative static exercises can be performed on the model under analysis by thoughtful introduction of once-and-for-all parametric shifts. Remember that such shifts have no effect on the growth rates of the per-capita variables involved these remain zero in the steady state. Rates of change can alter only if the parametric shocks occur not once, but continuously or periodically over time. In order to do so however, we would have to introduce a dynamic equation, which captures the behaviour over time of the parametric shock itself. Eschewing this complication at the moment, we suffice ourselves by pointing out that the inability of the steady-state analysis to offer an explanation for why rates of growth (of per-capita output for example) differ from zero, and, moreover, change over time- limits its usefulness as a model of long-run growth.

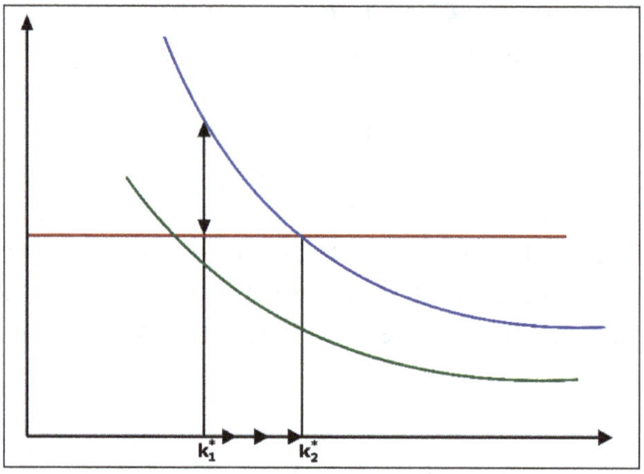

All shift in the rate of savings. Starting: Effect of a one-time parametric shock in the Solow from the position k_1^*, an increase in savings rate from-Swan model: The figure depicts the effect of a once s_1 to s_2 shifts the gross -and-for investment (per unit capital) curve upwards and to the right, as shown. Capital per person will increase until it reaches its new steady-state level, k_2^*.

Inter-temporal Equity and the Golden Rule of Capital Accumulation

Let us motivate this section by asking the question: If we provide the same amount of consumption to members of each current and future generations that is, if we do not provide less to future generations than (we do) to ourselves- then what is the maximum amount of per-capita consumption? The conditional statement highlighted in italics is the definition of what I have called intertemporal equity. We have avoided using the term intergenerational equity in deference to the many Ramsey type optimisation models in the early literature on growth models the emphasis is however the same. If we are to be fair to the generations that will come after us, our ability to consume in per-capita terms is to that extent limited and we call this level of per-capita consumption the golden rule for capital accumulation. In order to derive this rule for capital accumulation, let us first consider that for each unique steady-state value $k^* > 0$, there is a corresponding steady-state level of consumption, given by:

$$c^* = (1-s)f(k^*(s)),$$

Which can be rewritten by substituting the value for the fraction of income saved, $s \cdot f(k^*) = (n+\delta)k^*$ yielding:

$$c^*(s) = f\left[k^*(s)\right] - (n+\delta)k^*(s).$$

From the equation above, simple calculus will reveal that the maximum value of consumption per-capita, c^* when $f'\left[k^*\right] - (n+\delta).dk^*/ds = 0$, and since k' is positive, it must be that, for this maximum level of consumption, the required k (called k^{gold}) is:

$$f(k^{gold}) = (n+\delta)$$

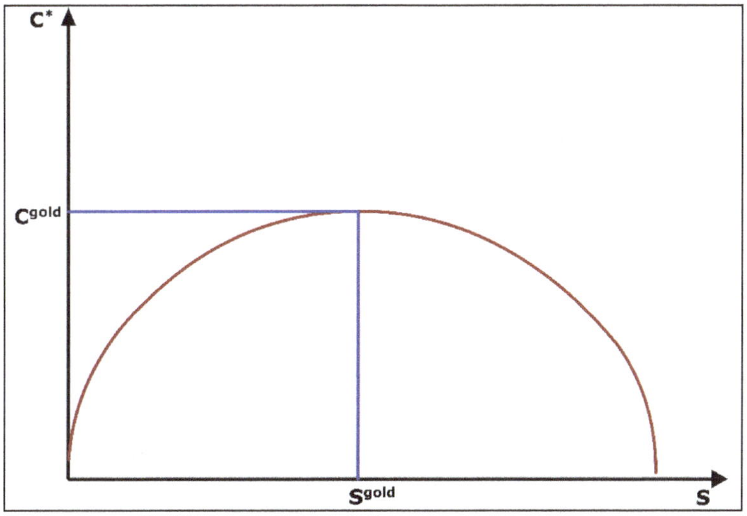

The Golden Rule of capital accumulation is the savings rate that maximises the steady-state level of per-capita consumption, shown on the vertical axis. This unique savings rate is denoted S^{gold}.

This is the golden rule of capital accumulation, as depicted in figure. The particular values of k, c and s can be called the golden rule values of the per-capita variables involved. Of note here is that savings rates that exceed the S^{gold} level are inefficient since the same level of capital accumulation could be attained with a higher per-capita consumption at all points in time. We say that the economy is oversaving. It could consume more at each point in its (short-run) transition as well as in the long-run steady state by lowering its savings rate. An economy that continually over saves is said to be dynamically inefficient.

Short—Run or Transitional Dynamics of the Solow- Swan model

The long-run implication of the Solow-Swan model is that the long-term rates of growth of the per-capita variables discussed above are static at zero in the steady state. We have also noted that the level-variables, K, L and Y increase at a rate exogenously determined by the rate of population growth, n. this is primarily due to our assumption that technology does not progress and that any technological shocks are of a once-and-for-all nature. The short-run dynamic of the model suggests that an economy's per-capita variables in particular we focus on per-capita incomes converge to their steady-state values. An especially intriguing implication of the short-run dynamic of the Solow-Swan model that has provided a fertile ground for much recent empirical research on growth is that it predicts that, over time, the per-capita income levels of countries in the world should converge. Empirical validation of this corollary of the Solowian framework has been attempted by many authors, some of whom have indeed found evidence for conditional convergence of per-capita incomes among the developed nations of the world, although unconditional convergence as predicted by the model has not yet been evidenced, though the continual improvement in the breadth, depth and quality of data available may eventually yield definitive answers.

To derive the dynamic path of any level variable of the type Y or K, let us reorganise that any level variable grows at a rate equal to the sum of the rate of per-capita growth (k/k) and the given rate of population growth, n.

$$\dot{K}/K = \dot{k}/k + n$$

Let us take the fundamental dynamic equation in intensive form, and dividing both sides by k, obtain:

$$\gamma_k = \dot{k}/k = s \cdot \frac{f(k)}{k} - (n+\delta)$$

Where γ_k denotes the rate of per-capita growth of the z-variable as defined by $\dot{z}/z$. With z= k, the above equation represents the per-capita rate of growth as the difference between the savings curve of the economy, a term which should be familiar to us as the one representing the stock of savings out of income, and the effective depreciation curve- a straight line at $(n+\delta)$. The following figure illustrates this dynamic:

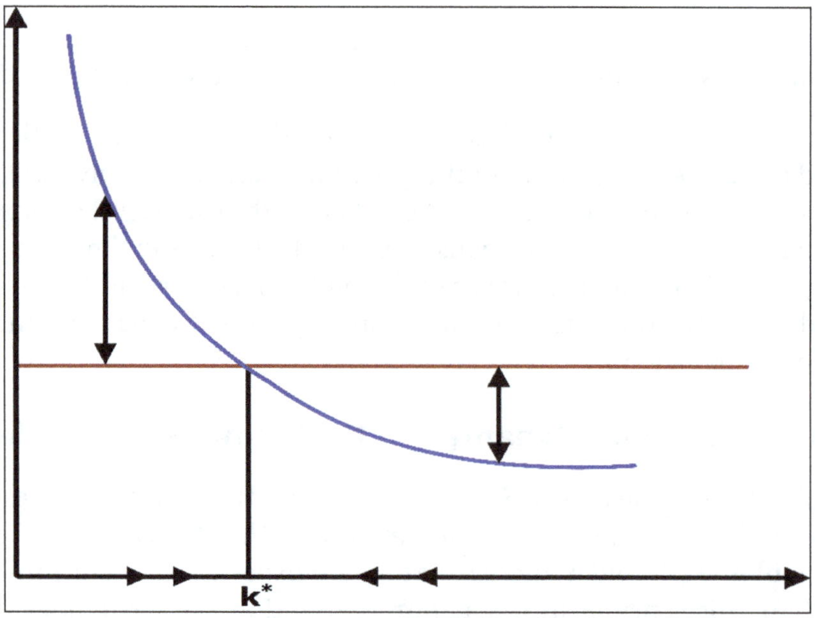

Dynamic behaviour in the Solow-Swan model: The growth rate of k is given by vertical difference between $s \cdot f(k)/k$ and the line of effective depreciation, $(n+\delta)$. The steady-state k^* is globally stable. For any $k < k^*$ the growth rate of k is positive. For the obverse case, $k > k^*$ the growth rate is negative, and k falls towards k^*.

In figure drawn above, the point where the savings curve crosses the effective depreciation line is the steady-state of the system. To the left of this steady-state, the savings curve lies above the effective depreciation level, and so the per-capita growth rate of capital is positive and increases the more left of the steady-state we move. The positive growth rate of capital per-person causes the level of k to rise. As k approaches k^* from the left, k/k goes to zero, hence, k^* is the leftward limit of k.

If we moved to the right of the steady state, effective depreciation outstrips savings, so that the rate of per-capita increase in capital is negative. This pushes k left, towards k^*. The closer k is to k^*, the smaller the value of $\dot{k}/k$, approaching zero from the right as well when k approaches k^*. The major short-run implication is that the economy asymptotically tends toward the steady-state, irrespective of where it began. For the purpose of the intensive form of the model, let us note that the reason for this asymptotic behaviour is our assumption of diminishing returns to factor (here, namely capital), which is the traditional microeconomic assumption in producer theory.

Therefore we find that the neoclassical production function exhibits global stability, such that, for any initial history, k(o) > o, the economy converges over time to its steady state, k^*>o.

The transitional behaviour of per-capita output, y, can also be charted in a similar fashion. The equation describing the short-run dynamic of per-capita output is:

$$\frac{\dot{y}}{y} = f'(k) \cdot \frac{\dot{k}}{f(k)} = \left[k \cdot \frac{f'(k)}{f(k)} \right] \cdot \left(\dot{k}/k \right).$$

Let us consider the term on the right hand side of the equation. The term in the brackets which weighs the per-capita growth rate is the share of capital in income. The relation between the corresponding per-capita rates of growth of output and capital is therefore sensitive to the share of rental income in total income. We can substitute $\dot{k}/k$ out of the equation above to get:

$$\frac{\dot{y}}{y} = s \cdot f'(k) - (n+\delta) k \cdot \frac{f'(k)}{f(k)}$$

Where $k \cdot \frac{f'(k)}{f(k)}$ is the share of capital income in total per-capita income. Let us denote this by $\text{Share}(k)$. To see how $\dot{y}/y$ changes with respect to a change in the per-capita stock of capital, k, we write down the partial differential:

$$\frac{\partial \left(\frac{\dot{y}}{y} \right)}{\partial k} = \left[\frac{f''(k) \cdot k}{f(k)} \right] \cdot \left(\frac{\dot{k}}{k} \right) - (n+\delta) \cdot \frac{f'(k)}{f(k)} \cdot \left[1 - \text{Share}(k) \right].$$

Since capital's share in income can be between zero and one, the second term on the right side of the equation given above is negative. Therefore, to the left of the steady state, where $\dot{k}/k$ is positive, the partial derivative of per-capita growth of output with respect to k is negative. Hence, $\dot{k}/k$ falls as k (and y) rises. To the right of the steady-state, the unambiguous result is that the same derivative will be negative whenever the economy is sufficiently close to the steady-state. Therefore, per-capita output has limited local stability to the right of the steady-state and limited global stability in case the initial level of output puts y to the left of the steady-state output, y^*. As a last aspect, consider that since consumption per-capita can be defined as a function of output, $c=(1-s)\cdot f(k)$, the dynamic of per-capita consumption mimics that of percapita output at all times, for any given rate of savings, s, that is $\dot{y}/y=\dot{c}/c$ at all times.

Convergence could mean one of two things in the context of the Solow-Swan model. One is that, since the derivative of $\dot{k}/k$ with respect to k is negative, this implies that the further away an economy is from its steady-state, the faster it converges to it. This is so since the negative derivative implies that smaller values of k are associated with larger values of $\dot{k}/k$. The mathematics is shown below:

$$\frac{\partial\left(\frac{\dot{k}}{k}\right)}{\partial k}=s\cdot\frac{\left[f'(k)-\frac{f(k)}{k}\right]}{k}<0.$$

This convergence of an economy to its steady state values could take two forms one is called absolute or unconditional convergence, which applies when one compares economies with reasonably similar (if not the exact same) parameter values, s, n and δ. With such economies, it is expected that countries which start out from a position of relatively poorer endowment of capital-labor ratio, k, will grow faster and eventually converge to the common steady state. Typically, such a country would also witness a higher rate of growth of output in per-capita terms. The second, and weaker, hypothesis is called conditional convergence, which applies to cases where there are significant differences in the parametric values, and, therefore occupy different steady-state positions. For such cases, we continue to make the claim that an economy converges to its own steady state values it grows faster the further away it is from its steady-state. This is true once the differences in parameters which determine the steady-state have been controlled for.

The second meaning of the term convergence is taken to imply that all economies in the world will eventually converge to the same level of per-capita income. In other words, it is the hypothesis that the dispersion of per-capita incomes across the world should fall over time.

Solow Growth Model

The concept of the growth rate is very important and you thoroughly need to understand it. Let x be an economic variable. Let x_0 be the initial value and x_1 be the subsequent value. The proportional change in going from x_0 to x_1 is simply,

$$\frac{x_1-x_0}{x_0}=\frac{\Delta x}{x_0}$$

The percentage change in going from x_0 to x_1 is simply 100 times the proportionate change:

$$\% \Delta x = 100(\Delta x / x_0)$$

If x is itself in percentage one has to be careful in expressing the change. For example, if unemployment decreases from 15% to 12% it is a reduction of 3 percentage points, but a $\frac{15-12}{15} \times 100 = 20\%$ fall in unemployment. People sometimes erroneously express it as a 3% fall.

Calculation of Growth Rate Assuming that the Rate of Growth is Constant

If we assume a constant rate of growth, the formula used for calculating the growth rate for more than one year is as follows: Let Y_0 be income in the initial year. Let n be the number of years. Let r be the constant compound annual rate of growth. Then income in the final year, Y_t, is given by:

$$Y_t = Y_0 (1+r)^n$$

$$= \log Y_t = \log Y_0 + n \log (1+r) \text{ where log stands for logarithm.}$$

$$= \log(1+r) = \frac{\log y_t \quad \log y_o}{}$$

$$\text{or } \log (1+r) = \frac{\log(y_t / y_o)}{}$$

$$= 1+r = \text{antilog}\left[\frac{\log(y_t / y_o)}{}\right]$$

$$\therefore r = \left\{\text{anti log}\left[\frac{\log(y_t / y_o)}{}\right] - 1\right\}$$

This assumes constant rate of growth, r (as in a constant rate of interest in compound interest formulations).

Calculation of Growth when the Rate of Growth is not Constant

When the rate of growth is not constant, it is say,

$$x_1, x_2, \ldots\ldots x_i \ldots\ldots x_t \text{ in say, years } t = 1, 2, \ldots, i, \ldots, t$$

$$\text{then } r = (x_1, x_2, \ldots\ldots x_t)^{\frac{1}{t}}$$

This is the geometric mean.

Exponential Growth

We know that growth can be written as $\frac{\Delta x}{x}$. This is in general terms.

Compound rates are the same as geometric growth. Continuous compound growth implies exponential growth,

$$v_t = v_o(1+g)^t$$

$$\Rightarrow \left(\frac{v_t}{v_o}\right) = (1+g)^t$$

$$\Rightarrow \left(\frac{v_t}{v_o}\right)^{1/t} = 1+g$$

$$\therefore g = \left(\frac{v_t}{v_o}\right)^{1/t} - 1$$

Let v_o equal the value of the variable in year 0 (the fast year) & v_t equal the value of the variable t years later. Further, let g equal the average compound annual growth rate. Then,

$$v_t = v_o(1+g)^t$$

$$\Rightarrow g = \left(\frac{v_t}{v_o}\right)^{1/t} - 1$$

If the growth rate is continuously compounded, then,

$$v_o\, e^{gt} = v_t$$

$$e^{gt} = \frac{v_t}{v_o}$$

$$g = \frac{1}{t}\ln\left(\frac{v_t}{v_o}\right)$$

We saw above that when the compound rate of growth is constant, $Y_t = Y_o(1+r)^t$. This means Y_o grows at 100r %. If compounding takes place m times a year (you may think of money in a bank earning compound interest), then in this case,

$$Y_t = Y_o\left(1+\frac{r}{m}\right)^{mt}.$$

As m gets larger and larger, and approaches infinity (theoretically, but this is conceptually very important), the term within the parenthesis acquires a definite value. We can write the above expression as,

$$Y_t = Y_o\left[\left(1+\frac{r}{m}\right)^{\frac{m}{r}}\right]^{rt}$$

Let m/r be denoted h then,

$$Y_t = Y_o\left[\left(1+\frac{1}{h}\right)^{h}\right]^{rt}$$

As m tends to infinity, so does h. A result in calculus states that Limit of $\left(1+\frac{1}{x}\right)^x$ as $x \to \infty$ is equal to e where e = 2.71828 approximately. This e is the inverse of natural logarithm. That is, for any number w, $e^{\ln w} = w$.

Hence as $h \to \infty$, $\left(1+\frac{1}{h}\right) \to e$.

Thus theoretically, $Y_t = Y_o\, e^{rt}$. This is called exponential growth. Exponential growth is the same as compound growth, where compounding is done instantaneously and constantly.

Depicting Growth in infinitesimal Terms

Let y = f(t) where t is time. Take natural logarithms of both sides,

$$\ln y = \ln(f(t))$$

Differentiating both sides with respect to time, we get,

$$\frac{d}{dt}(\ln y) = \frac{d}{dt}\ln(f(t))$$

$$= \frac{1}{f(t)} \bullet \frac{df(t)}{dt}$$

Using the fact of logarithmic differentiation and the chain rule. The right hand side above we can recognise as the instantaneous proportionate rate of growth,

$$\frac{\Delta x}{x} \text{ with } \Delta x \to 0 = \frac{1\, dx}{xdt}$$

Usually $\frac{dx}{dt}$, the time derivative of a variable x, is denoted $\dot{x}$.

Time as an Independent Explanatory Variable

If a variable y depends on x, and we postulate a linear relation between y and x, we can depict a statistical relationship under uncertainty $y_i = \alpha + \beta x_i + \varepsilon_i$ where i is the observation and α and β are coefficients to be estimated. When events takes place over time, we can show this in two ways. The first way is that we take the usual regression method, and use observations over time, what is called time–series data. Then the subscript will indicate time and is usually denoted by t. The second way is to say that time itself causes the change and can thus be considered like the variable x above, that is, time is considered as an independent variable in regression, as a regressor. This is how we get the concept of trend. A linear trend relationship can be denoted as:

$$y = \alpha + \beta T + \mu$$

where T indicates time. One has to appropriately define the origin, that is, the starting year or time period. Without disturbances, a constant growth series, as we have seen above, is given by the equation.

$$y_t = y_0(1+g)^t$$

where $g = \frac{(y_t - y_{t-1})}{y_{t-1}}$ is the constant proportionate rate of growth per period.

Taking longs of both sides of $y_t = y_0(1+g)^t$ given,

$$\ln y = \alpha + \beta t$$

where $\alpha = \ln y_0$ and $\beta = \ln(1+g)$

If we think that a series has a constant growth rate, plotting the log of the series against time provides an easy measure of growth. If the series is approximately linear, $\ln y = \alpha + \beta t$ can be fitted by least squares, regressing the log of y against time. The resultant slope coefficient then provides as estimates $\hat{g}$ of the growth rate.

The β coefficient of $y = \alpha + \beta T + \mu$ represents the continuous rate of change $\partial \ln y_t / \partial t$, whereas g represents the discrete case.

Some Concepts of Equilibrium Growth

An economy is said to be experiencing a steady-state growth if all variables are growing at a constant proportional rate or not at all. These rates may be different for different variables. An economy is said to be experiencing balanced growth if all variables are growing at the same constant proportional rate. Suppose in an economy, output per worker continues to grow at a constant 3%, savings rate continues to grow at 20%, capital per worker continues to grow at 8%, then this economy is showing steady state growth; if an economy is such where per-worker output, savings rate, capital per worker all grow at say 10 %, then this economy is experiencing balanced growth.

Kaldor's Stylised Facts about Economic Growth

Nicholas Kaldor, on the basis of his studies, presented in 1959 and 1961 works some "stylised facts" which he said could be observed with regularity, in the modern era, which we merely mention:

- In the long run, per capita output grows at a positive rate which shows no signs of diminishing.
- The capital-output ratio shows no perceptible upward or downward trend, that is, in the long run it remains roughly constant.
- The return to physical capital, that is, the profit rate, shows no perceptible upward or downward trend that is profit/capital remains largely constant.

- There is a great variety of growth rates of per capita income income across the world, that is, the rates of per capita growth vary substantially across nations.
- In the long run the capital labour ratio grows at a positive rate which shows no signs of diminishing.
- The income shares of labour and physical capital remain constant in the long run, and this, in turn implies that wage rate shows a rising trend.

The Solow Model

The model has certain assumptions which we state now and then set out the basic structure of the model.

Assumptions of the Solow Model

- The economy produces one composite good which can either be consumed or accumulated as a stock of capital. This is a simplified picture of reality. while we do not deny that lots of goods are produced in the economy, we consider, for purposes of building a model – a model, after all, is a parable or a fable only one 'composite' or 'aggregated' good.
- Labour supply is homogeneous. In other words, we do not distinguish between workers with different skills or between say, blue- and white-collared workers.
- There is a stock of capital which has been accumulated from the past. This capital and the labour are the factors of production, inputs to the production process.
- The production function exhibits constant returns to scale. This means that if labour and capital are increased by a certain proportion, say λ, output increases by the same proportion λ. If labour and capital are doubled, output is doubled. Thus there is an aggregate production function which is continuous and which displays constant returns to scale.
- The labour force grows at an exogenously given growth rate $g_L = n$. Thus labour force at time t is equal to $L_t = L_0e^{nt}$.
- People save a constant proportion of Income. If S denotes saving then S = sY. This assumption is the same as in the Harrod-Domar model. Some people feel that Solow made this deliberately to make a comparison with HarrodDomar model.
- There is no foreign trade.
- The government does not intervene in the economy; there are no taxes or government purchase.

Structure of the Model

Since we have assumed there is no depreciation, we consider the model here in the absence of depreciation. Later on, we shall discuss the case when there is depreciation of capital. To begin with consider the aggregate production function.

$$Y=F(K,L)$$

We have assumed that there are constant returns to scale. This means that if K & L are increases by a proportion λ, Y increases by the same proportion. The function F is homogenous of degree one.

$$Y = F(\lambda K, \lambda L) \text{ for all } \lambda > 1$$

For simplicity, let $\lambda = \frac{1}{L}$.

$$\text{Then } \frac{Y}{L} = F\left(\frac{K}{L}, \frac{L}{L}\right)$$

$$\text{or } \frac{Y}{L} = F\left(\frac{K}{L}, 1\right)$$

Let in denote quantities divided by L, by lower-case letters,

$$\text{So } y = F(k,1)$$

$$\text{Or } y = f(k)$$

This gives output per person as a function of capital labour ratio. Sometimes income is used synonymously with output. Denoting output by Q and output-labour ratio by q, we have,

$$q = f(k)$$

If we draw a picture of above the relationship we can show it as follows:

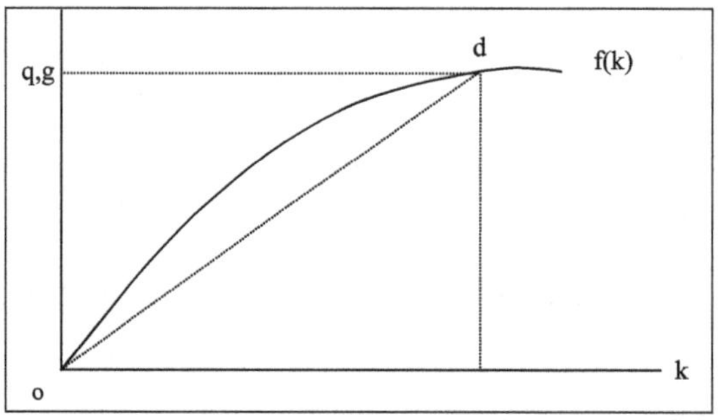

A ray d to any point d on the curve has a slope that gives the ratio of output to capital. This is because the of this ray is $= \frac{Q/L}{K/L} = \frac{Q}{K}$.

This is the is verse of capital output ratio v. Each point on the production function in the slow model is that Harrad-Domar model, l is not fixed or exogenous different points on the production function show different, capital output ratios.

Equilibrium Growth

We have $k = K/L$. Taking natural logarithms (denoted by Ln), we get,

$$\ln(k) = \ln\left(\frac{K}{L}\right)$$

$$\ln k = \ln \frac{K}{L}$$

$$\text{or, } \ln k = \ln K - \ln L$$

Differentiating with respect to figure, gives the proportional growth ratio:

$$\frac{d}{dt}(\ln k) = \frac{d}{dt}(\ln k) - \frac{d}{dt}(\ln L)$$
$$\frac{dk}{dt} \cdot \frac{1}{k} = \frac{dK}{dt} \cdot \frac{1}{K} - \frac{dL}{dt} \cdot \frac{1}{L}$$
$$\text{or } \hat{k} = \hat{K} - \hat{L}$$

Now $\frac{dK}{dt}$ on the right hand side is equal to investment I.

Investment = facing in equilibrium. So,

$$\frac{dK}{dt} = \dot{K} = S$$
$$S = SQ_t \text{ (as we have assumed)}$$
$$\text{So } \frac{dK}{dt} = sQ_t \text{ (t is the subscript denotes Q at a point of time)}$$

The Second term on the right hand side is $\hat{L} = \frac{dL}{dt} \cdot \frac{1}{L}$ which shows the proportional growth rate of labour. Which we have denoted n. So our equation, $\hat{k} = \hat{K} - \hat{L}$ can be written $\hat{k} = \frac{sQ}{K} - n$.

Dividing Q and K by L we get,

$$\hat{k} = \frac{sq}{k} - n = \frac{sf(k)}{k} - n$$

This gives $\hat{k}$, the rate of growth of k, is term of k itself. $\hat{k} = \frac{sq}{k} - n = \frac{sf(k)}{k} - n$ is the fundamental equation of the Solow model.

The equilibrium value of k is the one for which $\frac{dk}{dt} \cdot \frac{1}{k}$ is o, i.e. $\frac{dk}{dt} = o$ or where k once it reaches that value, does not change. Setting $\hat{k}$ =o in the equation above, we get,

$$\hat{k} = o = \frac{sf(k^*)}{k^*} - n$$

$$\text{or } \frac{sf(k^*)}{k^* = n}$$

where an * above k denotes its equilibrium value. The equilibrium q value is obtained as,

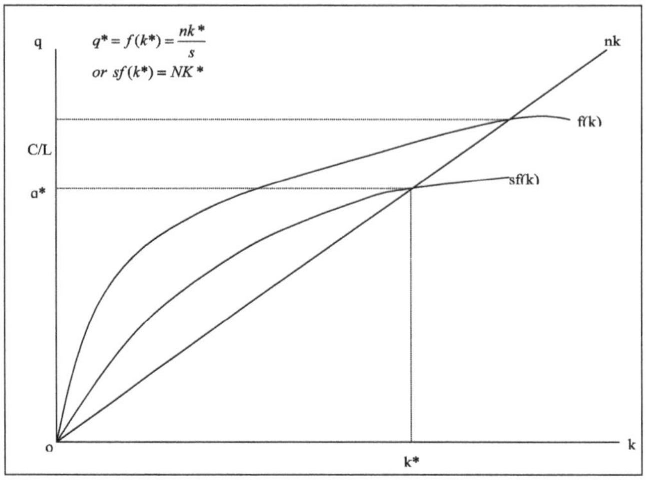

$$q^* = f(k^*) = \frac{nk^*}{s}$$
$$\text{or } sf(k^*) = NK^*$$

At any point to the left of k*, where k< k*,

$$f(k) > [(n/s)k]$$

This implies,

$$\frac{sf(k)}{k} > n$$

And from equation $\hat{k} = \frac{sq}{k} - n = \frac{sf(k)}{k} - n$, we can see that in this case $\hat{k} > o$, which mean that when k < k*, $\hat{k}$ increase.

Similarly we can show that whenever k>k* (to the right of k*), $\hat{k}$ is rising and where k>k*, $\hat{k}$ is falling. Thus k* is a stable equilibrium point. In equilibrium, when k equals k*, q reaches an equilibrium q*. As q* is a constant,

$$\frac{d\theta}{dt} \cdot \frac{1}{t} = \frac{dL}{dt} \cdot \frac{1}{t} = n$$

The economy thus converges to a steady state growth where $\hat{\theta} = \hat{K}$ and capital output ratio v is constant. However, $\hat{\theta}$ and $\hat{K}$ are not greater than L but equal to it. The equilibrium condition in the Solow model, $\frac{sf(k^*)}{k^*} = n$ can be written as $\frac{n}{s} = \frac{f(k)}{k} = \frac{q}{k} = \frac{Q/L}{K/L} = \frac{Q}{K} = \frac{1}{V^*}$, Where V is the capital output ratio.

So we have $n = \frac{S}{V^*}$, the Harrod-Domar condition for balanced full employment growth. However the Solow model allows V to vary and explains how the economy will turn toward a growth bath along with the Harrod-Domar condition is and there in the Solow model, the capital output ratio V* emerges as an equilibrium value, and not as a necessary technology assumption.

Consumption in the Solow Model

We know that in a closed economy with no government intervention in equilibrium,

$$Y = C + I$$

Where Y is aggregate output, C is aggregate consumption and I is investment.

Writing in per-worker, we have

$$\frac{Y}{L} = \frac{C}{L} + \frac{I}{L}.$$

We know, $\frac{Y}{L} = y = f(k)$,

So $f(k) = \frac{C}{L} + \frac{I}{L}$.

Now consider capital labour ratio, $k = K/L$. We have seen, $\frac{dk}{dt} \cdot \frac{1}{k} = \frac{dK}{dt} \cdot \frac{1}{K} - \frac{dL}{dt} \cdot \frac{1}{L}$.

$$\text{or } \hat{k} = \hat{K} - \hat{L}$$

Where $\wedge$ denotes proportional growth rate. We had already denoted $\hat{L}$ by n.

So we have,

$$\hat{k} = \hat{K} - n$$

or $\frac{\dot{k}}{k} = \frac{\dot{K}}{k} - n$ where $\dot{X}$ denotes $\frac{dX}{dt}$. Multiplying both sides by K/L we get,

$$\frac{\dot{k}}{k} \cdot \frac{K}{L} = \frac{\dot{K}}{K} \cdot \frac{K}{L} - \frac{nK}{L}$$

$$\text{or } \dot{k} = \frac{\dot{K}}{L} - nk$$

Alternatively putting it;

$$\frac{\dot{K}}{L} = \dot{k} + nk$$

Since one of the assumptions we had made was that there is no depreciation, hence,

$$\dot{k} = \frac{dK}{dt} = I$$

So we may write equation $\frac{\dot{K}}{L} = \dot{k} + nk$ as,

$$\frac{I}{L}=\dot{k}+nK$$

In equation $f(k)=\frac{C}{L}+\frac{I}{L}$ we can replace $\frac{I}{L}$ by the right hand side of the above equation. Equation $f(k)=\frac{C}{L}+\frac{I}{L}$ then becomes,

$$f(k)=\frac{C}{L}+\dot{k}+nK$$

This equation states the following: Output per worker (since we are taking θ as equal to Y and hence q=y) is put to three uses which are shown on the right hand side. First, consumption per worker $\frac{C}{L}$; a portion of investment nk, that maintains the capital labour ratio constant in the face of growing labour force; and a portion of investment, $\dot{k}$ which increases the capital labour ratio. When capital goods increase faster than the increase in labour, so that the capital-labour ratio rises, it is called capital deepening, while when capital goods rise merely to keep pace with the rise in labour force so that the capital labour ratio remains constant, it is called capital widening. Thus output per worker, in $f(k)=\frac{C}{L}+\dot{k}+nK$, is divided among consumption per worker, capital deepening and capital widening. We can arrive at $f(k)=\frac{C}{L}+\dot{k}+nK$ by a different route, from our fundamental equation of the Solow Model. Recall that the fundamental equation, $\hat{k}=\frac{sf(k)}{k}-n=\frac{sq}{k}-n$ is,

Since $\hat{k}=\frac{\dot{k}}{k}$, hence multiplying the above equation throughout by k, we get,

$$\dot{k}=sq=nk$$

Recall our assumption that q = y. We have,

$$\dot{k}=sq-nk$$

Since $y=\frac{Y}{L}$, we have $\dot{k}=\frac{sY}{L}-nk$.

We had made the assumption that S = sY.

Now in equilibrium S =Y-C = I. Hence we have, $\dot{k}=\frac{Y}{L}-\frac{C}{L}-nk$.

Now switching back in rotation f(k) for $\frac{Y}{L=y}$, we have,

$$\dot{k}=f(k)-\frac{C}{L}-nk$$

Or $f(k)=\frac{C}{L}+\dot{k}+nk$ which is $f(k)=\frac{C}{L}+\dot{k}+nK$.

What are the basic proposition and conclusion that we get from the Solow model? Does it provide some guidelines for studying the growth trajectories of actual economies? We give below some theoretical conclusions that emerge from the Solow model. First, given the assumptions as stated earlier, there exists a steady state (balanced growth) solution for the model. The balanced growth solution is stable. Stability is there in that whenever the initial values of all the variables, the economy eventually reverts to the steady state equilibrium value of y and k. The second conclusion we get that the balanced rate of growth (all variables grow at the same rate) is the constant exogenous grow the of labour force, which is n.

A Comparison with the Harrod-Domar Model

The first basic difference that the Solow model has with the Harrod Domar model is that in the Solow model the capital output ratio is not exogenously fixed. It is endogenously determined. The second difference is that process of adjustment in the variables is different in the two models. In the HD model, there are two knife-edges: the balance between the actual and warranted rates of growth, and between the warranted and natural rates of growth. Solow's model does not address this question, and instead assumes that planned investment equals planned savings at all times. This is, of course, again because s, v, n were all fixed in the HD model, whereas in the Solow model, there is a spectrum of values that that v, that is, the capital output ratio can take, and adjust to that value at which the warranted rate of growth equals the natural rate of growth.

Some Applications of the Neoclassical Model

Depreciation of Capital Stock

We know that in absence of depreciation, $\dot{K} = I$, Here I denote grow investment.

Let us now answer that a certain proportion δK of capital depreciates. We can now write,

$$I = \dot{K} + \delta K$$

Where I now is net investment and δ is the constant rate of depreciation of capital stock. Dividing by L, we obtain,

$$\frac{I}{L} = \frac{\dot{K}}{L} + \frac{\delta K}{L}.$$

We know from equation $\frac{\dot{K}}{L} = \dot{k} + nk$,

Substituting this expression for $\frac{\dot{K}}{L}$ into equation $\frac{I}{L} = \frac{\dot{K}}{L} + \frac{\delta K}{L}$, we obtain

$$\frac{I}{L} = \dot{k} + nk + \delta k$$

$$\text{or } \frac{I}{L} = \dot{k} + (n + \delta)k$$

Writing $\frac{I}{L}$ as $\frac{S}{L}$ (in equation) and they as sy or sf(k),

We have, $sf(k) = \dot{k} + (n+\delta)k$ or $\dot{k} = sf(k) - (n+\delta)k$

$$\text{Or, } \dot{k} = \frac{sf(k)}{k} - (n+\delta)$$

This is a modified form of the fundamental equation of the Solow model. The basic analysis that we studied, carrier over for the case of depreciating capital; we merely need to replace n by $(n+\delta)$.

Variable Savings Rate

We can use the Solow model to look at the situation where the saving rate is variable. Suppose the saving rate increases from s_1 to s_2. this means that the sf(k) curve shifts upwards. This means the sf(k) curve will cut the nk curve at a new point which is higher and to the right of the earlier point of intersection. This means equilibrium k and y will both rise. So an increase in the rate of savings does push up the output per man in the Solow model. But it is also important to note that in the Solow model, the savings rate is a key determinant of the level of capital per person. If the saving rate is high the economy will have a large capital stock and output. But saving has only a temporary effect on the growth in output per person. The economy will grow only till the economy reaches a new equilibrium capital per person level. The above observation that a permanent change in the savings rate has only a temporary effect on the economy's growth rate is called the Solowian paradox of thrift. This point is important to note since it is often suggested that developing nations should raise their savings rate as far as possible. this is supposed to push up the growth rates of per capita income. This proposition is present in the theories of development economists like Nurkse, Rostow and Lewis. Increasing the saving rate would push up growth rates only temporarily. The basic lesson of the Solow model is that permanent increase in the growth rate of per capita income comes about only through a change or improvement in technology.

Population Growth

We can now examine in the Solow model the effect of a growth in population. Capital accumulation by itself cannot explain long-term growth. This can come about through technical progress. The other source is a growth in population. Let us suppose that the population increase at a rate n. What effect does this have on the steady state growth? Once the number of workers rises, this will cause capital per worker k to fall.

We know that $\Delta k = sf(k) - nk$. So increase in population (not the rate, but the level) reduces k. of course, we had seen this while studying the basic model. The steady state level of k is determined from the pint where the curve sf(k) cuts the line nk. Dropping a perpendicular from this point to the horizontal axis (which measures k) gives us the steady state value k*.

Let us now see what happens when the rate of population itself changes, that is, n itself undergoes a change. Let the rate of population growth increase from n_1 to n_2. This means that the nk line will tilt upwards. If the sf(k) curve remains the same the new nk line will cut the sf(k) curve to the left of the earlier intersection point. This results in the steady state capital per worker k* to fall.

Since y = f(k), a reduction in k* results in y falling. Thus in the Solow model, if the rate of growth of population rises, output per worker will fall. This has lessons for developing nations. These nations should not allow the rate of population to increase as this may have detrimental effect on the per-worker output.

Money in the Neo-Classical Growth Model

James Tobin, in a paper published in 1965, presented a simple model of monetary growth which follows the Solowian model. Tobin had of course, earlier, independently developed a growth model in l955 which was similar to the Solow model but had the existence of government debt (net "outside" wealth). For our analysis, we assume that there is only one such type of outside wealth: money. Let money yield a certain rate of return, which we shall denote as R (we are concerned with a broad aggregate for money). In the original Solow model, physical capital was the only form of wealth that existed. However, money is an important alternative store of wealth. Tobin extended this to bring in outside government wealth in the form of money. How does this change the Solow model? Tobin used the simple quantity theory of money MV = PY. Assuming the velocity of money is constant, the growth in money equals the difference between the inflation rate and growth in nominal income.

$$\hat{M} = \hat{P} - \hat{Y}$$

where $\wedge$ represents the proportional growth rate of a variable x. Rewriting this, we see that the rate of inflation is merely the difference between the rate of money growth and the rate of output growth. The greater the difference, the higher will be the inflation rate. Note the important implication that if money stock is constant ($\hat{M} = 0$), then prices will fall at the rate of growth of output $\hat{Y}$ and real money balances, M/P, will grow at that same rate. Let real wealth (A) be held in two assets, real money (M/P) and physical capital (K), in a proportion such that:

$$A = \alpha(M/P) + (1 - \alpha)K$$

where α lies between 0 and 1. The value of α is determined through portfolio selection by households. The important thing Tobin did was to consider the real rate of return froom money as the difference between the nominal rate of interest and inflation rate. He suggested that people make a comparison between R and the marginal product of K. People do this comparing and in the economy it is determined how much wealth will be held and how much physical capital. This has implications thrugh the function f(k) on output growth. Thus in situations of inflation, people may hold less M/P because real value of money falls, people might hold more K. this leads to a fall in-marginal productivity of capital.

A limitation of Tobin's model is the fact that it treats money solely as a store of value and, in effect, does not consider its use in overcoming transactions costs, etc. they suggested extensions to the Tobin model where money directly enters the utility function.

Convergence and Poverty Traps

Convergence

If you look at the Solow model carefully, it might seem to you that the model suggests that the growth rates of different nations would tend to converge over time, that is, towards the same rate of growth. We can think of three reasons why the Solow model suggests this behaviour. First, the Solow model suggests the rate of return on capital is higher in countries with less capital per worker. Hence capital ought to flow from the rich nations to the poorer nations. Secondly, the Solow model predicts that countries eventually would converge to their balanced growth path. Finally, while there may be initial differences in incomes among countries because some countries have better stock of knowledge, eventually, as the poorer countries gain access to the latest technologies, such differences in incomes will shrink.

There are two types of convergence that is usually studied, absolute or unconditional convergence and conditional convergence. Absolute convergence states the following: suppose there is a group of countries. Suppose all these countries have access to the same technology f(.), and have the same population growth rate n, have the same propensity to save, that is, the same saving rate s, but differ, and this is the only point of difference, in their initial capital-output ratio. Then the Solow model suggests that all countries would converge to the same equilibrium steady state capital labour ratio, output per capita and consumption per capita (k^* , y^* , c^*) and the same growth rate n.

To understand this further, suppose that there are two countries, one rich and one poor. Supoose the poor country has capital labour ratio k1 and the rich country has k_2. Since $k_1$is < k_2 the absolute convergence predicts that both countries will ultimately converge to a level k^*, between k_1 and k_2. This means the poor country will grow much faster as its capital and output grow faster than n, while in the rich nation the capital and output will grow slower than n. in other words, since $k_1 <$ k_2, marginal product of k, that is, capital relative to labour is higher in the poor country than in the rich one, and thus the poor country will accumulate more capital and grow at a faster rate than the rich one. Conditional convergence is invoked in light of the fact that in the real world, rich and poor nations do not seem to be converging to a steady state growth rate, as implied by the Solow model.

Conditional convergence states that if nations are endowed with the same technological possibilities and population growth rates but differ in savings propensities that is, savings rate and the initial capital-labour ratio, then there will still be convergence to the same growth rate but not necessarily at the same equilibrium capital-labour ratio. Thus the conditional convergence hypothesis suggests that nations can differ in their capital-labour ratios and thus differ in their consumption per capita, but as long as they have the same population rate n, then all their level variables (as opposed to per capita) capital, output, consumption will eventually grow at the same rate. Of course, we usually see the absence of even conditional convergence, but that may be because nations differ in their population growth rates.

If we consider unconditional convergence, it might appear that nothing much of great importance is being talked about. After all if we assume that parameters like savings rate, population growth, capital depreciation are similar. It might seem common sense to argue that this is only to be expected. But note that the hypothesis of unconditional convergence does not assume that the initial level of per capita income or the capital stock is the same. If the parameters governing the evolution of the economies are similar the initial levels do not matter.

A well-known study to examine the empirical validity of the unconditional convergence hypothesis was conducted by William Baumol and published in a 1986 paper. Baumol used data compiled by noted economic historian Angus Maddison. Baumol studied a set of 16 countries that are among the richest today. Baumol plotted the 1870 per capita incomes for these countries on the horizontal axis and plotted the growth rate of per capita incomes of these countries over the period 1870-1979 on the vertical axis. If the unconditional hypothesis were true, we would get an inverse relationship between initial per capita income level and rate of growth of per capita income. Baumol indeed found a downward sloping scatter plot, which showed a negative relationship. Baumol also ran a regression where the dependent variable was the difference of the natural logarithms of the per-capita incomes of 1979 and 1870 and the dependent variable was the natural logarithm of the per capita income of 1870. The regression can be represented as,

$$\ln\left[\left(\frac{Y}{N}\right)\right]\ln\left[\left(\frac{Y}{N}\right)_{i,1979}\right]-\ln\left[\left(\frac{Y}{N}\right)_{i,1870}\right]=a+b\ln\left[\left(\frac{Y}{N}\right)_{i,1870}\right]+\varepsilon_i$$

(Y/N) is log of income per person and ε is an error term. The estimated values of a and b were 8.457 and (minus) 0.995 respectively. Since b is almost equal to -1, it shows almost perfect convergence.

Baumol's findings were challenged by Bradford De Long on two grounds. First, De Long pointed out that there were sample selection bias or, bias in the selection of the sample itself. When Baumol carried out the study, the countries chosen in his sample were already rich. In 1870, there was no way of knowing which countries were going to grow fast later. Ex-post knowledge cannot be a basis of ex-ante prediction. Historical data is constructed retrospectively. Those countries for which data is available over a long period are likely to be those that have grown rapidly in the past 100 years or so, and are industrialized today. On the other hand, countries that were already rich hundred years ago are likely to be included even if there subsequent growth has not been so fast.

The second point on which De Long challenged Baumol's findings is measurement error. Estimates of data for 1870 may not be precise. Those countries whose 1870 per capita income was overstated actually had grown faster than had been estimated. Those countries for which 1870 per capita income was understated had grown slower than had been measured. Either way, there was a bias towards showing convergence.

Poverty Traps

Empirically, the convergence hypothesis has not held up very well. The neo-classical model has not been very successful in showing why rates of growth differ across nations. One fact was staring everyone in the face: many rations of the world were poor. In a sense, what was going on was the exact opposite of what was suggested by the convergence hypothesis: some countries were showing stagnant growth, while others were progressing very fact. This idea that the poorer nations were actually caught is a trap has come to be called poverty trap. It is a trap because in spite of efforts, these nations stay at a low-level 'equilibrium'. There are two types of poverty traps: technological-induced and population induced. They can both be demonstrated in the Solow system.

1. Technological trap: If we consider the Solow production function $y=f(k)$, or $\frac{Y}{L}=F\left(\frac{K}{L}\right)$, and suppose there is a certain range where for certain values of L, K, the production function exhibits increasing returns to scale, then there will be multiple equilibrium. For certain values of k, say k*

if the economy grows at a level lower than k*, the economy will slump back towards a very low income and output level because the level k* may show a unstable equilibrium. The idea behind technological trap is that had such a hypothetical country received an initial injection of capital so as to give a value of k larger k*, it would have been pushed over the level. This idea is sometimes called the 'Big push Theory'. The idea of poverty trap being caused by low savings, low technology is sometimes called the vicious circle of poverty.

2. Population Trap: The second way in which poverty traps can arise is induced by population growth. In the neo-classical model, the rate of population growth was given exogenously. However for classical writers population growth was given endogenously. Robert Malthus in his 1798 work suggested that the rate of growth of population depends on per capita income. As per capita income rises, the rate of population growth rises ever faster. This has come to be knows as the theory of demographic transition. We can bring in the idea of demographic transition into the neo classical model. Recall that in the neo classical model population grows exogenously at a rate n. Now suppose population growth rate is dependent on y, as suggested by the theory of demographic transition. We know that y is a function of capital per person $y = f(k/l)$. Thus n, the population growth rate indirectly becomes a function of the capital labour ratio:

$$n = g(k/l)$$

We may think of some interval $k_2 - k_1$ where for values of k below k_1, n is < 0, but for values of k in the range $[k_2, k_1]$ n is >0; again for values of k > k_2, n may again become <0. Historically, in olden time in societies where k was below k_1, population was lost through wars, disease etc.

AK Model

An early version of AK theory was produced by Frankel, who argued that the aggregate production function can exhibit a constant or even increasing marginal product of capital. This is because, when firms accumulate more capital, some of that increased capital will be the intellectual capital that creates technological progress, and this technological progress will offset the tendency for the marginal product of capital to diminish. In the special case where the marginal product of capital is exactly constant, aggregate output Y is proportional to the aggregate stock of capital K:

$$Y = AK$$

where A is a positive constant that reflects the level of technology and 'K' here is taken in a broader sense as it includes physical as well as human capital. This model shows constant marginal product to capital (as $MP_k = dY/dK = A$) indicating that long run growth is possible. Thus, AK model is a simple way of illustrating endogenous growth. Assuming a closed economy, the savings are equal to investment under conditions of full employment. Since savings are the function f income and capital depreciates at a constant rate i.e. 'δ' the change in capital stock can be traced through following equations:

$$I = S = s.Y = s.AK$$

and, since capital depreciates at a constant rate, the change in capital stock i.e. $\dot{K}$ can be expressed as $\dot{K} = s.Y - \delta.K$. This change in capital stock can also be represented by a diagram given below:

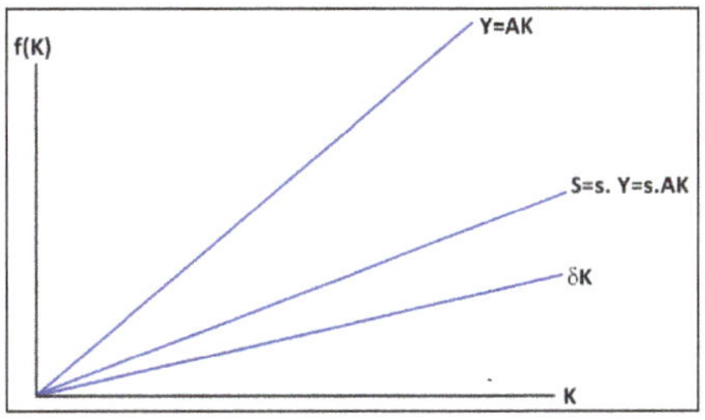

In this figure Y-axis show output per worker while the X-axis show the capital stock. The line $Y = AK$ having a constant slope shows the constant marginal productivity of capital; the line $S = s.Y$ is the gross investment line while the line δK shows the depreciation line or the total replacement investment. The difference between the gross investment line and the replacement line i.e. area between $S = s.Y$ line and δK line shows net investment in the economy which is positive and increasing. The growth of capital stock can be found by dividing both sides of the equation showing change in capital stock with 'K', we get, $\frac{\dot{K}}{K} = s.\frac{Y}{K} - \delta$.

Since, $Y = AK$, i.e. $Y / K = A$, therefore, above equation can be rewritten as:

$$\frac{\dot{K}}{K} = s.A - \delta$$

As, growth of output is equal to the growth of capital stock, $\frac{\dot{Y}}{Y} = \frac{\dot{K}}{K} = s.A - \delta$.

Further, assuming that $s.A > \delta$, the growth of capital stock as well as growth of output i.e. $\frac{\dot{Y}}{Y} > 0$, showing that the economy will be ever increasing as compared to the Solow model which shows that the income increases at a declining rate before stagnating for a given technology. We can easily compare how the paths of per capita income would differ in case of Solow model of exogenous growth and the AK model of endogenous growth. This comparison has been shown through figure.

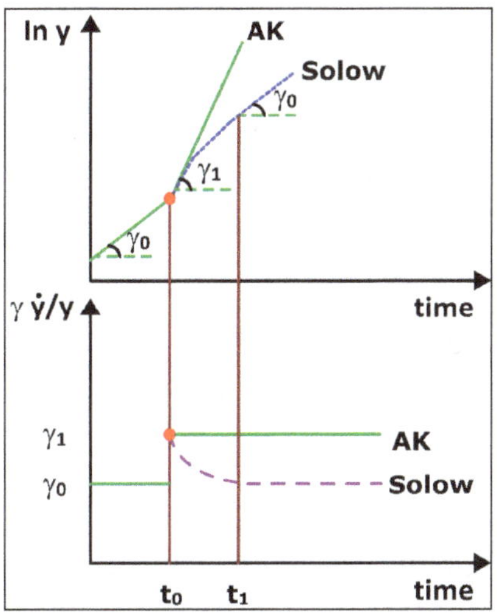

The AK Model and the Solow model compared for rising saving rate.

Figure compares the impact of rate of change in savings upon the growth of income. The top part of the diagram shows the levels of income and the bottom part shows the growth rate of the same. In the upper part, we can see that a once for all increase in saving rate in to time period leads to an ever growing income curve (shown as in y) in case of AK model while in case of Solow model, the income increases initially but ultimately reaches at the same level after t_1. This can be observed through the angle 'γ'. In case of Solow type growth path, as savings increase or say, due to exogenous change in technology in to time period, the income curve immediately and its slope rises as we can see that the size of angle 'γ' increases from γ_0 to γ_1 but after t_1 time period, it again comes back to the previous level i.e. γ_0. However, in case of AK type growth the increase in income is forever, shown by an ever increasing curve and once for all increase in the size of angle γ_0 to γ_1. The growth path can better be elaborated through growth rate of income in the lower segment of the diagram. We can see that in to time period, the growth rate of income increases immediately from γ_0 to γ_1 but the Solow type growth path shows that it comes back to γ_0 level while the AK growth path shows that growth of income is constant at stays at γ_1 level even in the long run.

AK Model with Human Factor

In its more realistic form, we can also add labour as an input along with capital. In this context, first of all, we can discuss Arrow's model with knowledge spillovers. In this model, the production function for final output can be written as,

$$Y = B.K^{\alpha}L^{1-\alpha}$$

which is a Cobb-Douglas type production function showing constant returns to scale with inputs K and L. In a model with technology and population growth as exogenous factors, the population, equal to labour input L, can be normalized to one and the individual firm takes total factor productivity B as given. However, we suppose that B is in fact endogenously determined. Specifically, the accumulation of capital generates new knowledge about production in the economy as a whole. In particular, we assume that, $B = AK^{1-\alpha}$, where, A is constant and is greater than zero i.e. $A > 0$. That is, an incidental by-product of capital accumulation by firms in the economy is the improvement of the technology that firms use to produce. Technological progress, modelled as a by-product of capital accumulation, is external to the firm. Combining the two preceding equations gives, $Y = A.K.L^{1-\alpha}$.

This is exactly the AK model above, noting that L = 1. However, in further formulation of the AK model, we can include human capital as a separate variable having a positive effect upon the level of output. Thus, more skilled labour force will be assumed to produce more output than an unskilled individual, and the total stock of such "skills" is called human capital. Crucially, human capital can be accumulated through education.

Thus, both types of capital can be accumulated this turns out to imply that the model has similar properties to the AK model. In this perspective, we can have a production function of the following type:

$$Y_t = A_t.K_t^{\alpha}.H_t^{1-\alpha}$$

where K_t is physical capital and H_t is human capital. So, growth is determined by,

$$\frac{\dot{Y}_t}{Y_t}=\frac{\dot{A}_t}{A_t}+\alpha\frac{\dot{K}_t}{K_t}+(1-\alpha)\frac{\dot{H}_t}{H_t}$$

Assuming that like physical capital, human capital also depreciates for given attainments. This can be understood in this way that if a person does not updates its knowledge, the knowledge accumulated so far depreciates in a dynamic economy. For simplifying the analysis, let us assume that both the physical as well as human capital depreciates at the same rate, then we can easily derive the equations for accumulation of each type of capital stock. This simplification is expected not to disturb the relevant conclusions of the model. Hence, the change in physical capital stock is defined as,

$$\dot{K}_t = s_k Y - \delta K$$

and the change in human capital stock can be defined as,

$$\dot{H}_t = s_H Y - \delta H$$

Similarly, we can also define the capital output ratios for both the physical and human capital. The capital output ratio for physical capital is, $x_K = \frac{K}{Y}$, while for human capital, it is, $x_H = \frac{H}{Y}$. For finding the growth rate of physical as well as human capital, we can divide the equations $\dot{K}_t = s_k Y - \delta K$ and $\dot{H}_t = s_H Y - \delta H$, respectively with 'K' and 'H' and substitute the above values of respective capital output ratios, we have $\frac{\dot{K}}{K}=\frac{s_K}{x_K}-\delta$ and $\frac{\dot{H}}{H}=\frac{s_H}{x_H}-\delta$. In AK model, for a steady growth path, the growth for physical and human capital stock should be the same i.e. $\frac{\dot{K}}{K}=\frac{s_K}{x_K}-\delta=\frac{s_H}{x_H}-\delta=\frac{\dot{H}}{H}$ .This implies that $\frac{s_K}{x_K}=\frac{s_H}{x_H}\Rightarrow\frac{x_K}{x_H}=\frac{s_K}{x_H}\Rightarrow\frac{K}{H}=\frac{s_K}{s_H}$. So, along the steady growth path, the stock of human capital can be written as, $H=\frac{s_H}{s_K}K$. This value of 'H' can be put in

$Y_t = A_t.K_t^{\alpha}.H_t^{1-\alpha}$, we get, $Y = AK^{\alpha}\left(\frac{s_H}{s_K}K\right)^{1-\alpha}$ or $Y = A.K\left(\frac{s_H}{s_K}\right)^{1-\alpha}$.

Again, under the steady growth path, growth of income is equal to the growth of capital stock, $\frac{\dot{Y}}{Y}=\frac{\dot{K}}{K}$, from equation $\frac{\dot{K}}{K}=\frac{s_K}{x_K}-\delta$ and putting the value of $x_K=\frac{K}{Y}$, we get, $\frac{\dot{Y}}{Y}=\frac{s_K Y}{K}-\delta = A.s_K\left(\frac{s_H}{s_K}\right)^{1-\alpha}-\delta$. Hence, $\frac{\dot{Y}}{Y}=A.(s_K)^{\alpha}(s_H)^{1-\alpha}-\delta$. Thus, allowing for both type of inputs- physical as well as human capital, which are continuously accumulated produce same results as that of the AK model as equation, $\frac{\dot{Y}}{Y}=A.(s_K)^{\alpha}(s_H)^{1-\alpha}-\delta$ is another form of growth of income in AK model with capital input only. In this case, the steady growth rate is $A.(s_K)^{\alpha}(s_H)^{1-\alpha}-\delta$ instead of $AS-\delta$ as in simple AK model. Here, the simple saving rate has been replaced with a geometric average of the two saving rates in the two factor model while leaving the broader implications unchanged. Lucas on the other hand tried to incorporate the role of human capital in terms of effective labour force and an attempt has also been made to measure the human capital accumulation in terms of allocation of time between production time and time spent in human capital accumulation. Thus the effect of human capital accumulation can be observed in the standard AK model. Although, we have already discussed the Lucas model in the lesson on endogenous growth models, yet it is important here to look at it briefly in AK framework. For this purpose, we now consider a simple endogenous growth model with human capital accumulation in which Y is a function in physical capital K and "effective labour" h. L, where 'h' is level of human capital per person and 'L' is the size of the labour force.

$$Y = K^{\alpha}(h.L)^{1-\alpha}$$

Lucas assumes that human capital per person evolves according to, $\dot{h}=(1-u)h$, where u is time spend working and (1 – u) is time spend accumulating skills. The growth rate of h is given by $\frac{\dot{h}}{h}=1-u$.

Since h enters the production function like labour-augmenting technological progress in the Solow model, we can conclude that the long-run growth rate of output is equal to the growth of human capital stock which is equal to the growth of physical capital stock on steady state equilibrium path. Hence, $\frac{\dot{Y}}{Y}=\frac{\dot{h}}{h}$ or $\frac{\dot{Y}}{Y}=1-u$. This implies that every policy measure which affects u has an impact on the long-run growth rate.

Thus, we have observed that AK model gives a new framework for the long run growth of the economies. However, there are still some reasons to doubt the predictions about long-run growth generated by this class of models. The first line of criticism is related with the non-accumulable factors. In the real world, there are factors of production that are in fixed supply, such as land, or that cannot simply be accumulated indefinitely such as energy. Remember that the AK model results are of a knife-edge variety: Any move away from all factors being accumulable, and we move back to the Solow model results. Moreover, similar treatment to all type of human capital is also criticised by many as they say that the strict parallel between human capital and physical capital in the model just described is probably not completely accurate. For instance, not all expenditures on education will produce the same effect on output. The marginal boost to aggregate output of primary teaching is altogether different to that of higher education; training the non-skilled informally and the formal training of the professional also differ in their marginal returns. By clubbing all these different types of human capital together hardly proposes an effective policy suggestion for countries with a varied structure of human capital. Another source of the difficulties faced by the AK model is that it does not make an explicit distinction between capital accumulation and technological progress. In effect it just lumps together the physical and human capital. Lastly, it also criticised for not giving any explanation for any possibility of convergence among the economies.

Nelson-Phelps Model

Take technology and human capital as the engines for economic growth. The first variable, technology, may be decomposed into two parts. The technology possibilities frontier will be variable $T(t)$ and a ready-to-use in production technology is represented by $A(t)$. In every time moment $A(t) \leq T(t)$; both variables are assumed to be positive quantities for all $t \geq 0$. We will be concerned with understanding the temporal evolution of a gap variable $\phi(t) \equiv A(t)/T(t)$, $\phi(t) \in [0,1]$, that has a straightforward interpretation: the higher the value of $\phi(t)$ the smaller is the gap between the values of the technology variable representing knowledge immediately available to produce and of the technology variable representing the scientific state of the art. Another fundamental variable is the growth rate of the technology frontier: $\tau(t) \equiv \dot{T}(t)/T(t), T(0) = T_0$ given. This growth rate is assumed as a control variable for the representative agent; that is, in what concerns technology decisions, the economy is able to choose the rate at which scientific progress occurs. Nevertheless, obviously this must be a constrained decision process because in order to allocate more resources to research activities one faces an opportunity cost related to the resources that remain available for other economic activities. In particular, we assume that the choice in terms of basic technology progress is constrained by the necessity of using economic resources to apply technology to the goods production process. Therefore, a trade-off emerges between our first two endogenous variables: $\phi(t)$ and $\tau(t)$. As far as technology choices are concerned, the basic economic goal is to maximize the intertemporal stream of $v[\phi(t), \tau(t)]$ functions, being a function v defined as follows:

1. Function v: The representative agent that makes technology choices faces a real valued objective function $v : \mathbb{R}^2_+ \mapsto \mathbb{R}$ that obeys the following properties:

- Continuity, concavity and smoothness.
- $v_\phi.\dfrac{\phi(t)}{v} = \theta \in (0,1); v_\tau.\dfrac{\tau(t)}{v} = \mu \in (0,1)$

The second condition in definition ensures that the utility of reducing the technology gap and the utility of increasing the pace of technological progress are both positive and diminishing for the representative agent. To simplify our treatment of the model we will work with a specific functional form of the above defined v function.

$$v[\phi(t), \tau(t)] = \phi(t)^{1/(1+\sigma)}.\tau(t)^{\sigma/(1+\sigma)}$$

The correspondence between parameters θ and μ in definition and parameter σ in equation $v[\phi(t), \tau(t)] = \phi(t)^{1/(1+\sigma)}.\tau(t)^{\sigma/(1+\sigma)}$ is the following: $\sigma = \mu/\theta$ and $\mu = 1 - \theta$. The trade-off between the two endogenous technology variables, $\phi(t)$ and $\tau(t)$, becomes explicit by considering the Nelson-Phelps technology constraint.

$A(t)=g[h(t)].[T(t)-A(t)], g(0)=0, g'>0, g''<0, A(0)=A_0$ states that the rate of increase of the index $A(t)$ is a function of human capital [$h(t)$ is a human capital per unit of labor variable or a human capital efficiency index] and of the gap that exists between the two technology variables. First and second derivatives of g indicate that there are positive but diminishing returns of human capital in the production of technology. The gap term translates the idea that the level of technology in practice will evolve faster when there is a large gap between technology possibilities and the stock of knowledge instantly available to produce. Recovering variable $\phi(t)$, from equation $A(t)=g[h(t)].[T(t)-A(t)], g(0)=0, g'>0, g''<0, A(0)=A_0$ we arrive at the final form of the first resource constraint of the optimal control problem:

$$\phi(t)=g[h(t)].[1-\phi(t)]-\tau(t).\phi(t), \phi(0)=\phi_0.$$

To complete the presentation of the model it is necessary to define a rule for the evolution of the human capital variable. On this respect we follow the standard form in most growth models, i.e., human capital evolves in time through a production process that involves a production function, f, and a constant depreciation rate, δ.

$$\dot{h}(t)=f[h(t)]-\delta.h(t), \delta>0, h(0)=h_0 \text{ given.}$$

The human capital variable is, alongside with variable $\phi(t)$, a state variable of the inter-temporal control problem. Equations $\phi(t)=g[h(t)].[1-\phi(t)]-\tau(t).\phi(t), \phi(0)=\phi_0$ and $\dot{h}(t)=f[h(t)]-\delta.h(t), \delta>0, h(0)=h_0$ are the motion equations that constitute the resource constraints to which the optimization problem is subject to.

The analytical tractability of the model demands that we take explicit functional forms for functions f[h(t)] and g[h(t)]. Assuming that it is possible to choose at each moment in time the shares of human capital to allocate to each of the two economic sectors (technology and education sectors), we define a new variable u(t) that represents precisely the share of human capital allocated to the generation of technology. Obviously $u(t)\leq 1, \forall t$. The properties of function g were set forth in equation $A(t)=g[h(t)].[T(t)-A(t)], g(0)=0, g'>0, g''<0, A(0)=A_0$. Positive and diminishing returns of human capital in the production of technology imply a function with the following shape:

$$g[h(t)]=a.[u(t).h(t)]^{\eta},\ a>0,\ \eta\in(0,1)\cdot$$

Function f may be defined in a similar way:

$$f[h(t)]=b.\{[1-u(t)].h(t)\}^{\beta}, b>0\cdot$$

For equation $f[h(t)]=b.\{[1-u(t)].h(t)\}^{\beta}, b>0$ we find it convenient to impose $\beta\in(0,1)$ in order to obtain a long run balanced growth path. Thus, one assumes that the education sector exhibits diminishing returns in the accumulation of human knowledge. This point was referred to earlier in the introduction and should be stressed since it constitutes an innovation relatively to conventional growth models. Where human capital contributes to the generation of physical goods solely in an indirect manner, we must assume diminishing returns in the accumulation of human capital in order to get a long term constant steady state growth. As a result of this assumption, the human capital per unit of labor variable will have a different behavior from those of the other inputs: its level will not grow in the long run in opposition to what happens to the several per capita variables, namely output, consumption and physical capital. Remembering that $h(t)$ defines average individual skills, intuitively it is hard to support the concept that human capabilities may be improved further and further indefinitely at a constant rate. Technology and machines can be expanded without limit, individual skills cannot this is a fundamental argument of our analysis. The optimal control growth problem has now all the necessary ingredients.

2. Control problem optimal solution: An optimal solution is a set of paths $\{\phi(t),h(t),\tau(t),u(t)\}$ that solve the maximization problem $\underset{\tau(t),u(t)}{\text{Max}}\int_0^{+\infty} v[\phi(t),\tau(t)].e^{-\rho.t}.dt$ subject to constraints $\dot{\phi}(t)=g[h(t)].[1-\phi(t)]-\tau(t).\phi(t),\phi(0)=\phi_0$ and $\dot{h}(t)=f[h(t)]-\delta.h(t),\delta>0,h(0)=h_0$ and where functions v, f and g are defined respectively by $v[\phi(t),\tau(t)]=\phi(t)^{1/(1+\sigma)}.\tau(t)^{\sigma/(1+\sigma)}$, $g[h(t)]=a.[u(t).h(t)]^{\eta}$, $a>0$, $\eta\in(0,1)$ and $f[h(t)]=b.\{[1-u(t)].h(t)\}^{\beta},b>0$. All variables assume non-negative values, initial values for state variables are given and shares $\phi(t)$ and $u(t)$ remain always below unity. Furthermore, it is obvious from the problem that we take an infinite horizon and that future technology accomplishments are discounted at a constant discount rate, $\rho>0$.

Optimal Solution and Steady State

Let $p_\phi(t)$ and $p_h(t)$ be co-state variables. We synthesize our model's information into a current value Hamiltonian function:

$$\aleph[\phi(t),h(t),\tau(t),u(t),p_\phi(t),p_h(t)]\equiv$$
$$\equiv v[\phi(t),\tau(t)]+\{a.[u(t).h(t)]^{\eta}.[1-\phi(t)]-\tau(t).\phi(t)\}.p_\phi(t)+$$
$$+\left(b.\{[1-u(t)].h(t)\}^{\beta}-\delta.h(t)\right).p_h(t)$$

Applying the Pontryagin's maximum principle, the first order optimality conditions can be computed:

$$\aleph_\tau=0\Rightarrow\frac{\sigma}{1-\sigma}.\left[\frac{\phi(t)}{\tau(t)}\right]^{\frac{1}{1+\sigma}}=p_\phi(t).\phi(t)$$

$$\aleph_u=0\Rightarrow\eta.a.u(t)^{-(1-\eta)}.h(t)^{\eta}.[1-\phi(t)].p_\phi(t)=\beta.b.[1-u(t)]^{-(1-\beta)}.h(t)^{\beta}.p_h(t)$$

$$\aleph_\phi=\rho.p_\phi(t)-\dot{p}_\phi(t)\Rightarrow\dot{p}_\phi(t)=\{\rho+a.[u(t).h(t)]^{\eta}+\tau(t)\}.p_\phi(t)-\frac{1}{1+\sigma}.\left[\frac{\tau(t)}{\phi(t)}\right]^{\frac{\sigma}{1+\sigma}}$$

$$\aleph_h = \rho.p_h(t) - \dot{p}_h(t) \Rightarrow$$
$$\dot{p}_h(t) = \left\{\rho + \delta - \beta.b.\left[1-u(t)\right]^{\beta}.h(t)^{-(1-\beta)}\right\}.p_h(t) - \eta.a.u(t)^{\eta}.h(t)^{-(1-\eta)}.\left[1-\phi(t)\right].p_\phi(t)$$
$$\aleph_{p_\phi} = \dot{\phi}(t) \Rightarrow \dot{\phi}(t) = a.\left[u(t).h(t)\right]^{\eta}.\left[1-\phi(t)\right] - \tau(t).\phi(t)$$
$$\aleph_{p_h} = \dot{h}(t) \Rightarrow \dot{h}(t) = b.\left\{\left[1-u(t)\right].h(t)\right\}^{\beta} - \delta.h(t)$$

$$\lim_{t\to+\infty} p_\phi(t).e^{-\rho.t}.\phi(t) = 0$$
$$\lim_{t\to+\infty} p_h(t).e^{-\rho.t}.h(t) = 0$$

Given conditions are sufficient conditions for optimality, given that the optimal Hamiltonian is concave in $[\phi(t), h(t)]$. The optimality conditions are the relations necessary to prove the following proposition.

Proposition: Existence and uniqueness of a balanced growth equilibrium. Under the condition $\beta + \rho/\delta < 1$ there exists a unique balanced growth path or unique steady state four dimensional point that satisfies given conditions.

Proof: To prove the existence of a unique steady state point one has to solve the system $\left[\dot{\phi}(t)\,\dot{h}(t)\,\dot{\tau}(t),\dot{u}(t)\right] = \bar{0}$. The solution for this system consists on a set $\left\{\bar{\phi}, \bar{h}, \bar{\tau}, \bar{u}\right\}$ of constant values. To solve the system one is compelled to find equations of motion for the two control variables. Let us start with $\tau(t)$.

Differentiating $\aleph_\tau = 0 \Rightarrow \frac{\sigma}{1-\sigma}.\left[\frac{\phi(t)}{\tau(t)}\right]^{\frac{1}{1+\sigma}} = p_\phi(t).\phi(t)$ with respect to time, the following relation involving growth rates is obtained: $\gamma_\tau = -\sigma.\gamma_\phi - (1+\sigma).\gamma_{p_\phi}$

Replacing γ_{p_ϕ} and γ_ϕ in $\gamma_\tau = -\sigma.\gamma_\phi - (1+\sigma).\gamma_{p_\phi}$ by the corresponding expressions from $\aleph_\phi = \rho.p_\phi(t) - \dot{p}_\phi(t) \Rightarrow \dot{p}_\phi(t) = \left\{\rho + a.\left[u(t).h(t)\right]^{\eta} + \tau(t)\right\}.p_\phi(t) - \frac{1}{1+\sigma}.\left[\frac{\tau(t)}{\phi(t)}\right]^{\frac{\sigma}{1+\sigma}}$ and $\aleph_{p_\phi} = \dot{\phi}(t) \Rightarrow$ $\dot{\phi}(t) = a.\left[u(t).h(t)\right]^{\eta}.\left[1-\phi(t)\right] - \tau(t).\phi(t)$, the motion equation for $\tau(t)$ comes as,

$$\dot{\tau}(t) = \left\{\frac{1}{\sigma}.\tau(t) - (1+\sigma).\rho - a.\left[u(t).h(t)\right]^{\eta}.\left[1+\sigma/\phi(t)\right]\right\}.\tau(t).$$

The time evolution of $u(t)$ is derived from the following relation that is true under $\aleph_u = 0 \Rightarrow \eta.a.u(t)^{-(1-\eta)}.h(t)^{\eta}.\left[1-\phi(t)\right].p_\phi(t) = \beta.b.\left[1-u(t)\right]^{-(1-\beta)}.h(t)^{\beta}.p_h(t)$:

$$\gamma_u = \frac{1-u(t)}{(1-\eta)-(\beta-\eta).u(t)}.\left[\gamma_{p_\phi} - \gamma_{p_h} - \frac{\phi(t)}{1-\phi(t)}.\gamma_\phi + (\eta-\beta).\gamma_h\right]$$

Finally, we can arrive at the result:

$$\dot{u}(t)=\frac{1-u(t)}{(1-\eta)-(\beta-\eta).u(t)}.\left\{\left[\frac{\phi(t)}{1-\phi(t)}-\frac{1-\sigma}{\sigma}\right].\tau(t)+\right.$$
$$\left.\left[\eta+(\beta-\eta).u(t)\right].b.\left[(1-u(t)).h(t)\right]^{-(1-\beta)}-(1-\beta+\eta).\delta\right\}.u(t).$$

Equations $\dot{\tau}(t)=\left\{\frac{1}{\sigma}.\tau(t)-(1+\sigma).\rho-a.\left[u(t).h(t)\right]^{\eta}.\left[1+\sigma/\phi(t)\right]\right\}.\tau(t)$ and above equation, alongside with the two resource constraints, constitute the system from which we derive the steady state solution. The system has in fact a unique solution, which is,

$$\begin{bmatrix}\bar{\phi}\\ \bar{h}\\ \bar{\tau}\\ \bar{u}\end{bmatrix}=\begin{bmatrix}\frac{(1-\sigma).\bar{g}}{\sigma.\rho+\bar{g}}\\ \left[\frac{b}{\delta}.(\beta+\rho/\delta)^{\beta}\right]^{1/(1-\beta)}\\ \frac{\sigma}{1-\sigma}.(\rho+\bar{g})\\ 1-\beta-\rho/\delta\end{bmatrix}$$

with $\bar{g}=a.(\bar{u}.\bar{h})^{\eta}$. If $\beta+\rho/\delta<1$ then we guarantee that $\bar{u}\in(0,1)$ and this is the only boundary condition that must be imposed in order to have above equation as a feasible four dimensional steady state point.

The steady state results deserve some comments. First, we notice that the share $\bar{u}$ depends upon parameters β, ρ and δ. The higher the elasticity parameter β and the discount rate, the lower is the value of the share of human capital allocated to technological development. The faster the depreciation of human capital, the more this form of capital is allocated to its own production relatively to a technological use. Second, the human capital efficiency index is indeed a constant amount on the balanced growth path. It depends on parameters b, δ, ρ and β. Third, we observe that $\bar{\phi}$ obeys the boundary condition $\bar{\phi}\leq 1$, because ρ>0 and $\bar{g}>0$. Fourth, the technology growth rate arises in the steady state depending on a multiplicity of factors, namely:

- The objective function parameter.
- The intertemporal discount rate.
- Both sectors education functions parameters (a and b).
- The elasticity parameters (β and η).
- The depreciation rate.

For the steady state growth rate result,

$$\bar{\tau}=\frac{\sigma}{1-\sigma}.\left(\rho+a.\left\{\left[(1-\beta)-\rho/\delta\right].\left[(b/\delta).(\beta+\rho/\delta)^{\beta}\right]^{1/(1-\beta)}\right\}^{\eta}\right).$$

We stress that the partial derivatives $\partial\bar{\tau}/\partial\sigma > 0, \partial\bar{\tau}/\partial a > 0, \partial\bar{\tau}/\partial b > 0$ and $\partial\bar{\tau}/\partial\eta > 0$ have unquestionable signs. The same is not true for β, ρ and δ because when changes in these factors benefit the accumulation of human knowledge (h rises) they affect negativelly the transference of human capital to innovation purposes (u falls).

At this stage, after the long term technology growth rate has been found, we could transform the model by adding a physical capital accumulation constraint that should include a labor augmenting aggregate production function; which would lead to an economic growth framework. Under such a scenario the growth rate in $\bar{\tau} = \frac{\sigma}{1-\sigma} \cdot \left(\rho + a. \left\{ \left[(1-\beta) - \rho/\delta \right] . \left[(b/\delta).(\beta + \rho/\delta)^{\beta} \right]^{1/(1-\beta)} \right\}^{\eta} \right)$ would be the steady state economic growth rate for the various per capita aggregates: physical capital, consumption and output. In such a model we have endogenous growth through technology choices, that is, long run constant per capita growth is obtained and is a function of several parameters of our analysis. These parameters concern the way in which the economy is able to create and diffuse technology and to invest in human capabilities. In fact, the growth rate obtained in this new framework is precisely the result of the particular way the economy handles the two true engines of growth: human capital and technology.

References

- Production-and-Costs: ncert.nic.in, Retrieved 02, February 2020
- The-neo-classical-growth-model-23005: ac.in, Retrieved 20, June 2020
- Investment-in-Humans-Technological-Diffusion-and-Economic-Growth-an-Optimal-Control-Interpretation-228458303: researchgate.net, Retrieved 16, March 2020

3

Theories of Development

Theories which deal with how desirable change in the society can be achieved are termed as theories of development. A few major theories studied within this field are Adam Smith's theory of development, Marxian theory of development, Ricardian theory of development, Schumpeter's capitalist development and Malthusian theory of economic development. All the diverse theories of development have been carefully analyzed in this chapter.

Adam Smith's Theory of Development

The father of Economics, Adam Smith, defined the concept of economics in his famous book, "An Enquiry into the Nature and Causes of the Wealth of Nations" in the year as the study of wealth. He analysed the basic economic factors that can help a nation to build its wealth; thereby giving the concept of development economics. He has, however, did not propound the systematic theory of development and this was left for the economist of later years.

Over the years, Development economics has emerged as a separate branch of economics which specifically deals with the developmental issues of middle and low-income countries. Its subject matter has changed over the years, for instance, in the decade of 1960-70s the developmental economists were preoccupied with deciding the superiority of state controlled or market owned economies which shifted the debate over traditional industries or the modern sector encompassing globalization in 1980s and 90s. In the recent years it has emerged as a more holistic concept to define objectives and economic policies for the emerging countries. In order to build the understanding of Development Economics, we will begin with the theory of Adam Smith. In his theory, he has explicitly focused on the six broad areas which are defined as follows:

- Determinant factors of economic development:
    - Nature law or laissez faire policy.
    - Division of labour and market perfections.
    - Capital accumulation is the engine of growth.
- Policy of balanced growth.
- Human resource /capital and economic development.
- Legends of development.
- Process of growth.
- Static state.

Determinant Factors of Economic Development

Economic development is based on several factors; however, Adam smith has classified and defined the following three major factors as determinants of economic development for low and middle-income countries:

- Natural law: Smith believed that growth and economic development can only be possible in an independent and free environment. Any restriction or interference with economic activities checks (stops) the process of economic development. He supports the obvious and simple system of natural liberty. According to Smith every individual is the best caretaker of his interest and any kind of intervention that prevents the individuals from carrying out the self interest thing may not lead to good market outcomes. Adam smith strongly supported the policy of free trade and laissez faire (minimum intervention) in economic activities. He asserted the existence of invisible hand or a system that brings about the equilibrium in perfectly competitive market and hence, maximises the national output.
- Division of labour and market perfection: Division of labour is the beginning point of the theory of economic growth. According to Smith, the development of a nation depends upon its level of production and quantity of output being produced that further depends upon the division of labour. The division of labour ensures the right placement of the workforce which enhances the total productivity. The benefits that an economy can derive from the division of its labour force can be listed out as follows:
    - Increased skill of each labour.
    - Saves time in production of the product.
    - Introduction of new innovations.
    - Increment in productivity.

  According to Smith, an economic model for development of the economies should be competitive in nature; existence of any form of monopolistic tendencies or monopoly and mal practices can act as an inhibitor for the process of development.
- Capital accumulation is the engine of growth: According to Smith, the growth of any society depends upon its capital accumulation which acts as an engine of growth. Capital accumulation reflects the productive capacity of any economic system and it further depends upon the real savings of the society. Also, according to him judicial expenses increase capital accumulation. In an economic system, the factor payments are made to four factors of production i.e. land, labour, capital and entrepreneur in the form of rent, wages, interest and profits. It would be unjust to expect savings from the labourers as the amount they receive in the form of wages is barely enough for their subsistence and is largely spent on their consumption. Therefore, savings should be channelized from the remaining factors of production as given below:
    - Wages: According to Smith, it is the capitalists and landlords who can do savings and not the workers as the wages earned by them are just enough to meet their basic requirements.

- Profit: Profit is the reward for the capitalist/ entrepreneur for bearing the risk. The level of profits can be enhanced by the expansion of economic activity that depends upon the investment of savings.

- Interest: Interest is the reward for the capital invested in the economic activity. According to Smith due to increment in prosperity, development, progress and population, rate of interest decline so as to increase in the supply of capital.

- Rent: Rent is the reward for the use of land for any economic activity. Smith thought that with the process of development, it is also possible that there will be increment of monetary and real rent. Rent as a proportion of national income can also increase national income.

Balanced Development Policy

Adam Smith was indeed a strong supporter of industrialization, he however, did not undermine the importance of agricultural and small scale industries in the initial stages of development. In order to achieve the sustained growth in long run, it is crucial to adopt the policy of balanced development in the starting phase of development which focus on all the sectors of economy i.e. agriculture, industries and trade and service sector rather than focusing only on the industrial sector. In the process of development, Smith favored the growth and development of agricultural sector in the first stage, followed by industrial sector in the second stage and in the last the trade and service which can be presented as follows:

Agriculture → **Industries** → **Trade**

Further, Smith also understood the role of externalities in the process of development.

Human Resource and Economic Development

According to Adam Smith, human resource (labour) is an active factor of development. He clearly indicates that "labour is that treasure which provides all the facilities and necessities for annual consumption to nation". Keeping in view the deficiency of capital, capital output ratio must be maintained so that the rate of development may not get slow down. Low standard population, however, must necessarily be controlled.

Legend of Development

According to Adam Smith following are the legend for economic development of any society:

- Farmers
- Trader
- Producer

It is impossible to attain the economic growth without the presence of these three economic legends as their presence is the pre-requisite for the process of capital accumulation and economic development. Also, as per the understanding of Smith, the working of these three is closely inter-related to each other and none of them can work in isolation.

Development Process

In the opinion of Smith, the process of economic development is a continuous, regular and cumulative process. The growth and development of agriculture, industries and commerce brings about the changes in various macroeconomic and developmental variables. A few of the macroeconomic and developmental variables are listed out below:

- Capital accumulation.
- Technological progress.
- Expansion of market.
- Population growth.
- Division of labour.
- Increase in profits.

A word of caution is that the changes continue to occur in the above mentioned variables with the process of economic development; however, this process of change does not continue at the same level.

Static State

Once the economy has developed its resources fully, then following changes will take place in the economic variables:

- Competition between labours is likely to bring the wage rate down at the subsistence level.
- Competition between the traders can reduce their profit level.

Once the reduction in the level of profit begins, it will continue further and will lead to the following:

- Reduction in increment.
- Capital accumulation stops.
- Population become static.
- Profits reached to minimum level.
- Wage rate reduced at minimum levels.
- Per capital income become static.
- Economy reached at a static condition and Smith called this condition as static state.

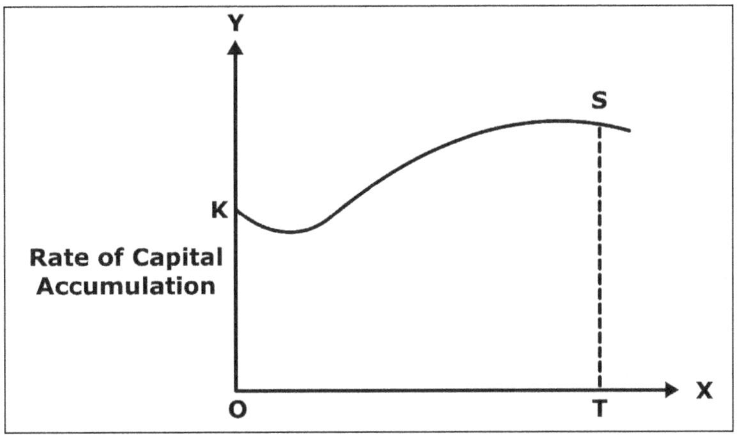

Explanation of Adam Smith model by diagram.

On X axis time period and on Y axis rate of capital accumulation $\frac{dk}{dt}$.

Economy grows till 'T' time from K to S. Once obtaining the position T, economy reaches to its static state. This is because rent became so high that profit became zero and hence capital accumulation stops.

Merits of the Adam Smith's theory

Adam Smith model has indicated the following features of development which are necessary for the development of any economy:

- Saving.
- Capital formation.
- Market expansion.
- Free trade policy.
- Balance growth.

In the opinion of Adam Smith improved technology has special importance for economic development. The use of technology enhances division of the labour force and expansion of market which further induces the production.

- Saving: Saving is very essential for the process of economic development as savings leads to capital accumulation which enhances the productive capacity of resources.
- Capital formation: Adam Smith assumed capital accumulation as main factor of economics of development which can be elaborated with the help of the following figure:

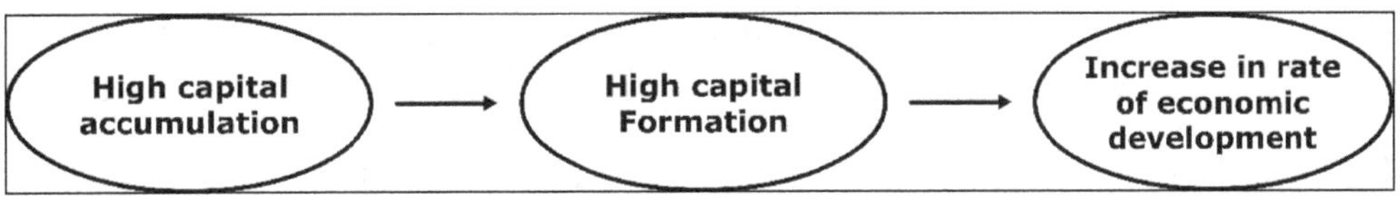

The high capital accumulation leads to increasing capital formation which enhances the rate of economic development.

- Expansion of market: The increasing rate of economic development will enhance the employment opportunities; thereby providing income to individuals which in turn will increase the purchasing capacity of individuals and increase the aggregate demand; thus leading to expansion of the market.
- Laissez faire policy: This approach of Adam Smith is relevant in many areas, for instance, international trade and production in private sector. This refers to minimum intervention of the government in economic activities.
- Balanced growth: According to Adam Smith there exist an inter dependency among farmers, traders and producers which is crucial for the process of economic development. The inter-relationship between the three can be understood as the expansion in the agricultural produce will provide increased amount of raw materials to industries; the expansion of industries will further encourage the trade and commerce. Therefore, balanced growth is required for the development of commerce and manufacturing industries; therefore, for the entire process of development.

  Smith principally viewed economic development: "As a process embedded in, and limited by a particular physical, institutional, and social environment. More specifically, Smith conceives of economic development as the filling-up with people and physical capital ('stock') of a spatial container ('country') that encompasses a given endowment of natural resources and is shaped internally and bounded externally by laws and institutions".

Demerits of the Adam Smith's Theory

The theory propounded by Adam Smith is criticized on the following grounds:

- Rigid division of society: This theory of Smith divides society in two parts which are as follows:
  - Capitalist or landlord class.
  - Labour class or land less class.

  It is, however, wrong to assume the existence of only two classes as in the real world, there also exists a third class known as Middle class and this class cannot be neglected.
- One side saving base: According to Smith only capitalist and landlords (money lender) saves money but this was not true always because even working class also saves money.
- Perfect completion is unrealistic assumption.
- Negligence of public sector due to his policy of laissez faire: Smith fails to explain the role of public sector in capital accumulation and economic development. In these days there is growth of public sector in every country which is helpful in capital formation.
- Negligence of industry and entrepreneurship: Smith neglected the important factors such

as industry and entrepreneurship but in reality entrepreneur organised all the factors and they brought new innovations which formed capital and development.

- Unrealistic assumption of static state.
- Static model: According to Hicks, Smith model is a static model because this model due not give any sequence of development for less developed countries.

Significance of Adam Smith Model in Less Developed Countries

The significance of Smith's model is quite limited in less developed countries because of various reasons. A few of them are listed below:

- Market size is small (limited): The size of the market in less developed countries is small which does not provide the economies of scale and therefore, the production is no longer profitable.
- Saving capacity is low: Savings are very essential for capital formation which is needed for the process of economic development. In less developed countries, however, the capacity of individuals to save is low which restricts the economic development.
- Lack of induced investment (because the level of profits is low in this economies): There is lack of induced investment in less developed countries owing to the lower levels of profit and this act as a barrier in the process of growth and economic development.
- Size of market depends upon level of income and output produced: The size of market in an economic system depends on the level of income and production of the society. Since in less developed countries the level of income and output is less and therefore the size of market also tends to be small.
- Productivity is low: Due to low level of savings there is lack of capital formation which lowers down the productivity of the economic system.
- Level of income is low due to low productivity: Owing to the low level of savings, capital formation and productivity, the size of income also tends to be on lower side in less developed countries.
- Vicious circles of poverty applied form both demand side and supply side: In less developed countries, there exists vicious circle of poverty from both demand and supply side. Owing to various factors such as low level of savings, investment etc., there tends to be low level of productivity and therefore low level of employment. This again leads to the problem of poverty in less developed countries.

Due to the above mentioned reasons Smiths' theory based on division of labour and size of the market does not apply on less developed nations. He further argued on the basis of following grounds:

- Perfect competition does not exist in these nations.
- The market structures are imperfect in these nations.

In the opinion of Smith, without the interference of government development in free economic activities is impossible and therefore, it is essential for the government to interfere in the economic activities of the state. Besides all this, the model of Smith told us about some factors which can enhance the process of development in less developed countries i.e.

- Saving.
- Balance growth.
- Three legants stated by Smith for under developed countries are farmers, producers and traders; these three legends increase production in their own sector and are helpful in capital accumulation and development of the nation.
- In the absence of free trade market system government can also help in increasing the production by giving the economic assistance.

Human Capital

The standard approach in labor economics views human capital as a set of skills/characteristics that increase a worker's productivity. This is a useful starting place, and for most practical purposes quite sufficient. Nevertheless, it may be useful to distinguish between some complementary/alternative ways of thinking of human capital. Here is a possible classification:

- The Becker view: Human capital is directly useful in the production process. More explicitly, human capital increases a worker's productivity in all tasks, though possibly differentially in different tasks, organizations, and situations. In this view, although the role of human capital in the production process may be quite complex, there is a sense in which we can think of it as represented (representable) by a unidimensional object, such as the stock of knowledge or skills, h, and this stock is directly part of the production function.
- The Gardener view: According to this view, we should not think of human capital as unidimensional, since there are many many dimensions or types of skills. A simple version of this approach would emphasize mental vs. physical abilities as different skills. Let us dub this the Gardener view after the work by the social psychologist Howard Gardener, who contributed to the development of multiple-intelligences theory, in particular emphasizing how many geniuses/famous personalities were very "unskilled" in some other dimensions.
- The Schultz/Nelson-Phelps view: Human capital is viewed mostly as the capacity to adapt. According to this approach, human capital is especially useful in dealing with "disequilibrium" situations, or more generally, with situations in which there is a changing environment, and workers have to adapt to this.
- The Bowles-Gintis view: "Human capital" is the capacity to work in organizations, obey orders, in short, adapt to life in a hierarchical/capitalist society. According to this view, the main role of schools is to instill in individuals the "correct" ideology and approach towards life.

- The Spence view: Observable measures of human capital are more a signal of ability than characteristics independently useful in the production process.

Despite their differences, the first three views are quite similar, in that "human capital" will be valued in the market because it increases firms' profits. This is straightforward in the Becker and Schultz views, but also similar in the Gardener view. In fact, in many applications, labor economists' view of human capital would be a mixture of these three approaches. Even the Bowles-Gintis view has very similar implications. Here, firms would pay higher wages to educated workers because these workers will be more useful to the firm as they will obey orders better and will be more reliable members of the firm's hierarchy. The Spence view is different from the others, however, in that observable measures of human capital may be rewarded because they are signals about some other characteristics of workers.

Sources of Human Capital Differences

It is useful to think of the possible sources of human capital differences before discussing the incentives to invest in human capital:

- Innate ability: Workers can have different amounts of skills/human capital because of innate differences. Research in biology/social biology has documented that there is some component of IQ which is genetic in origin (there is a heated debate about the exact importance of this component, and some economists have also taken part in this). The relevance of this observation for labor economics is twofold:
    - There is likely to be heterogeneity in human capital even when individuals have access to the same investment opportunities and the same economic constraints.
    - In empirical applications, we have to find a way of dealing with this source of differences in human capital, especially when it's likely to be correlated with other variables of interest.
- Schooling: This has been the focus of much research, since it is the most easily observable component of human capital investments. It has to be borne in mind, however, that the R2 of earnings regressions that control for schooling is relatively small, suggesting that schooling differences account for a relatively small fraction of the differences in earnings. Therefore, there is much more to human capital than schooling. Nevertheless, the analysis of schooling is likely to be very informative if we presume that the same forces that affect schooling investments are also likely to affect non-schooling investments. So we can infer from the patterns of schooling investments what may be happening to non-schooling investments, which are more difficult to observe.
- School quality and non-schooling investments: A pair of identical twins who grew up in the same environment until the age of 6, and then completed the same years of schooling may nevertheless have different amounts of human capital. This could be because they attended different schools with varying qualities, but it could also be the case even if they went to the same school. In this latter case, for one reason or another, they may have chosen to make different investments in other components of their human capital (one may have worked harder, or studied especially for some subjects, or because of a variety of choices/ circumstances, one may have become more assertive, better at communicating, etc.). Many

economists believe that these "unobserved" skills are very important in understanding the structure of wages (and the changes in the structure of wages). The problem is that we do not have good data on these components of human capital.

- Training: This is the component of human capital that workers acquire after schooling, often associated with some set of skills useful for a particular industry, or useful with a particular set of technologies. At some level, training is very similar to schooling in that the worker, at least to some degree, controls how much to invest. But it is also much more complex, since it is difficult for a worker to make training investments by himself. The firm also needs to invest in the training of the workers, and often ends up bearing a large fraction of the costs of these training investments. The role of the firm is even greater once we take into account that training has a significant "matching" component in the sense that it is most useful for the worker to invest in a set of specific technologies that the firm will be using in the future. So training is often a joint investment by firms and workers, complicating the analysis.
- Pre-labor market influences: There is increasing recognition among economists that peer group effects to which individuals are exposed before they join the labor market may also affect their human capital significantly. At some level, the analysis of these pre-labor market influences may be "sociological". But it also has an element of investment. For example, an altruistic parent deciding where to live is also deciding whether her offspring will be exposed to good or less good pre-labor market influences. Therefore, some of the same issues that arise in thinking about the theory of schooling and training will apply in this context too.

Human Capital Investments and the Separation Theorem

Let us start with the partial equilibrium schooling decisions and establish a simple general result, sometimes referred to as a "separation theorem" for human capital investments. We set up the basic model in continuous time for simplicity. Consider the schooling decision of a single individual facing exogenously given prices for human capital. Throughout, we assume that there are perfect capital markets. The separation theorem will show that, with perfect capital markets, schooling decisions will maximize the net present discounted value of the individual. More specifically, consider an individual with an instantaneous utility function $u(c)$ that satisfies the standard neoclassical assumptions. In particular, it is strictly increasing and strictly concave. Suppose that the individual has a planning horizon of T (where $T = \infty$ is allowed), discounts the future at the rate $\rho > 0$ and faces a constant flow rate of death equal to $\nu \geq 0$. Standard arguments imply that the objective function of this individual at time $t = 0$ is,

$$\max \int_0^T \exp(-(\rho+\upsilon)t)\, u(c(t))\, dt$$

Suppose that this individual is born with some human capital $h(0) \geq 0$. Suppose also that his human capital evolves over time according to the differential equation,

$$\dot{h}(t) = G(t, h(t), s(t)),$$

where $s(t) \in [0,1]$ is the fraction of time that the individual spends for investments in schooling, and $G : \mathbb{R}_+^2 \times [0,1] \to \mathbb{R}_+$ determines how human capital evolves as a function of time, the individual's stock of human capital and schooling decisions. In addition, we can impose a further restriction on schooling decisions, for example,

$$s(t) \in S(t),$$

where $S(t) \subset [0,1]$ and may be useful to model constraints of the form $s(t) \in \{0,1\}$, which would correspond to the restriction that schooling must be full-time (or other such restrictions on human capital investments). The individual is assumed to face an exogenous sequence of wage per unit of human capital given by $[w(t)]_{t=0}^{T}$, so that his labor earnings at time t are,

$$W(t) = w(t)[1-s(t)][h(t)+\omega(t)],$$

where $1-s(t)$ is the fraction of time spent supplying labor to the market and $\omega(t)$ is non-human capital labor that the individual may be supplying to the market at time t. The sequence of non-human capital labor that the individual can supply to the market, $[w(t)]_{t=0}^{T}$, is exogenous. This formulation assumes that the only margin of choice is between market work and schooling (i.e., there is no leisure). Finally, let us assume that the individual faces a constant (flow) interest rate equal to r on his savings. Using the equation for labor earnings, the lifetime budget constraint of the individual can be written as,

$$\int_0^T \exp(-rt)c(t)\,dt \le \int_0^T \exp(-rt)w(t)[1-s(t)][h(t)+\omega(t)]\,dt.$$

The Separation Theorem, can be stated as follows:

Theorem: (Separation Theorem) Suppose that the instantaneous utility function $u(\cdot)$ is strictly increasing. Then the sequence $[\hat{c}(t),\hat{s}(t),\hat{h}(t)]_{t=0}^{T}$ is a solution to the maximization of $\max\int_0^T \exp(-(\rho+\upsilon)t)u(c(t))\,dt$ subject to $\dot{h}(t)=G(t,h(t),s(t))$, $s(t)\in S(t)$, and $\int_0^T \exp(-rt)c(t)\,dt \le \int_0^T \exp(-rt)w(t)[1-s(t)][h(t)+\omega(t)]\,dt$ if and only if $[\hat{s}(t),\hat{h}(t)]_{t=0}^{T}$ maximizes, $\int_0^T \exp(-rt)w(t)[1-s(t)][h(t)+\omega(t)]\,dt$, subject to $\dot{h}(t)=G(t,h(t),s(t))$ and $s(t)\in S(t)$, and $[\hat{c}(t)]_{t=0}^{T}$ maximizes $\max\int_0^T \exp(-(\rho+\upsilon)t)u(c(t))\,dt$ subject to $\int_0^T \exp(-rt)c(t)\,dt \le \int_0^T \exp(-rt)$ $w(t)[1-s(t)][h(t)+\omega(t)]\,dt$ given $[\hat{s}(t),\hat{h}(t)]_{t=0}^{T}$. That is, human capital accumulation and supply decisions can be separated from consumption decisions.

Proof: To prove the "only if" part, suppose that $[\hat{s}(t),\hat{h}(t)]_{t=0}^{T}$ does not maximize $\int_0^T \exp(-rt)w(t)[1-$ $s(t)][h(t)+\omega(t)]\,dt$, but there exists $\hat{c}(t)$ such that $[\hat{c}(t),\hat{s}(t),\hat{h}(t)]_{t=0}^{T}$ is a solution to $\max\int_0^T$ $\max\int_0^T \exp(-(\rho+\upsilon)t)u(c(t))\,dt$. Let the value of $\int_0^T \exp(-rt)w(t)[1-s(t)][h(t)+\omega(t)]\,dt$

generated by $\left[\hat{s}(t),\hat{h}(t)\right]_{t=0}^{T}$ be denoted Y. Since $\left[\hat{s}(t),\hat{h}(t)\right]_{t=0}^{T}$ does not maximize $\int_0^T \exp(-rt)w(t)$ $\left[h(t)+\omega(t)\right]dt$, there exists $\left[\hat{s}(t),\hat{h}(t)\right]_{t=0}^{T}$ reaching a value of $\int_0^T \exp(-rt)w(t)\left[1-s(t)\right]$ $\left[1-s(t)\right]\left[h(t)+\omega(t)\right]dt, Y'>Y$. Consider the sequence $\left[\hat{c}(t),\hat{s}(t),\hat{h}(t)\right]_{t=0}^{T}$ where $c(t)=\hat{c}(t)+\varepsilon$. By the hypothesis that $\left[\hat{c}(t),\hat{s}(t),\hat{h}(t)\right]_{t=0}^{T}$ is a solution to $\max\int_0^T \exp(-(\rho+\upsilon)t)\,u(c(t))\,dt$, the budget constraint $\int_0^T \exp(-rt)c(t)\,dt \le \int_0^T \exp(-rt)w(t)\left[1-s(t)\right]\left[h(t)+\omega(t)\right]dt$ implies,

$$\int_0^T \exp(-rt)\hat{c}(t)\,dt \le Y.$$

Let $\varepsilon > 0$ and consider $c(t)=\hat{c}(t)+\varepsilon$ for all t. We have that,

$$\int_0^T \exp(-rt)c(t)\,dt = \int_0^T \exp(-rt)\hat{c}(t)\,dt + \frac{\left[1-\exp(-rT)\right]}{r}\varepsilon.$$
$$\le Y + \frac{\left[1-\exp(-rT)\right]}{r}\varepsilon.$$

Since $Y'>Y$, for ε sufficiently small, $\int_0^T \exp(-rt)c(t)\,dt \le Y'$ and thus $\left[c(t),s(t),h(t)\right]_{t=0}^{T}$ is feasible. Since $u(\cdot)$ is strictly increasing, $\left[c(t),s(t),h(t)\right]_{t=0}^{T}$ is strictly preferred to $\left[\hat{c}(t),\hat{s}(t),\hat{h}(t)\right]_{t=0}^{T}$, leading to a contradiction and proving the "only if" part. The proof of the "if" part is similar. Suppose that $\left[\hat{s}(t),\hat{h}(t)\right]_{t=0}^{T}$ maximizes $\int_0^T \exp(-rt)w(t)\left[1-s(t)\right]\left[h(t)+\omega(t)\right]dt$. Let the maximum value be denoted by Y. Consider the maximization of $\max\int_0^T \exp(-(\rho+\upsilon)t)\,u(c(t))\,dt$ subject to the constraint that $\int_0^T \exp(-rt)c(t)\,dt \le Y$. Let $\left[\hat{c}(t)\right]_{t=0}^{T}$ be a solution. This implies that if $\left[c'(t)\right]_{t=0}^{T}$ is a sequence that is strictly preferred to $\left[\hat{c}(t)\right]_{t=0}^{T}$, then $\int_0^T \exp(-rt)c'(t)\,dt > Y$. This implies that $\left[\hat{c}(t),\hat{s}(t),\hat{h}(t)\right]_{t=0}^{T}$ must be a solution to the original problem, because any other $\left[\hat{s}(t),\hat{h}(t)\right]_{t=0}^{T}$ leads to a value of $\int_0^T \exp(-rt)w(t)\left[1-s(t)\right]\left[h(t)+\omega(t)\right]dt$, $Y' \le Y$, and if $\left[c'(t)\right]_{t=0}^{T}$ is strictly preferred to $\left[\hat{c}(t)\right]_{t=0}^{T}$, then $\int_0^T \exp(-rt)c'(t)\,dt > Y \ge Y'$ for any Y' associated with any feasible $\left[s(t),h(t)\right]_{t=0}^{T}$.

The intuition for this theorem is straightforward: in the presence of perfect capital markets, the best human capital accumulation decisions are those that maximize the lifetime budget set of the individual. It can be shown that this theorem does not hold when there are imperfect capital markets. Moreover, this theorem also fails to hold when leisure is an argument of the utility function of the individual.

Schooling Investments and Returns to Education

We now turn to the simplest model of schooling decisions in partial equilibrium, which will illustrate the main tradeoffs in human capital investments. This model also enables a simple mapping from the theory of human capital investments to the large empirical literature on returns to schooling. Let us first assume that $T=\infty$, which will simplify the expressions. The flow rate of death, ν, is positive, so that individuals have finite expected lives. Suppose that $\dot{h}(t)=G(t,h(t),s(t))$, and $s(t)\in S(t)$, are such that the individual has to spend an interval S with $s(t)=1$ i.e., in full-time schooling, and $s(t)=0$ thereafter. At the end of the schooling interval, the individual will have a schooling level of, $h(S)=\eta(S)$, where $\eta(.)$ is an increasing, continuously differentiable and concave function. For $t\in[S,\infty)$, human capital accumulates over time (as the individual works) according to the differential equation.

$$\dot{h}(t)=g_h h(t),$$

for some $g_h \geq 0$. Suppose also that wages grow exponentially,

$$\dot{w}(t)=g_w w(t),$$

with boundary condition w (0) > 0. Suppose that,

$$g_w+g_h<r+\nu,$$

so that the net present discounted value of the individual is finite. Now using Separation Theorem, the optimal schooling decision must be a solution to the following maximization problem,

$$\max_S \int_S^{\infty} \exp(-(r+\nu)t)\omega(t)\,h(t)dt.$$

Now using $\dot{h}(t)=g_h h(t)$, and $\dot{w}(t)=g_w w(t)$,, this is equivalent to:

$$\max_S \frac{\eta(S)w(0)\exp(-(r-\nu-g_w)S)}{r+\nu-g_h-g_w}.$$

Since $\eta(S)$ is concave, the objective function in $\max_S \frac{\eta(S)w(0)\exp(-(r-\nu-g_w)S)}{r+\nu-g_h-g_w}$ is strictly concave. Therefore, the unique solution to this problem is characterized by the first-order condition,

$$\frac{\eta'(S^*)}{\eta(S^*)}=r+\nu-g_w.$$

Equation $\frac{\eta'(S^*)}{\eta(S^*)}=r+\nu-g_w$ shows that higher interest rates and higher values of ν (corresponding to shorter planning horizons) reduce human capital investments, while higher values of g_w

increase the value of human capital and thus encourage further investments. Integrating both sides of this equation with respect to S, we obtain,

$$\ln \eta\left(S^*\right) = \text{constant} + \left(r + v - g_w\right)S^*.$$

Now note that the wage earnings of the worker of age $\tau \geq S^*$ in the labor market at time t will be given by, $W(S,t) = \exp(g_w t)\ \exp\left(g_h (t-S)\right)\ \eta(S)$.

Taking logs and using equation $\ln \eta\left(S^*\right) = \text{constant} + \left(r + v - g_w\right)S^*$ implies that the earnings of the worker will be given by,

$$\ln W\left(S^*, t\right) = \text{constant} + \left(r + v - g_w\right)S^* + g_w t + g_h\left(t - S^*\right),$$

where $t-S$ can be thought of as worker experience (time after schooling). If we make a cross-sectional comparison across workers, the time trend term $g_w t$, will also go into the constant, where, in the cross section, log wage earnings are proportional to schooling and experience. Written differently, we have the following cross-sectional equation,

$$\ln W_j = \text{constant} + \gamma_s S_j + \gamma_e \text{ experience},$$

where j refers to individual j. Note however that we have not introduced any source of heterogeneity that can generate different levels of schooling across individuals. Nevertheless, equation $\ln W_j = \text{constant} + \gamma_s S_j + \gamma_e \text{ experience}$ is important, since it is the typical empirical model for the relationship between wages and schooling estimated in labor economics. The economic insight provided by this equation is quite important; it suggests that the functional form of the wage equation is not just a mere coincidence, but has economic content, the opportunity cost of one more year of schooling is foregone earnings. This implies that the benefit has to be commensurate with these foregone earnings, thus should lead to a proportional increase in earnings in the future. In particular, this proportional increase should be at the rate $\left(r + v - g_w\right)$.

Empirical work using equations of the form $\ln W_j = \text{constant} + \gamma_s S_j + \gamma_e \text{ experience}$, leads to estimates for γ in the range of 0.06 to 0.10. Equation $\ln W_j = \text{constant} + \gamma_s S_j + \gamma_e \text{ experience}$, suggests that these returns to schooling are not unreasonable. For example, we can think of the annual interest rate r as approximately 0.10, v as corresponding to 0.02 that gives an expected life of 50 years, and g_w corresponding to the rate of wage growth holding the human capital level of the individual constant, which should be approximately about 2%. Thus we should expect an estimate of γ around 0.10, which is consistent with the upper range of the empirical estimates.

Marxian Theory of Development

Karl Marx has presented certain arguments in order to build his theory of capital crisis. He has explained the following six logics to justify the theory:

1. Labor is absolute and ultimate source of all economic values and it is the result of pre-labor. In

the opinion of Marx, while considering factors of production labor force shall be considered before taking into account capital.

2. Minimum wages: According to Marx, real wage or subsistence wage should be determined by the quantity of labor force required to turn out the goods and services that constitute minimum level of subsistence necessary to maintain the labor force intact rather than focusing on the welfare of the labor force.

3. To earn surplus: Every capitalist tries to receive surplus from his labor force. And the surplus, also known as profit is defined as the difference between output produced per worker and minimum wages paid per worker. It is denoted by S.

4. Every capitalist wants to increase the surplus: The main objective of capitalists is to increase the surplus value. Therefore, the capitalist always tries to maximize the level of his profits. He can increase his profit by opting any of the following ways:

- By prolonged working hours: If the capitalists prolong the working hours then the amount of surplus will certainly increase.
- By increasing the productivity of labors.
- By decreasing the number of hours required to produce the output equivalent to labors subsistence.

In the opinion of Marx, second method i.e. increase in the productivity of labor is much more effective than the first and third method as these methods suffers from their own limitations. Therefore, the capitalists increase his surplus value by bringing the improvement in productivity of labor. In order to receive large stocks of capital, capitalists reinvest the surplus value earned by them. The productivity of labor is directly affected by the increased amount of capital. Profit or surplus is determined by the amount of capital invested in the process of production. Further, Marx splits the capital into two parts which are given below:

- Constant capital which is denoted by (c).
- Variable Capital which is denoted by (v).

The two types of capital can be defined as following:

- Constant capital (c): It includes plants, machinery and raw material used in the process of production.
- Variable Capital (v): Capital devoted to the purchase of labor powers in the form of wages is known as variable capital (v). It is also known as wage bill.

Now, the total output consists of the following three elements:

- Variable capital (v).
- Constant capital (c).
- Surplus Value (s).

Therefore, the value of total output denoted by o can be expressed in the following form:

$$o = (c + v) + s$$

where, $(c + v)$ is the total capital invested in the process of production.

Organic composition of capital: It is defined as the ratio of the constant capital to the variable capital. Mathematically, organic composition of capital can be expressed in the form of c/v.

The ratio of surplus: It is defined as the ratio of surplus value to the variable capital. Mathematically, the ratio of surplus can be expressed in the form of s/v. It is also known as the rate of exploitation.

Rate of profit: It is denoted by r and is defined as the ratio of total profit to total capital. Mathematically, the rate of profit can be expressed in the following form:

Rate of profit = Total profit / Total capital

$$\text{Rate of profit} = \frac{\quad}{+v}.$$

Now, dividing numerator and denominator by v, we get

$$\text{Rate of profit} = r = \frac{s/v}{\frac{c}{v}+1}+1$$

The formula depicted in equation above reflects the following conclusions:

- If s/v = constant then there is a negative relationship between organic composition of capital c/v and rate of profit (r).
- If s/v increase but less than the increase in c/v, then the rate of profit, r, will go down.
- If s/v increase faster than c/v, then it is possible to know that in the long run the rate of profit, r, will fall in any case.
- $\frac{\partial r}{\partial\left(\frac{\partial}{v}\right)} > o$ i.e., there is positive relation between r and s/v.
- $\frac{\partial r}{\partial\left(\frac{\partial}{v}\right)} < o$ i.e., there is positive relation between r and c/v.

5. The capitalist uses more of constant capital rather than variable capital to increase their surplus. Further, according to Marx:

- Constant capital is the production of pre-labor.
- Variable capital is the production of current labor.

6. The constant capital is used by capitalist and as a result of this the following will take place:

- There will be increase in the total production.

- There will be increase in the level of unemployment.
- There will be decrease in the wages of labor.

Further, Marx believed that the technological progress tends to increase the organic composition of capital (c/v). Since the rate of profit is inversely related to c/v, therefore it tends to decline with the capital accumulation. Marx explained this tendency of rate of profit as the "law of rate of profit to fall". Further, he explained this tendency with the help of the following formula and graph shown.

Formula for rate of profit: $r = \frac{s/v}{\frac{c}{v}+1}+1$.

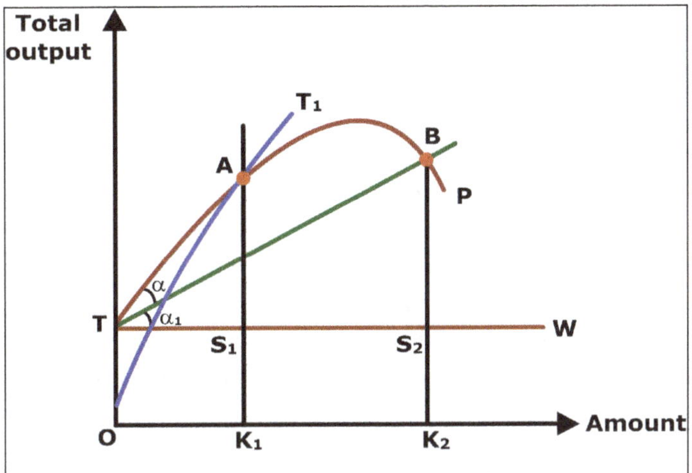

Tendency of rate of profit

The amount of capital is measured on horizontal axis and total output is measured on vertical axis. Total wage is OT, which is constant and parallel to horizontal axis. This horizontal line shows that labor supply is constant. With the initial amount of capital equals to OK, then the total production will be equal to AK and total profit of entrepreneurs will be equal to AS. Therefore, the rate of profit will be equal to:

$$\text{Profit rate} = \tan\alpha = \frac{AS_1}{AK_1}$$

If an entrepreneur increases the amount of capital from OK_1 to OK_2, then in this situation the total output will be equal to BK_2 and profit will be equal to BS_2. Therefore, the rate of profit will be equal to:

$$\text{Profit rate} = \tan\beta = \frac{BS_2}{BK_2}$$

where $\tan\beta = \tan\alpha_1$. Now, if we compare both the profit rates, we get:

$$\tan\alpha > \tan\beta \text{ or } \frac{AS_1}{AK_1} > \frac{BS_2}{BK_2}.$$

As more amount of capital is engaged in the process of production, then positively the rate of profit will decline.

Theory of Capital Crisis

It is the capitalist who increases the degree of exploitation either by reducing wages or prolonged working hours or increase in the productivity to stop the diminishing tendency of profit. Because each capitalist is busy in using labor saving and cost minimizing techniques, so ratio of labor (value of surplus) to total production reduces. And as a result of these factors, the rate of profit also gets reduced. Therefore, with the decline in the rate of profit, production will no longer remain profitable. Under these circumstances capital crisis starts to instigate in the economy. According to Marx, the cause of economic crisis is the poverty and low purchasing power of general public in the economy of the society. Economic crisis appears in the form of over production of goods as these goods face difficulties in finding new markets for themselves leading to fall in prices; thereby forcing the entrepreneurs to curtail down the production of goods on a large scale. The economy hence witnesses a rise in the level of unemployment, recession, cut in the wages of laborers, end of credit facilities and thereby destroying the small capitalists as a result of the economic crises.

However, in accordance with Marx it is not compulsory that the use of labor saving technology will always follow the above mentioned course of action. It is very much possible that the revival of economy begins quickly with the change in the technology as with the fall in prices, reduction in the wage rate and end of speculation crisis there are huge possibilities that the rate of profit might witness an increase. The increasing level of profit would then result into new investments and expansion of the economic activities. As pointed out by Karl Marx, crisis is always a starting point of new and large investment. Therefore considering the societal point of view these crisis form the base of next turn over cycle.

The cycle of crisis leads to a period of recession and as recession is always followed by recovery and therefore it ultimately leads to a situation of economic boom. The period of economic boom will soon be followed by the situation of crisis and again the same cycle will be initiated. This leads to the witnessing of Development of capitalist production. This sequence of action can be expressed with the help of the following figure:

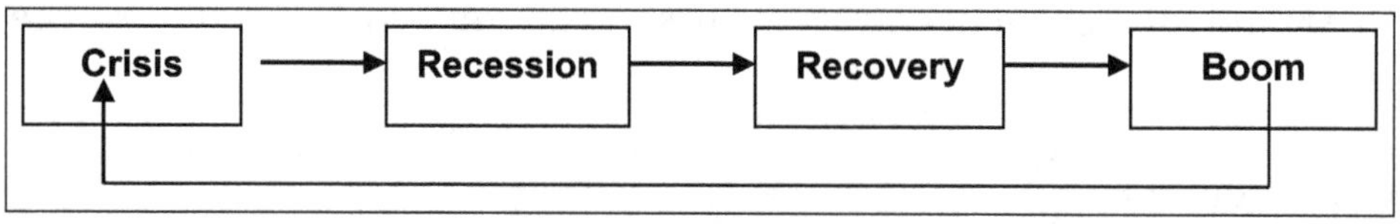

Cycle of crisis.

In each period of the crisis, bigger capitalist tends to ruins the smaller ones. Also there increases the exploitation of labor class and thereby towards the end, the "Dooms day" of capitalist finally arrives.

Criticism of the Marxian Theory

The theory of capital crisis as given by Karl Marx is an interesting theory in itself; it however suffers from certain limitations. For instance a few of its assumptions such as existence of surplus values, increasing unemployment due to technological innovations etc. have attracted the criticism from various other researchers. The criticisms of the Marxian theory of capital crisis are given below:

- The existence of surplus value being unrealistic: The entire analysis of the Marxian theory is based on the existence of surplus value. The critics, however, argued that in the real world the relationship between variables are based on real prices rather than being determined by the values.

- Technological progress helpful in increasing employment: According to Marx, the use of labor saving technology reduces the ratio of labor to total production and eventually it would lead to increase in the level of unemployment. Therefore he believed that the technological progress increases unemployment in the society. It is, however, nothing but the exaggeration of a short term phenomenon. Technological progress may replace a few of the laborers with the capital intensive technology but in the long run it will have exactly the opposite effect on the economy. In the long run, because of the technical progress there would be more generation of employment opportunities; thereby increasing the level of income as well as total demand. Hence it would be wrong to assume that owing to technological progress the level of unemployment would increase in the economy rather it reflects the pace of economic development of any society.
- The law of the tendency of the rate of profit to fall is not correct: In the opinion of Marx, with the process of economic development or technological progress there is an increase in the organic composition of capital i.e. c/v. Since the rate of profit is inversely related to organic composition of capital therefore the rate of profit tends to decline. In the entire context, Marx, however, failed to understand that it is not compulsory for technological innovation to be a labor saver technique. There is no denying from the possibility of the technological progress being capital savers. This would further lead to a decline in the capital output ratio as due to the technological innovation the productivity of capital increases and therefore lesser amount of capital would be required to produce the same level of output. The improvement in the productivity is mostly likely to increases the level of profits as well as an improvement in the wages being paid to the laborers.
- The cyclical theory is not appropriate: Karl Marx was the first person who assumed "cyclic" nature of the crisis as an integral part of his analytical structure. He stressed on the fact that with the increase in the capital accumulation, the demand for the consumption goods decreases and therefore, this would lead to decline in the level of profits. He, however, could not explain the fact that while the process of economic development is going on, it is not necessary that the proportion of wages in total income would decline and also the demand for consumption goods. There is no reason to believe that this decline in the wages and consumption goods would accompany the process of economic development.
- Static analysis: According to Schumpeter, the theory of capital crisis developed by Marx is static in its nature. The economy is, however, dynamic in its nature rather than being static and therefore this theory is criticized on the ground of its nature of analysis.

Marxian Economic System

The Marxian economic system is composed of four components are:

- The capitalist economic system.
- The labour theory of value.
- The theory of surplus value.

- The theory of capital accumulation.

The Capitalist Economic System

According to Marx, capitalism is an economic system with the following elements:

- A capitalistic society is divided into two classes: The capitalists, and the workers. The capitalists own the means of production, while the workers do not. The workers sell their services, i.e., labour power, to the capitalists for wages.
- A commodity forms the unit of production in a capitalistic society. A commodity is defined as the carrier of use-value (utility) and exchange-value (with other commodities).
- The growth of capitalism is based on the exploitation of labour. Labour produces surplus value which is appropriated by the capitalist.
- All commodities are produced with a profit motive and the exchange equation is m-C-M. The capitalist purchases commodity, C, (labour power) with money, m, with an intention to sell it (after production) for profit, M.
- The motive force behind capitalism is profit. The capitalist always reinvests the profit in his business to upgrade technology.
- Capitalists adopt labour saving machinery which creates a 'reserve army of the unemployed'. It results in growing the misery of the working class.

The Labour Theory of Value

According to Marx, the value of a commodity is determined by the quantity of labour required to produce it. One commodity has both use-value and exchange-value. When commodities represent use-values, they are qualitatively different due to the different forms of useful labour used in them. Marx was an advocate of the labour theory of value and believed that all production belongs to labour, because workers produce all value within society. Marx predicted that capitalism would produce growing misery for workers as competition for profit leads capitalists to adopt labour-saving machinery. The Marxian 'industrial reserve army' concept is another way of looking at 'technological unemployment'. It is not a biological law, but is an essential feature of the capitalist system. For Marx, a surplus population was largely the consequence of capitalistic tendencies of capital accumulation, labour displacing technological change, and the concentration of capital. The following points explain how the capitalistic process of production leads to the creation of an ever increasing population:

- Economic development under capitalism depends upon the accumulation of capital, which in turn, depends upon surplus value (or, profits). As long as there is profit, there will be continuous re-investment in the production process.
- In static conditions, capitalists accumulate capital and reinvest it to expand production, and to reap further profits. Since all round expansion in production results in an increase in demand for labour (i.e., higher wages), the surplus value has a tendency to fall. It provides additional reason to accumulate more capital.

- Under dynamic conditions, the greater amount of surplus value goes to those producers who are capable of producing advanced technology in production. Technological progress, according to Marx, means adoption of capital intensive and labour-replacing technology. Hence, the race for capital accumulation among the capitalists raises the capital output ratio, which reduces profits. Ultimately, the capitalist suffers.

The Theory of Surplus Value

Labour power has the unique characteristic of being capable of producing more than its own value when it is put to productive use. The excess of value produced by labour power over its own value is called surplus value. The aim of the capitalist is to, always, increase this surplus value. Surplus value refers to the extra labour of the worker, for which he receives nothing from the producer or employer. It is appropriated by the capitalist. This implies exploitation of labour. It is the only cause of class conflict, or class struggle. Marx's theory of surplus value can be explained by the following set of equations:

- $Y = C + V + S$.
- $s = S/V$.
- $k = C/(C+V)$.
- $\pi = S/(C+V) = s(1-k)^*$.

Where, Y = total income, C = constant capital, V = variable capital, S = surplus value, s = rate of surplus value, k = organic composition of capital (capital intensity) and π = rate of profit.

This equation shows that π is directly related to s, and inversely related to k. It means that the profitability of the producer depends, directly, on his capacity to exploit labour, and, indirectly, on the organic composition of capital. Due to severe competition, the capitalist tries to raise productivity. Therefore, the degree of automation rises, and, in turn, the organic composition of capital grows. It means that the rate of profit increases with the rise in exploitation of labour, and falls with the rise in constant capital. Therefore, the capitalist suffers from continual reduction of his profit and profitability. Capitalism has a built in doom. It will meet its natural death, eventually, in the long run:

$$\text{Proof}: \pi = S/(C+V) = SV/V(V+C)$$
$$= \frac{SV + SC - SC}{V(V+C)} = \frac{S(C+V) - SC}{V(V+C)}$$
$$= \frac{S}{V} - \frac{SC}{V(V+C)} = \frac{S}{V}\left\{1 - \frac{C}{C+V}\right\} = s(1-k)$$

The Theory of Capital Accumulation

Marx propounded the theory of capital accumulation. Marx contends that under static conditions capitalists are compelled to accumulate due to two reasons:

- The emergence of surplus value in capitalist production induces the capitalist to accumulate, and to re-invest.

- The mass effect of this all round expansion of production is an increase in the demand for labour, rise in wage rates, and reduction in surplus value, because surplus value is simply the excess of total produce over the subsistence produce. This provides another reason for an individual capitalist to accumulate.

A capitalist society is marked by continuous change. Under dynamic conditions, the larger share of surplus value goes to those producers who are able to introduce the most advanced and efficient technology in production. The race for capital accumulation among the capitalists', compel them to adopt new technology and gain huge profits. Capital accumulation depends upon the ability of the capitalists to raise the surplus value. Surplus value can be increased in three ways:

- By reducing the wage rates.
- By extending the working hours.
- By increasing the productivity of labour.

The first method cannot be pursued for a long time as it curtails labour supply. The second method can be relied upon only temporarily. Thus, Marx put more emphasis on the third method of increasing productivity of labour. This involves technological improvements. Capital intensive techniques increase the total output produced by a given labour force and, thus, increase surplus value.

Capital accumulation and technological progress leads to the following three tendencies the concentration of capital, immiserization of the proletariat and the falling rate of profit.

1. The Concentration of Capital: Competition compels capitalists to reduce the price of their commodities. This is done by increasing the productivity of labour through capital intensive technology. But the small capitalists fail in this competition, so they are compelled to exit from their business. Marx terms it as "expropriators are expropriated". This tendency of concentration has three effects:

- It results in a larger scale of production.
- The polarization between capitalists and workers is more sharpened.
- The capitalist production becomes social in nature, though in its property relations, it is still private.

  An individual worker is now a part of a large social productive process, and an individual capitalist is the trustee of the society.

2. Immiserization of the Proletariat: Capital accumulation results in the growing misery of the working class. The process of immiserization (i.e., increased unemployment, and reduction in wages) of the proletariat operates in the following two ways:

- Capitalism produces an industrial reserve army, or surplus toiling class. In other words, the capitalist system discards workers at a faster rate than it hires them. This is because of two reasons:
  - Under dynamic conditions, when labour saving technology is adopted widely, the industrial reserve army has a tendency to grow.

    - Due to the concentration of capital, larger capitalists prey on small capitalists. Thus, small producers who cannot face the competition from big producers also join the industrial army.

- The condition of the few workers who remain employed also deteriorates because:
    - Growing unemployment enables capitalists to reduce the wages to subsistence levels.
    - Capitalists also lengthen the working day and hours for more surplus.
    - Capitalists resort to hiring women and children at still lower wages than men.

The Falling Rate of Profit

Capital accumulation results in immiserization for the workers and falling rate of profits for the capitalists. According to Marx, the falling rate of profit is the consequence of two other basic tendencies:

- Extensive use of capital intensive technology tends to increase capital per man, or the organic composition of capital (k). With capital accumulation, capitalists try to get maximum production at minimum costs through the use of capital intensive technology.
- Marx assumes constant rate of surplus value (s). These two tendencies lead to the third eventuality, i.e., the falling rate of profit. This can be easily understood with the help of a fundamental equation, $\pi = s(1 - k)$. This equation implies that the rate of surplus value, the rise in organic composition of capital (k) reduces the rate of profit.

The Marxian Model of Economic Development

According to Marx, secular economic growth at full employment is a contradiction. There is a class struggle due to the impoverishment of the toiling class. Capital accumulation results in an ever increasing capital-output ratio, and declining profits. This economic development path is self destructive. Marx's theory of economic development is essentially an analysis of capital accumulation, and it effects. According to Marx, in order to reap greater profits, and to ensure their existence in the competitive economy, the capitalist producers tend to accumulate more and more capital, and to introduce mechanization in the process of production. This tendency of capital accumulation and technological change has three effects:

- It leads to the concentration of capital in the hands of a few entrepreneurs, and to the elimination of small entrepreneurs.
- It leads to the growing pauperization of the working class, and to the expansion of the industrial reserve army.
- It leads to the tendency of falling rates of profit.

All these effects are collectively responsible for the eventual breakdown of the capitalist system. Marx has contributed to the theory of economic development in three ways:

- He formulated the materialistic interpretation of history.

- He specified the motivating forces for economic development.
- He suggested an alternative path for planned economic development.

Symbolically, the Marxian theory of economic development can be summarized by the following equation:

- Total output (Q) depends on the size of labour force (L), amount of land (R), stock of capital (K), and technological progress (T).

  $Q = f(L, K, R, T),$

- Technological progress (T) depends on investment (I).

  $T = T(I)$

- Investment (I) depends on the rate of profit (π).

  $I = I(\pi)$

- The rate of profit (π) is the ratio of surplus value and capital.

  $\pi = S/(C+V)$

- Wages (W) depend on the level of investment and employment.

  $W = W\ (I, L)$

- Labour employment depends on the level of investment.

  $L = L(I)$

- Consumption Expenditure (E) depends on wage bill (W).

  $E = E(W)$

- Profits are determined by the level of technology and consumption.

  $\Pi = \Pi(T,E)$

- Total output (Q) is equal to profits (Π) plus wages (W). $Q = \Pi + W$.
- The economy has two sectors: Consumer goods and producer goods sectors. So, the total output is the sum of consumer goods and producer goods,

  $Q = Dg + Kg = E + I$.

The equation is determinate, because the number of equations and unknowns are equal. Let us have a look at the system of equations in the Marxian model.

Production	$Q = f(L, K, R, T)$
Technology	$T = T(I)$
Investment	$I = I(\pi)$
Profit	$\Pi = \Pi(T,E)$
Employment	$L = L(W)$
Wage	$W = W\ (I,\ L)$
Total Output	$Q = Cg + Kg$
WageBill	$W = wL$
Rate of Profit	$\pi = S/(C+V)$
Total Income	$Y = C+V+S$
Capital	K=C+V

Where, E = consumption expenditure, Π = profit, π= rate of profit, K= Capital, W= wage bill, w = Wage rate, Dg= consumer good, Kg= capital goods, C= Constant capital, V= Variable capital, S= surplus value, L = Employment We can observe the circularity of the Marxian model. Let us start with profit as the prime mover of the capitalist system.

High profit → Competition → Capital Intensive Technology → Capital-Output ratio → Profit fall. An increase in profits brings an increase in investment, and in the stock of capital, which permits capitalists to take advantage of the steady flow of improved technology. Intense competition leads to unemployment and a rise in the capital output ratio, and reduced profits. In order to remain in the competitive race, capitalists must continually introduce technological improvements, which means accumulating more and more capital, and using more and more capital intensive techniques. As a result, capital stock (K) increases relative to output. Under these conditions, the only way to maintain the prevailing rate of profit (π) is to increase the difference between output per man (q) and the wage rate (w). This objective can be achieved in the following ways:

- Reduce the wage rate to the bare minimum level.
- Add more labour saving techniques which raises q and keeps w at the minimum level.
- Increase hours of work, which raises q without increasing w.
- Strengthen the monopoly position, which raises prices without raising wages.

According to Marx, all these measures to maintain the rate of profit prove self defeating. In the short run, they produce economic fluctuations. In the long run, these factors lead to the breakdown of the capitalist system. This is illustrated in the diagram below. The OY axis represents income and the OX axis represents time periods.

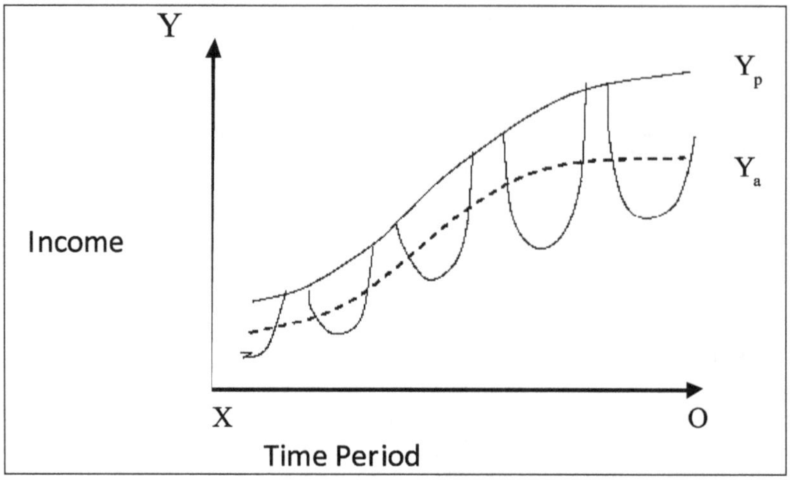

Marxian Model.

The classical economists were not concerned with the gap between potential and actual income. For them, the potential income would stagnate due to population growth. There is growth in income until the downfall of capitalism through a revolution of the working classes. The figure shows that Y_p is the upper limit of the growth process. It is stable, but Y_a is unstable. The gap appears between the trend of potential GNP and the trend in actual GNP. But, this gap is the product solely of increasing amplitude of cycles. Since the national income, in real terms, cannot rise above full employment levels, the increasing amplitude of fluctuations in real terms means increasingly severe downswings, which brings the trend of actual income further and further below the trend of potential income. In the short term, they produce economic fluctuations. In the long term, they lead to the breakdown of the capitalist system. Marx asserts that the capitalist system will ultimately collapse because of the following reasons:

- The falling rate of profit.
- Over production (market glut) due to high technology.
- Under consumption (low purchasing power) due to the immiserization process.
- Capital-intensive (labour-displacing) automations.
- Class struggle (conflict) due to rising income inequality.

The economic crises, according to Marx, will have the secular effect of producing deeper and deeper depressions, and shorter and weaker booms. Despite the best efforts made by the capitalists, the rate of profit will continue to decline. During a boom, capital accumulations temporarily create full employment conditions and bring a temporary increase in wages. An increase in wages causes the rate of profit to fall, which leads to reduced investment and to depression. Everything that the entrepreneurs do to maintain profits, increases the misery of the working class. Eventually, Marx predicts, the workers will not bear it, and, by sheer strength of their number, they will overthrow the capitalist system through revolution. Marx, however, refers to a number of offsetting factors which arrest the general law of the falling rate of profit. These factors are:

- Technological progress may reduce the cost of constant capital.

- The capitalist keeps constant profit by increasing the rate of exploitation.
- Intensified activities where weaker capitalists are expropriated.

But, Marx firmly believed that these counteracting forces are temporary in nature and do not nullify the general tendency towards economic collapse. Ultimately, the expropriators are expropriated. The internal contradictions in the capitalist system bring about its own collapse. Eventually, the success of capitalism is not sustainable.

Ricardian Theory of Development

Ricardo's greatest contribution to economics is the provision of engine of analysis. By using the technique of deductive or abstract reasoning, he constructed a rigorous model in which some selected economic variables were systematically placed to form a logic. Such a theoretical model helps to understand how a system works and how the change in variables affects the working of the system. Ricardo propounded no theory of development. He simply discussed the theory of distribution. This theory is based on the marginal and surplus principles. The marginal principle explains the share of rent in national output and surplus principle explains the division of the remaining share between wages and profits. The Ricardian theory is based on certain assumptions which are as under:

- Supply of land is fixed.
- Land is used for production of corn and the working force in agriculture helps in determining the distribution in industry.
- Law of diminishing returns operates on land.
- Demand for corn is perfectly inelastic.
- Labour and capital are variable inputs.
- Capital consists of circulating capital.
- There is capital homogeneity.
- All workers are paid subsistence wages.
- The state of technological knowledge is given.
- There is perfect competition.
- Demand for labour depends upon accumulation of capital.
- Demand and supply price are independent of the marginal productivity of labour.
- The supply price of labour is given and constant.
- Capital accumulation results from profits.

Ricardian system considers agriculture as the most important sector of the economy. The difficulty of providing food to expanding population is the main problem. According to Ricardo, there are three major groups in the economy. They are landlords, capitalists and labourers among whom the entire productive land is distributed. It is the capitalists who initiate the process of economic development in the society by reinvesting profits and, thus, increasing capital formation. The total national output is distributed among the three groups as rents, profits and wages, respectively and the share of each group can be determined as under:

- Rent per unit of labour is the difference between average and marginal product or total rent equals the difference between average product and marginal product multiplied by the quantity of labour and capital on land.
- The wage rate is determined by wage fund divided by number of workers employed at subsistence wage. Thus, output of total corn produced and sold, rent has the first right and the residual is distributed among wages and profits, while interest is included in profits.

Production Function

Ricardo's production function assumes the existence of three factors-land, labour and capital and it is subjected to the restriction of diminishing marginal productivity due to perfectly inelastic of land and its variable quality He regarded economic development as the process of these factors of production. The marginal productivity of land, labour and capital declines with the increase in cultivation. In agriculture, the rate of innovation introduced would be insufficient to affect the tendency for diminishing returns to set in at either intensive or extensive margin of cultivation. Thus, the introduction of improvements in the agriculture techniques might check the progress of diminishing returns it could have temporary effect on cost of agricultural production.

For the overall growth of the economy, it is necessary to examine as to which of these patterns prevail with respect to the output of industry and agriculture together. Ricardo is of the opinion that "Although, then it is probable that under the most favourable circumstances, the power of production is still greater than that of population, it will not long continue so, for the land being limited in quantity and differing in quality, with every increased portion of capital employed on it there will be a decreased rate of production while the power of population continues always to be the same". As Smithian economy grows at an accelerated rate, Ricardian economy develops at a progressively slower pace. Ricardian production function is given as:

$$Y = F(K, N, L)$$
$$K = \text{Capital}$$
$$N = \text{Labour}$$
$$L = \text{Land}$$

This production function is subjected to following constraints imposed by diminishing marginal productivity:

$$\frac{\partial^2 F}{\partial K^2} < 0 \frac{\partial^2 F}{\partial N^2} < 0 \frac{\partial^2 F}{\partial L^2} < 0$$

Since the pace of economy's technological progress regulates to a large extent the rate of onset of diminishing returns, we may write,

$$\frac{\partial^2 F}{\partial K^2} = g\left(\frac{ds}{dt}............\right)$$

$$\frac{\partial^2 F}{\partial N^2} = h\left(\frac{ds}{dt}............\right)$$

$$\frac{\partial^2 F}{\partial L^2} = j\left(\frac{ds}{dt}............\right)$$

Since ds/dt is one of the determinants of the extent of diminishing returns, it must also appear as a determinant of marginal productivity of the factors of production themselves. To simplify the calculations, we may introduce S in the production function i.e.

$$Y = f(K,N,L,S)$$

The rate of progress of the economy is obtained by differentiating the above equation,

$$\frac{dy}{dt} = \frac{\partial F}{\partial K}\cdot\frac{dK}{dt} + \frac{\partial F}{\partial L}\cdot\frac{dL}{dt} + \frac{\partial F}{\partial N}\cdot\frac{dN}{dt} + \frac{\partial F}{\partial s}\cdot\frac{ds}{dt}$$

$$\frac{dK}{dt} \rightarrow \text{Capital accumulation}$$

$$\frac{dL}{dt} \rightarrow \text{Labour growth}$$

$$\frac{dN}{dt} \rightarrow \text{Land increases}$$

$$\frac{ds}{dt} \rightarrow \text{Technological progress.}$$

Capital Accumulation

Ricardo emphasized the rate of capital accumulation as capital acts as an engine of growth. "Capital" is the part of the wealth of a country which is employed in production and consists of food, clothing tools, raw materials, machinery etc., necessary to give effect to labour. Capital accumulation depends upon two factors:

- Capacity to save.
- Will to save.

The capacity to save is more important in capital accumulation. This depends on the net income of society which is a surplus out of the total output after meeting the cost of workers subsistence. The larger the surplus, the larger will be the capacity to save. Landlords and capitalists invest through this surplus and the size of this surplus depends upon the rate of profit.

The Profit Rate

The rate of profit is the ratio of profits to capital employed. But since capital consists of working capital, it is equal to the wage bill. So, as long as rate of profit is positive, the process capital accumulation will continue and the economy will progress. The labour force will grow proportionately and the total wage fund will increase. The profit depends upon wages, wages on price of the corn and price of the corn on the fertility of marginal land. Hence, profits and wages are inversely proportional to each other. When there is improvement in agriculture, the productivity power of land increases and there is fall in the price of corn and as a result, subsistence wage also falls, but profits increase and there is more capital accumulation. This will increase the demand of labour and wage rate will rise, which will increase population and demand for corn and its price. Since the wages rise, the profit will decline and there will be less capital accumulation. The process of growth will continue till the profits fall to zero or the whole of the total product less rent is used for the maintenance of labour at subsistence level. At this stage, capital accumulation stops and the progress of the economy reaches a stationary state.

Increase in Wages

In Ricardian Scheme, wages play an active role in determining income between capital and labour. The wage rate depends upon the number of workers and wage fund. The wage rate falls with the increase in number of workers and vice-versa. If the wage rate is sufficient to enjoy the comforts of life by labourers, the population is expected to increase and if the wage rate is the lowest the working class cannot meet the necessities of life, the population will decrease. Thus, there is positive co-relation between wage rate and size of population. The increase in wages with the increase in population absorbs the rise in price of corn. Since wages also increase, profits decline. These opposite tendencies ultimately retard the capital accumulation.

Declining Profits in Other Industries

According to Ricardo, "The profits of the farmer regulate the profits of all other trades". Ricardo uses agricultural profits as a basis and it is the agricultural profit which determines the industrial profit. The money rate of profit earned on capital must be equal in equilibrium in both agriculture and industry. The rate of profit in the agricultural sector determines the rate of profit in the industrial sector of an economy. Thus, when the profit declines in the agricultural sector, it also declines in the industrial sector. The industry would have to raise the wages of labourers with the increase in price of corn and which in turn, reduces the profit. Thus, the price of corn determines the rate of profit in an industry. When profit declines in agricultural sector, it declines in all trades.

Other Sources of Capital Accumulation

Ricardo is of the view that economic development depends upon the difference between production and consumption. He stresses on increasing production and reducing unproductive consumption. The productivity of labour can be increased through technological changes and better organisation and thereby stimulating capital accumulation. But the use of machines will employ less workers which will lead to unemployment and reduced wages since the economic condition of workers decreases with the employment of more machines. So Prof. Ricardo regards the technological conditions as given and constant. Taxes are the source of capital accumulation in the hands of the government. According to Ricardo, taxes are levied only to reduce conspicuous consumption, otherwise the imposition of taxes on capitalists, landlords and labourers will transfer resources from these groups to government. Taxes adversely affect the investment. Therefore, Ricardo is not in favour of imposition of taxes, as taxes reduce income, profit and capital accumulation.

Prof. Ricardo is in favour of free trade as it is an important factor of development of the country. Free trade provides vast opportunities of investment to capitalists. The capitalists can make investment in export oriented industries and earn profits. The re-investment of profit by the capitalists will further enhance the developing activities. The capital accumulation can be raised by importing corn. But the import of corn leads to fall in demand for labour which deteriorates the economic conditions of labourers. On the other hand, landlords and capitalists do not think it fit to import cheap corn from the foreign countries, as a result, their profits decline. Ricardian theory has been illustrated with the help of a diagram.

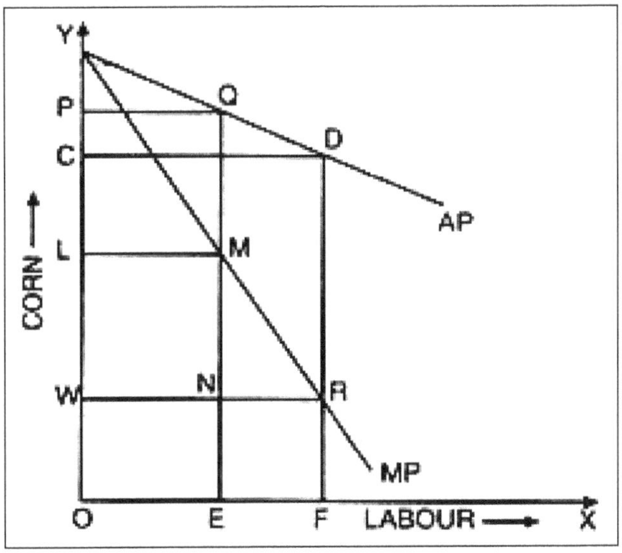

The quantity of corn is measured along the vertical axis and labour along the horizontal axis. The curve AP represents average product of labour and MP represents the marginal product of labour. With OE amount of labour, total corn produced is OPQE. Rent is shown by rectangle PQML, as the difference between AP and MP. At subsistence wage rate OW, the supply curve of labour WN is infinitely elastic and total wage is OWNE. Total profits WLMN, are the residue after deducting rent and wages from the total output:

$$\text{WLMN} = \text{OPQE} - (\text{LPQM} - \text{OWNE})$$

Stationary State

When the economic development proceeds real wage rate remains at the subsistence level and profit tends to fall. When the capital accumulation rises with increase in profit, total output increases which raises the wage fund. With the increase in the wage fund' population increases which raises the demand for corn and its price. As population increases, inferior grade lands are cultivated to meet increasing demand of corn. Ricardo assumes that labourers and landlords spend all their income on consumption and hence, save nothing.

The saving is done by the capitalist for profit earners. But as the society progresses, the share of profit begins to decline. Fall in the rate of profit slackens the process of capital accumulation and the development receives a set back and at this stage, there is no further increase in capital and the economy enters in a stationary state. In this state, capital accumulation stops, population does not grow, the wage rate is at subsistence level and technological progress ceases. "The basic casual force in this scheme is the fact of diminishing returns in agriculture, a grim tendency which can be postponed temporarily by technical progress. But technical progress cannot prevent the ultimate disappearance of profit and the onset of stationary state". The phenomenon of stationary state is explained with the help of a diagram. With the increase in capital accumulation, profits and wages tend to increase and the rise in wages bring about a decline in profits. The decline in profits will continue till a stage comes when the net product curve intersects the wage line OW at P. At this point, wages are equal to net product and the profit is nil. Any disturbance to the right of point P, will make the net product less than wage level which is impossible. So P is the point at which economy is in a stationary state.

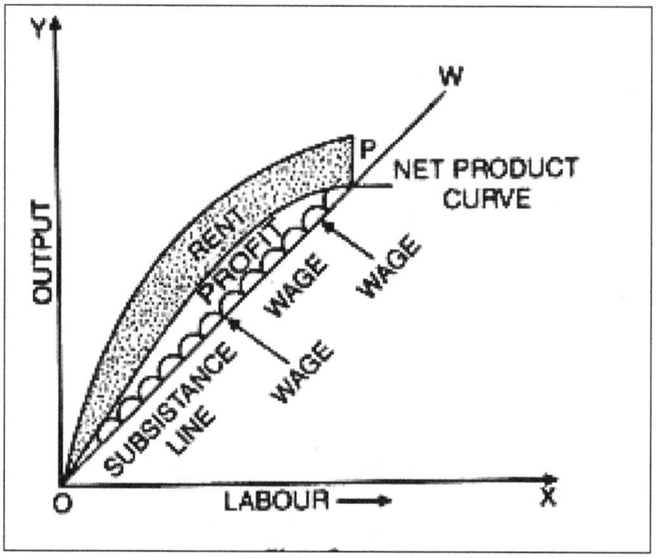

Thus, "Ricardian system of development formulated certain interrelations among capital, population and output on the basis of these relations, it traces the course of rent, wages and profits every time and finally it concedes with the celebrated forecast of the eventual advent of a stationary state".

Schumpeter's Capitalist Development

Schumpeter starts his analysis of development process with the concept of circular flow. It implies a condition where economic activity produces itself continuously at constant rate through time. It means a continuous activity and no destruction. It is the characteristics of an activity in stationary state. Circular flow is based upon a state of perfect competitive equilibrium in which costs are equal to revenue and prices to average costs. According to Schumpeter," The circular flow is a stream that is fed from the continually flowing springs of labour power and land and flow in every economic period into the reservoir which we call income, in order to be transformed into satisfaction of wants." The main features of circular flow are as under:

- All economic activities are essentially repetitive and follow a familiar routine course.
- All the producers know the aggregate demand for goods and adjust the supply of output accordingly. This means demand and supply are in equilibrium at each point of time.
- The economic system has the optimum level of output and its maximum use and there is no possibility of wastage of resources.
- The firms working in a system are in a state of competitive equilibrium.
- Under the stationary equilibrium, the prices are equal to the average cost of production and profits are zero. Interest rates tend to zero and there is less possibility of involuntary unemployment of resources.

These features imply that circular flow is used in a static setting. To make it dynamic and consistent with development, changes must take place in flow system. These changes can be brought through innovations.

Innovation

Innovation may be defined as a change in existing production system to be introduced by the entrepreneur with a view to make profits and reduce costs. The innovation is closely linked with Schumpeterian concept of development. He defined development as a "Spontaneous and discontinuous change in the channels of flow, disturbance of equilibrium which forever alters and displaces the equilibrium state previously existing." When changes takes place in the economy, circular flow is disturbed and the development process starts. He assumed that change is the basic element of dynamic process, and those changes come in the form of innovations. Any innovation may consist of:

- The introduction of a new product.
- The introduction of a new method of production.
- The opening up of a new market.
- The conquest of a new source of supply of raw materials or semi manufactured goods.
- The carrying out of the new organization of any industry like the creation of a monopoly.

The new combinations of these factors are essential for the development process to start. It is to be energized by the development agents are innovations or entrepreneurs. The entrepreneur is considered as the hero in the Schumpeterian drama of development.

Role of Entrepreneur

Entrepreneur or innovator is the key figure in Schumpeter analysis of the process of development. He occupies the central place in the development process because he initiates development in a society and carries it forward. Entrepreneurship is different from managerial activity. A manager simply directs production under existing techniques but entrepreneurship requires the introduction of something new. An entrepreneur is also different from a capitalist. The capitalist simply furnishes the funds while the entrepreneur directs the use of these funds. The entrepreneur is motivated:

- The desire to find a private commercial kingdom.
- The will to conquer and prove his superiority.
- The joy of creating, getting things done or simply of exercising one's energy and ingenuity.

Entrepreneurship is important because development is a discontinuous process which proceeds with spurts. According to Schumpeter, there is high degree of risk and uncertainty in economic world. Two things are necessary for the entrepreneurial function. Firstly, technical knowhow should be available to the entrepreneur for introducing new products and new combinations of production factors. This does not pose any problem because there always exists a reservoir of unused technical inventions which may be utilized by the entrepreneurs.

Prof. Schumpeter observes that, "It is no part of his function to find or to create new possibilities. They are always present, abundantly accumulated by all sorts of people." The second thing is the capital resource which can enable the entrepreneurs to have command over factors of production. For this, he needs purchasing power in the form of credit and capital which we can borrow from banks and other financial institutions. Thus, credit and bank plays a vital role in economic development. Schumpeter is of the opinion that the entrepreneur needs credit because credit promotes industrial development which in turn, delivers new goods. Credit enables the entrepreneur to buy producer's goods which he needs for conducting new experiments and innovations. The invention in one field of the economic activity will induce inventions in the related fields. Thus, credit creation becomes an important part of the development model and, therefore, growth necessarily becomes an uneven process because investment can be increased through bank borrowings.

Role of Profits

An entrepreneur innovates to earn profits. Profits are conceived "as a surplus over costs, a difference between the total receipts and outlay as a function of innovation." According to Prof. Schumpeter," under competitive equilibrium, the price of each product just equals its cost of production and there are no profits. Profits arise due to dynamic changes resulting from an innovation. They continue to exist till the innovation becomes general".

Breaking the Circular Flow

Schumpeter regards economic development as a dynamic and discontinuous process. The society progresses through trade cycle. That is why the entrepreneurial activity appears in a swarm like fashion. The swarm like appearance of entrepreneurs is responsible for cyclical nature of economic growth. In order to break the circular flow, the innovating entrepreneurs are financed by bank credit expansion. Since investment in innovation is risky, they must be paid bank interest on it. Once the innovation becomes successful and profitable, other entrepreneurs follow it in "swarm like clusters." Innovations in one field may induce other innovations in related fields. For example, the emergence of a motor car industry, may in turn, simulate a wave of new investments in the construction of highways, rubber tyres and petroleum products etc. but the spread is never hundred percent. The spread of innovation can be explained with the help of a figure where percentage of a firm is taken along Y-axis and time is along X-axis. The curve OL represents that firm adopt an innovation slowly to start but soon the adoption of innovation gains momentum but it never reaches 100 % adoption by firms.

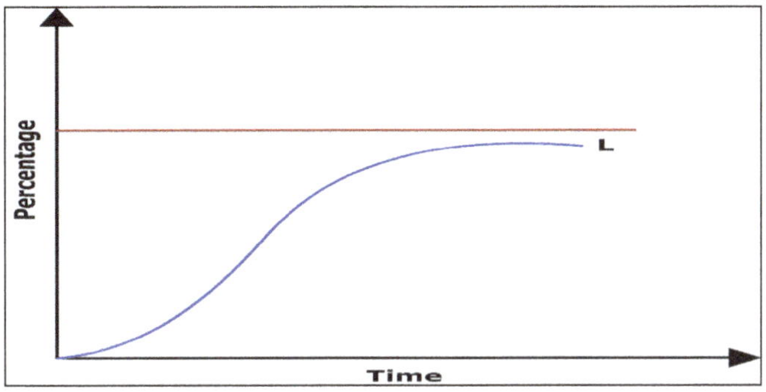

Cyclical Process

Since the investment is assumed to be financed by creating of bank credit, it increases money income and prices and helps to create a cumulative expansion throughout the economy. The increase in purchasing power of consumers increases the demand for the products of the old industries in relation to supply. Prices rise, profits increase and old industries expand by borrowing from banks. It induces a secondary wave of credit inflation which is super-imposed on primary wave of innovation. Over optimism and speculation add further to boom. After a period of gestation, the new products start appearing in the market replacing the old products and enforcing a process of liquidation, readjustment and absorption. The demand for old product decreases and there is fall in prices. The old firms contract output. As the innovators start repaying bank loans out of profits, the quantity of money is decreased and prices tend to fall and profits decline and as a result uncertainty and risk increase, the impulse for innovation is reduced and eventually comes to an end and depression begins. There are always ups and downs in the natural events.

Similarly, in the economic activities, there are wave-like movements. The forces that bring out spurt in economic activity and cause boom ultimately get exhausted and create counter forces. At last ultimately counter forces gain sufficient strength and power to overcome the original forces. This is how the boom starts fading away, giving place to depression. Schumpeter believes that new units of production enjoy advantage over old units of production when new plants start turning out production. They are naturally attracted by new products and they spend money to purchase those products. While the old plants cut their output or close down and the national output shrinks. Schumpeter describes this process of capitalist development as "creative destruction" where in the old economic structures of society are being continually destroyed and new structures are being continually created in their place.

The second reason for the down-swing phase is human psychology. Man is greedy by nature and this makes him over-ambitious and optimistic about future events. When an entrepreneur makes profit out of his investment, he thinks that he can go on making profit for ever without realizing the uncertainties and risks involved in business and as a result investment starts falling. It creates multiplier effect. Incomes begins to decrease, purchasing power shrinks, and prices fall and the stage of depression is reached. Schumpeter cyclical process of development is illustrated by a figure given as:

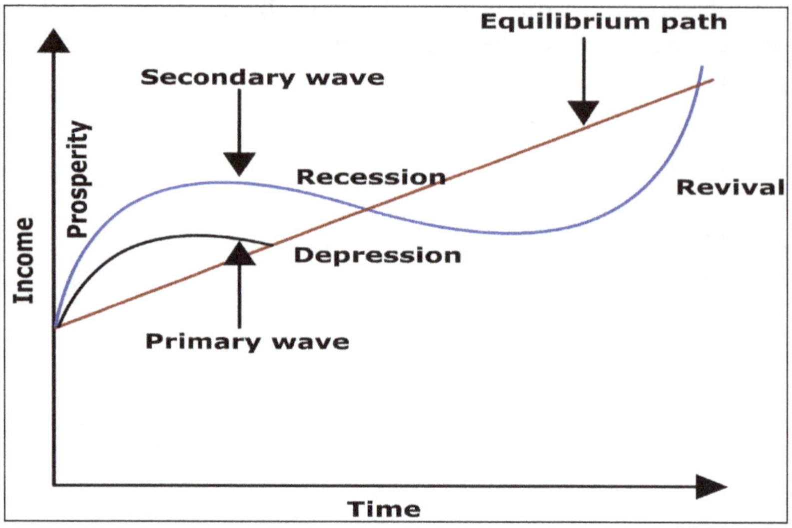

The secondary wave is super-imposed on the primary wave of innovation. With over optimism and speculation, development proceeds more rapidly in prospective phase When recession starts, the cycle continues downward below equilibrium level to dispersion phase and ultimately another innovation brings revival. Thus, entrepreneurs play a key role in the Schumpeterian analysis. They bring economic development in a spontaneous and discontinuous manner. And "cyclical savings are the cost of economic development under capitalism" a permanent feature of its dynamic path. Depression goes on for some time on its own momentum till the economy gets a new position of stability. The economy behaves like a man. When a man is tired, he takes rest and after taking rest, he become active and perform the various activities of life and similarly, when economy is tired, it needs rest i.e.it needs time to stabilize itself to a new position. Once stability is attained, a new swarm of innovators appear with a new sense of confidence and optimism. The innovators start making investment in the hope of making profits and in this way, the economy gathers momentum to move on the path of progress and development. Thus, business cycle forms an integral part of development theory.

Decay of Capitalism

The continuous technical progress results in an unbound increase in total and per capita output. As long as technical progress takes place, the rate of profit is positive. Hence, there can be no drying up of source of investible funds nor any vanishing of investment opportunities. "There is, therefore, no prior ceiling to the level of per capita income in a capitalist society. Nevertheless, the economic success of capitalism will eventually lead to its decay." The very success of capitalism undermines the social institutions which protect it and inevitably creates condition in which it will not be able to live and which strongly point to socialism as the heir apparent.

Capitalism can maintain itself only so long as entrepreneurs behave like knights and pioneers. Schumpeter holds a very pessimistic view about the survival of capitalism. He advocated capitalist system of production yet he was not unaware of the weakness of this system. Due to its drawbacks, capitalism disintegrates and yields place to socialism. Schumpeter gives the following reasons for the disintegration of capitalism:

- The obsolescence of entrepreneurial function.
- Destruction of institutional frame work of capitalist.
- Destruction of protecting political strata.

Prof. Schumpeter observes that the success of early captain of industry has made innovation a routine activity. It tends to degenerate into a depersonalized, routine activity carried on a big business through highly trained managers. The new lords of business are managers, depersonalized owners and private bureaucrats. This reduces the industrial bourgeois to a class of wage earners and, thus, undermines the function and the position of the entrepreneur as the "worrier knight." Another factor responsible for weakening the foundations of capitalism is the destruction of its institutional frame work. The entrepreneur by his own success tends to destroy not only his economic and social functions but also the institutional framework within which he works. The tendency towards concentration and increase in the size of production unit destroy capitalistic institutions like private property and freedom of contract. In case of big concerns, the proprietors are small and large shareholders who are dematerialized and defunctionalised by professional and salaried managers, and thus the proprietary interest is replaced by large and small stockholders. These changes tend to weaken the concept of private property and free individual contract.

The destruction of the protecting political strata will administer the last blow to capitalist system. With the progress of capitalism, not only the functions of the entrepreneur and the institutional framework of capitalism crumble but the group that protected early capitalism politically is also destroyed. The very success of capitalism is destroyed by the royal power. The progress of capitalism makes industrialists and merchants economically powerful and they begin to dominate in political field. The success of capitalism also creates active hostility against its own social order. He observes that the above factors simply weaken the economic and social foundation of capitalism but they are not sufficient to destroy the system. The capitalist is given more intellectual freedom and more means to practice his freedom. By extending educational facilities, capitalism increases the supply of educated and white collar groups. Capitalism also creates a labour movement. Here the intellectual finds a readymade class to which he can provide intellectual leadership.

The class conflict, industrial disputes, economic inequality, exploitation, fictions and frustration among the working groups are some of the factors which disrupt the capitalism. According to Schumpeter, the breakdown of capitalism would come only from the lack of appreciation of what capitalism can do. In this regard, Prof. Higgins writes, "According to Schumpeter, not the failure of capitalism but its very success, eventually leads to the slaughter of the goes that lays the golden egg". Schumpeter can be regarded as a prophet of doom of capitalism.

Mathematical Interpretation

Like classical and Marx's models, the Schumpeter model can be explained with the help of certain mathematical equations. Mathematical interpretation is based on certain propositions which are as under:

Proposition 1: The production function is same as in the classical economy i.e.

$$O = f(L, K, Q, T)$$

L = Labour force

K = Capital stock

T = Technology

Propostion 2: Savings depend upon wages, profits and interest rate. Workers and capitalist do savings of their incomes and their savings increase as their income rises. Schumpeter retained the neo-classical proposition that saving tends to rise with increase in interest rate is:

$$S = S(W, R, r)$$

S = Saving

W = Wages

R = Profits

r = Rate of interest.

Propostion 3: Total investment is the aggregate of induced investment and autonomous investment. Schumpeter distinguishes between two kinds of investment. First is the induced investment, which is stimulated by increase in income, output, sales and profits etc. second is the autonomous investment which is influenced by technological change, scientific discoveries etc.

$$I = I_i + I_A$$

I_i = Induced Investment

I_A = Autonomous Investment

Proposition 4: Induced investment depends upon the level of profits and interest rate. Induced investment tends to rise with the increase in profits and tends to fall as interest rate goes up. As this gap widens, the capital accumulation will induce investment.

$$Ii = I(Ri, r, Q)$$

$$\frac{dIi}{dR} > 0, \frac{dIi}{dr} < 0, \frac{dIi}{dQ} > 0$$

These inequalities show that the change in induced investment is due to change in profit and capital accumulation is positive whereas it would be negative due to change in interest rate.

Proposition 5: Autonomous investment depends resource discovery and technical progress. Prof. Schumpeter had laid great emphasis on innovation. Innovation can be in the form of discovery and technical progress which determines autonomous investment i.e.

$$I_A = Ia(K,T)$$
$$K = \text{Discovery}$$
$$T = \text{Technological progress}$$

Proposition 6 & 7: Technological progress and the rate of resource discovery depend on the supply of entrepreneurs. Entrepreneurs occupy a unique place in Schumpeterian analysis of development. His main function is to carry on innovations in the form of discovery of technological progress i.e.

$$T = T(E) \text{ and } K = K(E)$$
$$E = \text{Supply of entrepreneurs}$$

Proposition 8: The supply of entrepreneurs depends on the rate of profits and social climate. Schumpeter recognizes that ability, equality and capability of an individual depend upon social climate. The relationship between the supply of entrepreneurs, profits and social climate is expressed as:

$$E = E(R,x)$$
$$E = \text{Supply of entrepreneurs}$$
$$R = \text{Profits}$$
$$x = \text{Social climate}$$

The supply of entrepreneurs is dependent variable whereas profit and social climate are dependent variables.

Proposition 9: GNP depends upon relationship between savings and investment and super multiplier. An excess of investment over saving will raise GNP through multiplier effect. The increase in GNP will be some multiple of gap between investment and savings i.e.

$$O = R(I,-S)$$
$$O = \text{Gross national output}$$
$$R = \text{Multiplier}$$
$$I = \text{Investment}$$
$$S = \text{Saving}$$

Proposition 10: The wage bill depends upon the level of investment.

$$W = W(I)$$

This equation shows that there is direct relationship between wage income and investment. An increase or decrease in income will tend to increase or decrease wage income.

Proposition 11: The social climate is reflected by distribution of income. The concept of social climate is complex. It reveals that income of social climate. If income distribution raises the level of profits of the entrepreneurs that will create favorable social climate for development and vice-versa. The ratio of profits to wages is a short hand expression influencing social climate.

$$X = X\left(\frac{R}{W}\right)$$

X = Social Climate

R/W = Ratio of profits to wages

Any increase or decrease in this ratio will favorably affect the social climate.

Propostion 12: GNP is equal to profits + wages. To close the system, a familiar identity is used as $O = R + W$.

Here, O = GNP

R = Profits

W = Wages

As the system contains 12 equations and 12 unknowns so it is a determinate system.

Critical Appraisal

Schumpeterian analysis of economic development is modified and refined version of Marx's model of growth. His theory is based on the development experiences of capitalist countries during 18th and 19th century. He correctly emphasized the rate of entrepreneur in the development of capitalism. In the capitalistic societies, entrepreneurs were the prime movers of development process and innovations played an important role in the development of capitalism. Despite all this, this theory is criticized on the following grounds:

- Role of Innovator Emphasized: Schumpeter theory highlights the role of innovator as the prime mover of economic development. The analysis of the entrepreneurial innovation is highly useful in the development of capitalism. Innovations are only one of many factors causing cyclical fluctuations in a capitalistic economy. The functions of innovators in the large business corporations are performed by a large and changing number of individuals. It is difficult to differentiate their innovating activity from their ordinary business activity. The innovational activities have become a matter of routine these days and there is no need of special agent like innovator for carrying on such activities. Thus, Schumpeter has over glorified the rate of innovator in his model.

- Role of Savings Ignored: Schumpeter assumed that innovations are financed by the bank credit and this assumption is not much convincing. Banks usually grant short term loans, but the innovations and development activities require long term loans. He assumes that innovations are financed by the borrowings from credit creating banks. In this way this theory ignores the important sources of real savings such as deficit financing, budgetary savings, public borrowings and other fiscal measures. In present time, the sources of savings play a vital role in financing the development projects and innovations.

- Analysis of Capitalist Process not Convincing: "Schumpeter's" broad socio-economic analysis of capitalist process is generally admired. Yet few seem prepared to accept its conclusion. His arguments are stimulating but not completely convincing. This theory explains that rational behavior of innovators and intellectual class is responsible for the success of capitalism. The

Schumpeter's Hero i.e. innovator or entrepreneur is a forward looking man in the economic matters and he is an adaptable individual who can overcome all sorts of difficulties and obstacles. But in social and political field, he may be quite inapt and weak. The entrepreneur may not be capable of adjusting to political changes. It is, therefore, not convincing that capitalist process always works on the basis of rationality and dispassionate ideas.

- Emergency of socialism not based on sound reasoning: Schumpeterian analysis about the emergence of socialism is provocative yet it seems it be one sided and over emphasized. He himself is not quite sure about the way in which socialism will take place of capitalism. His unawareness about this factor is clear from these words, "We know nothing as yet about the precise way by which socialism may be expected to come, expect that there must be a great many possibilities ranging from gradual bureaucratization to the most picturesque revolution." Schumpeter says about the changing condition of the capitalism may be finally replaced by a system different from socialism. So it is very difficult to conclude that the decomposition of capitalism will eventually lead to composition of socialism.
- Circular Flow based on Say's Law of market: Circular flow is the first component of the Schumpeterian analysis of economic growth and its features reveals that this concept is very much similar to Say's law of market. The circular flow or Say's law is valid in a stationary society which is not in tune with development process which is dynamic one. It is dynamic setting which is more conductive to economic development. Hence the assumption of circular flow are incompatible with the development process.

Schumpeter and UDC

Schumpeter's theory forms the foundation of stone of modern thinking on the problem of development. Yet his analysis is not applicable to UDC, it is due to the following reasons:

- Not applicable to socialist countries: This theory is not applicable to majority of UDC which has socialist system. For example, the introduction of social security measures and highly progressive income taxes are harmful to the development of an entrepreneurial class because they tend to reduce the profits.
- Institution Change and Innovations not needed: In UDC, the class innovation is very small due to small extent of market and low expectation of profit. Schumpeter contends private innovator as the prime mover of economic growth, but in poor countries the government is the biggest innovator. He observed that for sustained growth there should be combination of several factors like organizational structures, business practices, skilled labours and appropriate values, attitudes and motivation.
- Lack of entrepreneurship: The Schumpeter's analysis rests on the existence of entrepreneurial class but UDC lacks inadequate entrepreneurship. In such economies, profits are low and low state of technology does not enhance innovational investments in new plant. Moreover, the lack of adequate power, transport, skilled personnel act as disincentives to entrepreneurial activity.
- Different Socio-Economic Order: UDC have got a socio economic structure which is entirely different from the socio economic order that prevailed in western Europe and America in

18th and 19th centuries and which has been the basis of Schumpeterian analysis of problem of development. In these centuries, certain essential of growth like economic and social overheads, suitable attitudes and values for economic development already existed but in UDC such essentials does not exist.

- Neglects savings: Schumpeter's exclusive emphasis on bank credit obscures the rate of savings in investment. It also considers the importance of deficit financing, budgetary savings, public credit and other fiscal measures in the economic development.
- Neglects Consumption: The Schumpeterian analysis is production oriented and the development process is consumption oriented. This is applied in the current trend towards the welfare state in which demand and consumption play a leading role.
- Neglects population growth: Schumpeter theory is also inapplicable to UDC because it neglects the effect of growth of population on wealth. In these countries, population is the main hurdle in the process of development and any theory that neglects population problem, cannot be very useful to them.
- Neglects external factors: The development is due to the changes that arise from within the economy. But in UDC changes do not take place from within the economy; rather they are outcome of imparted ideas, technology and capital.
- Unsatisfactory explanation of inflationary forces: In this theory, inflationary impulses from an integral part of the process of development but in involve no secular inflation. The long term price is stable. In an UDC inflationary forces are very powerful. "Social demand working through political and labour union channels seeks to extract from the economy more than what through domestic production and international trade. It can be made to yield. It is not only development and the associated investment that are responsible for inflationary tendencies but the entire social climate of demand oriented economy".
- Assimilation of innovation: The development process in UDC is based not on innovations but on existing innovations. For example, entrepreneurs in UDC are not in position to innovate; rather they adapt innovations taking place in advanced countries.

Malthusian Theory of Economic Development

Malthus showed more appreciation than most of his contemporaries of the importance of a distinct and systematic theory of growth. Book I of his Principles of Political Economy was concerned with value and distribution; book II with "The Progress of Wealth". In his famous work, Malthus posited his hypothesis that (unchecked) population growth always exceeds the growth of means of subsistence. He argued that while population rises geometrically, food supply increases arithmetically. Actual (checked) population growth is kept in line with food supply growth by "positive checks" (starvation, disease and the like, elevating the death rate) and "preventive checks" (i.e. postponement of marriage, etc. that keep down the birth rate), both of which are characterised by "misery and vice".

Malthus's hypothesis implied that actual population always has a tendency to push above the food supply. Because of this tendency, any attempt to ameliorate the condition of the lower classes by increasing their incomes or improving agricultural productivity would be fruitless, as the extra means of subsistence would be completely absorbed by an induced boost in population. As long as this tendency remains, Malthus argued, the "perfectibility" of society will always be out of reach. He defines the problem of development as explaining any difference between potential gross national product ("Power of Producing riches") and actual gross national product (actual riches).

There is nothing automatic about economic growth, Malthus warns. To say that population growth by itself is enough to bring economic advance is absurd. In the first place, population growth-despite the strength of the psychological and physiological forces tending to bring it down is an end product of the whole economic process; "an increase of population cannot take place without a proportionate or nearly proportionate increase of wealth". As evidenced, that the natural tendency toward population growth is no guarantee that either population or income will grow, he cites examples of Spain, Portugal, Hungry, Turkey, "together with nearly the whole of Asia and Africa and the greatest part of America". Secondly, mere increases in numbers do not provide a stimulus to economic expansion; population growth encourages development only if it brings an increase in effective demand. "A man whose only possession is his labour is, or is not, in demand by those who have the disposal of produce". And the demand for labour, in turn, depends on the rate of capital accumulation.

Effective Demand

In elaborating his theory of effective demand and its relations to savings and investment, Malthus anticipated some of the basic ideas of such modern writers as Keynes and Kalecki. He flatly repudiated 'Say's law', which said in effect that supply creates its own demand and that savings are just a demand for capital goods. Saving in the sense of planned or ex-ante saving or abstinence, means not consuming; and not consuming in itself brings a decline in effective demand, profits and investment. Malthus drew attentions to a circularity of a kind quite different from the one spelled out by the other classical economists, which has been restated more systematically by Kalecki and others. We have national income (or output) equal to profits plus wages. As we know that,

$$O = R + W$$

$$\text{Or } R = O - W$$

Where $R = \text{Profit}$

$W = \text{Wages}$

$O = \text{National output}$

Since workers, as a class are too poor to save, they spend all their income on consumption. Let us denote workers' consumptions as C_w. Capitalists (C_c), however, do save; these savings create income in so far as they are invested. So we may write,

$$R = (I + C_c + C_w) - C_w = I + C_c \qquad \because O = I + C_c + C_w$$

National income or output is generated by investment, capitalists' consumption and workers' consumption. Profit are national income less wages; wages equal worker's consumption and so according to Malthus, profits are equal to investment plus capitalists' consumption.

Role of Capital

Malthus, does not, of course, deny the need for saving and investment for economic growth. But he suggests a concept of 'optimum propensity to save'. Up to a certain point saving is needed to finance (without inflation) the investment for which profitable opportunities exist. Beyond that point, however, saving will reduce. Consumer spending to such an extent that investment too will be discouraged. High rates of growth do not occur with high levels of ex-ante saving (abstinence) on the part of the upper income groups, but with high levels of ex-post (realized) savings and investment, which are in large degree the result of growth, and do not require reductions in consumer spending. Like Smith and Ricardo, Malthus also believed in free enterprise and considered that the wealth effects of free trade are very high.

Structural Change

Malthus also noted the phenomenon which much later Colin Clark has stressed; economic development entails structural change of a sort which diminishes the relative importance of agriculture in the economy. He argued that technological progress tends to increase employment and that tapering-off of the growth of income and output causes unemployment. He suggested land reform as one means of expanding output. Malthus envisaged the economy as consisting of two major sectors, industrial and agriculture, the latter triggers the growth of the former.

The Malthusian picture of economic development seems to have been one is which capital was invested in agriculture until all the arable land was brought into cultivation, stocked and improved; after that there were no more opportunities for profitable investment in that sector, and investment opportunities existed only is the industrial sector. Diminishing returns to increased employment on the land could be avoided only if technological progress in the industrial sector was rapid enough, and if enough investment took place, to absorb most of the population growth in the industrial sector and to reduce the cost of living of workers on the land, permitting reductions in their corn (goods) wage rates. Let us assume once again that the rate of technological progress in the industrial sector depends only on the amount of capital available for utilising the steady flow of improvements. Malthus explicitly recognised the possibility of unemployment arising from inadequate investment, so the level of industrial employment can also be treated as a function of investment. Thus we can regard industrial output as depending solely on the amount of capital invested in the industrial sector.

$$O_i = a \,.\, Q_i$$

Where O_i is the output of industrial sector, Q_i is the amount of capital in industrial sector, and 1/a is the capital-output ration for the sector. Differentiating the above equation with respect to time.

$$\delta O_i / \delta t = a \,.\, \delta Q_i / \delta t + Q_i \,.\, \delta a / \delta t \text{ where a is constant}$$

$$\delta O_i / \delta t = a \,.\, \delta Q_i / \delta t$$

If technological progress is 'neutral', the capital output ratio can be considered as constant and the second term drops out. The trend of industrial output through time depends only on the rate of capital accumulation (investment) in the industrial sector the rate of investment in turn depends upon the level of profits and in this model, the rate of profits will depend on the wage rate (which is turn depends upon the cost of producing wage goods, especially food stuffs) and effective demand, which depends on capitalists' consumption and investment. Malthus also, makes some suggestions about sectoral interaction in underdeveloped areas, which help to explain why they remain underdeveloped. First, he points out that each sector constitutes the market for the output of the other sector (in the absence of international trade). Thus failure of either sector to expand acts as a drag on the growth of the other; 'balanced growth' is necessary if we are to have growth at all. The development of the industrial sector of underdeveloped countries is limited by the poverty of the agricultural sector. The continuing poverty of the peasant agriculture sector does not arise from scarcity of fertile land; poverty persists because large land owners have no incentive for more intensive cultivation with the present limitations of the marker, whereas the peasants lack capital that would be needed for efficient cultivation, which alone would permit them to pay enough to induce land lords to rent some of their land. Thus the industrial sector (including large-scale agriculture) remains limited in total size. Because of its land-and-capital intensive nature it provides employment for relatively few people. The bulk of population, meanwhile, lives in poverty by means of labour-intensive peasant agriculture, which provides no effective demand for further growth.

A Critical Appraisal

There is no doubt that Malthus made a valuable contribution to the theory of economic growth. This repudiation of say's law and emphasizing the importance of effective demand and its relation to saving and investment are indeed noteworthy for their modern touch. A great deal of what he wrote on the subject is applicable to an under-developed economy, especially relating to the theory of dualism.

J.S Mill's Theory of Development

J.S. Mill made a valuable contribution to the theory of economic development. He analyzed various factors of economic growth. He regarded economic development as a function of land, labour and capital. While land and labour are two original factors of production and capital is stock previously accumulated of the products of former labour. The wealth of a nation can increase only if land and capital help to increase production faster than labour force. Wealth refers to those things which can be kept for sometime before they are put to use. It consists of tools, machines and the skill of labour force. Mill emphasizes the materiality of the product. He also distinguishes between productive consumption and unproductive consumption. Productive consumption is that which goes to maintain and increase the productive powers of the community. Only the productive consumers are productive labourers but all consumption is not productive. Worker's consumption of subsistence goods is productive while that of luxuries is unproductive.

- Control of Population Growth: Mill believed in Malthusian theory of production. The law of population growth throws light on the tendency of population to increase faster than the increase in the means of living. The result is restriction on population growth by the checks or preventive checks. Positive checks are made in UDC and among laboring classes, preventive checks are generally practiced among the middle classes of advanced countries. Emigration is an effective measure to relieve the excessive population problem.

- Wage Fund: The elasticity of labour supply is very high in response to rise in wages. Wages generally exceed the subsistence level. Wages are paid out of capital and hence they are limited by the existing fund of capital. Wages are determined by the demand and supply of labour. By capital, Mills means "only circulating capital and not even the whole of that but the part of which is expanded in the direct purchase of labour" and by population is meant "the numbers only of the laboring class, or rather of those who work for hire". Any change in wage rate is affected by change in capital or population. Mill pointed out that wages cannot rise buy by an increase of the aggregate funds employed in hiring labourers, or a diminution in the number of the competitors for hire, nor fall except either by a diminution of the funds devoted to paying labour or by an increase in the numbers of labourers to be paid. Thus, the rise and fall in wages depends upon whether capital grows faster than population or population than capital. This is based on Mill's notion that, "demand for commodities is not demand for labour". It implies that income invested on advances of wages to labour create employment and not income spent on consumer goods. Thus, increase in consumption will lead to decline in the investment. So increase in investment leads to increase in the wage fund and it leads to economic progress.
- Role of Capital Accumulation: Capital is defined as the stock previously accumulated of the products of formal labour. Greater the capital larger will be the size of wage fund and higher will be the demand for productive labour. Capital is the result of saving and saving means the abstinence from present consumption for the sake of future goods. According to Mill, capital accumulation depends upon:
    - The amount of fund from which saving can be made.
    - The strength of the disposition to save which, in turn, depends upon the rate of return of saving or the rate of profit and the willingness to save at a given rate of profit.

  For Mill, profit depends upon cost of labour, so that rate of profit is the ratio of profit to wages. When profit rises or wages fall, the rate of profit increases which, in turn, increases the rate of capital accumulation. Similarly, the rate of capital accumulation can be increased by increasing the desire to save.
- Rate of Profit: According to Mill, the ultimate tendency in an economy is for the rate of profit to decline due to diminishing returns in agriculture and increase in population at a Malthusian rate. In the absence of technical improvements in agriculture and the growth rate of population being higher than rate of capital accumulation, the rate of profit is "within a hand's breadth of minimum", and the country is "on the verge of stationary state". The preventive measures for minimum rate of profits are as under:
    - Capital losses during crisis.
    - Technical improvements.
    - Expansion of foreign trade.
    - Government borrowing for unproductive expenditure.
    - By capital exports to colonies to produce consumer goods for home country.

But none of these factors can continue indefinitely so ultimately the profits would have the tendency to be at the minimum level and the rate of accumulation declines.

- Role of State: J.S. Mill was a staunch supporter of the policy of laissez-faire. Every departure from it unless required by some great good is a certain evil. He, therefore, assigned the minimum role to the state in economic affairs. Mill recognized a number of exceptions to the general rule of Laissez-faire and felt the necessity of government intervention. The government has an important function to civilize the citizens by educational facilities. Education must be compulsory. Mill was first to put forward an economic justification for government intervention in the field of education. 'The uncultivated cannot be competent judges of cultivation' i.e. the buyer of education is not a competent judge of commodity. Mill did not think of education as an investment in human capital which directly stimulates economic growth, but education contributes to economic growth indirectly by raising the character of people, by promoting civic peace and by reducing the numbers. Mill further favoured free trade and was against protection and defended the imposition of protective duties temporarily in the case of infant industries.
- Stationary State: Mill thought that stationary state was imminent "at the most a few years ahead and no more" its arrival postponed by above factors. He welcomed the stationary state as it leads to improvement in income distribution and large remuneration for labour. But this is possible only through control on increase in numbers of working classes, through provident habits and education. Thus, "In Mill's stationary state, there could be no increase in either population or stock of capital, profit having reached the minimum necessary to prevent net disserving by the economy as a whole. However, there might still be a rising standard of living due to improvements in the art of living and increased leisure through technical progress".

References

- Ricardian-theory-of-development-explained-4524: economicsdiscussion.net, Retrieved 22, July 2020
- Mills-theory-of-development-explained-4542: economicsdiscussion.net, Retrieved 06, January 2020

4

Dual Economy Models

The existence of two distinct economic sectors within one country, which have different levels of development, patterns of demand and technology, is termed as dual economy. A few models studied in relation to dual economy are vicious circle of poverty, balanced and unbalanced growth and Leibenstein critical minimum effort theory. The diverse facets of these theories have been thoroughly discussed in this chapter.

Role of State

The concept of vicious and virtuous circle of poverty as formulated by Ragnar Nurkse describes the state in which the underdeveloped countries (UDCs) are entrapped in, where poverty seems to be the cause and effect of poverty. It means that if you are poor, you are bound to remain poor. This holds true for both individuals and societies. Nurkse argued that it is due to the impoverish state of these economics that any development effort to shift these economics to a higher growth path fails to fructify. "Poverty, according to Nelson, is a circular constellation of forces tending to act and react upon one another in such a way as to keep a country in a state of poverty". It implies that in the presence of such forces, achieving higher levels of economic growth becomes no longer automatic or spontaneous. This is because poverty hinders the inducement to invest, especially given the small size of the markets in the UDCs. Thus it results in a shortage of capital accumulation in these economies. Due to this reason, lack of capital accumulation is the central problem faced by the UDCs in their path of development. Capital investment especially social overhead capital is 'lumpy' in nature i.e. it cannot be acquired in small increments but must be obtained in large, discrete units and has a long gestation period. This works as a deterrent for the private investor to invest in capital formation in the small market economy. Another factor contributing to the vicious circle of poverty is the inelasticity of demand faced by the UDCs at the early stages of development.

Working of the Theory of the Vicious Circle of Poverty

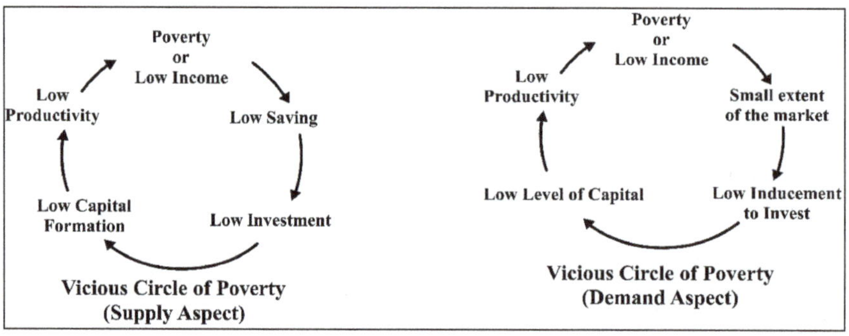

Vicious Circle of Poverty (Supply Aspect)

Vicious Circle of Poverty (Demand Aspect)

Nurkse looked at the problem of vicious circle of poverty from both sides, the supply side and the demand side wherein he gave more emphasize to the supply side problem. The supply side argument explains that the capacity to save of UDCs is severely limited by their low level of income earned. Hence, the mobilisation of savings into investment generates low levels of investment in an economy. Due to shortage of investment in the economy, productivity levels are also adversely affected which in turn results in an overall low level of income produced.

The demand side argument on the other hand explains the low level of income resulting in a lack of demand by the consumers and producers leading to a limited size of the market. The small size of the market works restraints the incentive to invest in that market. Hence the lack of effective investment results in low levels of income. According to Nurkse, in addition to these two vicious circles of poverty, the UDCs also face one other circle of poverty that operates in terms of Market Imperfections. These economies work in a manner that resources are not optimally utilised. There are no economies of scale. The scale of production is low and cost of production is high. There is lack of competitiveness and thus the UDCs are losers in international market. So in such a scenario the question is how the UDCs will break the vicious circle of poverty and move to higher path of growth. Nurkse borrowed the idea from 'Allyn Young' to provide the solution for the same. He quoted the famous example of the Shoe Factory which highlights that if a firm is only producing one product i.e. shoes then it is bound to fail. This is because the workers (then consumers) engaged in the factory will not spend their income entirely on the purchase of shoes. This is so because human wants are diverse.

So the demand for shoes will be less than the supply of shoes and hence a glut of shoes will be created which will result in the price to fall. Thus the firm will suffer losses. He said it might be acceptable in the Short run but not in the Long run. So the way out is to set up a number of factories producing different goods that are market-wise and technologically interdependent so that workers working in one firm are the buyers of another firm and vice-versa i.e. there should be a synchronized application of capital in a number of factories simultaneously so as to cater to the complementarities of demand. If such kind of investment is made then the size of the market will expand, there'll be no deficiency of demand and all benefits will be realized in terms of cheap goods both domestically and internationally. He said this will result in a frontal attack on poverty. According to him a single factory fails and many factories succeed to come out of the vicious circle of poverty through their forward and backward linkages. Backward linkages can be defined as "the growth of an industry leads to the growth of the industries that supply inputs to it". Forward linkages exist when the growth of an industry leads to the growth of other industries that uses its output as input. Before Nurkse, Adam Smith propagated the idea of division of labour and expansion of the size of the market to accelerate the process of economic development. Nurkse seems to have been influenced by his ideas also.

Critical Appraisal of the Theory

- The approach promotes practices like Division of Labour that ensure economies in terms of time, money and effort.
- It promotes development of various ancillary industries through working of vertical linkages.
- It accelerates the pace of economic development by developing a large number of sectors simultaneously.

- The approach suggests that the UDCs can move on the path of economic progress by massive investment simultaneously in all sectors appears totally impractical because the central problem faced by the UDCs is the dearth of capital and other resources.
- There could be problems of coordination. If large number of interdependent industries will be established then underperformance of few might disrupt the whole chain. Hence this theory is good on paper only but in practice lack of technical knowledge and skills will restrain growth.

Circular Causation

The classical economists are of the view that the expansion of international trade can be taken as an important source of economic development as it has equalizing effect i.e. it has developed both export and import countries irrespective of type of goods traded. But some of the recent economists have argued that international trade cannot encourage growth especially in underdeveloped countries. It may only help to the developed country. The theory of circular causation is one of the explanations to this.

Circular causation can be defined as a common complex situation with several interconnected causes and effects, where an action is controlled or affected by its own outcome or results. Circular causation is a theory developed by Swedish economist Gunnar Myrdal in the year 1956. It is a multi-causal approach where the core variables and their linkages are delineated. The idea behind it is that a change in one form of an institution will lead to successive changes in other institutions. These changes are circular in that they continue in a cycle, many times in a negative way, in which there is no end, and cumulative in that they persist in each round. The change doesn't occur all at once but in small changes because that would lead to chaos.

The Theory

According to Gunnar Myrdal "Economic development results in a circular causation process leading to rapid development of developed countries while the weaker countries i.e. underdeveloped countries in Asia and Africa continent tend to remain behind and poor". He further argues that "economic theory has disregarded these so called noneconomic factors and kept them outside the analysis. As they are among the main vehicles for the circular causation in the cumulative processes of economic change, this represents one of the principal shortcomings of economic theory".

Evolution of Theory

Gunnar Myrdal developed the concept from Knut Wicksell and developed it alongside with Nicholas Kaldor when they worked together at the United Nations Economic Commission for Europe. Myrdal concentrated on the social provisioning aspect of development, while Kaldor concentrated on demand-supply relationships to the manufacturing sector. About Economic Theory and Underdeveloped Regions Myrdal wrote that 'the argument moves on a general and methodological plane in the sense that the theory is discussed as a complex of broad structures of thought'. His aim was to submit 'broad generalizations, as a 'theory' is permitted to be, grasp the social facts as they organize themselves into a pattern when viewed under a bird's-eye perspective into this general vision, the specific characteristic. Myrdal developed further the circular cumulative causation concept and stated that it makes different assumptions from that of stable equilibrium on what can be considered the most important forces guiding the evolution of social processes. These forces characterize the dynamics of these processes in two diverse ways.

It is generally recognized that Myrdal's work on development and underdevelopment made three important contributions. He proposed accumulative causation approach in opposition to the dominant one, which he called the stable equilibrium approach. He pointed out that analyses of development processes, which only focus on economic factors, are irrelevant and misleading because historical, institutional, social and cultural factors also matter. He disputed the existence of a body of economic thought that is 'objective' in the sense that it is value-free.

Development Processes and Cumulative Causation

Myrdal's cumulative causation theory is the theory of development. His theory includes institutional and political factors to determine the development process besides demand and supply factors of an economy. Concerning institutional factors he insisted both economic and non-economic factors should be included in the analysis of causes of development as both have substantial importance. Again, Myrdal's cumulative causation theory allows the possibility and necessity of the social reform by introducing policies. Myrdal's methodology on policies is so unique that it might as well be called "the political implications in the evolutionary economics". Myrdal's cumulative causation theory can be a kind of indicator of the direction for the further development of cumulative causation theory.

Balanced and Unbalanced Growth

There are three approached to the theory of Balanced Growth that are commonly followed, first given by Nurkse, is considered to be the most fundamental approach to the BGS, that runs in accordance with the size of the market which seem to be an extension of Adam Smith's ideas; second given by W.A. Lewis runs in terms of the difference between social and private productivity that reconcile the benefits to both individual and society according to the principle of maximum social advantage and third approach is given by P.N.R.Rodan that explains the BGS in terms of the theory of Big Push.

Nurkse's Approach

Underdeveloped countries (UDCs) are in a firm grip of vicious circle of poverty where poverty seems to be the cause and effect of poverty. That means if a nation is poor, it is bound to remain poor. It holds in respect of both individuals and societies. If you are caught in the orbit of poverty, then you continue moving in that trap. He looked at the problem of vicious circle of poverty from two sides which are operating simultaneously. They are:

- The supply side argument explains that the capacity to save of UDCs is severely limited by their low level of income earned. Hence the mobilisation of savings into investment generates low levels of investment in an economy. Due to shortage of investment in the economy, productivity levels are also adversely affected which in turn results in an overall low level of income produced.

- The demand side argument on the other hand explains the low level of income resulting in a lack of demand by the consumers and producers leading to a limited size of the market. The small size of the market works restraints the incentive to invest in that market. Hence the lack of effective investment results in low levels of income.

According to Nurkse, in addition to these two vicious circles of poverty, the UDCs also face one other circle of poverty that operates in terms of market imperfections. These economies work in a manner that resources are not optimally utilised. There are no economies of scale. The scale of production is low and cost of production is high. There is lack of competitiveness and thus the UDCs are losers in international market. So in such a scenario the question is how the UDCs will break the vicious circle of poverty and move to higher path of growth. Nurkse borrowed the idea from 'Allyn Young' to provide the solution for the same. He quoted the famous example of the Shoe Factory which highlights that if a firm is only producing one product i.e. shoes then it is bound to fail. This is because the workers (then consumers) engaged in the factory will not spend their income entirely on the purchase of shoes. This is so because human wants are diverse. So the demand for shoes will be less than the supply of shoes and hence a glut of shoes will be created which will result in the price to fall. Thus the firm will suffer losses. He said it might be acceptable in the Short run but not in the Long run.

So the way out is to set up a number of factories producing different goods that are market-wise and technologically interdependent so that workers working in one firm are the buyers of another firm and vice-versa i.e. there should be a synchronized application of capital in a number of factories simultaneously so as to cater to the complementarities of demand. If such kind of investment is made then the size of the market will expand, there'll be no deficiency of demand and all benefits will be realized terms of cheap goods both domestically and internationally. He said this will result in a frontal attack on poverty. According to him a single factory fails and many factories succeed to come out of the vicious circle of poverty through their forward and backward linkages. Backward linkages can be defined as "the growth of an industry leads to the growth of the industries that supply inputs to it". Forward linkages exist when the growth of an industry leads to the growth of other industries that uses its output as input. It is the role of the state to undertake measures that promote industrial linkages, division of labour and hence expansion in the size of the markets (as the private sector is driven by profit motives and thus is shy in commencing investment with long gestation period and where the returns are uncertain and low). These measures include investment in social overhead capital, reduction in transport cost and adoption of the policy of laissez faire in international trade. He also argued that as the domestic production rises, there is expansion of foreign markets also.

Critique of Balanced Growth

The doctrine of balanced growth is based on wrong assumptions. Every underdeveloped country starts from a position that reflects previous investment decisions—and previous development. The theory of balanced growth requires balanced investment to meet the growing demand and as a result there is existence of increasing returns. If simultaneous investments are made in all related fields, bottlenecks arise, due to the shortage of raw materials, prices, factor shortages etc. There is ever likelihood of operating decreasing returns. It involves the simultaneous start of several productive activities at one instance. But in an underdeveloped country, there is an acute shortage of capital resource, technical and managerial skills etc. The whole system is self-contradictory.

Scholars such as Hirschman, Rostow, Fleming and Singer propounded the theory of unbalanced growth as a strategy of development to be used by the underdeveloped countries. This theory stresses on the need of investment in strategic sectors of the economy instead of all the sectors simultaneously. According to this theory the other sectors would automatically develop themselves through what is known as "linkages effect". Unbalanced growth theory which creating imbalances in the system are the best strategy for growth. Owing to the lack of availability of resources in the less developed countries, the little that is available must be used efficiently. Accordingly, strategic sectors in the economy should get priority or precedence over others where income is concerned.

Rodenstein Rodan's Approach

According to the theory of 'Big Push', if we want to pull out the underdeveloped economies from the low levels of equilibrium trap then we must choose a strategy that is market wise and technology wise interdependent. More particularly, in order to launch UDCs on a higher growth path and to sustain it, there is a need to put in a certain minimum amount of investment to overcome obstacles to development in an UDC. Thus this approach puts a lot of emphasis on the role of State to play. There are three mechanisms for generating big push in an economy. They are:

- Indivisibility in production function: Production function explains a technological way in which inputs can be transformed into output. This transformation leads to increase in production, economies of scale and externalities. Rodan regards investment in social overhead capital (SOC) vital for this transformation. The services of social-overhead capital comprising basic industries like power, transport, and communications are indirectly productive and have a long gestation period. They cannot be imported installations require a "sizeable initial lump" of investment. So excess capacity is likely to remain in them for some time. Thus SOC is characterised by four indivisibilities, it is irreversible in time and, therefore, must precede other directly productive investments. Second, equipment of SOC has high minimum durability. Lesser durability is not technically possible and is also less efficient. Hence it's lumpy in nature. Third, development of SOC needs a long gestation period. Last, it is an irreducible minimum industry mix of different kinds of public utilities i.e. investment in one set of infrastructure is not adequate but investment in multiple services or other complimentary inputs for SOC to work effectively. These indivisibilities of supply of social overhead capital are all of the principal obstacles to development in underdeveloped countries.

- Indivisibility of Demand: The indivisibility or complementarities of demand requires simultaneous setting up of interdependent industries in interdependent countries to enlarge the size of the market. For this to be successful there is a need to adopt practices like division of labour that save time, tools and promote new inventions. This would result in large scale production at a decreased cost and allows substitution of inputs. Hence it would make a firm competitive in comparison to his rivals.

- Indivisibility in savings: The central problem of the third world country in the process of economic growth is that there is dearth of capital in the form of plant, machinery, equipment etc. due to the low levels of savings in these economies. Rodan argued that if these countries are able to accelerate their incremental savings ratio, then it could be translated into development of large stock of capital. However, capital is seen as only a necessary but not a sufficient condition to move to higher trajectory of income. The focal point is how gainfully this stock of capital is employed in productive projects which require exchange of ideas. Therefore, exchange of ideas is even more important than provision of capital.

Hence they play an excessive role in the process of economic growth.

Merits of the Theory of Balanced Growth Strategy

- Ragnar Nurkse, in his doctrine of balanced growth has stressed on the importance of private investment. When investment is made in different sectors of the economy, there would be increase in the importance of private entrepreneurs. He asserts, that the private entrepreneurs can contribute considerably to economic development.
- The theory stresses on setting up a number of industries simultaneous to cater to complementarities of demand. By doing so, the size of the market will increase and hence economies of scale could be realized. And increase in the scale of production will lead to reduction of cost in the long run.
- The theory promotes practices like Division of Labour that ensure economies in terms of time, money and effort.
- It promotes development of various ancillary industries through working of vertical linkages.
- It accelerates the pace of economic development by developing a large number of sectors simultaneously.
- The development of SOC encourages private investment to take place by creating an infrastructure congenial for its growth and expansion.

Short-comings of the Theory of Balanced Growth Strategy

- It is argued that the adoption of BGS would induce inflationary pressures in the economy. Such dangers are more pronounced in the Short run. When a number of industries are set up in one go, a number of workers get employed. This would result in increase in their income and further an increase in aggregate demand. With the high rise in demand in the short period it may not be to increase supply to that extent which would result in rise in the price levels in the economy.
- There could be problems of coordination. If large number of interdependent industries will be established, then underperformance of few might disrupt the whole chain. Hence this theory is good on paper only but in practice lack of technical knowledge and skills will restrain growth.
- In underdeveloped countries there is an acute shortage of capital and other resources like entrepreneurial ability, technical know-how, infrastructure and institutional constraints.

To suggest that they can move on the path of economic progress by massive investment simultaneously in all sectors appears totally impractical. The balanced growth doctrine requires huge amounts of precisely these resources whose limited availability is the basic characteristic of the underdeveloped economies.

- This theory overlooks the role of agriculture sector in the process of growth. Economist H.W. Singer argued that if underdeveloped countries are to launch a large investment package in industries without paying much attention to agriculture, they are bound to run into difficulties like shortage of food and raw material shortages. Hence, development of industries requires development of agriculture sector as well. But whether it is in the capacity of UDCs to carry out investment in both the sectors or not is debatable.
- This theory overlooks the role of international trade as an engine of economic growth. However, there are two contrasting views regarding the impact of International trade on UDCs.
- This theory neglects the role of technology as it lays more or undue emphasis on capital formation.

Unbalanced Growth Strategy

Unbalanced growth strategy theory stresses on the need for deliberate unbalancing of the economy as per a pre-designed strategy' as the best method to enable a country to achieve higher trajectory of income. Therefore, the most efficient path towards economic development is a somewhat disorderly path and that path will be in tune with bottlenecks and shortages of three things, skills, facilities and services of products. Competitions, tensions, pressures as well as inducements are inevitable outcomes of unbalancing growth. According to this theory, industrial development will proceed largely through backward linkages that'll work its way from the last industries to intermediate industries and to the basic industries i.e. strategic investment in potent sectors will benefit the lagged sectors through the working of linkages. Hirschman stresses on the importance of import substitution to improve the balance of payments (i.e. the capability of the nation to mobilise and utilise its resources), particularly in the Third World Countries (TWCs), to achieve higher levels of growth. If the economy is to be kept growing over high rate of growth, basic task of development policy is the ability of using the resources which is woefully absent in the TWCs, so it is necessary to create distortions, disequilibrium, tensions and imbalances.

The choice of technique on the basis of which leading sectors are selected in which investment is induced is best guided by Harvey Leibinstein's method of Social Marginal Productivity/ Output criteria. According to this criterion those sectors are selected for investment whose social benefits exceed their cost rather than those which are worthwhile from private point of view. Some other criteria's that conventionally play a role in determining a project are 'how entrepreneurship and supply of savings, consumption habits and population growth' are affected when a projected is selected or rejected.

However, Hirschman suggested an alternate criterion whereby which while make a choice between two projects, the decision must dwell on the distinction between 'Postponement choice' and 'Substitution choice'. Substitution choices are mutually exclusive choices i.e. in the case of two events, if we choose one; we are permanently discarding the other. So in this case the two events cannot happen simultaneously i.e. one event happens at the expense of other. This is especially applicable to the TWCs which are suffering from the dearth of resources. Postponement choices describe a sequence of projects as no project is permanently discarded or selected. One project is postponed until the resources are not available for its execution. So here, discarding is temporary, something which is not relevant in the first case.

Hirschman suggested that an optimal sequence is one that involves minimum amount of expenditure from the available projects. If two projects involve equal minimum expenditure, then that one is chosen that generates more resources for the next project. He defined two series of investment i.e. Convergent series (investments that appropriate more economies from the proceeding investments than what they create) and Divergent series (investments that create economies which will be appropriated by their succeeding investments), out of which he divergent series of investment over convergent series of investment. Divergent series of investment are in Social Overhead Capital (SOC) which is high on social profitability rather than private profitability whereas convergent series of investment is guided by Directly Productive Activities (DPA) whose main objective is private profitability.

Hirschman defines SOC as those investments that include all public utilities like drainage system, irrigation, power, communication and transport, public health, education and law and order. These activities facilitate the operations of a great variety of other economic activities. These activities are provided by all countries subject to some public control and they cannot be imported. SOC is characterised by lumpiness and high capital output ratio. They have a long gestation period and are irreversible in time. Hirschman replied heavily on investing in SOC for creating imbalances because investment in SOC creates more external economies than what it appropriates. Its backward linkages are weak but forward linkages are strong. It encourages private investment in DPA and is safer than DPA. Its base is diversified and wider than that of DPA.

Merits of Unbalanced Growth Strategy are:

- The developing countries do not have the adequate capital to invest in all sectors of economy. So if investment is concentrated at the potential and selective sector only, then the developing countries can get their economy with better growth.
- The unbalance condition of economy creates the balanced condition which further makes the economy unbalance and finally economy is balanced. It is a non-ending process.
- This theory decentralises the mechanism of decision making and hence will be more useful for the underdeveloped areas.

Demerits of Unbalanced Growth Strategy are:

- This theory puts undue emphasis industrialization notwithstanding the significance of agriculture sector. This reflects the possibility of lop-sided development in the society.
- Due to long gestation period in the industries, in the short-run there might be some degree of inflationary pressures.
- Thirlwall criticizes the theory by arguing that it may lead to concentration of production in one or two commodities and this may adversely affect the BOP if these commodities are

price inelastic and income inelastic in demand. He also criticizes the theory for leaving too much matter of chance and for the possibility of waste and excess capacity.

- Paul Streeten criticizes the theory by saying that it is an incomplete theory which has paid no attention to the composition, time and direction of investment projects (though it has propounded optimum degree of disorderly model). He also argued that the theory focuses on the stimuli and expansion but tends to neglect or minimize the resistances caused in the UDCs.

Leibenstein Critical Minimum Effort Theory

The main idea of the theory is that economic growth in the underdeveloped and overpopulated countries in not possible unless a certain minimum level of investment is injected into the system as a consolidated dose that pulls the system out of doldrums. This minimum level of investment is called 'critical minimum effort'. According to Leibenstein, "A sufficiently large minimum effort is necessary at the outset if the necessary minimum is to be achieved." It is necessary for the sustained economic growth of underdeveloped countries that a certain minimum sum of money is invested. Prof. Leibenstein has further added, "In order to achieve the transition from the state of backwardness to the more developed state, where we can expect steady secular growth, it is necessary, though not always sufficient condition, that at the same point or during the same period, the economy should receive a stimulus to growth that is necessary than a certain critical minimum size."

Shocks and Stimulants

According to Leibenstein, every economy is under the influence of two forces, 'shocks' and 'stimulants'. Shocks refer to those forces which reduce the level of output, income, employment and investment etc. In other words, shocks dampen and depress the development forces. Stocks depress development forces which reverse the wheel of development. On the contrary, stimulants refer to those forces which raise the level of income, output, employment and investment etc. In other words, Stimulants impress and encourage development forces. They are called 'Income Generating forces' which lubricate the wheel of development. Stimulants have the capacity to raise per capita income above equilibrium level.

The long run economic development does not take place in backward and undeveloped countries as the magnitude of stimulants in those countries is quite small. A country is said to be underdeveloped if the impact of shocks in stronger than the impact of stimulants. On the contrary, a country is said to be developed if the impact of shocks is weaker than the impact of stimulants. Leibenstein is of the view that the underdeveloped countries are under the influence of shocks and stimulants. But in the long run, the magnitude of shocks and stimulants is too small and there is no process of development. Thus, the efforts to escape from economic backwardness, the spontaneous or forced, are below the critical minimum effort required for persistent growth. In order to break the circle of poverty, backwardness and other imperfection in underdeveloped country, they must get critical effort sufficient in magnitude to move the economy on the path of development. The theory of critical minimum effort has been illustrated in the figure.

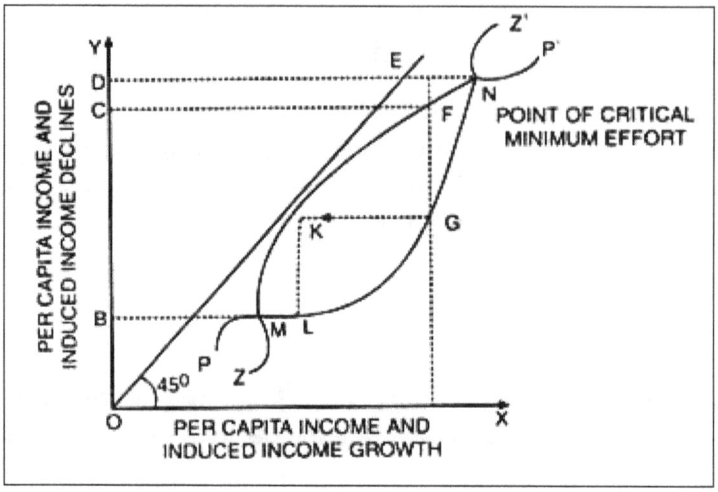

The diagram shows the outcome of the struggle between the stimulants and shocks and also enables to find out stimulants of sufficient magnitude as below:

- OX-axis of the diagram represents per capita income and induced income growth.
- OY-axis indicates per capita income and induced income declines.
- The 45° line measures induced increases and decreases in income.
- P' curve represents stimulants and Z' curve shows stocks.
- OM is the subsistence living standard.
- At M' curve P' Z' intersect each other indicating the equality between growth rate of population and the growth rate of income so that the income is caught in the vicious circle of poverty.
- If the income level is raised from OB to OC which is not in accordance with the critical minimum effort, the rising population will neutralize the increased income. The system will once again hand on the subsistence level of living. Shocks being more powerful than the stimulants. At OJ level of income raising forces are just FE while the depressants up to GM. This will bring the income level down to M again which is just the subsistence level.
- Solution of this problem for such a rise in the level of national income where stimulants are stronger than the shocks so that the growth in income becomes self-sustaining.
- If the per capita income is raised beyond OD' the economy, can be pulled out of the vicious circle of poverty. Thereby, growth in income becomes self-sustaining beyond point D. The per capita income has been shown by the arrows.

Attitudes, Motivation and Incentives

According to Leibenstein, the generation of stimulants depends on attitudes and motivation of the people and the incentives given to them. However, the motivation and incentives are useless without the main factors of economic development. The main factors of economic development are the entrepreneurs, the inventors, the discoverers, the innovators, and those who can accumulate and utilize wealth, and those who can accumulate skills and spread knowledge. No doubt the activities of such persons are endless, but we are to study only those activities which are in a position to generate stimulants and promote economic growth. It requires continuous efforts of various agencies necessary for economic development. It requires special type of human response to attitudes, motivations and incentives which are created by economic and social environment.

Incentives

According to Leibenstein, there are two types of incentives that are found in the underdeveloped countries:

- Zero-sum Incentives: Zero-sum incentives are those which exercise zero effect on economic growth. They do not increase national income. It includes trading risk, non-trading or speculative activities and transference of income and profit from one section of people to another. The zero-sum incentives have distributive effect only. They are carried on in order to secure greater monopolistic position, political power and local prestige. They do not add to aggregate resources of the community. In fact, it is wastage of scarce resources. In short, we may say that zero-sum incentives are not conducive for economic growth.
- Positive-sum Incentives: The positive-sum incentives lead to economic growth and enhance the national income. The positive-sum activities are essential for economic development. These activities consists the productive investment, use of technical know-how, exploration and exploitation of the new markets and the use of scientific discoveries and innovations etc. These are conducive for economic growth as they change the attitudes, motivations and aspirations of the people. They try to raise the level of income, output, investment, saving and employment. Leibenstein is of the opinion that mere creation of positive-sum activities is not sufficient to solve the problems of economic development. Because such activities are unfortunately directed towards zero-sum activities for want of growth oriented environment. It is, thus, essential that the minimum effort should be enough to create such a favourable environment congenial to the persistence of positive sum incentives.

In underdeveloped countries certain influences which work against the positive change or depress their per capita income, are as follows:

- The zero-sum entrepreneurial activities directed towards the maintenance of present economic privileges.
- The conservative attitude of both organised and unorganized workers.
- The attraction of traditional ideas and resistance to the new ideas and knowledge.
- Increase in non-productive consumption expenditures that could otherwise be used for capital accumulation.
- Greater population growth, other things being equal that reduces the amount of capital available per worker.
- High capital-output ratio.

Leibenstein stresses that these influences can be overcome by a sufficiently large critical minimum effort which would stimulate the positive-sum incentives, counteracting the zero-sum activities. It would, thus, restore a rapid rate of economic growth in underdeveloped economies. As a result, the per capita income would rise and tend to increase the level of saving and investment in the economy. A critical minimum effort, in turn, would lead to:

- An expansion of the growth agents.
- An increase in their contribution to per unit of capital, as the capital-output ratio declines.
- A fall in the effectiveness of factors restricting growth.
- The creation of an environment that stimulates socio-economic mobility.
- The expansion of secondary and tertiary sectors.

Role of Growth Agents

The critical minimum effort theory is based on the sum of positive-sum activities and such activities are carried on by some growth agents. According to Leibenstein, "By growth agents we mean those individuals who have the capacities to carry out the growth contributing activities." Leibenstein's growth agents are not land, labour and capital, but his growth agents are the entrepreneurs, investors, discoverers, savers and innovators.

Leibenstein found that entrepreneur is the most crucial agent of growth. He is a person of rare qualities and he is out to explore new investment opportunities so as to mobilize essential resources for production and promotion of new ventures etc. He promotes, encourages and sustains positive-sum activities which are essential for the economic growth of a country. The critical minimum theory is based on the presence of certain favourable conditions which are created by the expansion of the growth agents in the process of economic development. These conditions lead the income increasing forces at a higher rate than the income depressing forces. The growth of contributing activities includes the creation of entrepreneurship, expansion of workers' skill and the increase in the rate of savings, investment, capital formation and technical know-how etc.

Population Growth and Per Capita Income

Leibenstein's theory recognizes population growth as a function of per capita income. It is related to the various stages of economic development. At the subsistence equilibrium level of income, fertility and mortality rates are the maximum consistent with the survival rate of population. Now if the per capita income is raised above the subsistence equilibrium position the mortality rate falls without any drop in the fertility. The result is an increase in the growth rate of population. Thus, an increase in the per capita income tends to raise the growth rate of population. It is only up to a point. Beyond that the increase in the per capita income lowers the fertility rate and as development gains momentum, the rate of population growth declines.

The Leibenstein argued that with the increase in per capita income, the desire to have more children declines. Specialization leads to increasing income levels and the consequent-social and economic mobility make it a difficult and costly affair to support a large family. Hence, growth rate of population becomes constant and then starts declining gradually as the economy gradually advances towards the path of sustained development. According to Leibenstein, a biologically maximum growth rate may be about 3 or 4 per cent. Leibenstein, thus suggests to make sufficiently the necessary critical minimum effort so as the control such a very high population growth. The relationship between population growth and per capita income is illustrated in the figure.

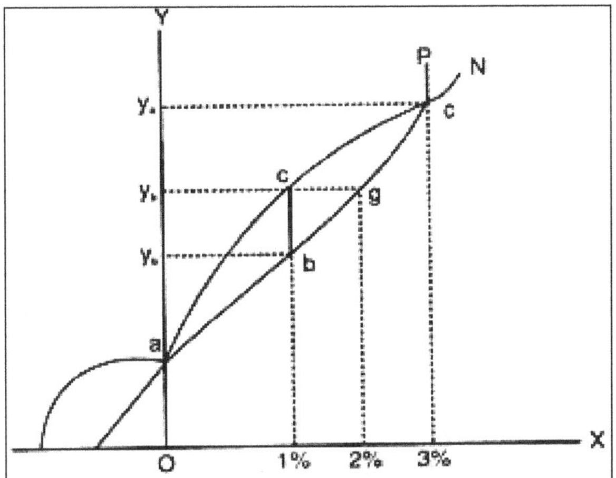

RATE OF POPULATION GROWTH OR RATE OF NATIONAL INCOME GROWTH

In above figure, rate of population growth or rate of national income growth is shown on the horizontal scale and per capita income on the vertical scale. Curve P indicates the population growth and curve N indicates the level of per capita income. Let us start from the point a which represents the subsistence equilibrium point. Here the population growth or national income growth is zero. When the per capita income rises to y_b, the population growth rate and national income growth rate both are equal to 1%. When per capita income rises to y_c, we have the points c and g on curves N and P respectively. These points signify that at the y_c, level of per capita income, the population growth rate is 2% whereas national income growth rate is 1%. Thus, this is a disequilibrium state and cannot represent a level of income that can sustain itself.

Therefore, the level of per capita income should be raised to that level at which population growth rate starts declining and national income growth rate starts rising. The only such point is y. At this level of per capita income the population growth rate is 3%. The growth rate of population, according to Leibenstein is maximum biologically determined. After ye level of per capita income, the population starts declining and national income starts rising. Thus ye level of per capita income is critical minimum per capita income which can sustain itself or which can generate the process of self-sustained growth. According to Leibenstein, the less developed countries must raise their per capita income to this level, if they want to achieve the substained growth.

Theory of Dualism

In Boeke's terminology, "eastern" and "dualistic "are synonymous terms. This is on account of the fact that "eastern" lands possess all the characteristics of a dual society. They are typically pre-capitalistic but at the same time have come into contact with "west". However, though the "west" has penetrated these lands it has been able to absorb them culturally and socially. Both east and west represents a definite culture, a definite philosophy of life, but culture and philosophies of life that have clashed without blending. Thus “eastern” economies are the same as “dualistic” economies. The important features of dualistic economy is overriding importance of social needs which said that the relatively greater importance of social needs as compared to western economies. As contrasted with western society, human needs are very much limited in eastern societies. Because of limited human needs, economic motivation to produce more either does not exist in the eastern society or is very weak, which in turn leads to a low level of economic activity. In this society the supply curve is sloping backward.

The eastern society has family as the unit and individual self-sufficiency is the dominate idea. People are not easily induced to organize production or to collective investment. The idea of income does not fit in an eastern society. Income is a thing that a man gets more or less regularly from outside as a result of acts of exchange usually in the shape of money. In eastern society, the results of cultivating food crops grown for the maintenance of the household cannot be termed “income” in the strict sense .Whereas agriculture is the basis of life in an eastern society, industry is merely supplementary. He also pointed out that there are five type of unemployment problem exist in underdeveloped countries those are seasonal unemployment, unemployment of casual workers, unemployment of regular labourers, unemployment of urban white collar workers, and unemployment among Eurasians’. Due to above character Boeke argued that the under developed countries are should be left by alone by developed countries as there is significant differences between the eastern and western societies. Thus western economic theory is totally inapplicable to the eastern societies. The social dualistic theory has been criticized by Professor Benjamin Higgins on the following grounds:

- Wants are not limited: It has been observed that the desires of people in Indonesia are limited because there the values of MFC and MPM are higher. Therefore, the government of Indonesia has to enforce import restrictions. Moreover, whenever the harvest is good the farmers become wealthy and the demand for expensive (luxurious) goods rises.
- Casual Labor are not Unorganized: Boeke’s version that casual workers are disorganized and inactive may be true in case of agricultural sector but they are organized in tea, rubber, coffee and plantation etc.
- Eastern Labor is not immobile: According to Boeke eastern labor is immobile. It is not so because of attraction of recent and modern facilities of life in the urban areas. Moreover the high income incentives force the labor to move from rural areas to urban areas.
- Dualistic theory is not particular to underdeveloped countries only: According to Boeke, the eastern society exists in only in underdeveloped economies, which is not true. It does exist in Canada, Italy and even in the United States.
- Applicability to western society: Professor Higgins observed that a majority of the characteristics of eastern society, as given by Boeke, are present even in the western societies. For example, during hyperinflation, speculation is preferred to investment. This means that the people in the western countries also have a strong desire to keep their capital safe and in liquid form. The western society also believes in conspicuous consumption. The backward bending supply curve of efforts has also been experienced by Australia during post war period and by US in the decade of fifties.

- Not a theory but a description: It is challenged that the Boeke's dualistic theory is a mere description of facts rather than being a theory. His findings are based upon neoclassical theory which has the limited applicability in the western world.
- It does not provide any solution to the problem of unemployment: Boeke's dualism focuses more on socio-cultural aspects rather on economic. According to him the government is not in a position to remove unemployment from the economy. Moreover, he did not put forward any remark on the situation of under employment. Therefore his theory is full of shortcomings.

Technological Dualism

As a substitute to Boeke's sociological theory of dualism, Benjamin Higgins in 1956 has put forward the theory of technological dualism. The theory of Technological dualism implies the use of separate production functions in the advanced sector and the traditional sector. According to him traditional rural sector possesses agriculture and handicrafts or very small industries. The technical coefficients of production in this sector are variable so that the products can be produced with wide range of techniques and alternative combinations of labour and capital and the factor endowment is such that labour and capital and the factor endowment is such that labour is relatively abundant factor of production, so that techniques of production are labour intensive. In contrast, the modern sector comprises of plantations, mines, or large scale industry.

The theory of dualism assumes a bifurcation of economic and social structures of different sectors so that they can be differentiated in terms of organization, level of development, and goal structure. Usually the concept of economic dualism distinguishes between two sectors of economy. Economic and regional dualism is often the result of a social dualism. Economic dualism, most broadly defined, refers to the coexistence of two or more economic systems. In the 18th and early 19th centuries, economic dualism existed in Western Europe as a combination of institutions congruent with preindustrial and industrial society. The "industrial" refers to the application of science and technology rather than tradition to the productive process. It can be argued that a dualistic development is not a specific feature of some individual country, due to the reason that it has been observed in many transition economies experienced at different periods of time in the course of transformation. In this sector, there is very limited degree of technical substitutability of factors so that production is characterized by fixed technical coefficient and the production process are relatively capital intensive.

Higgins claims his concept of technological dualism as more fruitful than the concept of social dualism as annunciated by Boeke. This is because of its more realistic approach to the problems of the underdeveloped countries. Placing the underdeveloped countries in their world settings Higgins finds that the actual pattern of demand has been such as to bring increasing conflict between the objectives of optimal output and full employment. While demand for exports grew at a higher rate due to rapidly expanding industrial economy basically in Europe, the demand for output of the rural sector grew only at the rate at which the total population increased. But according to the critics, the empirical relevance of the theory of technological dualism in doubt.

Boeke's theory of dualism is different from western dualism which states that economic activity in western countries was based on all the powerful economic needs, while the activity in the countries outside western world and colonial countries guided fundamentally by "social needs". Boeke characterizes a society in the economic sense by the social sprit, the organizational forms and the technique dominating it. According to Boeke, it is not necessary that a society be dominated exclusively be one social system. If one social system does prevail, the society in question is a homogeneous society. When, on the contrary, two social systems appear simultaneously, we have a dual society. Boeke has spelled out a dual society as the one where one of the two prevailing social systems in fact always the most advanced one, will import from abroad and gain from its existence in the new environment without being able to oust or to assimilate the divergent social system that has grown up there, with the result that neither of them becomes general and characteristic for that society as a whole.

The two sectors have little connection & interdependence and develop each according to its own pattern. The contemporary sector can be considered an economic territory of industrial countries, and its multiple-factor and growth effects will benefit the industrial countries but have little effect on internal market. Development in dualism concepts is the conquest of traditional sector by concentrating on and expanding the modern sector. In time, it is assumed that the trickledown effects will decrease and eliminate dualism. In this the major problem is that of capital formation because the degree or amount of capital formation determines the scope and speed of expansion of the modern sector. But the original model of Boeke emphasized one singe feature of dualism, either behavioral or technological parameter difference between sectors, which produce the single commodity or are characterized by identical demand and demographic parameters. The reason behind the underdevelopment is not due to "economic dualism" rather "social dualism".

According to him the development guided due to social needs rather economic needs. The core of his theory the reasons of underdevelopment in western capitalist societies are not applicable to the Asian and African colonial societies where capitalism lives side by side with a peasant economy which largely ruled by pre capitalistic relationships. According to Boeke's view the introduction of fracture of capitalism into pre capitalist peasant economy not only unbalanced the equilibrium of the latter economic system, but also congested the gradual development of capitalistic forms comparable to those in the evolution of the western economy. But later scholars adopted and extended a multidimensional approach. Several authors stress the dualism of specific factors which is different from original dualistic theory of Boekes. Professor Higgins has attempted to present how disguised unemployment gradually rises in the rural sector of dualistic society. But the theory has following defects:

- Assumption of fixed technical coefficient: Higgins wrongly assumes fixed technical coefficient in the industrial sector without any empirical verification.
- Factor prices do not entirely depend upon factor endowment: This theory indicates how the factor endowment and different production functions result in disguised unemployment. So disguised unemployment is connected with the factor prices. But it has been found out that the factor endowments do not entirely determine the factor prices.
- Ignoring the institutional factors: There are many institutional and psychological factors which have been ignored by Higgins in connection with their effect on factor proportion.
- Ignoring the use of labor absorbing techniques: According to Higgins that industrial sector employs highly capital intensive techniques which are imported. But practically we find

that all imported techniques are not labor saving. For example, Japan's agricultural development is not due to capital intensive techniques.

- Size and nature of disguised unemployment is not assessed: Higgins does not clarify the nature of disguised unemployment in the rural sector and excess labor supply in the industrial sector. Moreover, he does not tell about the extent of disguised unemployed due to technological dualism.

But economists like Higgins who propose technological dualism argument differ from Boeke, according to him "dualism is the situation in which development is not due to the reason of lack of effective demand but due to the constraint of natural resource and technology and according to him dualism cannot elapse only diminishing due to the reason that "some degree of dualism exists in virtually every economy. In the advanced economies like USA and Canada ,have areas in which techniques lag behind those of the most advanced sectors, and in which standards of economic and social welfare are correspondingly low. This notion emphasizes the simultaneous presence of both well performing and poorly-performing sectors in an economy, reflecting different stages of their development as the economy evolves. Now the structure and dimension of dualism changes ,the changes from social dualism to structural dualism that is private and public sector exist simultaneously exist in most of the countries and adding to that dynamic sector with stagnant sector also exist.

Big Push Theory

The theory of 'big push' first put forward by P.N. Rosenstein-Rodan is actually a stringent variant of the theory of 'balanced growth'. The crux of this theory is that the obstacles of development are formidable and pervasive. The development process by its very nature is not a smooth and uninterrupted process. It involves a series of discontinuous 'jumps'. The factors affecting economic growth, though functionally related with each other, are marked by a number of "discontinuities" and "hump." Therefore, any strategy of economic development that relies basically upon the philosophy of economic "gradualism" is bound to be frustrated. What is needed is a "big push" to undo the initial inertia of the stagnant economy. It is only then that a smooth journey of the economy towards higher levels of productivity and income can be ensured.

Unless big initial momentum is imparted to the economy, it would fail to achieve a self- generating and cumulative growth. A certain minimum of initial speed is essential if at all the race is to be run. A big thrust of a certain minimum size is needed in order to overcome the various discontinuities and indivisibilities in the economy and offset the diseconomies of scale that may arise once development begins. According to Rosenstein-Rodan, marginal increments in investment in unrelated individual spots of the economy would be like sprinkling here and there a few drops of water in a desert. Sizable lump of investment injected all at once can alone make a difference.

Rationale for the Big Push

The basic rationale of the 'Big Push' like the 'Balanced Growth' theory is based upon the idea of 'external economies'. In the theory of welfare economics, external economies are defined as those unpaid benefits which go to third parties. The private costs and prices of products fail to reflect these. And the market prices have to be corrected if an account of these external economies is to be taken. However, the concept of external economies has a different connotation in growth theory. Here, they are pecuniary in nature and get transmitted through the price system. To explain the emergence of such external economies and their transmission, let us consider two industries A and B. If the industry A expands in order to overcome the technical indivisibilities, it shall derive certain internal economies. This may result in the lowering of the price for the product of the industry A. Now if the industry B uses A's output as an input, the benefits of A's internal economies shall then be passed on to the industry B in the form of pecuniary external economies. Thus, "the profits of industry B created by the lower prices of product. A call for investment and expansion in industry B, one result of which will be an increase in industry B's demand for industry A's product. This in turn will give rise to profits and call for further investment and expansion of industry A."

Following such a line of argument, Prof. Rosenstein-Rodan contends that the importance of external economies is one of the chief points of difference between the static theory and a theory of growth. "In the static allocative theory there is no such importance of the external economies. In the theory of growth however," remarks Prof. Rodan, "external economies abound because given the inherent imperfection of the investment market, imperfect knowledge and risks, pecuniary and technological external economies have a similarly disturbing effect on the path towards equilibrium. Now, the basic contention of the "big push" theory is that such a mutually beneficial way of output expansions is not likely to occur unless the initial obstacles are overcome. There are "non- appropriabilities" or "indivisibilities" of different kinds which if not removed through a "big push" will not permit the emergence and transmission of 'external economies' – which lie at the back of a self-generating development process.

Associated with the removal of each set of indivisibilities is a stream of external economies. A 'bit by bit' approach to development would not enable the economy to cross over certain indivisible economic obstacles to development. What is required is a vigorous effort to jump over these obstacles. As such, for the economy to be successfully launched on the path of self-generating growth a "big push" in the form of a minimum size of investment programme is necessary. In essence, therefore, an all-or-nothing approach to development is stressed in big-push approach to development.

Requirements for Big Push

The hallmark of the 'big-push' approach lies in the reaping of external economies through the simultaneous installation of a host of technically interdependent industries. But before that could become possible, we have to overcome the economic indivisibilities by moving forward by a certain "minimum indivisible step". This can be realised through the injection of an initial big dose of a certain size of investment. Prof. Rodan distinguishes three kinds of indivisibilities and externalities with a view to specify the areas where big push needs to be applied. They are:

- Indivisibilities in the production function, i.e., lumpiness of capital, especially in the creation of social overhead capital.
- Indivisibility of demand, i.e., complementarity of demand.
- Indivisibility of savings, i.e., kink in the supply of savings.

Indivisibilities in the Production Function

Prof. Rodan argues that it is possible to generate enormous pecuniary external economies by overcoming the 'indivisibilities of inputs, processes and outputs.' The emergence of such externalities would bring about a wide range of increasing returns. To corroborate his contention he cites the case of United States. He feels that the fall in the capital-output ratio in U.S.A. from 4:1 to 3:1 over the last eighty years was chiefly due to the increasing returns made possible by the levelling down of production indivisibilities. The most important case of indivisibilities and external economies on the supply side resides in the social overhead capital which is now called infrastructure. The most important effect of jumping over this indivisibility is the "investment opportunities created in other industries". Social overhead capital consists of all the basic industries such as transport, power, communications, and such other public utilities.

The construction of these infrastructures involves 'lumpy' capital investments. And the capital-output ratio in the social overheads is considerably higher than in other industries. Moreover, these services are only indirectly productive and involve long gestation periods. Besides, their "minimum feasible size" is large enough. As such it is well-nigh difficult to avoid excess capacity in these, at least in the initial periods. Above all, there is a "minimum industry mix of public utilities" that must be required to divert at least 30 to 40 per cent of their total investment in the creation of social overhead capital. In this view, therefore, it is possible to distinguish four types of indivisibilities of creating social overhead capital. They are:

- Indivisibility of Time: The creation of social overhead capital must precede other directly productive industries so that it is irreversible or indivisible in time.
- Indivisibility of Durability: The infrastructures generally last long. The overhead capital with lesser durability is either technically not feasible or is very poor in efficiency.
- Indivisibility of Long Gestation Periods: The investments in social overhead capital, by all counts, involve a highly protracted period of time for their fruition as compared with investments in other directly productive channels.
- Indivisibility of an Irreducible Industry Mix of Public Utilities: Social overhead capital must grow collectively. There is an irreducibly minimum industry mix of different public utilities that have to be created all at one stroke.

As it is impossible to import the infrastructures, they have got to be produced domestically. And because of the existence of above explained indivisibilities, it is necessary to make 'lumpy' investments in them. And their creation is a precondition to the investments in directly productive and other quick-yielding productive activities. Only then the way for a self-generating economy can be paved. Thus the absence of adequate social overhead capital constitutes the most important bottleneck in the development of developing countries.

Indivisibility of Demand

This refers to the complementarity of demand arising from the diversity of human wants. The very fact that there is an indivisibility of complementarity of demand requires simultaneous setting up of interrelated industries in countries to initiate and accelerate the process of development.

Indivisibility of demand generates interdependencies in investment decisions. As such, if each investment project was undertaken independently, it is in most cases likely to flop down. This is because individual investment projects generally have "high risks because of uncertainty as to whether their products will find a market," This point can be clarified with the help of the following well known example given by Rosenstein-Rodan for a closed economy. To start with, let us suppose that 100 disguisedly unemployed workers in an underdeveloped country were withdrawn and employed in a shoe factory. The wages of the newly employed workers would provide an additional income to them. Now, if they spend all their newly received purchasing power on the shoes, an adequate market for the shoe industry would be ensured. As a result, the industry would succeed and survive.

But the fact is that human beings having diversity of wants cannot simply afford to survive simply by the consumption of shoes and nothing else. As such, they will not spend all their earnings on the purchase of shoes. The market for the shoe industry will, therefore, remain limited as before. Therefore, the incentives to invest will be adversely affected. As a result, the shoe factory investment project might end in a fiasco. Now let us make a somewhat different assumption to see how an atmosphere congenial to the undertaking of investments can occur. Suppose that instead of only 100 workers being engaged in the shoe factory, 10,000 workers are put to work in 100 different factories producing a variety of consumer goods. These new factories provide larger employment and thus purchasing power to their workers. There is an increase in the total volume of purchasing power and the total size of the market. This is because the "new producers would be each other's customers".

In a way, what has happened is that due to the complementarity of demand, the risk of limitedness of market is greatly reduced. The result is that the incentives to invest are increased. "Thus provided that the total volume of employment and purchasing power is increased by a minimum indivisible step, each factory Will have enough market to reach full capacity production and the point of minimum cost per unit." We, therefore, find that the indivisibility of demand requires the simultaneous production of a "bundle" of large number of wage goods on which the newly employed workers could spend their income. That alone would ensure adequate market for the product of each producer. In terms of investment the implication is that "unless there is assurance that the necessary complementary investments will occur, any single investment project may be considered too risky to be undertaken at all."

This, as Prof. Higgins remarks, results into indivisibility in the decision-making process. A large-scale investment programme based on complementarity of demand undertaken as a unit may bring forth large increases in national income. But each of the individual investment projects undertaken singly may not fructify at all. The essence of the whole analysis is that a high minimum quantum of investment in interdependent industries is needed to overcome the indivisibility of demand and hence that of decision-making. That, according to the big push theory, is the only reliable way of overcoming the smallness of the market size and low inducement to invest in the developing economies.

Indivisibility in the Supply of Savings

A high minimum package of investment cannot be undertaken without an adequate supply of savings. But it is not possible to have such high volume of savings in underdeveloped countries due to an extremely low price and high income elasticities of the supply of savings. The savings are low primarily because incomes are low. This, thus, constitutes the third indivisibility. "The way out of the vicious circle," remarks Rosenstein-Rodan, "is to have first an increase in income and to provide mechanisms which assure that in every second stage the marginal rate of savings will be very much higher than the average rate of savings." The Smithian advice that 'frugality is a virtue and prodigality a vice' has to be adapted to a situation of growing income." But in the ultimate analysis the initial big increase in income has got to be provided through an initial big increase in investment.

The existence of the three indivisibilities outlined above make it abundantly clear that the solution to all these lies in a high minimum quantum of investment. Thus, a big push through a minimum indivisible step forward in the form of a high minimum quantity of investment could alone make it possible to jump over the economic obstacles to development in the underdeveloped countries. Lastly, Resenstein-Rodan considers the role of international trade vis-a-vis the strategy of big push in generating a self-sustaining process of development. In this regard he is of the view that international trade cannot be a substitute for "big push." The provision of some of the needed wage goods through imports can at best help in narrowing down the range of fields which call for a 'big push'. The historical experience provided by the nineteenth century corroborates Rosenstein- Rodan's conclusion that international trade cannot by itself obviate the need for 'big push' altogether. Once the process of development by an initial application of 'big push' is underway, its sequel course would tend to follow simultaneously three sets of balanced growth relations. They are:

- A balance between the social overhead capital and the directly productive activities (in both the consumer and capital goods sectors).
- A vertical balance between capital goods and consumer goods (including the intermediate goods).
- Lastly, there should be the horizontal balance between various consumer goods industries due to complementary nature of expanding consumer demand.

The Need for Balanced Growth of Centralised Planning

The mutual benefits arising from the external economies for industrialisation cannot be included in the cost calculations of entrepreneurs to the fullest possible extent without recourse to some sort of centralized 'balanced growth' planning. This is because of a number of reasons. First, due to the imperfections in the market, the free market price system does not adequately give proper signal to the private investors for the future possibilities of expansion in complementary industries.

Second, in developing countries due to the imperfections of knowledge and risks, the response of the private entrepreneurs to any given price signal is quite imperfect and unsatisfactory. Thus, due to the failure to take advantage of the external economies to the fullest extent, investments which may be profitable in terms of 'social marginal net product' remain unprofitable in terms of 'private marginal net product'. In this view, therefore, there is a need for an integrated investment scheme to be carried out in complementary industries. The best way to do that would be to carry out the investment programme under the direction of some centralised planning authority. An individual entrepreneur in a developing country cannot hope to have all the necessary data which the central planning authority can draw upon.

The crash programme of investment envisaged by the 'big-push' theory cannot by its very nature be made just at random. It has to take into consideration the various balances – horizontal as well as vertical. Only then could the achievement of self-generating, cumulative and harmonious growth of the economy is possible. For this what is necessary is a unified decision-making process. "Allocation of capital," remarks Prof. Higgins, "on the basis of individual estimates of short-run returns on various marginal investment projects is the very process by which the underdeveloped countries got where they are.

The basic reason for government action to promote development is that each of a set of individual private investment decisions may seem unattractive in itself, whereas a large scale investment program undertaken as a unit may yield substantial increase in national income." Prof. Rosenstein-Rodan's theory is essentially a theory of development and thus helps us to examine the path towards development rather than restricting itself simply to the study of conditions at the point of equilibrium. The theory highlights the inefficiency of price system of signalling the desirable directions for investment. It is big-push investment through a centralised planning that could put the developing countries on a self-generating development process.

Evaluation of Rosenstein's Big Push Strategy

However, Prof. Rosenstein-Rodan's all-or-nothing approach is not perfect in itself in all respects. It suffers from a number of lacunae. First, the main implication of the 'big-push' theory is State intervention and centralised planning. It is argued that due to imperfections of market the free price system fails to register and thus communicate properly the economic events, much less their future course. But the pertinent question involved here is, will the prevailing circumstances of the developing countries warrant a conclusion to the contrary? The actual fact of the matter is that the current institutional and administrative set-up of the government machinery of the poor developing countries is too weak to cope with the dictates of the 'big push' theory. It is, therefore, quite doubtful whether the government sponsored brand of communication system about the future events would at all be more effective than the free price mechanism. The governments of developing countries may somehow manage to draw up their initial integrated economic plans. But they are bound to be faced with tremendous difficulties in the execution of these plans. In any comprehensive programme comprising a complex set of related projects, delays and continued revision of the original time-bound schedules are inevitable. These are indeed formidable hurdles for the developing countries to cross.

Besides, on account of the poor and incompetent institutional set-ups of the developing countries, there is bound to be insufficient knowledge about the local conditions and an "inefficient feedback of this vital local knowledge from different parts of the country to the central planning machinery." Mere improvement in the standard type of statistical information would not remedy all this. Above all, the process of unified decision-making and coordination becomes all the more difficult in mixed economies like India. This is so because not often, the public and private sectors rather than being complementary are in fact competitive with each other. Thus, it may so happen that the "private enterprise is inhibited by uncertainties not only about the general economic situation but also about the future intention of the government regulations."

Thus, it is quite clear that the application of a 'big push' programme in the developing countries with their weak and incompetent institutional and administrative machinery is likely to die its own death. Secondly, the chief plank on which the 'big push' theory is founded is the emergence of a wide range of external economies. International trade can provide much more external economies than does the domestic investments. However, the developing countries being primarily primary producing countries, engage a large part of their total investment for their exports and marginal import substitutes, the field where the external economies are found to be very- negligible.

Thirdly, the 'big push' theory concentrates mainly on the industrial sector, viz., capital goods, consumer goods and social overhead capital. The manufacturing sector is considered inherently to be a better vehicle of economic growth. But in the developing countries, the most dominant sector is composed of agricultural and primary production. For a balanced growth of the economy, agriculture also requires a corresponding 'big push'. Any neglect of the agricultural sector in these countries is bound to jeopardise the 'big push' effort. Fourthly, the major part of the 'lumpy' investments involved in the 'all-or-nothing' approach is called for by the 'technical indivisibilities' embodied in the creation of social overhead capital. Not only is the quantum of investment enormously 'lumpy' but also the capital-output ratio high in the provision of social overhead services than in other directions. Thus, due to the inherent capital scarcity in the developing countries, it is really a matter of dubious wisdom to require these countries to overstrain their meagre resources in the provision of a complete outfit of infrastructures.

The 'big push' theory recommends a 'starting from scratch' concerted action in the creation of social overheads. This is on the implicit assumption that these services are totally non-existent in these economies. However, for most of these countries, "the practical question is not whether to have a completely new outfit of these services starting from scratch but how to extend and improve the existing facilities."

Further, the 'big push' theory by its very nature requires the 'lumpy' investments in different social overheads to be made simultaneously and once for all. With the very long gestation periods usually associated with such investments, there are bound to be inflationary pressures in the economy due to the shortage of consumption goods. In an inflationary atmosphere, the process of construction of the social overheads is bound to be a protracted one. In this light it would be better to spread the infrastructure-building activity over a period of time through phasing and changing the time dimension of the projects. This requires selection of a suitable economic size of the social overhead investments.

Lewis Model of Unlimited Labour Supply

The Nobel Laureate, W. Arthur Lewis in the mid 1950s presented his model of unlimited supply of labor or of surplus labor economy. By surplus labor it means that part of manpower which even if is withdrawn from the process of production there will be no fall in the amount of output. Lewis model makes the following assumptions:

- There is a duel economy i.e., the economy is characterized by a traditional, over-populated rural subsistence sector furnished with zero MPL, and the high productivity modern urban industrial sector.
- The subsistence sector does not make the use of 'Reproducible Capital', while the modern sector uses the produced means of capital.

- The production in the advanced sector is higher than the production in traditional and backward sector.
- According to Lewis, the supply of labor is perfectly elastic. In other words, the supply of labor is greater than demand for labor.

The followings are the sources of unlimited supply of labor in UDCs:

- Because of severe increase in population more, than required number of labors are working with lands, the so called disguised unemployed.
- In UDCs so many people are having temporary and part time jobs, as the shoe-shines, loaders, porters and waiters etc. There will be no fall in the production even their number are one halved.
- The landlords and feudals are having an army of tenants for the sake of their influence, power and prestige. They do not make any contribution towards production, and they are prepared to work even at less than subsistence wages.
- The women in UDCs do not work, but they just perform house-hold duties. Thus they also represent unemployment.
- The high birth rate in UDCs leads to grow unemployment.

Basic Thesis of the Lewis Model

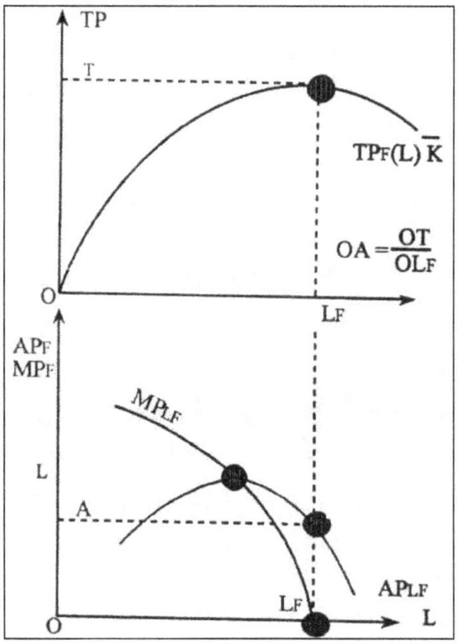

Traditional Sector.

Lewis model is a classical type model which states that the unlimited supplies of labor can be had at the prevailing subsistence wages. The industrial and advanced modern sector can be developed on the basis of agri. to traditional sector. This can be done by transferring the labor from traditional sector and modern sector. Lewis says that the wages in industrial sector remain constant. Consequently, the capitalists will earn 'surplus'. Such surplus will be re-invested in the modern sector leading to absorb the labor which are migrated from subsistence sector. In this way, the surplus labor or the labor which were prey to disguised unemployment will get the employment. Thus both the labor transfer and modern sector employment growth are brought about by output expansion in that sector. The speed with which this expansion occurs is determined by the rate of industrial investment and capital accumulation in the modern sector. Though the wages have been assumed constant, yet Lewis says that the urban wages are at least 30% higher than average rural income to induce the workers to migrate from their home areas. The process of migration and capital formation is shown with the help of figure.

In the figure, the production function regarding traditional sector has been demonstrated. Here in the upper part of the figure, by employing LF of labor, the OT of food production has been produced, while the amount of capital is fixed here. In the lower part of figure we have APL and MPL in the subsistence farming sector which have been derived from the TPF curve in the upper part of the figure. This is the behavior of a UDC where 80% to 90% of population lives and works in rural areas. Lewis makes two assumptions regarding traditional sector:

- There is surplus labor because MPL = 0 (as MPLF curve cuts x-axis).
- All rural workers share equally in the output so that rural real wage is determined by the APL, and not by MPL. Thus it is OA, which has been attained by dividing OT by OLF labor in subsistence sector.

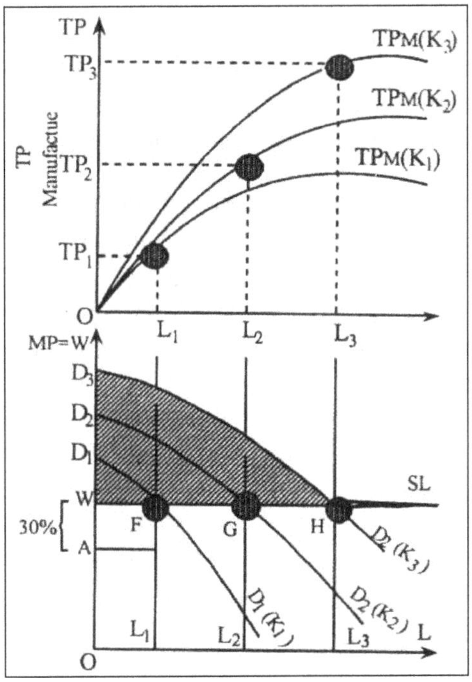

Modern Sector.

In the figure the upper segment we have the production functions regarding modern industrial sector. In case OL_1 labor are employed, having the production function $TPM(K_1)$, TP_1 is being produced. In the lower segment of figure, the demand for labor is $D_1(K_1)$ at the constant wages (OW) which are 30% higher than the average rural wages. In the Lewis model, the modern sector capital stock is allowed to increase from K_1 to K_2 and K_3 as a result of reinvestment of profits by capitalist industrialists. This causes the TP curve in the upper part of figure, to shift upward from $TPM(K_1)$ to

$TPM(K_2)$ and to $TPM(K_3)$. The process that will generate these capitalistic profits for reinvestment and growth is illustrated in the lower part of figure. The modern sector MPL curves have been derived from the TPM curves of the upper part of the figure. These curves are demand for labor curve because of assumption of perfect competition.

The OA in both lower parts of figures represents the average level of real subsistence income in the traditional rural sector. But in the modern sector the real wages have been represented by OW (the 30% higher than rural wages). At such wages the supply of rural labor is assumed to be unlimited or perfectly elastic as shown by WSL curve in figure. This means that modern sector employer can hire as much labor as he likes without any fear of rise in wages. It is also told that in traditional sector the supply of labor is in the millions, while the employment in modern sector is in thousands. In the modern sector the employment is made by the employer to the point where MPL = W. (the point F in the lower part of figure. Thus the basic employment is OL_1, with this employment of labor CD_1FL, output in manufacturing sector is being produced. While the share of such employed labor will be $OWFL_1$.

The balance of output shown by the shaded area WD_1F would be the total profits (surplus) that accrue to the capitalists. As Lewis assumes that all of these profits are reinvested, the total stock of capital in the modern sector will rise from K_1 to K_2. As a result, TPM will shift from $TPM(K_1)$ to $TPM(K_2)$ which in a turn leads to increase MPL. In other words, the demand for labor will increase as shown by the curve $D_2(K_2)$ in the lower part of figure. Now the new equilibrium in the modern sector takes place at point G where OL_2 labor are being employed. The total output rises to OTP_2 or OD_2GL_2 while total wages and profits increase to $OWGL_2$ and WD_2G, respectively. Once again, these larger (WD_2G) profits are reinvested, the total stock of capital will increase to K_3. Again the TP curve will shift upward, as the $TPM(K_3)$, and demand for labor curve will shift to $D_3(K_3)$.

This process of modern self sustaining growth and employment expansion will remain continue till all the surplus rural labor is absorbed in the new industrial sector. Thereafter, additional workers can be withdrawn from agri. sector only at a higher cost of lost food production because this will decrease the labor to land ratios. In this way, the MPL will be no more zero. Here, labor supply curve will become positively sloped along with the growth of modern sector. The structural transformation of the economy will take place through shifting traditional rural agriculture to modern urban industry.

Criticism on the Lewis Model

Although Lewis two-sector development model is simple and roughly it is in conformity with the historical growth in the West, but it has following flaws and most of its assumptions do not fit in the institutional and economic realities of UDCs:

- Proportionality between employment creation and capital accumulation: Lewis model assumes that there exists proportionality in the labor transfer and employment creation in modern sector and rate of capital accumulation in the modern sector. The faster the rate of capital accumulation, the higher the growth rate of the modern sector and faster the rate of new job creation. But if the capitalists reinvest their profits in the labor-saving capital equipment rather increasing the labor employment (what has been assumed in Lewis model) the jobs will not be created and modern sector will not expand. Now we employ a diagram where we shall show that labor demand curves do not shift uniformly outward. It is so because that increase in capital stock will embody labor saving technology.

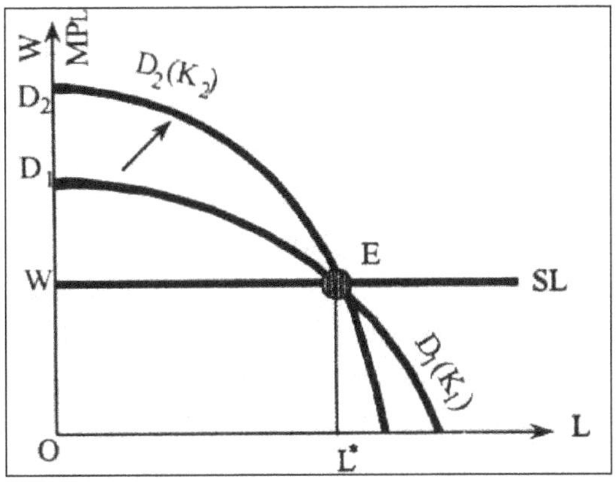

In figure, it is obvious that even though the total output has grown substantially, i.e., $OD_2\,EL^* > OD_1EL^*$. But the total wages remained $OWEL^*$ and the employment also remained OL^*. Both remained unchanged. All of increase in output has accrued to capitalists in the form of excess profits. This may be given the name of "Anti-development" economic growth, all the extra income and output growth went to a few capitalists while the income and employment levels for the masses of workers remained unchanged. In this way, total GNP would rise, but there would be no or little improvement in aggregate social welfare.

- Peak harvesting and sowing season: Lewis did not pay attention to the pattern of seasonality of labor demand in traditional agri. sector. Labor demand varies considerably and such demand is at its peak during the sowing and harvesting season. Thus during some months of the year the MPL may be above-zero. In such situation, the positive opportunity costs will involve in transferring the labor from agriculture sector. As a result, the labor transfer will reduce agriculture output.

- Rise in urban wages: The absorption of surplus labor itself may end pre-maturely because competitors (producers) may alter wage rates and lower the share of profit. It has been shown that rural-urban migration in Egyptian economy was accompanied by increase in wage rate of 15% and a fall in profits by 12%. Moreover, the wages in industrial sector were forced up directly by unions, civil service wage scales, minimum wage laws and MNCs (multi-national corporations) hiring practices tend to negate the role of competitive forces in the modern sector labor market. Again, the wages in subsistence sector may go up indirectly through rise in productivity in this sector.

- Full impact of growing population: Lewis model underestimates the full impact on the poor economy of a rapidly growing population, i.e., its effects on agri. surplus, the capitalist profit share, wage rates and overall employment opportunities. Similarly, Lewis assumed that the rate of growth in manufacturing sector would be identical to that in agri. sector. But, if industrial development involves more intensive use of capital than labor, then the flow of labor from agri. to industry will simply create more unemployment.

- Ignoring the balanced growth: Lewis ignored the balanced growth between agri. sector and industrial sector. But we know that there, exists a linkage between agri. growth and industrial expansion in poor countries. If a part of profits made by capitalists is not devoted to agri. sector, the process of industrialization would be jeopardized (perhaps, due to reduced supply of raw material). Because of this flaw, Ranis-Fei model considers the balanced growth of both sectors. This will be discussed after this model.

- Ignoring the role of leakages: Lewis has ignored the role which the leakages can play in the economy. As Lewis assumed that all of increase in profits are diverted into savings. It means that savings of producers are equal to one. But, practically it is not so. The increase in profits may accompany the increase in consumption. As in Pakistan during 2nd plan the capitalistic class diverted their increased profits to palacious houses and conspicuous consumption. In such tike situation the MPS out of profits will be less than one. Again, it is not necessary that the capital formation will be made by the capitalistic class. The same may be done by the farmers producing cash crops. As the small farmers producing cash crops in Egypt have shown themselves to be quite capable of saving the required capital. Again, the World's largest Coca industry in Ghana is the result of creation of small enterprise capital formation.
- Process of migration is neither smooth nor costless: Lewis assumed that the transfer of unskilled labor from agri. to industry is regarded as almost smooth and costless. But, practically it is no so as industry requires different types of labor. If this problem is removed with the help of investment in education and skill formation, the process of migration will become costlier and expensive.

Ranis and Fei Model

Like Lewis model, Fei-Ranis model is also based on the Nurkse's model of Economic Development. Fei-Ranis model tries to overcome the limitations of the Lewis model by incorporating certain major departures from it due to which Fei-Ranis model is seen as an improvement over the Lewis model. These departures are as under:

- Lewis model invariably underscores the significance of the agriculture sector, it talks about a model of growth in which there is no interaction between the capitalist sector and agriculture sector, except that the surplus labour force moves from agriculture sector to the capitalist sector. In this model, one sector continues to grow while the other to lag behind, i.e. capitalist sector grows at the expense of the agriculture sector. However, Fei-Ranis model emphasize that the interaction between K sector and agriculture sector is significant and this interaction accelerates the process of overall economic development in the economy.
- Fei-Ranis model is closer to reality prevailing in the LDC as it takes into account the impact of population growth on labour force. This feature is completely missing in Lewis model.
- Lewis model does not assign any role to the landlord i.e. landlord is a passive factor and does not have any important role to play. But in Fei-Ranis model landlord plays an important role in the sense that he maybe prompted to introduce innovation and technological progress in the agriculture sector under two circumstances:
    - If the price of agriculture sector products is allowed to rise.

- In case of subsidization of input cost.

- In Lewis model, the speed of transfer of labour force from agriculture to capitalist sector depends upon the growth of profits of the capitalist sector only. In Fei-Ranis model, it depends upon rate of growth of population, nature of technological progress and growth of industrial capital. Industrial capital depends upon growth of profits of industries and surplus generated in agriculture sector.

- In the Lewis model, the end result is a lopsided pattern of development because capitalist sector grows at the expense of agriculture sector. The two cannot grow simultaneously and the gap tends to increase overtime. In the Fei-Ranis model on the other hand, balanced growth of capitalist and agriculture sector is necessary because otherwise the end product will be stagnation.

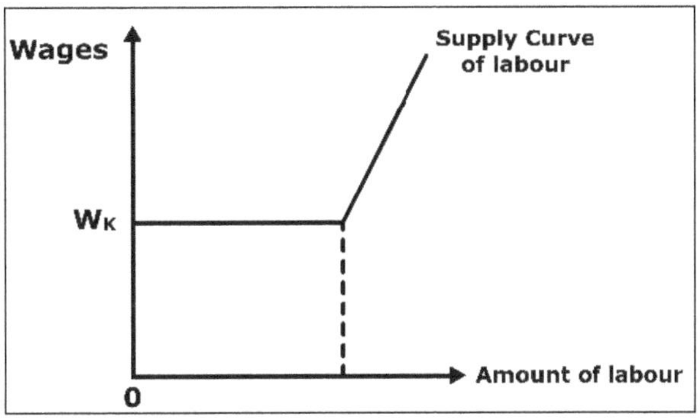

- In Fei-Ranis model when the surplus labour force is exhausted, the supply of labour curve turns upward implying thereby that higher wage rate must be paid to the workers if more labourers are to be employed. In Lewis model, the supply curve is perfectly elastic.

Three Stages of the Process of Transition

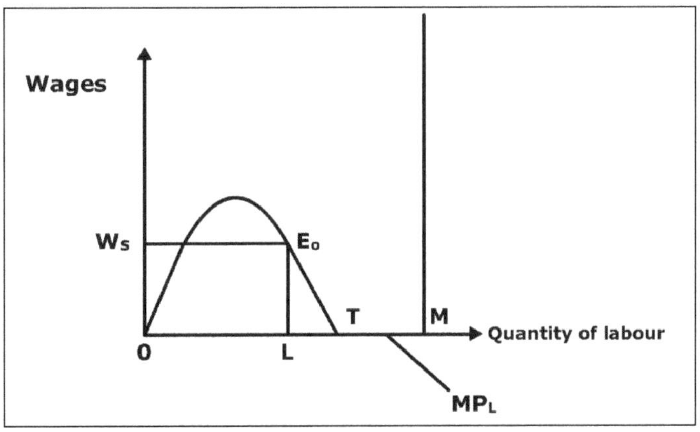

OM is the total quantity of labour force, which is fixed while the demand for labour is given by the marginal product curve of labour which is MP_L. OL amount of labour force is productively employed and LM is underemployed or unemployed. In the first stage, that labour will get transferred from A Sr to K Sr whose marginal product is negative or zero so that there is no difference on the performance of A sector with the departure of that labour force. In the second stage, that labour force is transferred whose marginal product is positive but less than the subsistence wage rate.

This departure would make a difference to the A Sr output. In the third stage, there is commercialization of agriculture whereby the agriculture sector and K Sr compete with each other for labour force. Hence, they bid the wage rate and whosoever provides an increased wage rate will succeed in getting the surplus labour force.

Assumptions of Fei-Ranis Model

- There is a presence of dual economy. Traditional or agriculture sector is passive and stagnant in nature while the capitalist sector is active and progressive in nature.
- Supply of land is fixed, and both A sector and K sector makes use of the land.
- Population is an exogenous factor i.e. it is determined by factors other than those present in the model.
- Real wage rate in the industrial sector is fixed. This wage rate is equal to initial level productivity and is also called constant institutional wage rate.
- There are constant returns to scale with respect to labour where labour acts as a variable factor in both A Sr and K Sr.
- There is no accumulation of K in the A Sr. except in one form, i.e., land reclamation. It means that if there is no technological breakthrough in agriculture, the sector will become non-remunerative and it will be characterized by fatigue. Therefore, land's fertility has to be maintained.
- Output of the A Sr. depends upon land and labour, while that of the K Sr. depends upon labour and capital.
- Marginal product of labour is zero at some points and such labour force can be transferred from A Sr to K Sr, where the productive capacity is more without any loss to A Sr.

Functioning of Agriculture Sector

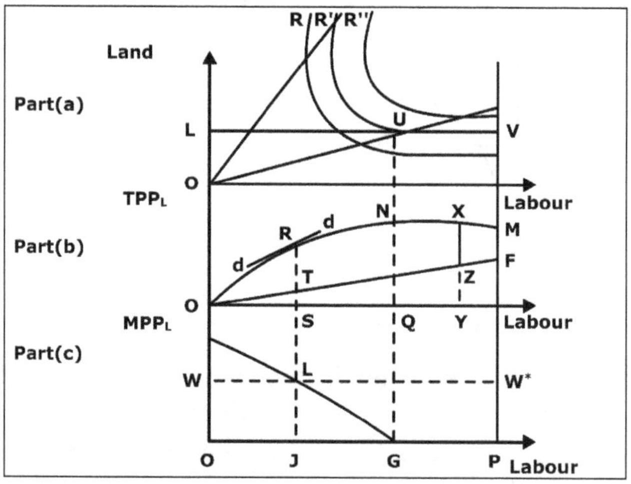

In part (a), the total supply of labour in the economy is fixed at OP on the x-axis and the total amount of land available is OL on the y-axis. OA and OB are the ridgelines, they are the boundaries within which there is a possibility of substitution between various factors of production i.e. land and labour. The curves joining the two lines, R, R', R" are the production frontier lines. Labour force productively employed is LU, therefore, labour force and surplus is UV. In part (b), we have amount of labour on the x-axis and the total product of labour on the y-axis. Total product of labour is OM, after N it slightly diminishes. OF is the corresponding wage bill.

In part (c), quantities of labour lies on the x-axis while the marginal product of labour on the y-axis. OW is the initial wage rate fixed at subsistence level. At G, MPL is zero; therefore, beyond G there is all surplus amount of labour force (GP). In the first stage of transition, let us assume for the sake of convenience that from the surplus labour force (UV=QP=GP) we withdraw YP [from part (b)]. We make use of OY labour force to produce XY level of output and the total wage bill is ZY. Therefore, the total agricultural surplus is XZ. In the Fei-Ranis model, this XZ is the source of hidden savings which can be mobilized; leading to higher capital accumulation and can put the economy on the path of higher growth. If these savings are not visualized for the K Sr., they will remain hidden. Hence, agriculture sector makes two important contributions to the process of growth–surplus labour force and surplus output for the growth of K[ist] Sr. In the second stage of transition, that labour force is transferred whose marginal productivity is positive but less than the constant institutional wage rate SQ. Finally, in the third stage, there will be commercialization of agriculture and both the sectors will compete for OS amount of labour force.

Functioning of Industrial Sector

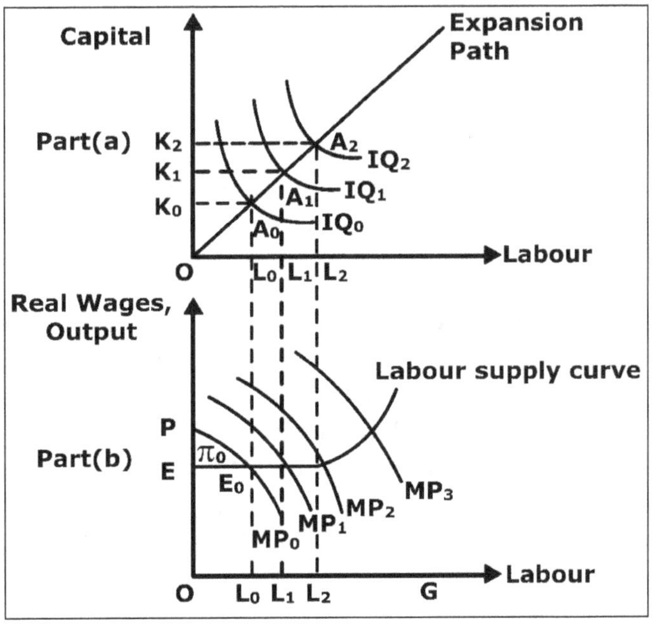

Part (a) has labour on the x-axis, while capital lies on the y-axis. IQ_0, IQ_1 and IQ_2 are the isoquant curves representing various combinations of L and K for a given level of output. Higher isoquant represents higher level of output. OM is the expansion path of K Sr corresponding to OK_0, if we apply L_0 amount of labour force we get MP_0 curve. It tells us that if the wage rate is OE and OL_0 labour force is applied, then the total wage bill is OExOL_0, and the total output is OPE_0L_0. Therefore, the total surplus is EPE_0. Every capitalist is tempted to increase its surplus and hence he ploughs back this surplus in the business. This leads to increase in capital to K_1 and increase in labour to L_1

corresponding to a higher marginal product MP_1 and surplus will be even higher. This surplus will again be ploughed back only till the point where labour force gets fully exhausted from A Sr (till E_2). Beyond this, any further amount of labour force will only be available at a higher wage rate.

Interaction of A Sr. and K Sr.

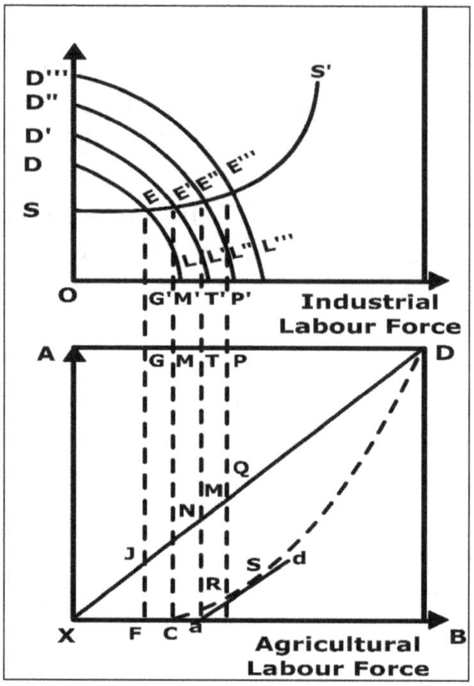

In Part (a), SS' is the labour supply curve in the K Sr. and DL is the marginal product of labour. Initially the K Sr. uses OG' amount of labour force and correspondingly AG part of labour force gets transferred from A Sr. to K Sr. Corresponding to G, we have point F and J in Part (b). OX is the total wage bill and OF is the total physical productivity curve in the A Sr.

With OG' amount of labour force, the total surplus of the K Sr. is DSE corresponding to which the total wage bill is OSEG'. So the capitalist is prompted to reinvest DSE in the K Sr. due to which the DL curve shifts upward to D'L' and E' is the new point of equilibrium corresponding to which M' is employed in the K Sr. For M' amount of labour force, OM is withdrawn from the A Sr. leading to MN wage bill and NC agricultural surplus. Now with M' amount of labour force in the K Sr. the total surplus in the K Sr. amounts to D'SE' which will again be reinvested in the business. This process of transfer of labour force from A Sr. to K Sr. will continue to happen until point "S" where the gap between the total physical productivity and the wage bill is maximum.

Criticism of Fei-Ranis Model

- Agricultural output in first phase of Ranis-Fei model will not remain constant and may fall whereas FR model assumed that MPL is equal to zero in agricultural sector in initial stage.
- This model has been criticized on the grounds that capital also play major role in determining output in agricultural sector which was neglected by the Ranis-Fei model which maintained that output is only determined by land and labour .

- As Fei and Ranis model assumed closed economy, so it has neglected the role of foreign trade.
- Last but not least, in LDC the subsistence agricultural sector has low productivity which caused the sluggish nature of industrial sector, but according to Jorgenson, who argued that for improvement of the modern sector drive the traditional sector.

Harris Todaro Migration Model

While criticising the Lewis model J. R. Harris and M. P. Todaro have developed a new model of economic development which is relevant for labour surplus countries. It is the best known model of internal migration in the context of present-day developing countries. The model has focused on migration of labour from rural to urban areas induced by certain incentives. They have referred to two types of migration induced migration and internal migration. According to this model migrating workers are essentially participants in a lottery of relatively high-paid jobs in the towns. When new urban jobs are created the lottery becomes more attractive to potential migrants. Depending on their responsiveness to this improved opportunity, more than one worker are likely to migrate for each job created. If so, the output foregone may be that of two or more agricultural workers, not just one. If the migrants bring some of their family members to urban areas more output will be lost. The reason is that the wife and children of migrants find fewer employment opportunities in towns than in the rural areas because they do not have land in the towns on which to grow food.

Internal Migration

Most of the internal labour migration which occurs in the course of economic development is from rural to urban areas. The model sets out to explain why the observed high rates of small-urban migration found in most developing countries is quite natural from an economic view point. In this model the expected real wage-differential between urban and rural areas is the main motivating force behind migration or the main determinant of the migration decision. The potential migrant first calculates the real income which he would get in the urban area for a job with his present effort. He next makes a personal judgement of the probability of obtaining such a job.

He then compares the expected income with that which he hopes so obtain in the rural area. His migration decision is based on the difference. For example, suppose the expected rural income is \$ 1000 per month, and that real income of an urban job which is commensurate with his qualification is \$ 2000. However, this information alone is not sufficient to make the migration decision. If the subjective probability of getting the urban job was 0.4, than the expected income would be \$ 800 and no migration would take place on this case expected urban wage = actual urban wage × the probability of getting a job.

$$800 = 0.4 \times \$\ 2000$$

If the probability were 0.8 the expected income would be \$ 1600 (= 0.8 × \$ 2000) and the worker would migrate. (To this one may, of course, add the cost of transfer.) Thus the model brings into focus the role of economic incentive in the migration decision.

The Basic Model

The Harris-Todaro model assumes that migration from rural to urban areas depends primarily on the difference in wages between the rural and urban labour markets. That is:

$$M_t = f(W_u - W_r)$$

where M_t is the number of rural to urban migrants in time t, is response function, W_u is the urban wage and W is the rural wage. Since there is unemployment in the town (and it is assumed that there is no unemployment in rural areas), and every migrant cannot expect to find a job there, the model postulates that the expected urban wage with the rural wage. The expected urban wage is the actual urban wage times the probability of getting a job, or

$$W_u^e = PW_u$$

where W_u^e = expected urban wage and p = probability of getting a job. Here p is expressed as

$$p = \frac{E_u}{E_u + U_u} = \frac{E_u}{L}$$

where E_u is urban employment, U_u is urban unemployment and L is total urban work force. Harris and Todaro assume that all members of the urban labour force have equal chances of obtaining the jobs available. So W_u^e becomes simply the urban wage times the urban employment rate. Migration in any given time then depends on three factors:

- The urban-rural wage gap.
- The urban employment rate.
- The responsiveness of potential migrants to the resulting opportunities.

Thus, $M_t = h\,\alpha(pW_u - W_r)$, where Mt = migration in period t and h = the response rate of potential migrants.

As long as $W_u^e > W_r$ the rural-urban migration will continue. It will stop only when migration has forced down the urban wage or forced up urban unemployment so much that expected urban wage (W_u^e) is covated to existing rural wage (W_r). If $W_r > W_u^e$ there will be a flow of disappointed urban jobseekers back to the rural areas. This is known as reverse migration.

Theoretical Implication of the Model

There is no denying the fact that any development project can be evaluated using social cost-benefit analysis. An important part of the social cost of any input is opportunity cost, its value in its next best alternative use. Labour hired for an urban formal-sector project might well be drawn from the urban informal sector also. The worker who moves out of the urban informal sector may, in turn, be replaced by someone from the rural sector. In this case, the output lost is that of the worker who was formerly in the rural sector, i.e., the worker at the end of the employment chain. For this reason, some analysts believe that the wage paid to casual agricultural labourers provides a good measure of the social cost of unskilled labour.

However, this measure, although a good indicator of output foregone through labour reallocation, probably understates the true social cost of employing labour, which has other components that are likely to be significant. One such component is induced migration. No doubt there are both pull and push factors behind internal labour migration that occurs in the course of economic development from rural to urban areas. Such migration can result either from favourable economic developments in the towns or from adverse developments in the rural areas. The Harris-Todaro model integrates these two sets of forces in their analysis of the process of labour reallocation that is likely to occur during economic development. This is why the model was sort of innovation in the literature of development economics when it appeared for the first time in 1970.

The Policy Implications of the Model

The H-T model has far-reaching implications from the policy point of view. For example, if the government of the country concerned were successful in fostering industrial development in an urban area, employment would increase there. The effect would be to increase the subjective productivity of getting urban employment in the minds of rural inhabitants. Migration would increase and the eventual effect of the new industrial development could be that urban unemployment becomes higher that the level prevailing before the new development took place.

There will be some level of urban employment which ensures equilibrium in the sense that no further migration takes place. Potential migrants may take a long-term view in arriving at a decision. They may consider that their desireness of obtaining an urban job will be higher after a waiting period of some months. Thus they will compare the present value of the sum of expected urban earnings with that of expected rural earnings. They may be content to accept a low wage in the urban informal sector for some time. This might be a rational decision on a long-term basis. The root of the problem is the large difference between earnings in the modern industrial sector and those in the rural areas. Often the former are well above the market clearing levels for varies reasory. The long-term solution to the problem lies in adopting policies for both urban and rural areas which reduces the real income differences between the two areas.

Low Level of Equilibrium Trap

Richard R. Nelson in his theory 'Low Level of Equilibrium Trap' that he outlined in 1956 argued that if we look at the Third World Countries (TWC), there exists a vicious circle of poverty where poverty is the cause and effect of poverty. In order to pull the TWCs out of the trap, an investment over and above a certain minimum is required and only then it will have the capacity of moving the economy on higher paths of economic development. He stressed on the Balanced Growth Strategy where in large investment in made through way of synchronized application of capital to cater to complementarities of demand. He revealed certain structural characteristics that are peculiar to the TWC. They are as under:

- He postulated that population growth is a function of per capita income of the country. There exists a positive relationship between population growth and per capita income at the initial stages of development i.e. as the per capita income increases, rate of growth of population also increases. After that with increase in per capita income, rate of growth of population is constant till a certain level. Beyond that level with further rise in the per capita income, population growth will fall.

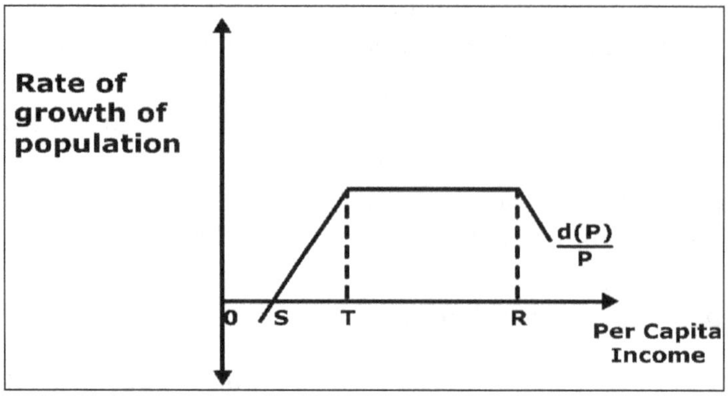

On the x-axis, we have the per capital income and on the rate of growth of population. Initially the economy is at 'S' i.e. at a low level of income which is stable at subsistence levels. As the per capita income increases the population growth also increases. Population growth is maximum at 'P' level of per capita income and thereafter it remains constant at that level till 'R' levels of per capital income. If he per capital income increases beyond 'R' then the rate of growth of population actually falls.

- He postulated that addition to the capital stock takes place in two forms. One by the increase in the quantum of natural resources which he assumes to be negligible and second by the savings created capital per capita (the latter is roughly the same as investment in the industrial sector i.e. it represents additions to stock of tools and equipments). Hence, he assumes that addition to the capital stock is equal to savings created capital per capita which assumes the following relationship with per capita income.

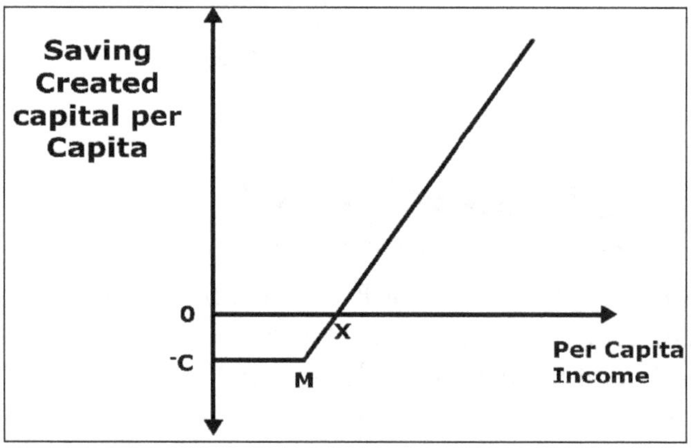

On the x-axis, we have per capita income and on the y-axis we have savings created capital per capita. At 'M' level of per capita income, there are dis-savings (equal to –c). If per capita income increases, then capital per capita is linearly correlated to it.

- Regarding output growth, he postulated that output is a function of factors of production i.e. assumed to be labour and capital. $O = T.f(L, K)$, where 'O' stands for output, 'T' stands for index of technical productivity, 'L' stands for labour and 'K' stands for capital.

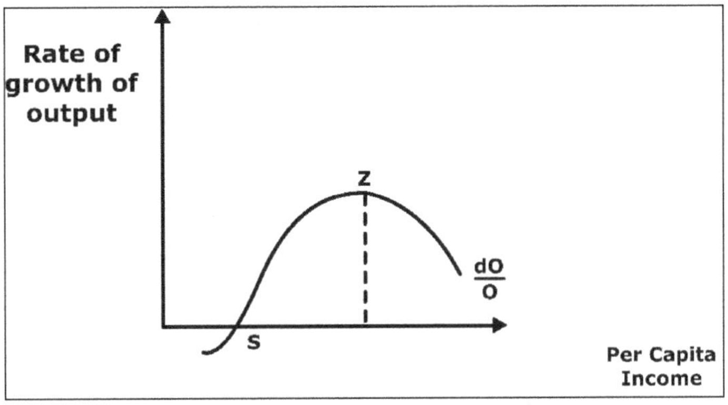

At 'S' level of per capita income, the economy is at the subsistence level with rate of growth of population and rate of growth of output equal to zero i.e. stationary. When the exceeds the 'S' level, then due to increases in labour supply and growth of savings created capital per capita, the output in the economy initially increases then reaches a maximum (Z) and then falls.

- Nelson postulated that there is this availability of arable uncultivable land in the TWCs. And as the population grows, more and more land is brought under cultivation and hence the supply of land becomes smaller and smaller. However he also claimed that the techniques of production used by the TWC are obsolete and inefficient.
- He further postulated that there is certain inertia at both economic and cultural levels in the TWCs. People are fatalist and risk-averse due to which the investors are shy in making huge investments.

Working of Nelson's Model

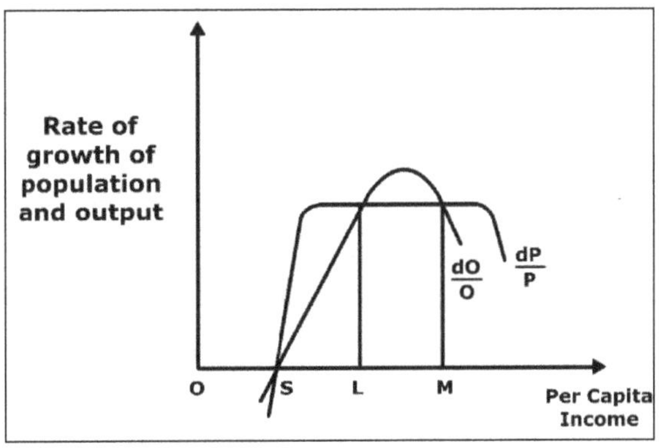

Nelson argued that TWCs are operating at the subsistence level of equilibrium (S). With the working of forces motivated to achieving a greater economic development, if the per capita income rises between OS and OL, then there is this tendency of the economy to move back to the original level (S). This is so because between OS and OL, the rate of growth of population is higher than that of the rate of growth of output. So, Nelson propagated that if the TWCs want to move to higher and sustained levels of income, any developmental investment must be able to bring about a rise in the per capita income beyond OL. He further argued that positive impact on growth of economy would continue till OM level of per capita income. So, OL according to him measures the strength of trap for the TWCs beyond which they can achieve a sustained growth of per capita income.

Moreover, Nelson suggested few strategy measures that ensure the TWCs to reach that level of sustained economic development. He stressed on the need for stabilizing socio-political conducive environment in the country. He favoured the route of foreign aid to raise the capital and output by obtaining funds from abroad i.e. particularly international institutions. He suggested that TWCs should not use the latest methods of production but vigilantly so as to make productive use of the latest resources that are congenial to its growth and prosperity. He suggested that TWCs need to adopt such methods that help them change their distribution of income in the desired direction. Changes in the social structure of the society with emphasis on large social overhead investment by the government and breaking of socio-economic and cultural inertia.

Criticism of Nelson's Theory by H. L. Myint

- The application of Nelson's theory to TWCs is not easily possible as it is not possible to establish a function between rate of growth of per capita income and rate of growth of population. The main factor of growth of population is that Death Rate has declined in recent times due to improvement in public health and control of epidemics.
- Functional relationship between level of per capita income and rate of growth of output is not as simple as it is assumed by Nelson. This relationship is highly complex. It takes place in two steps:
  - Relationship between level of per capita income and rate of growth of savings gets modified by a number of factors such as the pattern of income distribution and efficiency and effectiveness of financial institutions in mobilisation of savings.
  - Relationship between invention and resultant output depends upon a stable overall capital-output ratio rather it depends upon the extent to which a productive organisation of the country is improved and to what degree land saving innovations can be adopted to check the operation of diminishing returns.
- If the time element is introduced in Nelson's model then it creates problems in analysis. For instance growth in population and growth in income over the period of time might change the functional relationship between the two variables. Moreover, if the time factor is taken into account, the movement from L to M will be accompanied by permanent and irreversible additions to capital stock and skills and other variables.
- Nelson's model neglects the role of state completely.

References

- Leibenstein-critical-minimum-theory-with-diagram-4646: economicsdiscussion.net, Retrieved 25, August 2020
- Lewis-model-of-unlimited-supply-of-labor: economicsconcepts.com, Retrieved 13, May 2020
- Model-of-labour-migration-and-reallocation-economics-26765: economicsdiscussion.net, Retrieved 04, February 2020

5

Planning and Governance

Planning and governance have a significant impact on growth and development of an economy. Some of the major areas of study related to planning and governance with respect to economic growth and development are trade in developing world, role of MNC's in developing countries and dual gap analysis. The topics elaborated in this chapter will help in gaining a better perspective about these aspects of planning and governance.

Trade in Developing World

Traditional Heckscher-Ohlin (H-O) theory focuses on relative endowments of internationally immobile production factors across countries and on differences in factor intensities across goods. Set in the general framework of a competitive market structure, which implies constant returns of scale at the firm level, the theory predicts that an economy exports goods whose production uses intensively the factor with which the country is comparatively well endowed and imports the other goods. Differences in countriesí relative factor abundance also determine the extent to which industrial activities are spread across the global economy or concentrated in just a few countries. H-O does not consider forward and backward linkages, which are of no importance in a world of perfect competition. While fully applying only in a world of costless trade, the theoretical framework implies that a decline in trade costs leads to increased specialization of countries in sectors of relative factor abundance.

The new trade theory provides a systematic treatment of increasing returns to scale at the firm level and imperfectly competitive market structures. Regarding the pattern of trade, new trade models give a theoretical explanation of how market size can provide a basis for comparative advantage. Building on this insight, the new economic geography models focus on pecuniary externalities that occur in increasing returns to scale industrial sectors and are created by the existence of forward and backward linkages manufacturing firms use both primary factors and other manufactures as production inputs and sell their output to both consumers and other manufacturing firms and make firms decide to locate close to other firms that supply some of their inputs and provide some of their markets. The new economic geography models predict that firms in increasing returns to scale industries that face positive trade costs will tend to locate in a large market. This is:

- Because of forward (cost) linkages having more firms in a location means more competition and implies that more intermediate inputs are available locally and that these intermediate inputs tend to be cheaper than elsewhere allowing downstream firms to produce more efficiently and enjoy higher short-run profits, and
- Because of backward (demand) linkages having more firms in a location enlarges the market for intermediate goods, allowing upstream firms to produce at a more efficient scale and raise short-run profitability in order to save trade costs.

As a result, economies with large markets will get a disproportionally large share of increasing return activities. However, forces related to product and factor market competition work in the opposite direction, i.e. towards a dispersion of industrial activity. This is because the presence of a large number of firms will tend to drive wages up and output prices down, thereby lowering the short-term profitability of firms. Tension between forward and backward linkages on the one and product and factor market competition on the other hand determines the degree to which industrial activity is characterized by agglomeration or dispersion. The result of this tension on industrial location is likely to be non-monotonic. "At high trade costs, the dominant force in determining location is the need to be close to final consumption, preventing any strong geographical concentration of manufacturing. At low trade costs, the dominant determinant of location is wage costs, again mandating dispersed manufacturing to keep labor costs down. Therefore the linkage forces that can cause agglomeration are strongest relative to other forces at intermediate values of trade costs". Accordingly, in new economic geography models, the structure of production in individual countries is determined, as in traditional trade theory, by the interaction between country characteristics and industry characteristics. But while traditional trade theory focuses on relative factor endowments of countries and factor intensities of goods, the mechanisms of new economic geography models also take account of market size and countries' geographical distance from the markets of main developed countries, as well as of transport intensity of industrial sectors, including the size of transport costs and the dependence on intermediate inputs.

What does this imply for the evolution of industrial structure in developed and developing countries as globalization forces gain strength? "The reliance on very special and sometimes opposite assumptions makes [the new economic geography] literature appear as a collection of special cases; and it is not always clear what each case buys, nor how they relate to each other. Furthermore, as the models have become more complex they have als relied increasingly on numerical methods, making comparisons even more difficult." Consequently, there is no unified theoretical model with a consistent set of assumptions that could be applied to test a set of specific empirical predictions regarding the evolution of countries' industrial structure and trade patterns. While keeping the absence of a unified theoretical model in mind as a caveat for the interpretation of the empirical findings, a number of general predictions can be distilled from this literature regarding development issues. These broad predictions can be based on an analysis of how specific exogenous changes impact on the balance between forces that pull towards agglomeration and those that pull towards dispersion. Cost and demand linkages between industries pull towards agglomeration, while cross-country differences in the endowment of immobile production factors, the cost of trade between countries, and the strength of final consumer demand in locations other than the industrial centre pull towards dispersion. The changes and their effects were:

- The change in balance between agglomeration and dispersion brought about by the decline in communication and transport costs and the resulting increased tradability of intermediate production inputs that has given rise to international production fragmentation.

- How these changes might have impacted on the spread of industrial activities from developed to developing countries.

- How trade liberalization and preferential trade arrangements, whose importance in the world trading system has risen strongly over the past few years, might have influenced the spread of industry in addition to the decline in communication and transport costs.

All three subsections distil broad predictions on the evolution of manufactured exports and manufacturing value added that the following sections subject to empirical scrutiny.

Trade in Intermediate Inputs and International Production Fragmentation

The decline in communication and transport costs over the past few years has made it economically viable to break up integrated production processes and undertake downstream production activities in one country, and upstream production activities in another. The optimal location of industrial activities is likely to change when this kind of production fragmentation occurs in industrial sectors with increasing returns to scale at the firm level because transport and communication costs on intermediate goods determine where pecuniary externalities occur. The new balance between agglomeration and dispersion forces is then determined by the degree to which final goods production relies on intermediate goods inputs, the relative factor intensities of upstream and downstream production, whether or not transport and communication costs also decline for final goods, and where final output is consumed.

This mechanism can be described as follows, if there is variation in factor intensity across production stages and the downstream activity (e.g. assembly) is more labour intensive than the upstream activity (including the provision of product designs and process technology, and the production of intermediate goods) but trade costs (i.e. transport and communication costs, tariffs, non-tariff barriers, etc.) fall only for the upstream product, the downstream activity moves from the developed to the developing country, while the upstream activity remains in the developed country. The reason for this is that a decline in trade costs makes firms less sensitive to the pecuniary externalities created by forward linkages and more sensitive to international differences in factor prices. The level of final goods production activities in the developing country depends on the costs of shipping the final good. If these are high, final goods production in the developing country will become more profitable because of the availability of cheaper production inputs, but not rise above the amount sufficient to supply the developing country market, while the developed country will retain final goods production to supply its domestic market. Taken together this means that the developed country produces all intermediate goods, while the developed and the developing country share final goods production.

If trading costs for the final good also fall below a certain threshold, final goods production in the developing country will increase. This is because final goods producing firms in the developed country will find shipping the intermediate good to the developing country and the final good back home more profitable than producing both the intermediate and the final good at home. On the other hand, a decline in trade costs for the final good will make final goods imports from the developed country cheaper and raise competition for final goods producers in the developing countries, reducing their profitability. The outcome for final goods producing firms in the developing country will be more favourable the higher is the share of imported intermediate goods in the production of the final good and the larger is the market for the final good in the developing country. By contrast, if final goods demand in the developing country is small, the cost saving effect of fragmentation must be very high in order to make up for shipping the intermediate good from the developed to the developing country and the final good back to the developed country. In other words, the wage difference between the two countries must be high and/or trade costs must be very low, for example, because of close geographical proximity between the developed and the developing country, for international production fragmentation to occur. The resulting broad empirical predictions are:

- A strong rise of exports from both developed and developing countries in sectors where production stages are easily separable, components are less labour-intensive than final goods, and demand for final goods is small in the low-wage (i.e. developing) country.
- Manufactured exports grow more rapidly in developing than in developed countries.
- Manufacturing value added declines in developed and rises in developing countries but the bulk of manufacturing value added remains in developed countries.
- Manufactured exports in developing countries grow much more rapidly than manufacturing value added.

The Spread of Industry from Developed to Developing Countries

According to new economic geography models, economic development is not a smooth process of many developing countries catching up with the industrialized countries. Rather, starting from a situation where a rich and a poor group of countries coexist, the models outline mechanisms that make industrialization spread in waves from country to country causing a few countries to make a rapid transition from the poor to the rich club. As outlined above, these mechanisms work on the basis of the interplay between pecuniary externalities and trade costs but with a crucial role also for differences in wages between the industrialized and the developing countries. Agglomeration of industrial activities in a developed country becomes less sustainable the larger is the wage gap with the developing country, the lower are trade costs between the developed and developing country, the lower are forward linkages (because of a low degree of intermediate input use in final good production) and backward linkages (the benefit from being close to industrial consumers) in the developed country, and the higher are forward and backward linkages in the developing country.

Initially, the industrialized countries have higher wages than the developing countries but the positive pecuniary externalities created by linkages among industrial firms compensate for the higher wage costs. The spread of industry is triggered by an exogenous increase in world demand for manufactures, relative to demand for other tradable goods, which increases demand for labour in the established industrialized countries and opens up a larger and larger wage gap between the industrialized and the other countries. At some point the wage gap becomes too large to be compensated by the benefits coming from linkages in the industrialized country, and industrial firms start to relocate to low-wage economies.

However, the dispersion of industry does not lead to steady industrial development in all low-wage economies. Very small initial cross-country differences will determine which of the low-wage countries attract relocating firms if all countries are identical, it will simply be a matter of chance. "The pertinent dimensions of difference are those which determine the profitability of the first firms to relocate, so include labour market factors, internal infrastructure, as well as institutional characteristics of a country. Since the first entrants will be highly dependent on imported intermediate and capital goods and on export markets for final sales, they will tend to go to locations close (or with good transport links) to established centres. The first sectors to become detached from an existing agglomeration will typically be those that are intensive in immobile primary factors (the prices of which are high in the centre), and that are not too heavily dependent on linkages with other firms. These may be firms with low usage of intermediate goods, low levels of sales to other industrial sectors, or that do not need to cluster with related activities to gain new technology. As these sectors relocate, so they may begin to create linkages and attract other sectors. The sequence in which industries enter then depends on their factor intensities, their tradability, and the way in which they benefit from linkages to other activities, and create their own linkage effects."

The importance given to differences in wages across countries and differences in factor intensity and intermediate input use across industrial sectors departs from the standard new economic geography models that focus on two countries with similar underlying characteristics and on the industrial sector as a whole. This allows for the formulation of predictions that can be tested empirically for a sample that includes different industrial sectors and countries with different underlying characteristics. However, the spread of industry will follow the path outlined in the preceding paragraphs only if initially linkages do not exceed a critical mass in any developing economy. If this is the case, firms looking for lower prices of immobile factors will move industrial activity earlier than firms looking to exploit linkages in the developing country who will move industrial activity only after the creation of sizable linkage effects in developing countries.

By contrast, if there is a developing country that has the critical mass of domestic linkages already before the spread of industry sets in, both types of firms move industrial activity at the same time but to different developing countries: firms primarily wanting to exploit factor price differences will go to the developing countries with few linkages and among them to those that are geographically close, while firms primarily looking to benefit from linkages in the new location will go to the already relatively more industrialized developing country with geographical proximity playing a secondary role.

The impact on the developing country's structures of manufactured exports and manufacturing value added depends on the type of firm that moves industrial activity. If the developing country does not have a critical mass of linkages that provide pecuniary externalities to industrial firms because of insufficient domestic production of intermediate inputs or insufficient domestic demand from either other industrial firms or final consumers, the developing country will import a large fraction of production inputs and export the bulk of output without much domestic value added. As a result, the country's manufactured exports will strongly rise, while manufacturing value added will go up only little. By contrast, a developing country with established domestic linkages will provide a large share of intermediate inputs from domestic production and a large share of output will go into further domestic production or consumption. As a result, the country's manufactured exports will rise much less, while its manufactured value added will rise much more than in the first case. The resulting broad empirical predictions on the spread of industry are:

- Developing countries geographically close to a main developed country market benefit from industrial dispersion in labour-intensive sectors earlier than others provided that non-tradable goods and immobile factors are readily available.
- If all developing countries have a low level of wages and linkages, the spread of industry will differ in time with early movers looking for both close geographic proximity and lower

prices of immobile factors relative to more industrialized countries, and later movers (after a critical mass of firms is created in some sectors) looking to exploit newly created linkages in the economically less developed regions. If developing countries differ regarding the level of wages and linkages, firms with different underlying motivations will move industrial activity at the same time with firms primarily looking for lower prices of immobile factors moving activity to the geographically close and relatively less industrialized developing countries, and firms looking to exploit linkages in the new location moving activity to the relatively more industrialized developing countries. The spread of industry from firms looking to exploit linkages will lead to a strong change in the developing country's manufacturing value added and a small change in its manufactured exports, while the opposite holds when the other firms move.

Trade Liberalization and Preferential Trading Arrangements

The characteristics of an individual country's external trading regime strongly influence the country-specific effects of shifts in the balance between agglomeration and dispersion forces discussed above. This is because trade barriers (such as tariffs and non-tariff measures) are essentially just another form of trade costs, which come in addition to communications and transport costs. Accordingly, the forces triggered by trade liberalization and preferential trading arrangements (PTAs) are very similar to those coming from a decline in transport and communication costs. The main additional feature of trade barriers is the possibility of discriminatory policies favouring one country over another. Therefore, the following discussion of the mechanisms features two developing countries, in addition to one developed country, in order to emphasize the effects of discriminatory trade policy. Two cases without discrimination (multilateral and unilateral trade liberalization) and two cases with discrimination (PTAs between the developed and one of the developing countries, and PTAs among the two developing countries) are considered.

Multilateral trade liberalization leads to an equal decline in the trade barriers on both the intermediate and the final good in all three countries and has the same effects as a decrease in transport and communication costs for the two goods, as discussed above. Unilateral trade liberalization for the intermediate good in one of the developing countries has the same effect as a decline in transport costs for the intermediate good. The effects of unilateral trade liberalization by one of the developing countries for both the intermediate and the final good are less clear because cheaper intermediate goods imports decrease production costs for final goods producers in the liberalizing country, while cheaper final goods imports decrease their domestic sales. Given only unilateral trade liberalization, this decline in profitability cannot be compensated by higher exports. "Under unilateral liberalization the continuing barriers to developing countries' exports mean both that it takes a lower tariff rate to start industrialization [in developing countries] and that, once industrialization has started, [the developing country] has a lower share of manufacturing than it would in the multilateral case".

When the two developing countries engage in a PTA with each other, industrial activity rises if the enlargement effect from combining the size of the two markets is sufficient to create additional pecuniary externalities for firms through either rising demand or falling costs. If PTAs between developing countries lower restrictions on the movement of labour, labour migration between the two developing countries can cause such a decline in costs by enlarging the pool of workers required by firms. When the developed and one of the developing countries form a PTA, the effects for the two countries are essentially the same as in the case of multilateral trade liberalization. By contrast, the other developing country will be relatively worse off because it will not attract additional industrial activities and lose market shares for its industrial exports in the developed country market. The resulting broad empirical predictions on the spread of industry that weaken or reinforce the pure geographical effects, which were discussed in the last section, are:

- Industrial activity moves most in sectors where trade barriers on intermediate goods are low in developing countries or where trade barriers on final goods are low in developed countries ñ these are likely to be sectors where international production fragmentation has played an increasingly important role, i.e. wearing apparel, electrical and non-electrical machinery, and transport equipment.
- Industrial activity in developing countries rises more in sectors favoured by preferential trading arrangements among developing countries provided that the market enlargement creates additional pecuniary externalities for industrial firms.
- Under preferential trading arrangements between a developed and a developing country, the developing country that is part of the arrangement attracts more industrial activity than excluded developing countries, provided that differences in the geographical distance and/or the wage level and/or the excluded developing country's market size do not outweigh the effects coming from discriminatory trade policy. Empirical scrutiny of this prediction requires an examination of sector-specific data on effectively applied tariffs and on bilateral trade.

Agriculture and Globalisation

Structural Adjustment Programmes (SAPs) is nothing but the changes in the structure of the economy from public to private and from restriction to openness, which ultimately integrates the domestic economy to the world economy. The openness or globalization is not only confined to industrial and services sector, but also to agricultural sector. When the size of Government reduces, its expenditure in almost sector reduces including agriculture leading thereby decline public investment and Gross Capital Formation in agriculture. There are broadly two policies responsible for agricultural globalization. One is the policy of liberalization, privatization and globalization or famously known as the structural adjustment programme. In most cases, institutional, fiscal and trade policy changes strongly impinging on agriculture has been prescribes and implemented. Secondly the policy prescribed in Uruguay Round or Agreement on Agriculture (AA) under the WTO.

Agricultural Globalisation before Agreement on Agriculture

World economic slowdown together with the build-up of third world external debt in the aftermath of the oil crisis prepared the conditions for the transition of the 1980s. In all countries undergoing stabilization and structural adjustment under Fund/Bank tutelage, large changes in macro prices (exchange rates, interest rates and real wages) and the fiscal stance were essential parts of the overall package. Most notably, cuts in public expenditures, drastic in many instances, were prescribed not merely to correct external and public sector deficits but also to diminish the role of government in long-term growth in favor of the market. The internal and external market liberalization under agriculture involved the following:

- Reduction or abolition of export taxes and quotas.
- Reduction or elimination of government controls on agricultural trade, and disbanding of state marketing agencies or boards.
- Reduced import tariffs, and elimination of import licensing, quotas or prohibitions.
- Elimination of internal market regulations or controls (including pan-territorial or pan-seasonal pricing) and of restrictions on the private sector in product and input marketing.
- Decline in public production and infrastructural services including research and extension, product distribution, input supply and agricultural credit.

As part of the reforms, agricultural subsidization has generally been reduced. The share of Government expenditure on agriculture fell particularly sharply in countries undergoing structural adjustment. One part of the reductions came in the form of reductions in input subsidies. Another was through cuts in public good or services provision. Although it is widely acknowledged that public expenditures promoting agriculture were often disproportionately cut in structural adjustment programs, these are often attributed to political motivation on the part of the relevant governments rather than to Bank or Fund instigation. Consider the instance of expenditures on agricultural research. Many countries, particularly in Latin America and sub-Saharan Africa have had to cut back sharply on already low levels of allocations to agricultural research. Whereas such expenditures grew rapidly during the 1960s and 1970s, they experienced real absolute declines thereafter in many cases. In sum, numerous developing economies had already gone the distance toward agricultural liberalization, privatization and globalization prior to the Uruguay Round.

The Agreement on Agriculture

To advance global agricultural trade, the AA includes the following provisions in regard to tariffs and quotas:

- All quantitative and other non-tariff restrictions to be converted to tariff equivalents, added to existing tariffs and the tariffs bound. For Developing Economies, staples in traditional diets were exempted.
- Advanced economies (AE) to reduce bound tariffs by an average of 36 percent and a minimum of 15 percent on each item by the end of 1999.
- Developing economies (DE) to reduce tariffs by 15 percent on average and a minimum of 10 percent on each item by the end of 2004.

But the actual implementation of these accords has involved widespread "dirty tarrification" of quotas. In particular, AEs have chosen greatly inflated tariff equivalents for the base period 1986-88. Even after implementation of the accords, the average tariff will be as high as 36 percent in AEs and 20 percent in DEs. On a trade weighted basis, agricultural tariffs in the AEs remain almost six times higher than those in the industrial sector.

At the same time, the AA makes an egregious provision that allows AEs but not DEs the power to invoke "special safeguard" measures i.e., to limit imports in the event of unexpectedly large import increases or declines in world (import) prices! On export subsidies, which are a major plank of AE policies, the AA standards include:

- Total fiscal expenditure on export subsidies to be cut by 36 percent in AEs and by 24 percent in DEs.
- The volume of subsidized exports to be cut by 21 percent in AEs by 2000 and by 14 percent in DEs by 2004. It is noteworthy that the vast majority of DEs have no export subsidies in the first place. In consequence, they would be precluded from imposing any such subsidies in the future.

The accord also introduced a set of requirements in regard to domestic support for agriculture that may well prove to be the most consequential for DEs. After being capped at base 1986-88 levels, the Agreement requires reductions in the "aggregate measure of support" (AMS) to the tune of 20 percent over a six-year period in AEs and by 13 percent over a ten-year period in DEs. But the provision excluded the EU compensation program under the 1992 CAP reform and the US deficiency payments program. Apart from the de minimis provisions, there are two critical exemptions for DEs:

- Agriculture and rural development measures: Input subsidies to low-income or resource poor producers and general investment subsidies.
- "Green Box" measures: These include general services to agriculture such as research and extension, pest control, environmental programs, crop insurance. The key proviso is that such measures be minimally trade- or production-distorting.

The Rationale for Agricultural Globalisation

The general belief is that globalization of agriculture provides market access to developing economies and increase in income of the economy including the farmers. It is because the Advanced Economies give huge subsidies to their farmers that are quite low in Developing Economies, which distorts the market. Removal of subsidies in advanced economies will push up the process of agricultural goods and Developing Economies benefits from exporting these economies. Is agricultural underdevelopment primarily due to the price/trade regimes within DEs and in the world at large? A major FAO report unhesitatingly avers that "the past policy bias against agriculture [within] these countries and distortions on world agricultural markets due to the protection and subsidization of this sector in many developed countries" are the two key factors explaining agricultural underdevelopment. By implication, producer prices are taken to be powerful determinants of supply within DEs. In the conventional view, production and trade subsidies in AEs have served to raise AE output and exports world-wide while production and trade taxes, whether explicit or implicit, in the developing countries have reduced DE output and net exports. Hence, at a global level, the two sets of policies have worked against each other so far as their impact on world supplies and world prices is concerned.

Once there is abolition of the distorting measures in the form of subsidies and other forms of supports and secondly provision of market access particularly to the products of developing countries, ultimately there will be increase in real income and welfare of the population. In turn, this implies that liberalization is expected, on the one hand, to reduce AE outputs and exports and therefore raise world agricultural prices and, on the other, to open up their markets for exports from the rest of the world. Trade expansion due to increased import market access will raise net world demands, because world prices to rise and generate supply responses in the DEs. Although benefits will primarily accrue to the established DE exporters (Argentina, Brazil and Thailand among others), additional benefits will accrue also to others who are poised to become exporters at the higher prices and to producers everywhere in the DE, many of whom are impoverished. While the dismantling of both DE taxation and AE subsidization of agriculture will hurt net importers of previously subsidized products, economy-wide trade liberalization is presumed to produce net benefits for all liberalizing countries.

Agricultural globalization in the neo-liberal claim is promoted on the ground that it promotes food security of the people and equitable development in the developing countries by enabling the developing countries specialize in the production and securing gains from trade. In most DEs, food consumption levels remain low and agriculture remains underdeveloped, whether in terms of labor or land productivity. Agricultural underdevelopment explains not merely the low supply of food products but also the low effective demand for food because agriculture accounts for a large share of total employment and income. The relative price of food is of overwhelming importance for consumers in these countries. It is also a principal determinant of the real distribution of incomes both directly, via the share of rent, real wage levels and the overall rate of profits, and through its influence on core inflation.

Implications

During the post reform period and in response to Globalization and WTO there is growing domestic and export demand for non-cereal items of food, there has been a discernible shift in the allocation of resources in Indian agriculture in the recent periods away from cereals, particularly coarse cereals to dairy farming, poultry, edible oils, meat , fish, vegetable to fruits, etc. These enterprises, being labor intensive, are suited to small holders and lead to rise in wage employment. There is also rise in income of farmers growing high value products. There have, however been some disturbing trends in the postreform periods. Apart from stagnant or declining public investment, the post-reform period has witnessed a decline in institutional credit for small and marginal farmers, increasing risk and uncertainty in agriculture due to Globalisation and WTO, increase in farmer's suicide, less emphasis to research and extension and rise in regional disparities. The neo-liberal economic reforms in the last decade has led to public expenditure cuts, a credit squeeze, and collapse of employment growth in rural areas. The crisis has been intensified due to full trade liberalization, which has exposed farmers to the volatility of the global commodity markets against a background of recession in the capitalist world.

Green Revolution

Much of the success was caused by the combination of high rates of investment in crop research, infrastructure, and market development and appropriate policy support that took place during the first Green Revolution (GR). We can distinguish the first GR period as 1966-1985 and the post-GR period as the next two decades. Large public investment in crop genetic improvement built on the scientific advances already made in the developed world for the major staple crops, wheat, rice, and maize and adapted those advances to the conditions of developing countries. The GR strategy for food crop productivity growth was explicitly based on the premise that, given appropriate institutional mechanisms, technology spillovers across political and agroclimatic boundaries could be captured. However, neither private firms nor national governments had sufficient incentive to invest in all of the research and development of such international public goods. Private firms operating through markets have limited interest in public goods, because they do not have the capacity to capture much of the benefit through proprietary claims; also, because of the global, nonrival nature of the research products, no single nation has the incentive to invest public resources in this type of research.

International public goods institutions were needed to fill this gap, and efforts to develop the necessary institutional capacity, particularly in plant breeding, were a central part of the GR strategy. Based on the early successes with wheat at the International Maize and Wheat Improvement Centre (CIMMYT) in Mexico and rice at the International Rice Research Institute (IRRI) in the Philippines, the Consultative Group on International Agricultural Research (CGIAR) was established specifically to generate technological spillovers for countries that underinvest in agricultural research, because they are unable to capture all of the benefits of those investments. After CGIAR-generated knowledge, invention, and products (such as breeding lines) were made publicly available, national public and private sectors responded with investments for technology adaptation, dissemination, and delivery.

Despite that success, in the post-GR period, investment in agriculture dropped off dramatically into the mid-2000s. However, the need for continued investments in agricultural innovation and productivity growth is as important today as it was in the early years of the GR. Low income countries and lagging regions of emerging economies continue to rely on agricultural productivity as an engine of growth and hunger reduction. However, sustaining productivity gains, enhancing smallholder competitiveness, and adapting to climate change are becoming increasingly urgent concerns across all production systems.

Since the mid-2000s and heightened after the 2008 food price spikes, there has been renewed interest in agricultural investment, and there are calls for the next GR, including those calls made by the former Secretary General of the United Nations Kofi Annan and Sir Gordon Conway. Simultaneously, there is recognition of the limitations of the first GR and the need for alternative solutions that correct for those limitations and unintended consequences. GR 2.0 must address these concerns both where the GR was successful and in low income countries and lagging regions, where agricultural productivity is still low.

First GR: Diffusion and Impact of Crop Genetic Improvements

Positive impacts on poverty reduction and lower food prices were driven in large part by crop germplasm improvements in CGIAR centers that were then transferred to national agricultural programs for adaptation and dissemination. The productivity gains from crop germplasm improvement alone are estimated to have averaged 1.0% per annum for wheat (across all regions), 0.8% for rice, 0.7% for maize, and 0.5% and 0.6% for sorghum and millets, respectively. Adoption rates of modern varieties in developing countries increased rapidly, reaching a majority of cropland (63%) by 1998.

However, global aggregates mask great geographic disparities. In Asian countries (including China), the percentage of area planted to modern varieties was 82% by 1998, whereas improved varieties covered only 27% of total area planted in Africa. This difference may be, in part, because of the later introduction of CGIAR research programs focused on Africa as well as the lag in breeding efforts for the orphan crops, crops that did not benefit from a backlog of research conducted before the GR period but had improvement that came during the GR and post-GR periods, such as cassava, sorghum, and millets which are of greater relative importance to the African poor. For instance, the first CIMMYT maize program focused on Africa only began in the late 1980s. Although the International Institute for Tropical Agriculture research for cassava started in 1967, its impact was felt only since the 1980s. Although it lagged behind in the GR period, Africa has witnessed positive growth in the post-GR period. Adoption of improved varieties across sub-Saharan Africa reached 70% for wheat, 45% for maize, 26% for rice, 19% for cassava, and 15% for sorghum by 2005.

Impact on Productivity and Food Prices

The rapid increase in agricultural output resulting from the GR came from an impressive increase in yields per hectare. Between 1960 and 2000, yields for all developing countries rose 208% for wheat, 109% for rice, 157% for maize, 78% for potatoes, and 36% for cassava. Developing countries in southeast Asia and India were the first countries to show the impact of the GR varieties on rice yields, with China and other Asian regions experiencing stronger yield growth in the subsequent decades. Similar yield trends were observed for wheat and maize in Asia. Analysis of agricultural total factor productivity (TFP) finds similar trends to the partial productivity trends captured by yield per hectare [TFP is defined as the ratio of total output to total inputs in a production process]. For the period 1970–1989, change in global TFP for agriculture was 0.87%, which nearly doubled to 1.56% from 1990 to 2006.

Crop genetic improvement focused mostly on producing high-yielding varieties (HYVs), but the decrease in time to maturity was also an important improvement for many crops, allowing for an increase in cropping intensity. The rapid spread of the rice–wheat system in the Indo-Gangetic plains (from Pakistan to Bangladesh) can be attributed to the shortening of the crop growing period. Other improved inputs, including fertilizer, irrigation, and to a certain extent, pesticides, were also critical components of the GR intervention. Asia had already invested significantly in irrigation infrastructure at the start of the GR and continued to do so throughout the GR and post-GR periods.

Widespread adoption of GR technologies led to a significant shift in the food supply function, contributing to a fall in real food prices. Between 1960 and 1990, food supply in developing countries increased 12–13%. Estimates suggest that, without the CGIAR and national program crop germplasm improvement efforts, food production in developing countries would have been almost 20% lower (requiring another 20–25 million hectares of land under cultivation worldwide). World food and feed prices would have been 35–65% higher, and average caloric availability would have declined by 11–13%. Overall, these efforts benefited virtually all consumers in the world and the poor relatively more so, because they spend a greater share of their income on food.

Access to Crop Genetic Improvements

The CGIAR's numerous crop improvement networks allowed for the best breeding materials and knowledge to be widely and freely available and used across the developing world. National

Agricultural Research Systems (NARS) in developing countries generally used varieties or crosses from CGIAR centers as parents and then adapted those varieties for particular agroecological environments or preferences. Enabling such adaptive transfers significantly improved research efficiency, reduced research costs, and greatly expanded the pool of genetic resources and varieties available to the national programs. Such an uninhibited system of germplasm exchange with the best international materials allowed countries to make strategic decisions about investing in plant breeding capacity. In general, large NARSs engaged in adaptive transfers rather than direct use of CGIAR-generated varieties and crosses, whereas small NARSs used the material directly. The CGIAR content of modern varieties was high for most food crops; 36% of all varietal releases were based on CGIAR crosses, although it varies greatly by crop. In addition, 26% of all modern varieties had a CGIAR-crossed parent or other ancestor.

Returns to Crop Improvement Research Investment

The returns to research investments in the GR strategy of germplasm improvement have been measured in great detail by several economists over the last few decades. These studies have found high rates of returns that, for the most part, compare favorably with alternative public investments. A recent metareview of trends and characteristics of the rates of return to agricultural research and development, examining 292 case studies with 1,900 estimated rates of returns, found a median annual rate of return estimate ranging from 40% to 60%. More importantly, it found no evidence that the rates of return to research had declined over time. The overall benefits of CGIAR contributions to crop genetic improvement are estimated in billions of dollars mostly because of the benefits from the improved three main staples. Spring bread wheat, rice (in Asia only), and maize (CIMMYT contribution only) have produced estimated benefits of $2.5, $10.8, and $0.6–0.8 billion, respectively.

There is evidence of continuing high rates of return for crop breeding improvements that have wide adaptability, such as those improvements for wheat, rice and maize. The more recent evidence also shows high returns for improvements in orphan crops in the post-GR period. No studies have found evidence of significant decline in rates of return to agricultural research in the post-GR period, likely because of continued investment in breeding for improved stress tolerance in addition to yield growth. For example, a recent estimate of the total benefits of resistance to all types of wheat rust was estimated to generate between $600 million and $2 billion per year. The spread of crop genetic improvement for marginal production environments and orphan crops adds to the continued high returns that have been observed in the post-GR period. In Africa, for instance, the internal rates of return to CGIAR investments from 2000 to 2020 in the dual purpose cowpea, which was developed through a collaboration between International Institute for Tropical Agriculture and the International Livestock Research Institute, have been estimated between 50% and 103%, depending on the assumptions used.

Limitations of GR-Led Growth Strategies

The GR contributed to widespread poverty reduction, averted hunger for millions of people, and avoided the conversion of thousands of hectares of land into agricultural cultivation. At the same time, the GR also spurred its share of unintended negative consequences, often not because of the technology itself but rather, because of the policies that were used to promote rapid intensification of agricultural systems and increase food supplies. Some areas were left behind, and even where it successfully increased agricultural productivity, the GR was not always the panacea for solving the myriad of poverty, food security, and nutrition problems facing poor societies.

Poverty and Food Insecurity Persisted Despite the GR Success

There is a large econometric literature that uses cross-country or time series data to estimate the relationship between agricultural productivity growth and poverty. These studies generally find high poverty reduction elasticities for agricultural productivity growth. In Asia, it has been estimated that each 1% increase in crop productivity reduces the number of poor people by 0.48%. In India, it is estimated that a 1% increase in agricultural value added per hectare leads to a 0.4% reduction in poverty in the short run and 1.9% reduction in the long run, the latter arising through the indirect effects of lower food prices and higher wages. For low income countries in general, the impact on the poverty headcount has been found to be larger from agricultural growth relative to equivalent growth in the nonagriculture sector at a factor of 2.3 times. In sub-Saharan Africa, agriculture's contribution to poverty reduction was estimated to be 4.25 times the contribution of equivalent investment in the service sector.

Because the GR strategy was based on intensification of favorable areas, its contribution to poverty reduction was relatively lower in the marginal production environments. In South Asia, the poorest areas that relied on rain-fed agriculture were also the slowest to benefit from the GR, contributing to widening interregional disparities and an incidence of poverty that still remains high. Technologies often bypassed the poor for a number of reasons. Among these reasons were inequitable land distribution with insecure ownership and tenancy rights; poorly developed input, credit, and output markets; policies that discriminated against smallholders, such as subsidies for mechanization or crop and scale bias in research and extension; and slow growth in the nonfarm economy that was unable to absorb the rising numbers of rural unemployed or underused people. Migration from less-favored rural areas has been cited as a strategy for poverty reduction; however, when migration out of rural areas occurs faster than the growth in employment opportunities, only a transfer of poverty results rather than true poverty reduction associated with agricultural transformation.

Sex played a major role in determining the distribution of benefits from the GR. Women farmers and female-headed households are found to have gained proportionally less than their male counterparts across crops and continents. Technology transfer largely focused on male farmers, with few measures to address women's technology needs or social conditions, and thus, they largely missed women farmers. Cross-country empirical evidence shows that women farmers are no less efficient than their male counterparts when using the same productive assets; however, women consistently face barriers to accessing productive resources and technologies.

Nutrition: Calorie Availability Increases but Micronutrient Intake Is Still Lagging

Between 1960 and 1990, the share of undernourished people in the world fell significantly. Improved availability and decreased staple food prices dramatically improved energy and protein consumption of the poor. The pathways through which the GR improved nutritional outcomes depended on whether a household was a net producer or net consumer; however, for virtually all consumers, the supply shifts and GR-driven rise in real incomes had positive nutritional implications. A 10-y study in southern India found that increased rice production resulting from the spread of HYVs accounted for about one-third of the substantial increase in energy and protein consumption of both farmers and landless workers, controlling for changes in nonfarm income sources. The fall in staple prices as a result of the GR also allowed for more rapid diet diversification, even among poor populations, because savings on staple food expenditures improved access to micronutrient-dense foods. In Bangladesh, for example, the steady fall in real rice prices from 1992 to 2000 led to greater expenditures per capita on nonrice food and a significant improvement in child nutrition status. The amount of rice consumed did not change, but households spent more on nonrice foods as their rice expenditures declined.

Nutritional gains of the GR have been uneven; although overall calorie consumption increased, dietary diversity decreased for many poor people, and micronutrient malnutrition persisted. In some cases, traditional crops that were important sources of critical micronutrients (such as iron, vitamin A, and zinc) were displaced in favor of the higher-value staple crops. For example, intensive rice monoculture systems led to the loss of wild leafy vegetables and fish that the poor had previously harvested from rice paddies in the Philippines. Price effects of such supply shifts also limited access to micronutrients, because prices of micronutrient-dense foods rose relative to staples in many places. In India, the increasing price of legumes has been associated with a consequent decline in pulse consumption across all income groups.

Policy and structural impediments, as well as a weak private sector, limited the supply responsiveness for vegetables and other nonstaples. Policies that promoted staple crop production, such as fertilizer and credit subsidies, price supports, and irrigation infrastructure (particularly for rice), tended to crowd out the production of traditional nonstaple crops, such as pulses and legumes in India. More recent evidence does suggest that diets are shifting in urban and rural Asia to include fewer cereals and more milk, meat, vegetables, and fruits. Evidence from India shows a marked increase in protein and fat intake between 1975 and 1995 across all income groups, suggesting that all consumers have benefitted from some nutritional improvements. However, micronutrient deficiencies among the poor persist, indicating that this dietary shift has not yet fully compensated for the decline in vitamin intake associated with cereal-dominant diets. Biofortification (breeding micronutrients into staple crops, such as the vitamin A-enhanced, orange-fleshed sweet potato) offers a new solution for improving nutrition outcomes, particularly for the rural poor, who depend on their own production for a large proportion of their daily caloric intake.

Environment: Impacts Have Been Mixed

GR-driven intensification saved new land from conversion to agriculture, a known source of greenhouse gas emissions and driver of climate change, and allowed for the release of marginal lands out of agricultural production into providing alternative ecosystem services, such as the regeneration of forest cover. HYVs more responsive to external inputs were central to the productivity achievements; however, in many cases, appropriate research and policies to incentivize judicious use of inputs were largely lacking. Unintended consequences in water use, soil degradation, and chemical runoff have had serious environmental impacts beyond the areas cultivated. The slowdown in yield growth that has been observed since the mid-1980s can be attributed, in part, to the above degradation of the agricultural resource base. These environmental costs are widely recognized as a potential threat to the long-term sustainability and replication of the GR's success.

The environmental consequences were not caused by the GR technology per se but rather, the policy environment that promoted injudicious and overuse of inputs and expansion of cultivation into areas that could not sustain high levels of intensification, such as the sloping lands. Output price protection and input subsides especially fertilizer, pesticide, and irrigation water distorted incentives at the farm level for adopting practices that would enhance efficiency in input use and thereby, contribute to sustaining the agricultural resource base. Where the policy incentives were corrected, farmers quickly changed behavior and adopted more sustainable practices. For example, the removal of pesticide subsides in Indonesia in the early 1990s led to a dramatic drop in insecticide use.

Marginal Production Environments

The original purpose of the GR was to intensify where returns would be high, with a focus on irrigated or high rainfall areas. The international breeding programs aimed to provide broadly adaptable germplasm that could then be grown across a wide set of geographies, but adoption was greatest in favorable areas. Technologies in the GR period did not focus on the constraints to production in more marginal environments, especially tolerance to stresses such as drought or flooding. Whereas HYVs of wheat provided yield gains of 40% in irrigated areas with modest use of fertilizer, in dry areas, gains were often no more than 10%. Almost full adoption of wheat and rice HYVs had been achieved in irrigated environments by the mid-1980s, but very low adoption in environments with scarce rainfall or poor water control (in the case of rice) had been achieved. In India, specifically, adoption was strongly correlated with water supply. Worldwide, improved seed–fertilizer technologies for wheat were less widely adopted in marginal environments and had less of an impact there than in favored environments.

More often than not, marginal environments were left behind, because the climate and resource constraints were such that returns to investment in GR varieties were low. Despite relatively low adoption of improved varieties, people living in marginal environments benefitted from the GR through consumption and wage linkages, such as lower food prices. Farm employment and growth in the nonfarm rural economy provided labor benefits to the landless rural poor and those people living in marginal production environments. Multicountry case studies of rice environments in Asia show that labor migration to more productive environments resulted in wage equalization and was one of the primary means of redistributing the gains of technological change from favorable to marginal areas. Similar results were found for wheat grown in high- and low-potential environments in Pakistan. There is also a growing body of evidence of spillovers from the productive regions that benefit the more marginal environments. These spillovers involve not only technology transfer and capital investments but also the software of development, such as local institutions, property rights, and social capital.

Poorly endowed environments, nevertheless, pose a tremendous challenge to researchers and policymakers alike to identify new agricultural research and development (R&D) opportunities and facilitate adoption of technologies and appropriate institutions to meet the needs of the poor living there. In the post-GR period, new investments in R&D for stress-tolerant crops and increased demand for feed grains have changed the prospects for agricultural production in marginal areas. Drought- and pest-resistant varieties, such as submergence-tolerant rice and drought-tolerant maize, provide options that reduce farmers' risk and improve incentives to invest in productivity-enhancing technologies. Changing market contexts also create new opportunities for farmers in more marginal areas to produce for the feed and biofuel markets.

Gains in Africa Lag Significantly but Are Catching Up

Africa was the main exception to the success of the GR in the developing world. The GR strategy was not appropriate where population densities were low and/or market infrastructure was poor. Also, the agricultural resource base could not sustainably support productivity growth, and the poor depended largely on orphan crops rather than the three main staple cereals. The package of innovations that spurred GR success in Asia was largely inappropriate for the African context at that time. However, emerging success stories of agricultural productivity growth in recent decades show that:

- The context for agricultural development has shifted dramatically.
- Investments in research to address the crops and constraints relevant to the continent's agriculture yield high returns.

First, during the GR period, the demand for intensification in Africa was quite low, because land was relatively abundant. Farmers had little incentive to intensify land use, because they had no incentive to save on land costs. However, there are some areas in Africa today where the land/labor ratios are now similar to what they were in Asia during the GR. For instance, in eastern and southern Africa, the amount of arable land has risen only marginally, but the percentage of households engaged in agriculture has grown threefold. The demand for yield-enhancing technologies is consequently rising in the region.

Second, improvements in rice, wheat, and maize largely addressed the main food security concerns in Asia. Africa, however, has huge diversity of cropping systems, and many orphan crops are central to food security. Even where the major cereals are grown in Africa, few suitable varieties were available for those agroecologies until the end of the GR and beginning of the post-GR period. In the 1960s and 1970s, national and international programs may have sought to short cut the varietal improvement process in sub-Saharan Africa by introducing unsuitable varieties from Asia and Latin America. This pattern remained until the 1980s, when more suitable varieties finally became available based on research specifically targeted to African conditions. Improved varieties of sorghum, millet, and cassava also started to emerge around the middle to late 1980s. The productivity gains from such investments are now starting to emerge; benefits from CGIAR investments in Africa for maize alone are estimated to exceed $2.9 billion. Yields growth for roots and tubers rose sharply between 1980 and 2005, increasing 40% during this period.

To a GR 2.0

GR 2.0 is already beginning to take place, and it is happening in low income countries as well as emerging economies. Low income countries, many of them in sub-Saharan Africa, still have very low productive agricultural systems. In these areas, chronic hunger and poverty continue to be daunting problems, and they face the age-old constraints to enhancing productivity growth, such as the lack of technology, poor market infrastructure, inappropriate institutions, and an enabling policy environment. Emerging economies, including much of Asia where gains from the first GR were concentrated, are well on their way to agricultural modernization and structural transformation. The challenge for agriculture now is to integrate smallholders into value chains, maintain their competitiveness, and close the urban-rural income gap. Enhancing staple crop supplies and sustaining productivity gains continue to be important, despite declining per capita cereal consumption, to meet the demands of population growth and demand for feed grain.

A confluence of factors has come together in recent years to generate renewed interest in agriculture and spur the early stages of GR 2.0. In the low income countries, continued levels of food deficits and the reliance on food aid and food imports have reintroduced agriculture as an engine of growth on the policy agenda. African leaders have acknowledged that agriculture plays a critical role in their development process and that lack of investment in the sector would only leave them farther behind. The Comprehensive Africa Agriculture Development Program (the agricultural program of the New Partnership for Africa's Development, an initiative of the African Union) declaration of 2006 and resulting pledges by African Heads of State to increase agricultural investments showed their commitment to improve the agriculture sector. There is also an increasing awareness of the detrimental impacts of climate change on food security, especially for tropical agriculture systems in low income countries.

In the emerging economies, growing private sector interest in investing in the agricultural sector has created an agricultural renaissance. Supermarkets are spreading rapidly across urban areas in emerging economies and encouraging national and multinational agribusiness investments along the fresh produce value chains in these countries. Consequently, traditional staple crop systems are diversifying into high-value horticulture and livestock production. Private sector has also made significant investments in other commercial crops for fiber and biofuel. For example, private R&D and supply chains have been the primary driver behind the rapid rise of Bt cotton production across Asia and Latin America. Despite these positive developments, interregional differences in productivity and poverty persist in many emerging economies. Rising demand for feed and biofuels and technological advances in breeding for stress tolerance could result in a revitalization of these areas. The rapid rise of hybrid maize production in eastern India is a case in point.

Finally, at the global level, there has been an increased tightening of food markets driven by population and income growth as well as diversion of food grain for biofuel and livestock feed. As a consequence, the long-term declining trend in real food prices, observed worldwide since 1975, leveled off by 2005. The food price crisis of 2008, sustained high prices, and more recent peaks observed in 2011 and 2012 have brought agriculture back onto global and national agendas.

By 2050, global population is projected to increase by about one-third, which will require a 70% increase in food production. To meet this need, GR 2.0 must continue to focus on shifting the yield frontier for the major staples. Increasing cereal productivity not only meets demand for staples, it also allows for the release of land to diversify into high-value crops and movement of labor out of agriculture, where other economic opportunities provide greater returns. GR 2.0 must also focus on improving tolerance to stresses, both climatic and biotic (pest and disease). Improved varieties that are tolerant to drought or submergence enhance smallholder productivity in marginal environments and provide tools to adapt to climate change. Epidemics such as the recent UG-99 wheat stem rust infestation, a new virulent strain resistant to improved varieties that emerged at a time when research on rust resistance had largely stopped (assuming that the problem had been solved), underscore the necessity of continued investments to maintain resistance to pests and diseases to avoid future shocks. Finally, technologies to increase input use efficiency and improve management practices are necessary to ensure the competitiveness and sustainability of production systems.

International public goods research continues to play a critical role, but in contrast to the first GR, the context in which the CGIAR operates has changed significantly. NARSs in many emerging countries have become research leaders in their own right, which is especially true of China and Brazil. The multinational life sciences companies are now the leading source of innovation in agricultural science, especially biotechnology. New partnerships can channel the expertise of the private sector and advanced national programs in emerging countries to benefit the low income countries. In 2007 the CGIAR began a major reform process to better address this changing context. It is still too early to say whether the system itself will be able to reorient itself, but there are definite signs that individual centers are starting to work innovatively. For example, IRRI partnered with the Beijing Genomics Institute to carry out genetic fingerprinting of IRRI's entire gene bank collection, which will then become publicly available data. Similarly, CIMMYT is developing drought-tolerant maize for Africa through a partnership with Monsanto, which provided proprietary germplasm that CIMMYT incorporated into high-yielding maize varieties adapted to African conditions.

There are also emerging examples of advanced NARSs leading global public good efforts with the CGIAR as a partner and collaborator. Exemplary cases include the partnership between IRRI and China to develop photosynthesis-efficient C4 rice as well as the global cassava partnership for genetic improvement, an international alliance of research institutes. The CGIAR also needs to become clearer in terms of the work on which it focuses and when it is hands off to the NARS. For instance, the CGIAR centers could hand over improved breeding material to the NARS and leave it up to them to complete the adaptation and varietal development process. The CGIAR should also devolve the activities associated with technology diffusion to the NARS, private sector, and nongovernmental organization partners.

The CGIAR has had limited success in generating and diffusing technologies and practices that enhance resource and input use efficiency, thereby contributing to improved competitiveness and sustainability. Improved understanding of tropical and subtropical agroecologies is an important global public good that contributes to innovation and new sustainable resource management practices. The emphasis of global public good research in resource management must be on such strategic knowledge generation rather than development of location-specific techniques and products. The emerging Digital Revolution provides new opportunities for smarter use of agricultural resources. Remote sensing and spatial mapping technologies allow for better targeting and monitoring of agricultural investments. Cell phones and other information and communication technologies can contribute to smarter application of water, fertilizers, and other inputs. The adaptation of precision agriculture techniques for developing country smallholder agriculture conditions could have significant global public good benefits.

Prebisch and Singer: Theory of International Trade

Consider a two country, two commodity (2×2) model in which the advanced centre produces and exports manufacture goods with income elasticity of demand greater than unity, and the backward periphery produces and exports primary commodities with an income elasticity of demand less than unity. Let us assume that income elasticity of demand for manufactures (E_m) is 1.3, and the income elasticity of demand for primary commodities (E_p) is 0.8. Assume to start with that the growth rate of income of both centre and periphery are equal to 3 per cent, that is ,$G_c = G_p = 3.0$. What will be the growth of exports (X) and imports (M) in the centre and periphery?

For the center we have,

$$X_c = G_p \times E_m = 3.0 \times 1.3 = 3.9 \text{ per cent}$$
$$M_c = G_c \times E_p = 3.0 \times 0.8 = 2.4 \text{ per cent}$$

For the periphery we have,

$$X_p = G_c \times E_p = 3.0 \times 0.8 = 2.4 \text{ per cent}$$
$$M_p = G_p \times E_m = 3.0 \times 1.3 = 3.9 \text{ percent}$$

With imports growing faster than exports in the periphery, this is not a sustainable position, unless the periphery can finance an ever growing balance of payment deficit on the current account by capital inflows. If it cannot, the balance of payments equilibrium on the current account is requirement, there must be some adjustment to raise the rate of growth of exports or reduce the rate of growth of imports. Now suppose we rule out the possibility that relative prices measured in a common currency can change as an adjustment mechanism, the only adjustment mechanism left (barring protection) is a reduction in the periphery's growth rate to reduce the rate of growth of imports in line with the rate of growth of exports. From the model, we can solve for necessary growth rate of the periphery to keep trade balanced. On the assumptions outlined, we must have M = X or GE = X, and therefore,

$$G_p = X_p / E_m = 2.4 / 1.3 = 1.846.$$

Thus the growth rate of the periphery is constrained to 1.846 per cent, compared with 3 per cent in the centre. In these circumstances both the relative and the absolute gap in income between periphery and centre will widen. Notice, in fact, that since the growth of the periphery's exports is equal to $G_c \times E_p$, we can write the above equation as,

$$G_p = G_c \times E_p / E_m$$

And dividing through by G, we reach the interesting result that the relative growth rate of the periphery and centre will equal the ratio of the income elasticity of demand for two countries' commodities:

$$G_p / G_c = E_p / E_m$$

This result will hold as long as current account equilibrium on the balance of payments is requirement, and relative price adjustment in international trade is either ruled out as an adjustment mechanism to rectify the balance of payment disequilibrium or does not work. To avoid the consequences of this model, Prebisch argued the case for protection, which in effect is a policy to reduce E_m, which for the periphery is the propensity to import manufactured goods.

Technical Progress and the Terms of Trade

The barter terms of trade might be expected to move in favor of the developing countries. For one thing, primary-product production tends to be subject to diminishing returns, and for another, technical progress tends to be more rapid in manufacturing industry than in agriculture. If prices are related to costs one would expect that in the theory the ratio of primary product prices to industrial prices would rise. According to Prebisch, however the ratio had shown a long run historical tendency to fall. He advanced two explanations for this. His first explanation concerns the relation between incomes and productivity from supply side. He suggested that whereas factor income tends to rise with productivity increases in developed countries, they rise more slowly than productivity in the developing countries because of population pressure and surplus labor. So there is upward pressure on final goods prices in developed countries and, thereby, causing the ratio of prices to move in the opposite direction to that suggested by the pace of technical progress. If we look from the perspective of demand side, we will find that demand for primary products grows more slowly than that of industrial products because of mainly two reasons:

- Income elasticity of demand for primary products is low.
- Primary products are substituted by synthetic material.

This is illustrated in the given figure which is likely to happen.

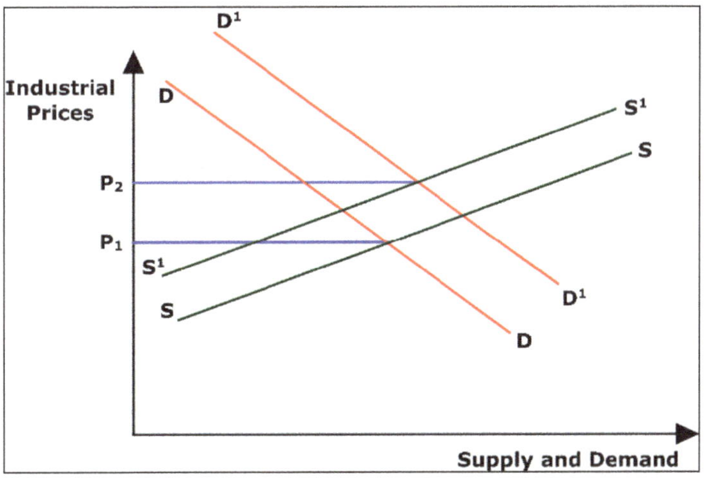

The supply and demand curves for industrial products are relatively elastic in the center, and the demand curve and the supply curve for primary products are relatively inelastic in the periphery. We assume that supply and demand curves intersect at the same point in both sectors so that the prices of industrial and primary products are equal i.e. terms of trade is equal to 1. In the center, technical progress will shift the supply curve SS outwards, but let us assume that increase in wage costs push it backward to S_1S_1. In the periphery the technical progress shifts the supply curve outward to S_1S_1 but there is no inward shift due to rising wage costs. In the center, the demand for industrial goods grows strongly from DD to D_1D_1, while in the periphery the demand for primary goods grows slowly. The price of industrial goods rises to P_2 while the price of primary products has actually to P_2 in periphery. The terms of trade of primary products has deteriorated for fundamental economic reasons associated with the nature of the products and the institutional structures of the countries that produce them.

Prebisch also put forward a separate independent hypothesis of the secular deterioration in the terms of primary products: the operation of a ratchet effect, with the prices of primary products relative to those of manufactured goods falling during cyclical downturns by more than they rise relative to the prices of manufactured products on the upturns. Such a symmetrical cycle, illustrated in figure.

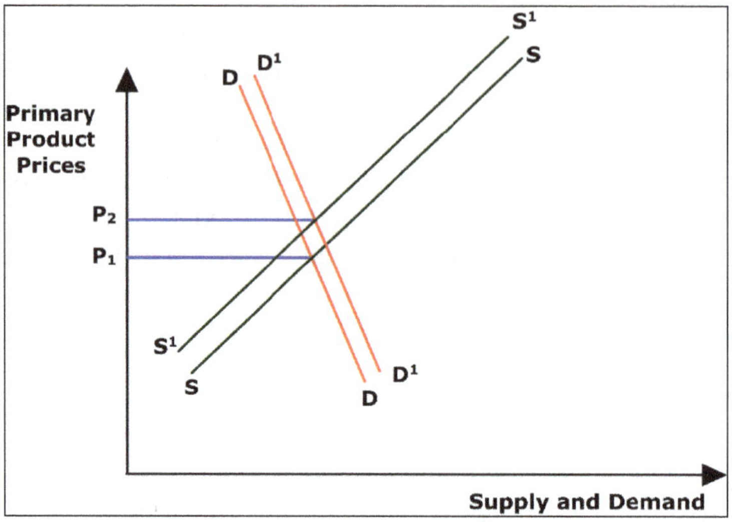

As it happens, the asymmetry hypothesis does not seem to be supported in the years since the Second World War, except for a few commodities such as rice, cotton rubber, and coffee. And even then the difference between the elasticity of prices on the downswing and on upswing is quite small.

The Income Elasticity of Demand for Products and the Balance of Payments

According to Prebisch, the second factor working to the disadvantage of developing countries is the balance of payments effects of differences in the income elasticity of demand for different type of products. As mentioned, it is generally recognized and agreed that the income elasticity of demand for primary commodities is lower than that of manufactured products. On average, the elasticity is probably less than unity, resulting in decreasing proportion of income spent on those commodities. In the two countries, two commodity case the lower income elasticity of demand for primary commodities means that for a given growth of world income the balance of payments of primary-producing, developing countries will automatically deteriorate vis-a-vis the balance of payments of developed countries producing and exporting industrial goods.

Suppose that the income elasticity of demand for the exports of the developing countries is 0.8 and the growth of world income is 3.0 per cent: exports will then grow at 2.4 per cent. Now suppose that the income elasticity of demand for exports of developed countries 1.3 and growth of world income is 3.0 per cent; exports of developed countries will then grow at 3.9 per cent. Since there are only two sets of countries, the exports of developing countries are the imports of developed countries and the exports of developed countries are the imports of developing countries. Thus developing countries' grow at 2.4 per cent but imports grow at 3.9 per cent; developed countries exports grow at 3.9 per cent and imports 2.4 per cent. Starting from equilibrium, the balance of payments of the developing countries' automatically worsens while that of the developed countries shows a surplus. This has further repercussions on terms of trade. With imports growing faster than exports in developing countries, and balance of payments deteriorating, terms of trade will also deteriorate through depreciation of the currency, which may cause the balance of payment to deteriorate even more if imports and exports are price elastic.

Now we will consider per capita income growth between developing and developed countries. The growth rate of population is faster in developing countries; the growth of income must also be faster than in the developed countries if the per capita income growth rate is to remain same. But this will mean even faster growth rate of imports into developing countries and further more deterioration of terms of trade and consequently in balance of payments. And if the goal is to narrow the relative or absolute differences in per capita income between developed and developing countries, the balance of payment implications will be even more severe. In the previous example, we ignore the differences in population growth. It is easily seen that the price of balance of payments equilibrium is slower growth for the developing country.

If their exports are growing at 2.4 per cent , import growth must be constrained to 2.4 per cent, which means that with income elasticity of demand for imports 1.3 per cent, income growth in the developed countries must be restrained to 2.4/1.3 = 1.85 per cent for balance of payments equilibrium. In the absence of foreign borrowings to bridge the foreign exchange gap, or a change in the structure of the exports, the result of different income elasticities of demand for primary and manufactured products is slower growth in the primary producing countries – perpetuating the development gap. In the absence of protection, the only alternative is deliberate depreciation of the currency. This has several disadvantages. For one thing the price elasticities of exports and imports may not be right for foreign exchange earnings to be increased, and second, depreciation will encourage production in existing activities, the concentration on which contributed to the balance of payments difficulties in the first place.

There is certain equilibrium mechanisms in existence that may reverse the tendencies referred to, but they are likely to be weak and fairly slow in operation. First it cannot be assumed that the industrial structure of the developing remains same. Over time it is natural that the proportion of total resources employed in the production of manufactured goods should increase, decreasing the rate of increase of imports of manufactured goods. Second, assuming that money income and the population grow at the same rate in both sets of countries, if the terms of trade are deteriorating for the developing countries, then real per capita income cannot be growing so rapidly in the developing countries. Thus even with a high income elasticity of demand for imports in developing countries, the absolute increments in imports may eventually equal exports through a terms of trade effect.

Prebisch recognized this later equilibrating mechanism, but rejected reliance upon it because of the sacrifice of real growth that it clearly involves. For terms of trade and balance of payments reasons (which are connected), Prebisch therefore argued for the protection of certain domestically produced goods, and for monopoly exports pricing by developing countries to protect their interests. Prebisch's balance of payment argument reinforces the classical infant-industry and optimum tariff argument for protection. There are several benefits that Prebisch expected from protection:

- Protection would enable scarce foreign exchange to be rationed between different categories of imports, and could help to correct balance of payments disequilibrium resulting from a high income elasticity of demand for certain types of imports.

- It could help arrest the deterioration in the terms of trade by dampening down the demand for imports.
- It could provide the opportunity to diversify products and to start producing and exporting goods with a much higher income elasticity of demand in world market.

Recent Trends in the Terms of Trade

Primary Commodities

Whether the terms of trade have moved unfavourably against primary commodities and the developing countries is an empirical question. Prebisch originally suggested an average deterioration of the terms of trade for primary commodities between 1876 and 1938 of 0.9 per cent per annum. Work by Singer at the United Nations in 1949 also suggested a trend deterioration of 0.64 per cent per annum over the same period, and thus Prebisch Singer thesis of the declining terms of trade for primary commodities was born.

Developing Countries

The terms of trade of primary commodities relative to manufactures is not necessarily the same as the terms of trade of developing countries relative to industrial countries, relative to industrial countries, because both sets of countries export and import both types of goods (albeit in different ratios), but in practice there is likely to be a close overlap and parallel movement between the two. Researchers have looked at the export prices of developing countries, and also at the prices of exports from developing to developed countries relative to the prices of imports from developed countries into developing countries (both excluding fuel). In the first case the trend deterioration was 0.51per cent per annum; in the second case the relative deterioration was 0.93 per cent per annum.

Over the period 1955-89 a 1 per cent deterioration in the terms of trade of primary products translated into a 3 percent deterioration in the terms of trade for developing countries as a whole, although this would have been substantially greater for Africa and Latin America, which are more commodity-dependent than Asia It has been estimated by UNCTAD that terms of trade losses for developing countries as a whole were equivalent in the 1980s to a loss of nearly $300 billion of foreign exchange, equal to more than twice the net inflow of resources into developing countries in 1980.

Economists have also looked at the terms of trade of manufactures exported by developing countries relative to those of developed countries over the period 1970-87, and find a deterioration of approximately 1 per cent per annum. If this were the case, it would appear that the developing countries suffer double jeopardy. Not only do the price of their primary products decline relative to those of manufactured goods, but also the prices of their primary product decline relative to those of manufactured but also the prices of their manufactured exports decline relative to those of developed countries, reflecting, no doubt, the commodity composition of their exports their lower value added and lower income elasticity of demand in world markets.

From the point of view of development, measured by per capita income, the income terms of trade is perhaps the more relevant concept to consider than the barter terms of trade. It may well be, for instance, that the prices of exports fall relative to those of imports owing to increase efficiency in the exporting country, and this releases resources for furthers exports which subsequently expend more than proportionately to the fall in price. The barter terms of trade will have worsened, but development will be stimulated. It is also worth remembering that when a country devalues is currency a deliberately worsens its barter terms of trade in the hope that balance of payments will improve, providing scope for a faster growth of real income through rapid improvement in the income terms of trade. On the other hand, if demand for a county' exports inelastic, then a decline in the barter terms of trade will also mean a deterioration in the income terms of trade. In the long run, if world trade is buoyant, all countries can experience an improvement in their income through terms of trade. The question is not who the gainers are and who are the losers, as in the case of barter terms of trade, but are the relative rates of improvement in the income terms of trade?

Prebisch's Views on Structuralism

Roul Prebish tried to establish the intellectual machineries of structralist economics. Prebisch theory states that the global system was not a uniform market place with producers and suppliers freely making mutually beneficial contracts. In fact it was divided into powerful central economies and relatively weak peripheral economies, the issue of peripheral economies was addressed directly by the economics of structuralism while formal model mapping of orthodox economies was rejected by it. On this bases, Prebisch was actively involved in the newly established institutional mechanism which served to order the global system in the post, Second World War period in 1998, ECLA, the special economic commission for Latin America, was setup in United Nations, for which Prebisch was a key figure. It was only due to Prebisch effort that UNCTAD was ready to discuss the international economic relations linking industrialized and less developed countries.

Prebisch's principle was based on ideas of orthodox Ricardian. It was inspired by economy theory that international specialization conferred benefits upon all those who are involved in it. He stated that a preference for industrialization behind protective tariff barriers was favored in these economies. Prebisch argued that the orthodox theory condemned Latin American economies to a secondary and relatively declining position as primary product exporters. He rejected the argument in favor of international specialization. In addition to challenging the orthodox conception of Latin American economies with in the world economy mapping concurrent reworking of the explanations of the nature of peripheral economies. The market equilibrium model of new classicism is rejected in favor of an empiricist-style, pragmatic and problem oriented approach known as structuralism. It found that economies of Latin America should be analysis as a loosely integrated set of separate sectors. The new policy solution was to pursue national programs of industrialization behind protective tariff barriers.

Prebisch and Structuralism II

It was held that most Latin American countries were facing the problems of balance of payments and inflations. As a consequence, some of these countries entered into international monetary fund agreements to stabilize their economies. Most of the time, the IMF recommendations were indirect conflict with the policies being recommended by ECLA. The main constraint on growth was seen by the Structuralists it as of scarcity of foreign exchange. Latin American countries needed to plan their economic development and to increase the size of their markets through economic integration. Planning being new to most Latin American governments, ECLA provides both training and direct collaboration in the preparations of plans. Infect, a United Nation Institute, ILPES (Institute Latino Americano, be planificationeconomica Y social) was created in the early sixties to assist Latin American countries in the preparation of their development plans.

Prebisch became the first director of IELPS thus focusing the importance to planning in the early sixties. Along with the planning effort, ECLA also recommended that Latin American countries needed to move on to a second stage of imports substitution for this reason Prebisch concluded that further Import substitution would have to take place at reasonable level. Thus in the sixties, ECLA became the champion of regional economic integration. According to Prebisch, "Trade between Latin American countries forms only 10 percent of their total foreign trade and industrial exports are relatively very small by contrast with countries such as Italy, Japan , and other with similar income levels. All this had resulted in the splitting of the industrialization process into as many watertight compartments as there are countries, without the advantages of specialization and the economics of scale".

WTO and Developing Countries

About two thirds of the WTO's around 150 members are developing countries. They play an increasingly important and active role in the WTO because of their numbers, because they are becoming more important in the global economy, and because they increasingly look to trade as a vital tool in their development efforts. Developing countries are a highly diverse group often with very different views and concerns. The WTO deals with the special needs of developing countries in three ways:

- The WTO agreements contain special provisions on developing countries.
- The Committee on Trade and Development is the main body focusing on work in this area in the WTO, with some others dealing with specific topics such as trade and debt, and technology transfer.
- The WTO Secretariat provides technical assistance (mainly training of various kinds) for developing countries.

In the Agreements: More Time and Better Terms

The WTO agreements include numerous provisions giving developing and least developed countries special rights or extra leniency "special and differential treatment". Among these are provisions that allow developed countries to treat developing countries more favourably than other WTO members. The General Agreement on Tariffs and Trade (GATT, which deals with trade in goods) has a special section on Trade and Development which includes provisions on the concept of non-reciprocity in trade negotiations between developed and developing countries when developed countries grant trade concessions to developing countries they should not expect the developing countries to make matching offers in return. Both GATT and the General Agreement on

Trade in Services (GATS) allow developing countries some preferential treatment. Other measures concerning developing countries in the WTO agreements include:

- Extra time for developing countries to fulfil their commitments (in many of the WTO agreements)
- Provisions designed to increase developing countries' trading opportunities through greater market access (e.g. In textiles, services, technical barriers to trade)
- Provisions requiring WTO members to safeguard the interests of developing countries when adopting some domestic or international measures (e.g. In anti-dumping, safeguards, technical barriers to trade)
- Provisions for various means of helping developing countries (e.g. to deal with commitments on animal and plant health standards, technical standards, and in strengthening their domestic telecommunications sectors).

Legal Assistance: A Secretariat Service

The WTO Secretariat has special legal advisers for assisting developing countries in any WTO dispute and for giving them legal counsel. The service is offered by the WTO's Training and Technical Cooperation Institute. Developing countries regularly make use of it. Furthermore, in 2001, 32 WTO governments set up an Advisory Centre on WTO law. Its members consist of countries contributing to the funding, and those receiving legal advice. All least-developed countries are automatically eligible for advice. Other developing countries and transition economies have to be fee-paying members in order to receive advice.

Least-developed Countries: Special Focus

The least-developed countries receive extra attention in the WTO. All the WTO agreements recognize that they must benefit from the greatest possible flexibility, and better-off members must make extra efforts to lower import barriers on least-developed countries' exports. Since the Uruguay Round agreements were signed in 1994, several decisions in favour of least-developed countries have been taken. Meeting in Singapore in 1996, WTO ministers agreed on a "Plan of Action for Least-Developed Countries". This included technical assistance to enable them to participate better in the multilateral system and a pledge from developed countries to improved market access for least-developed countries' products. A year later, in October 1997, six international organizations the International Monetary Fund, the International Trade Centre, the United Nations Conference for Trade and Development, the United Nations Development Programme, the World Bank and the WTO launched the "Integrated Framework", a joint technical assistance programme exclusively for least-developed countries.

In 2002, the WTO adopted a work programme for least-developed countries. It contains several broad elements: improved market access; more technical assistance; support for agencies working on the diversification of least-developed countries' economies; help in following the work of the WTO; and a speedier membership process for least-developed countries negotiating to join the WTO. At the same time, more and more member governments have unilaterally scrapped import duties and import quotas on all exports from least-developed countries.

A 'Maison' in Geneva: Being Present is Important, but Not Easy for All

The WTO's official business takes place mainly in Geneva. So do the unofficial contacts that can be equally important. But having a permanent office of representatives in Geneva can be expensive. Only about one third of the 30 or so least-developed countries in the WTO have permanent offices in Geneva, and they cover all United Nations activities as well as the WTO. As a result of the negotiations to locate the WTO headquarters in Geneva, the Swiss government has agreed to provide subsidized office space for delegations from least-developed countries. A number of WTO members also provide financial support for ministers and accompanying officials from least-developed countries to help them attend WTO ministerial conferences.

Committees

Work specifically on developing countries within the WTO itself can be divided into two broad areas:

- Work of the WTO committees.
- Training for government officials (and others) by the WTO Secretariat as mandated by the committee.

Trade and Development Committee

The WTO Committee on Trade and Development has a wide-ranging mandate. Among the broad areas of topics it has tackled as priorities are: how provisions favouring developing countries are being implemented, guidelines for technical cooperation, increased participation of developing countries in the trading system, and the position of least-developed countries. Member countries also have to inform the WTO about special programmes involving trade concessions for products from developing countries, and about regional arrangements among developing countries. The Trade and Development Committee handles notifications of:

- Generalized System of Preferences programmes (in which developed countries lower their trade barriers preferentially for products from developing countries).
- preferential arrangements among developing countries such as MERCOSUR (the Southern Common Market in Latin America), the Common Market for Eastern and Southern Africa (COMESA), and the ASEAN Free Trade Area (AFTA).

Sub-committee on Least-Developed Countries

The Sub-committee on Least-Developed Countries reports to the Trade and Development Committee, but it is an important body in its own right. Its work focuses on two related issues:

- Ways of integrating least-developed countries into the multilateral trading system
- Technical cooperation. The sub-committee also examines periodically how special provisions favouring least-developed countries in the WTO agreements are being implemented.

The Doha agenda committees: The Doha Ministerial Conference in November 2001, added new tasks and some new working groups. The Trade and Development Committee meets in "special sessions" to handle work under the Doha Development Agenda. The ministers also set up working groups on Trade, Debt and Finance, and on Trade and Technology Transfer.

WTO Technical Cooperation

Technical cooperation is an area of WTO work that is devoted almost entirely to helping developing countries (and countries in transition from centrally-planned economies) operate successfully in the multilateral trading system. The objective is to help build the necessary institutions and to train officials. The subjects covered deal both with trade policies and with effective negotiation.

Training, seminars and workshops: The WTO holds regular training sessions on trade policy in Geneva. In addition, it organizes about 500 technical cooperation activities annually, including seminars and workshops in various countries and courses in Geneva. Targeted are developing countries and countries in transition from former socialist or communist systems, with a special emphasis on African countries. Seminars have also been organized in Asia, Latin America, the Caribbean, Middle East and Pacific. Funding for technical cooperation and training comes from three sources: the WTO's regular budget, voluntary contributions from WTO members, and cost-sharing either by countries involved in an event or by international organizations.

The present regular WTO budget for technical cooperation and training is 7 million Swiss francs. Extra contributions by member countries go into trust funds administered by the WTO Secretariat or the donor country. In 2004, contributions to trust funds totalled 24 million Swiss francs. A WTO Reference Centre programme was initiated in 1997 with the objective of creating a network of computerized information centres in least-developed and developing countries. The centres provide access to WTO information and documents through a print library, a CD-ROM collection and through the Internet to WTO websites and databases. The centres are located mainly in trade ministries and in the headquarters of regional coordination organizations. There are currently 140 reference centres.

Some Issues Raised

The Uruguay Round saw a shift in North-South politics in the GATTWTO system. Previously, developed and developing countries had tended to be in opposite groups, although even then there were exceptions. In the run up to the Uruguay Round, the line between the two became less rigid, and during the round different alliances developed, depending on the issues. The trend has continued since then. In some issues, the divide still appears clear in textiles and clothing, and some of the newer issues debated in the WTO, for example and developing countries have organized themselves into alliances such as the African Group and the Least-Developed Countries Group. In many others, the developing countries do not share common interests and may find themselves on opposite sides of a negotiation. A number of different coalitions among different groups of developing countries have emerged for this reason. The differences can be found in subjects of immense importance to developing countries, such as agriculture.

Developing Country Status at WTO

There are no WTO definitions of "developed" and "developing" countries. Members announce for themselves whether they are "developed" or "developing" countries. However, other members can challenge the decision of a member to make use of provisions available to developing countries.

The WTO Agreements contain special provisions which give developing countries special rights. These provisions are referred to as "Special and Differential Treatment" (S&D) provisions. The special provisions include:

- Longer time periods for implementing Agreements and commitments,
- Measures to increase trading opportunities for developing countries,
- Provisions requiring all WTO members to safeguard the trade interests of developing countries,
- Support to help developing countries build the capacity to carry out WTO work, handle disputes, and implement technical standards, and
- Provisions related to least-developed country (LDC) Members.

Benefits to Developing Countries in the WTO

- The Agreement Establishing the World Trade Organization (also known as "the WTO Agreement") specifies that international trade should benefit the economic development of developing and least-developed countries.
- General Agreement on Tariffs and Trade (GATT) gives developing countries the right to restrict imports, if doing so would promote the establishment or maintenance of a particular industry, or assist in cases of balance-of-payments difficulties.
- Part IV of the GATT includes provisions on the concept of non-reciprocal preferential treatment for developing countries, i.e. when developed countries grant trade concessions to developing countries they should not expect the developing countries to make matching offers in return. However, developing countries claim that Part IV has been without practical value as it does not contain any obligations for developed countries.

Issues

Recently, U.S. President had put pressure on the WTO to change how it designates developing countries, singling out China, with which the United States is engaged in a trade war, for unfairly getting preferential treatment. The United States also recently proposed, that in current and future negotiations, following should not invoke the self-declaration option:

- Members of the Organization for Economic Cooperation and Development (OECD)
- Members of the Group of 20 (G-20),
- High income countries as per the World Bank definition, or
- Countries that account for 0.5% or more of global merchandise trade.

In a rebuttal to the US approach, China, India, South Africa, and others submitted a proposal of their own. While reiterating that self-declaration is appropriate in the WTO context, they make the point that per capita indicators must be given top priority when assessing development levels. WTO members can consider the following steps to help integrate developing countries in global trade:

- Countries can decide to follow South Korea's example and not claim differentiated treatment, without the need to declare themselves "developed."
- Negotiations should provide for differentiated treatment taking into account the policy making challenges in developing countries without establishing permanent exemptions. These provisions should either be time-bound or have clear threshold and phase-out criteria, as in the WTO Agreement on Subsidies and Countervailing Measures.

Problems with Current U.S. Policy

Key Problems

- Washington has promoted free trade principles only in sectors that benefit the U.S. economy; in other sectors, like textiles, protectionism reigns.
- U.S. agricultural and patenting policies will not meet the food needs of a growing world population.
- Further liberalization in selected issues, old and new, will give Northern corporations more access to the resources of the South, thereby further debilitating the domestic economies of developing countries.

U.S. influence in the WTO has more often meant U.S. domination than responsible leadership. Instead of promoting beneficial goals for all, the U.S. is too often concerned with aggressively expanding its own markets. As much as domestic politics permit, it pursues a corporate-driven menu of liberalization that marginalizes the development needs of the poor. The inequities within the WTO are stark. Exports from developing countries continue to face significant market access impediments. Recent UN studies confirm that tariff peaks and tariff escalation still hamper developing country exports and their attempts to export new products such as beef, cigarettes, clothing, footwear, and wood articles.

To gain new market access in developing countries, the developed countries–acting in the interests of transnational corporations (TNCs) have rapidly imposed new agreements in telecommunications, information technology, and financial services. The Millennium Round talks (scheduled to commence in late 1999) will advance economic liberalization in both traditional and new sectors even further, contrary to the interests of developing countries. Washington has creatively interpreted WTO agreements to protect key industries. In textiles and clothing, the U.S. has selectively opened its markets, but this liberalization has proved of little benefit to developing nations. Similarly, the U.S. has misused the transitional safeguard measures designed to protect domestic industries from sudden increases in imports. It has also introduced its own Rules of Origin (rules used to identify where a textile or clothing product comes from), changing the conditions of competition and adding to the restrictions against the low-cost textile exports of other countries.

Using creative calculations and interpretations of the Agreement on Agriculture (intended to reduce domestic support and open up markets), the U.S. made a few relatively insignificant changes in its policies to comply with its commitments under the agreement. Thus the agreement institutionalizes subsidies to U.S. agroexporters while prohibiting developing country governments from introducing new forms of support for their own disadvantaged farmers. Under the WTO's "Green Box" policies, direct income subsidies to U.S. agroexporters are exempted from reductions on the specious grounds that they are "decoupled" from production or are somehow "non-trade distorting." The 1996 Farm Bill reduced direct payments to U.S. farmers, but it increased expenditure for export subsidies, thereby providing a net benefit to U.S. agroexporters.

U.S. led WTO agricultural policies will not meet the food needs of a growing world population. These policies promote food availability through trade and discourage countries from developing food self-sufficiency. Most developing countries are short of foreign exchange and cannot afford to buy food from the world market, despite low pricing and availability. New rules regarding plant information will have both agricultural and medical implications. The Trade Related Intellectual Property Rights Agreement (TRIPS) fiercely protects the rights of corporations but easily allows the shared knowledge of indigenous communities to be patented by others. When fully implemented, developing countries will lose billions in rent transfers to rich countries, as TNCs will continue to control virtually all the patents of developing countries.

TRIPS, which was strongly supported by the Clinton administration, provides the U.S. biotechnology industry with a very favorable legal environment. But biotechnology is not the answer to food shortages. Genetically modified seeds and plants (GMOs) raise costs for farmers and promote monocropping, which increases the incidence of diseases and pests, encourages the use of chemicals, and threatens the biodiversity and genetic purity of plant species. Furthermore, although the U.S. has not done long-term research on the health impact of GMOs, other countries are unable to halt their imports unless those countries can present scientific proof of harmful effects. In sum, TRIPS will be catastrophic for both health and sustainable agricultural systems in developing countries. Washington intends to introduce a broad spectrum of issues at the Millennium Round talks with the aim of enlarging the market for U.S. goods, services, and investments. High on the agenda will be the controversial Multilateral Agreement on Investment, which seeks to gain national treatment and rights for corporations operating in all countries. Small- and medium-sized enterprises in developing countries are unlikely to be able to withstand such competition, leading to the destruction of domestic economies in the LDCs.

Washington also intends to conclude an initial agreement on transparency in government procurement by the Third Ministerial Conference. Such an agreement will eventually bring about the full-scale opening of government procurement, a trillion dollar business, to foreign companies. Like the investment agreement, this will be detrimental for developing countries, whose enterprises will not be ready for such intense competition. It is precisely because the WTO is a multilateral avenue with an effective enforcement capability that the U.S. is putting an increasing number of issues under its auspices. But Washington fails to recognize that such liberalization policies often fail to promote the kind of sustainable international development that it purports to support.

Toward a New Foreign Policy

Key Recommendations

- The WTO should consider its top priority to be the development needs of its members.
- Sections of agreements that work to the disadvantage of developing countries must be changed, including agriculture, TRIPS, textiles, and the dispute settlement system.

- U.S. domination should end, decision-making should be democratic, and each government should consult regularly with its broader society on trade deliberations.

A change from a "trade creates wealth" perspective to one that stresses broad-based development is necessary if trade is to improve the living standards of the world's poor and ensure the long-term sustainability of resources. The WTO should emphasize greater self-sufficiency of economies nationally and regionally. Domestic markets, rather than foreign markets, should be the main stimulus of growth. Resources should be used sustainably to support local and national communities. People and the preservation of the environment, rather than capital, should be the primary objectives of any expansion of global trade. Countries must be free to choose if they want overseas investments and, if so, what kind of investments. They must also be able to decide on their tariff rates and other trade barriers in order to protect their industries, as the developed countries have been doing.

The U.S. should use its influence to encourage the WTO to become a democratic institution that provides space for a diversity of economic interests. Governments should hold regular consultations with their citizens and legislatures, especially when negotiations are in process. U.S. officials should insist that the working documents and minutes of WTO meetings be readily available to the public. Mechanisms must be developed that allow representatives of organized civil society sectors to participate in WTO rule-making processes, including intervening in the dispute settlement system. Certain practices and rules in the WTO must be changed to incorporate the realities and broader development agenda of the Southern members, including the following:

- All members should be equipped with the technical expertise and human resources to participate fully in the multilateral negotiations. Liberalization on the "fast track" must be stopped. Instead changes should be made to rules that effectively disadvantage the economies of developing countries.

- Decision-making in the WTO must involve all members. This has not been the case to date; instead the "quad" (U.S., EU, Japan, and Canada) has made many decisions on behalf of all.

- The dispute settlement system must consider the development needs of countries (especially the most vulnerable), not just whether free trade rules have been violated. For instance, in the recent dispute over the banana trade, the WTO ruled in favor of the U.S. over the EU's traditional arrangement of preferential access for Caribbean banana exporting countries–a ruling that may have devastating economic consequences for Caribbean economies that depend solely on banana exports.

- If developed and developing country farmers are to compete in the same markets, then the $280 billion in annual subsidies that developed countries provide to their farmers should be reduced to the negligible amounts developing countries provide. Otherwise, developing countries should be allowed to increase both their subsidies and their tariffs to protect their markets from the highly subsidized exports of the developed countries. Small farms in both developed and developing countries should be encouraged, not squeezed out–especially in developing countries, where farming is the source of livelihood for millions.

- TRIPS should be abolished and the control of intellectual property should be returned to the pre-Uruguay institutions such as the World Intellectual Property Organization. At minimum, seeds, plants, and drugs should be exempt from TRIPS in order to preserve basic health care and agricultural systems in developing countries. Currently, TRIPS even contradicts the principles of the Convention on Biodiversity.

- Developed countries should eliminate the tariff escalation on product chains of interest to developing countries. And if the WTO continues to force all countries down the liberalization path, the protected sectors in the U.S. must also be liberalized to open up new export markets for developing nations.
- The WTO should caucus with relevant UN agencies and use the international standards established in UN conventions to ensure that development goals are in concert with its trade agenda. The final test of the WTO's success is not the volume of world trade or the extent to which trade barriers have been lowered, but whether and to what extent living conditions in all nations–particularly the developing countries, which constitute three-fourths of its members–are improving.

Smart Cities

'Smart' communities are defined by the Canadian Federal Government (CFG) as those communities in which local leaders and stakeholders, by use of electronic networks and the Internet, are forming alliances and partnerships in order to innovate and extract new economic and social value. In this definition, emphasis is placed on the network deployment (transport and ICTs), but also on investments in human and social capital in support of sustainable community objectives and quality of life, by means of engaging social participation as well as user-specific technologies and community-building applications. The idea of a 'wired' city as the main development model and of 'connectivity' as a source of growth is brought to the forefront for increasing local prosperity and competitiveness. A broader definition, provided at the Smart Cities Workshop, defines a 'smart' city as 'a city that makes conscious effort to innovatively employ ICTs in support of a more inclusive, diverse and sustainable urban environment', a definition that is also adopted by the California Institute for Smart Communities. An alternative approach for defining 'smart' communities' is to place placing emphasis on the importance of social and environmental capital in urban development. This implies communities whose citizens are taught to learn, adapt and innovate. It has a strong focus on social inclusion and on participation in community affairs and decision-making processes in order to reach social and environmental objectives.

The terms 'community informatics', 'virtual community', digital community', and 'smart community network', used by various researchers, seem to have very close meanings to the CFG definition. 'Networked communities', on the other hand, relates to communities that have deployed digital broadband capability and make maximum use of it on behalf of their citizens, targeting economic development, organizational performance and high quality of living. 'Community networks' are defined as publicly controlled networks, at the service of the community, namely, individuals who use the network for communicating with friends, playing games, acquiring information, obtaining training etc.; and organizations running a variety of work tasks through the network. An 'intelligent community', on the other hand, is a community that perceives broadband communication services as a vital new collaborative opportunity for economic growth and social welfare. The distinctive attribute of such communities is the view of local users of ICT networks not as simple customers and consumers, but also as 'producers and creators of content, products and services'. At least five different descriptions can be encountered for 'intelligent cities', as follows:

- Intelligent cities are meant as virtual reconstructions of cities or virtual cities. The term has been broadly used as an equivalent to 'digital city', 'information city', 'wired city', 'telecity', 'knowledge-based city', 'electronic communities', 'electronic community spaces', 'flexicity', 'teletopia', 'cyberville', covering a wide range of electronic and digital applications relating to digital spaces of communities and cities.
- World Foundation for 'smart' communities defines 'intelligent' cities as 'smart' cities which, based on the adoption and use of ICTs, are paving a 'smart' development. This implies a conscious effort to use ICTs to transform life and work within a certain region (California Institute for Smart Communities 2001).
- 'Intelligent' cities were also defined as intelligent environments with embedded ICTs, targeting the creation of interactive spaces that bring computation into the physical world. From this perspective, 'intelligent' cities (or more generally 'intelligent' spaces) refer to physical environments in which ICTs and sensor systems disappear as they become embedded into physical objects and the surroundings in which we live, travel, and work.
- Along the same lines, 'intelligent' cities (communities, clusters, regions) were defined as multi-layer territorial systems of innovation that bring together knowledge-intensive activities, institutions for cooperation in learning and innovation, and digital spaces for communication and interaction, in order to maximize the problem-solving capability of the city. The distinctive characteristic, in this respect, is highly innovative performance, as innovation and solving new problems are the main features of intelligence.

The goal behind 'smart' city development is the provision of qualitative and innovative services to the public, to the economic activities, and also to the visitors of a city, together with the production of a safe, pleasant and inclusive urban environment. To this end, the development of a 'smart city' presupposes the proper integration of three layers:

- Physical layer, incorporating human capabilities and knowledge-intensive activities.
- Institutional layer that incorporates proper institutional mechanisms for social cooperation towards knowledge and innovation development.
- Digital infrastructure layer that incorporates a range of ICT infrastructure, tools, applications and content in support of both individual and collective action.

The concepts of 'smart' and 'intelligent' cities are treated in the available literature as being quite relative. However, in 'smart' cities, the emphasis is placed more on embedded systems, sensors and interactive media that support knowledge diffusion and interaction. 'Intelligent' cities, on the other hand, seem to rely more on collective/collaborative intelligence, innovation systems and web-based collaborative spaces. In both cases, the focus is on the integration of the three dimensions of urban space i.e. the physical, institutional and digital dimension.

Going 'smart': Critical factors

In its effort to explore the best practices amongst the world's Intelligent Communities adapting to the demands of the Broadband Economy, The Intelligent Community Forum (ICF), a think tank that studies the economic and social developments of 21st Century communities, defines five critical success factors for the creation of 'smart/intelligent communities', which are also used as evaluation criteria for assessing and rewarding the efforts undertaken by various cities towards 'going smart'. These are as follows:

- Deployment of broadband communication infrastructure, used for the evaluation of the local capacity for digital communication. It should be noted that connectivity choices made by a 'smart' city need to be evaluated through both the prism of that city's local vision, and the affordability of costs incurred for the users.
- Effective education and training of local labour force, strengthening high rates of adoption/ use of ICT infrastructure. This results in increasing the capacity of this workforce to perform knowledge-intensive activities, while transforming 'individuals' into 'citizens', and enhancing the potential of participation in knowledge creation processes.
- Policies and programs that promote 'digital democracy' by bridging the digital divide among different groups of society, ensuring that everyone will reap the benefits of the broadband revolution (i.e. digital inclusion);
- Innovation capacity, assessing the level of creation of an innovation-friendly environment that attracts highly creative people and businesses.
- Marketing of 'smart' communities as advantageous places for living, working and running a business, which leverages the community's potential to attract talented employment and investments.

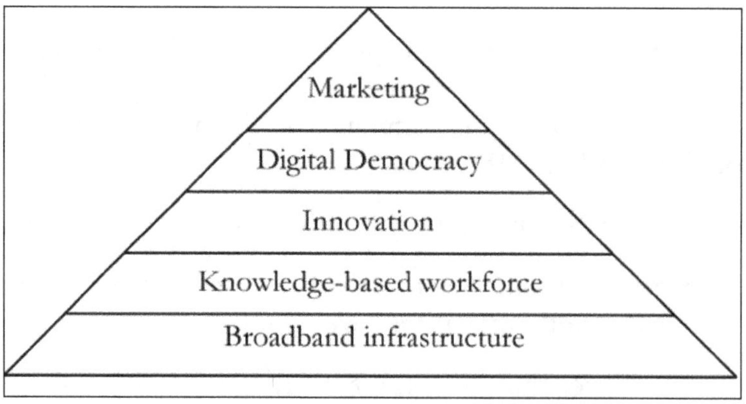

Critical success factors for cities 'going smart'.

It should be noted that although technology forms the basis for community interaction, it is in fact the last factor that worries leaders of smart communities, as it constitutes a success factor that changes rather quickly. As experience from world pioneer smart cities shows, of critical importance are the rest of the factors presented in figure above, as well as effective policies to challenge local people to use broadband. The key issue, in this respect, is not 'what' type of technology is available, but how 'effectively' this technology is used.

Digital Dimensions of 'smart cities'

The 'smart' city can offer local citizens and businesses a range of tools and ICT applications that can steer innovative behaviour. These applications create virtual environments, supporting both individual choices and group communication-collaboration options. The whole range of applications can be classified in the following groups:

- e-Information: Refers to the provision of various types of information to a wide range of audiences, e.g. citizens, visitors, businesses, institutions.
- e-Business: Refers to the potential offered to businesses for the exploitation of e-business opportunities, adoption of business-to-business (B2B) and business-to-client (B2C) interaction models, adoption of new innovative strategies for e-marketing their products etc.
- e-Marketing: Supports a range of e-marketing possibilities for a city/municipality in the promotion of the city's image (products, archaeological sites, cultural assets etc.).
- e-Government: Refers to the provision, in a more effective way, of services to citizens, businesses, and governmental institutions (G2C, G2B and G2G interaction).
- e-Innovation: refers to the potential for e-cooperation and on-line development of new products.
- e-Participation: Refers to the increasing potential for e-inclusion of citizens, thus strengthening active participation in the decision-making processes (e-Democracy).

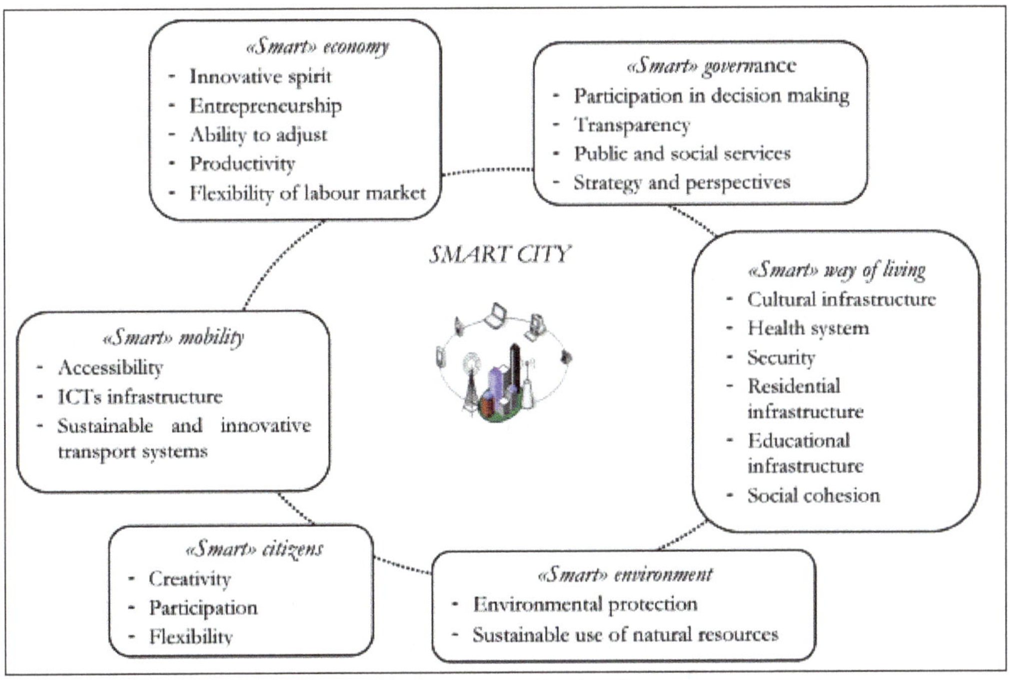

Dimensions of smart city development.

Based on a search of 'smart cities' literature, it is evident that this term does not carry a holistic meaning gained by the integration of certain city attributes/functions. Instead, it is used to describe innovative aspects available to a city that are based on the adoption/use of ICTs. These aspects can be associated with the economy, local population, governance, citizens' participation etc. With regard to the economy, a 'smart' city can be a city hosting a 'smart' industry (i.e. an industry that is either a producer or a heavy user of innovative ICTs,) or a city which develops highly ICT-based business parks in its territory. It is also used to describe a city with 'smart' inhabitants (i.e. highly educated local human resources or a city where G2C (government to citizen) interaction is heavily based on ICTs (e-governance); or a city exhibiting a strong, ICT-enabled, public participation in local decision-making processes (e-democracy). Moreover, it may refer to a city which makes use of modern ICTs in urban processes in order to improve the quality of life for its inhabitants (e.g. 'smart' transport systems in support of urban traffic management). Finally, the term is used to describe a city that makes use of ICTs to improve services in several fields, e.g. security/safety, health, 'green' urban development, or sustainable energy consumption.

In the European Smart Cities Project (Vienna University of Technology), six dimensions of 'smartness' were identified, referring to the economy, local citizens, governance, mobility, environment and way of life. These are shown in figure above, together with a range of indicative issues raised within each category.

'Smart cities' and Community Development

Getting access to effective and affordable ICT systems is crucial for reaping the benefits of communication and driving community development processes in the broadband economy context. This places new challenges in front of planners and regional policy-makers regarding the bridging of the 'digital divide' at community level, and coping with ICT illiteracy. The UNESCO Report (1980) entitled 'Many voices one world', stresses the need for a 'democratization of information flow', implying more equal access to information for larger groups of society, together with the need for policy action towards this end, dealing with the development of high-quality broadband connectivity. It also articulates and legitimizes the idea of 'the basic human right to communicate' and be informed about whatever might affect daily life in order to support autonomous decision-making. Moreover, emphasis is placed on the role of citizens and stakeholder groups as carriers of change at the community level, based on participation and access to information.

Today the scope of citizens' and stakeholders' right to information has been considerably broadened, in alignment with the huge development of ICTs and their applications that has given rise to a further increase in interaction and networking potential both between and among different groups of society, thus contributing to a more equitable share of knowledge and information, and a relative shift of power relationships affecting decision-making processes at the community level.

A crucial objective of the 'smart' cities' perspective relates to community development, seeking to empower local individuals and groups by providing them with the necessary skills and information to affect changes in their own communities. Community development represents a process of change, where participation and collective action is of crucial importance. It implies a community where individuals are assisted to acquire skills and competences and to develop their own views and attitudes, a requirement for their democratic participation in a wide range of community problems. Community development creates the foundation for building communities that are based on justice, equality, mutual respect and cooperation; it also forms the cornerstone for the creation of relationships and networking, thus strengthening bonds and understanding among local citizens, as well as the creative exploitation of local knowledge and experience. Moreover, it is considered as a step for influencing power relationships and their role on policy decisions, by changing the position of ordinary people and their potential to affect local decision making.

The key aspects of community development, are presented in figure below, where the role that 'smart cities' can play towards this end is also shown.

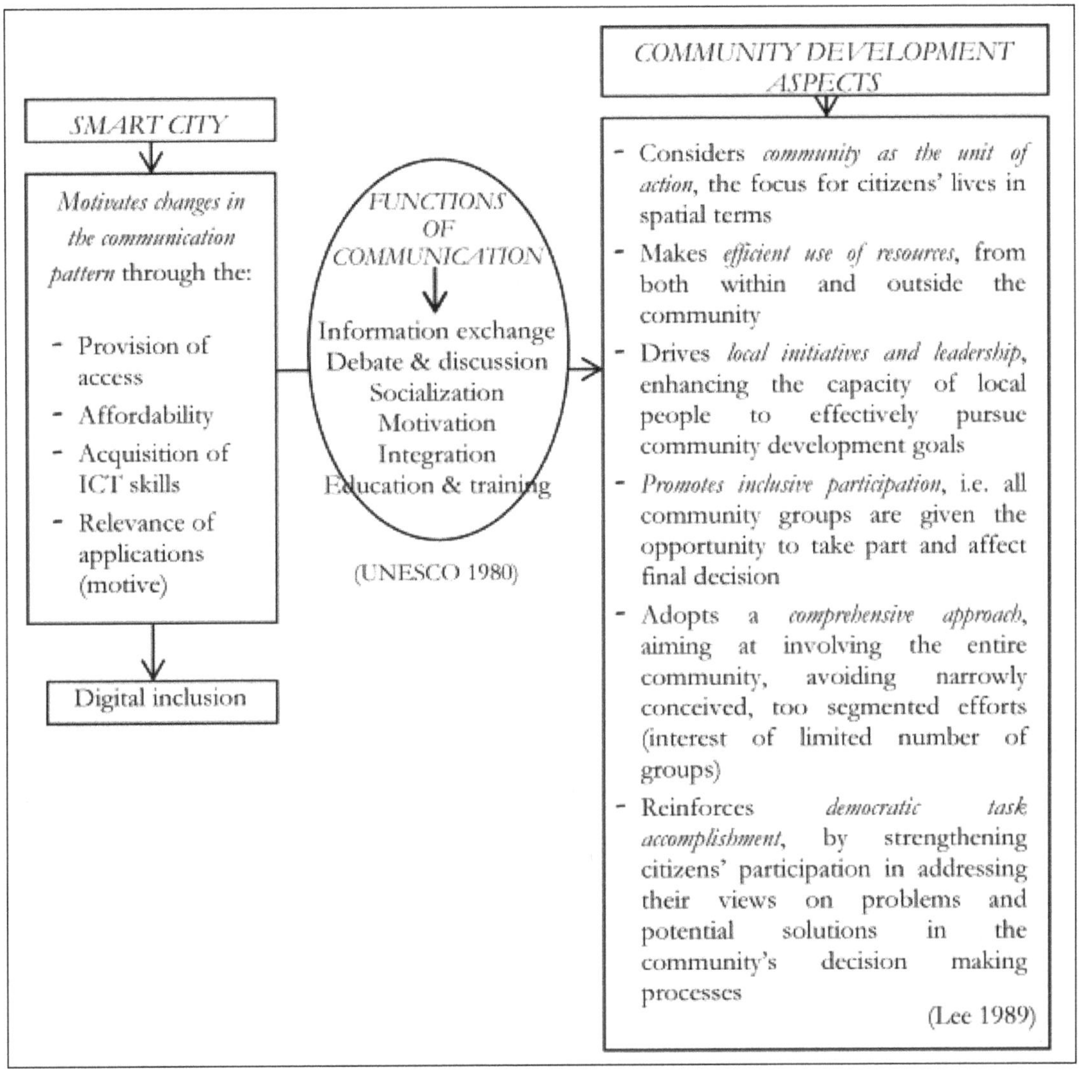

Smart cities for community development.

Dual Gap Analysis

Dual gap analysis which is also called two gap analysis was made in the context of foreign aid or foreign borrowing of capital by developing countries required for achieving rapid economic development. The question raised was what constrains acceleration of investment which is required to achieve a certain target growth rate of economic development in the developing countries. The first important factor mentioned in this connection is the domestic saving rate in the country on which investment depends. Therefore, Harrod-Domar model which was generally used for development planning laid stress on the saving rate (and therefore investment) and capital-output ratio, as the two factors that determine economic development. Thus, according to Harrod-Domar model,

$$g = s/k$$

Where, g is the growth rate of GDP, s the saving rate of the economy (i.e., ratio of saving to national income) and k is the capital-output ratio. Capital-output ratio (which is the reciprocal of output-capital ratio) in this model is taken as given and rate of investment and therefore rate of economic growth depends on the domestic saving rate of the economy.

However, Harrod-Domar model was a closed economy model and foreign trade was not incorporated in it. However, every developing country even if it followed import-substitution development strategy needed imports of certain capital goods and raw materials which they could not manufacture themselves and required them for their industrialisation. Therefore, in Harrod-Domar model foreign trade was to be introduced so as to explain the role of foreign exchange required to import capital and intermediate goods and raw materials needed for industrial growth. Accordingly, the extension of Harrod-Domar model was made by adding the term for foreign trade balance (namely, imports minus exports) as per cent of national income. The extended Harrod-Domar model was written as,

$$g = \frac{s}{k} + \frac{b}{k}$$

$$\text{where, } b = \frac{\text{Imports} - \text{Exports}}{\text{National Income}}$$

The significance of this extended version of Harrod-Domar model was that the growth of exports of developing countries was limited, imports could exceed exports only if foreign aid (both grants and concessional loans) or private foreign investment was available to enable the developing countries to get the required foreign exchange for importing capital goods and industrial raw materials so that more investment than domestic saving can occur to achieve target growth rate. However, even if domestic saving could be raised to achieve the required investment for attaining target growth rate, the foreign exchange needed to import essential capital goods and raw materials would not be there as the domestic savings and foreign exchange (provided by foreign aid and foreign investment) are not perfect substitutes of one another. Thus, the higher domestic saving would not make up the deficiency of foreign exchange to import the required Capital goods and industrial raw materials more than value of exports.

For example, for imports of capital goods and industrial raw materials we require dollars and not rupees. And the dollars can be obtained by either increasing exports or through foreign aid or foreign investment. This implies foreign exchange gap or bottleneck as distinct from saving gap to achieve the desired growth rate. Since it was not possible for the developing countries in the initial stages of development to achieve sufficient growth in exports (except the oil producing Arab countries), foreign exchange gap was faced by them. It was therefore pointed out that to meet the foreign exchange gap, foreign aid or foreign investment was needed to help them achieve the desired rate of economic development in the fifties and sixties of the 20th century.

Now, it is important to note that in view of lack of substitutability between domestic saving and foreign exchange resources economic development could be constrained by whatever factor, domestic saving or foreign exchange reserves, is the most binding factor. Foreign capital (both in the form of foreign aid or borrowed funds) can play an important role in supplementing domestic resources in order to relieve both domestic saving constraint and foreign exchange constraint. Therefore, this was called dual gap analysis of foreign assistance by Chenery and Strout. It was argued by them that the most developing countries either face lack of domestic saving to finance the required investment to achieve the desired rate of economic growth or shortage of foreign exchange required to import necessary capital goods and raw materials for industrialisation.

Besides, it was generally assumed by the exponents of two-gap analysis that the two gaps were unequal in size and were independent of each other, that is, there did not exists any substitutability between domestic saving and foreign exchange. We explain below these two gaps in some detail:

- Saving Gap or Saving Constraint.
- Foreign Exchange Gap.

Saving Gap or Saving Constraint

The implication of the dual gap analysis that either of the two gaps will be binding for any developing country at any particular point of time. The saving gap is said to be binding or dominant when domestic savings are inadequate to support the desired rate of economic growth though it has adequate foreign exchange earnings for importing the necessary capital goods and raw materials. Given the assumption of full employment or capacity output, the shortage of saving can be viewed as lack of productive resources such as manpower or other productive resources in the economy for being used for increasing investment to achieve higher growth rate, though the adequate foreign exchange resources are available and are not being used fully. In such a situation saving-gap constraint implies that the excess foreign exchange might be used for importing luxury consumer goods rather than capital goods and industrial raw materials for bringing about higher industrial growth rate.

Todaro and Smith therefore rightly say, if, for example, the savings gap is dominant, this would indicate that the economy is operating at foil employment and not using all of its foreign exchange earnings. It may have enough foreign exchange to purchase additional capital goods from abroad but there is not enough excess domestic about or other productive resources to carry out additional investment projects. As a result, 'excess' foreign exchange, including foreign aid, might be spent on the importation of luxury consumption goods. Such a country is said to have a shortage of productive resources which from a different viewpoint can be regarded as a shortage in saving. Thus, in such a case a developing economy is said to be incapable of absorbing foreign exchange for purposes of economic growth.

It is worth mentioning that such a saving gap was faced by oil-exporting countries of Middle East in the 1970s when they suddenly had a flush of petro-dollars due to rise in oil prices by OPEC. These petro-dollars were spent by these countries for importing luxury consumer goods rather than using them for additional domestic investment. However, in later years they realised the importance of their petro-dollars which they started using for buying capital goods and hiring manpower from abroad. In this way they were able to overcome their domestic saving gap by using their foreign exchange earnings. This means saving gap countries do not need foreign aid to increase their investment for attaining higher growth rate.

Foreign Exchange Gap

On the contrary the saving-gap countries, the countries facing foreign exchange gap cannot overcome it by using their excess domestic saving. Therefore, for them foreign exchange gap is binding for achieving a desired rate of economic growth. In their case foreign exchange resources are inadequate for supporting higher rate of economic growth that is permitted by their domestic saving rate. Most of the developing countries are assumed to fall in this category as they face a situation where the foreign exchange gap is binding. These countries have enough domestic saving or productive resources such as labour and other inputs but lack adequate foreign exchange resources to import capital and intermediate goods, such as machines, oil, certain industrial raw materials which they cannot produce themselves. In such a situation due to lack of complementary foreign exchange resources, a certain part of domestic savings may remain unutilised.

The availability of domestic savings or resources would permit them to undertake new investment projects if they receive foreign capital inflows through foreign aid or through FDI and FIIs so that they can import new capital and intermediate goods (including oil and petroleum products).

It is important to mention here a confusion which usually arises because in national income accounting of an open economy such as ours saving-investment gap is said to be equal to import-export gap (i.e., current account balance). If this were so, then question arises where does the problem lie? We state below the national income account identity of an open economy,

$$Y = C + I + X - M$$

Where, Y stands for national income, C for consumption, I for investment, X for exports and M for imports. (Note that both exports and imports include both goods and services),

$$Y - C = I + X - M$$

Since $Y - C$ = national saving(S)

Therefore, $S = I + X - M$

$$\text{or } I - S = M - X$$

Thus the above equation $I - S = M - X$ shows that saving-investment gap equals import-export gap. How does it happen? As a matter of fact, the above national income identity is only in accounting or ex-post sense and not in ex-ante or intended sense. Despite the trade deficit (or current account deficit) this identity will hold good. This is because import-export gap is somehow financed either by foreign capital inflows which may occur either through commercial borrowing or foreign assistance or private capital inflows through FDI and FIIs or ultimately by withdrawal from accumulated foreign exchange reserves of the past years held by the Central Bank of a country.

Thus, the real problem remains how to relieve foreign exchange gap to undertake necessary additional investment which requires import of capital goods and raw materials. In fact, it was in this context that dual gap theory was used to show the crucial importance of foreign aid and other forms of capital flows to finance a deficit in the current account balance of payments (that is, the excess of imports of goods and services over their exports).

A Critical Appraisal of Dual Gap Theory

Two-gap theory was put forward to bring out the crucial role of foreign assistance to relieve foreign exchange gap faced by developing countries. Of course foreign aid has been helpful for accelerating economic growth in developing countries but it has been often tied to development projects in which donor countries were interested. It has been rightly asserted by Bruton that even developing countries which pursued import-substitution development strategy.

Dual gap analysis overemphasized the lack of substitutability between saving and foreign exchange. As the oil-rich Arab countries used their own foreign exchange resources to buy both manpower and capital goods from abroad to relieve their shortage of domestic savings. Further, if you can cut down consumption of some goods which have export potential (and therefore save more) the foreign exchange earnings from exports so made can be used to import capital goods and raw materials for their development. The dual gap model underplayed the export potential of developing countries. Therefore, after the mid-seventies of the last century, the emphasis was shifted from "aid" to "foreign trade," Many countries such as Japan, South Korea, Taiwan and Singapore by adopting export-led growth strategies succeeded in achieving higher economic growth without much foreign aid.

Payments and Tariff Protection

The principal tool for the analysis of the monetary aspects of international trade is the balance of payments settlement.

Concept and Uses of Balance of Payments

Balance of payments (BOP) is a systematic record of all international economic transactions, visible and invisible, of a country during a given period usually a year. In other words, the statement is a device for recording all the economic transactions within a given period between the residents of a country and the residents of other countries. The BOP of a country, technically speaking, always 'balances'. Such equality in the debit and credit sides of the BOP, known as equilibrium, has no economic significance. It simply results from the double entry book-keeping procedure which is used to record the transactions. The analysis of the BOP can be done in terms of its two major sub-divisions, Current account, and Capital account.

- Current Account: The current account can be broken in to two parts, viz. one, balance of trade, and two, balance of invisibles. The balance of trade (BOT) deals only with exports and imports of merchandise (or visible items). The balance of invisibles (BOI) shows the net receipts on account of invisibles. These include the remittances, net service payments, etc. It is not necessary that BOT should always balance; more often than not it will show either a surplus or a deficit. Similarly, the BOI will always show either a surplus or a deficit. A surplus on BOT may be matched with a surplus or deficit on BOI. If the surplus on BOI equals the deficit on BOT, the current account will show a net balance. But then there is no reason why these two balances should always be equal, again, always in opposite directions. As a matter of fact, the balance on current account can always show a deficit or a surplus. A surplus on current account leads to an acquisition of assets or repayment of debts previously contracted, and a deficit involves withdrawal of previously accumulated assets or is met by borrowings.

- Capital Account: The capital account presents transfers of money and other capital items and changes in country's foreign assets and liabilities resulting from the transactions recorded in the current account. The deficit on the current account and on account of capital transactions can be financed by external assistance (loans and grants), borrowings from the International Monetary Fund and allocation of the Special Drawing Rights. Uses: The BOP account provide a link between the increase in gross external debt and the portfolio and spending decisions of the economy.

Uses: The BOP account provide a link between the increase in gross external debt and the portfolio and spending decisions of the economy.

Thus, increase in gross external debt = Current account deficit – direct and long-term portfolio capital changes + increases in official reserve + other private capital outflows:

The above equation shows that an increase in external debt can have three broad sources:

- Current account deficits not financed by long-term capital inflows.
- Borrowing to finance a reserve build-up, and iii) private outflows of capital.

BOP and Developing Economies

It is well-known in development economics that developing economies invariably start as debtor economies. In the process of development itself these economies have to import a great deal of capital goods, consumer goods, food and raw materials, and spares and components. They also have to import some new technologies and hence, the total exchange outgo cannot be matched by export earnings. But it is expected that soon, as the new capital goods and technologies begin to become effective and their products are directed towards exports, export goods and services become competitive in cost and quality. In that case, the volume of exports expands and, in due course, begins to overtake exports. A developing economy then moves on from being a debtor country to a balanced one in terms of BOP and, finally, becomes a creditor country exporting more than it imports and giving credit to buyers. Thus, from being a net debtor in the beginning, it becomes a net creditor in the end and, in fact, begins to invest abroad rather than have others bending to and investing in it.

Tarrifs and Effective Protection

More generally, governments do not adhere to free trade despite the strong case for the efficiency and welfare gains from trade that has been clearly established and accepted. Policymakers have proven very resourceful in generating different devices for restricting the free flow of goods and services. Among these, the most important are import tariffs. Tariffs, generally speaking, are of two types, specific tariff, and ad valorem tariff.

- A specific tariff is an import duty that assigns a fixed monetary (rupees) tax per physical unit of the good imported. The total import tax bill is levied in accordance with the number of units coming into the importing country and not according to the price or value of the imports. Tax authorities can collect specific tariffs with ease because they need to know only the physical quantity of imports coming into the country, not their monetary value. However, specific tariff has a fundamental disadvantage as an instrument of protection for domestic producers because its protective value varies inversely with the price of the import.

- The ad valorem tariff is levied as a constant percentage of the monetary value of 1 unit of the imported good. Thus, if the ad valorem tariff is 10 per cent, an imported good with a world price of \$ 100 will have \$ 10 tax added as the import duty. If the price rises to \$ 200 because of inflation, the import levy rises to \$ 20.

  Although the ad valorem tariff preserves the protective value of the trade interference for home producers as prices increase, there are difficulties with this tariff instrument because customs inspectors need to make a judgment on the monetary value of the imported good. Knowing this fact, the seller of the good is tempted to under-value the good's price on invoices in order to reduce the tax burden. On the other hand, customs officials may deliberately overvalue a good to counteract undervaluation or to increase the level of protection and tariff revenue. Nevertheless, ad valorem tariffs have come into widespread use.

Effective Tariff Rate

An issue relating to trariffs concerns the choice of the appropriate tariff rate when evaluating the impact of tariffs. The issue involves the distinction between the nominal tariff rate on a good and the effective tariff rate, more commonly known as the effective rate of protection (ERP). The nominal rate is simply the rate listing in a country's tariff schedule, whether it is an ad valorem tariff or a specific tariff that can be converted to an ad valorem equivalent by dividing the specific tariff amount per unit by the price of the good. The ERP is defined as the percentage change in the value added in an industry because of the imposition of a tariff structure by the country rather than the existence of free trade. When using the ERP we are concerned about the extent to which "value added" in the domestic import-competing industry is altered by the existence of the whole tariff structure. The ERP can be illustrated with a numerical example.

Consider a situation in which good F is the final good and goods A and B are intermediate inputs used in making F. Assume that A and B are the only intermediate inputs and that 1 unit each of A and B is used in producing 1 unit of the final good F. Intermediate goods A and B can be either imported or produced in their country but compete with imports and thus have their prices influenced by the tariffs on the competing imports. Suppose that, under free trade, the price of the final good (P_F) is \$ 1,000 and the prices of the inputs are P_A = \$ 500 and PB = \$ 200. In this free trade situation, the value added is \$ 1,000 – (\$ 500 + \$ 200) = \$ 1000 – \$ 700 = \$ 300. B Now consider a situation where protective tariffs exist: a prime mark next to a price (P') indicates a tariff-protected price. Suppose that the tariff rate (t_F) on the final good is 10 per cent and that the tariff on input A (t_A) is 5 per cent and on input B (t_B) it is 8 per cent. If we assume that the country is a small country then the domestic prices of the goods with the tariffs in place are,

P'_F =\$ 1000 + 0.10 (\$ 1000) = \$ 1000 + \$ 100 = \$ 1100

P'_A = \$ 500 + 0.05 (\$ 500) = \$ 500 + \$ 25 = \$525

P'_B = \$ 200 + 0.08(\$ 200) = \$ 200 + \$ 16 = \$ 216

The value added in industry F under protection is \$ 1,100 – (\$ 525 + \$ 216) = \$ 1,100 – \$ 741 = \$ 359. The industry has experienced an increase in its value added because of the tariffs, and therefore the factors of production working in industry F are able to receive higher returns than under free trade. There is thus an economic incentive for factors of production in other industries to move into industry F. Since the effective rate of protection is the percent change in the value added when moving from free trade to protection, the ERP in this example is,

$$\frac{\text{Value added under protection} - \text{Value added with free trade}}{\text{Value added with free trade}}$$

$$= \frac{VA' - VA}{VA} = \frac{\text{Rs.}359 - \text{Rs.}300}{\text{Rs.}300}$$

$$= 0.197, \text{ or } 19.7\%$$

Thus, the factors of production in industry F have benefited from the tariffs, although consumers have lost. A more common formula for calculating the ERP for any industry j utilizing inputs designated as i is:

$$ERP_J = \frac{t_j - \sum_i a_{ij} t_j}{1 - \sum_i a_{ij}}$$

Where a_{ij} represents the free-trade value of input i as a percentage of the free-trade value of the final good j, t_j and t_i represent the tariff rates on the final good and on any input i, respectively, and Σ_I means that we are summing over all the inputs. In the example, the a_{ij} for input A is \$ 500/\$ 1000 or 0.50, and the value of the a_{ij} for input B is \$ 200/\$ 1000 or 0.20. This method of calculating the ERP has the advantage of illustrating three general rules about the relationship between nominal rates and effective rates of protection. These rules are as follows:

- If the nominal tariff rate on the final good is higher than the weighted-average nominal tariff rate on the inputs, then the ERP will be higher than the nominal rate on the final good.
- If the nominal tariff rate on the final good is lower than the weighted-average nominal tariff rate on the inputs, then the ERP will be lower than the nominal rate on the final good.
- If the nominal tariff rate on the final good is equal to the weighted average nominal tariff rate on the inputs, then the ERP will be equal to the nominal rate on the final good.

Overall, the nominal tariff rate is useful for assessing the price impact of tariffs on consumers. For producers, however, the effective note is more useful because factors tend to flow toward industries with relatively higher ERPs. In the assessment of development prospects and economic planning in the developing countries, a strong case can be made for ERPs as analytical tools, even more so than nominal rates of protection.

Project Evaluation and UNIDO Guidelines

Project level evaluation covers only individual projects but programme level evaluation includes comprehensive evaluation applied to such groups of projects as those that share the same overall goal and development issues. It is also directed by a set of projects under a specific-cooperation schemes. Programme level evaluation is classified into two types as follows:

- Country Program Evaluation: This comprehensive evaluation examines the overall effects of a project on the development of a targeted country across projects.
- Thematic Evaluation: This evaluation looks at a number of projects by focusing on specific sectors, issues (environment, poverty, gender, peace building etc.). It also considers effective approaches and methods to implement projects focusing on the specific theme.

Evaluation Types by Stages during the Project Cycle

Project level evaluation is classified into four types conducted at different stages during the project cycle:

- Ex-ante evaluation or planned evaluation: It is conducted on a Project request by a recipient country. It involves a study of the project to determine its necessity as well as its conformity.
- Mid-term evaluation: It is conducted at the mid-point of projects. It aims at examining the achievements and process of the project, focusing on the efficiency and relevance among the five evaluation criteria. Based upon its results, the original project plan may be revised.
- Terminal Evaluation: Terminal evaluation is performed upon completion of a project, focusing on its efficiency, effectiveness and sustainability.
- Ex-Post Evaluation: Ex-Post Evaluation is conducted after a certain period has passed since the completion of a target project and it is conducted with emphasis on the impact and sustainability of the project.

There are three phases in evaluation:

- Assessment of the project performance.
- Value judgment based on the five evaluation criteria.
- Making recommendations, drawing lessons learned and providing feedback.

Evaluation study basically consists of the following six steps:

- Confirmation of the evaluation's purpose.

- Organisation of information on a target project.
- Making plans for the implementation of the evaluation.
- Collection and analysis of data.
- Interpretation of data and putting the result together.
- Reporting evaluation results.

1. Evaluation as a Management Tool: Evaluation is a practical tool for effectively managing a project. It provides all stakeholders throughout all levels and stages of project management with information about the process, such information includes what the needs of a target society are, whether a project is being carried out as planned, how a project is affecting a target society or what the factors that affect project management are.

2. Framework of Evaluation: Evaluation is the act of making a value judgment backed up by evidence of recommendations and lessons learned to the future operation is essential.

Three Phases of Project Evaluation

- Assessing the Performance of a Project Results, implementation process and causal relationships: Three kinds of assessment are indispensable for analyzing the actual situation and the performance of the project. Measurement of results is to see what is achieved in a project and to what extent. Examination of implementation process is to analyze what is happening in the process towards its achievement and how it affects the performance, lastly, examination of casual relationship is to examine whether the project performance resulted from project intervention by looking at casual relationships between the project and whatever effects (in care of ex-ante evaluate).

  Theory Failure and Implementation Failure: Theory failure refers to finding out a problem in casual relationship at the planning phase, while implementation failure refers to a problem in the implementation process of a project. Theory failure implies that it is theoretically impossible to cause effect and achieve project objectives as expected even after project implementation. In that care, no effects might be observed even though outputs are delivered as planned. Theory failure may indicate that there was a problem in the original project plans.

On the other hand, implementation failure implies that there is a cause of failure in the project implementation (inputs, activities, outputs and internal conditions etc.) or management system. It is important to distinguish the two types of failure and analyze them respectively. This distinction is based on a definition of project in which inputs, activities and output are controllable by administrators (managerial interest) and thus, should totally be managed, while changes in a target group at the levels of project objectives are not controllable because they may be inevitably influenced by external factors.

- Value judgment based on the five evaluation criteria: Five evaluation criteria such as relevance, effectiveness, efficiency, impact and sustainability are used to evaluate the value of conducting a project from a comprehensive point of view. The evaluator examines the effects of a project as well as the appropriateness of the volume of resources for producing the effects (i.e. efficiency). The value of conducting a project would possibly decrease if it costs more than necessary even though it produced enormous effects or if effects were limited despite the fact that a large scale of inputs were used. Also, in order to judge the validity of an aid intervention, the relevance of strategies is examined as well as the sustainability of the effects after the termination of the assistance. Thus evaluating a project using the five criteria makes it possible to see the value of a project from different viewpoints and as a result, various factors that influence the success or the failure of the project can be specified, when evaluating projects, whether to assess performance or to foresee the future, perspectives will differ depending on the timing of evaluation study in operating cycle, focus of each criterion also will vary among projects.

- Make Recommendations, Learn lesson and feedback: Results of an evaluation are meaningful only when they are utilised. It is indispensable to specify the hindering or contributing factors influencing a project when making such recommendations and understanding what has been learned, for example, when the project is found to be ineffective, the hindering factors should be identified by examining both the implementation process and the causal relationship and based on those factors, recommendation or lessons learned should be proposed.

Reasons for Unutilisation of Evaluation

The reasons for unutilisation of evaluation are:

- Lack of administrators' participation and involvement in the evaluation process.
- Conflicting interest of program officials & evaluators of the program.
- Lack of emphasis on providing solution to problems, rather than accurate description of events and activities only.

Evaluation may be especially fearful when the evaluation researchers are an outsider to the organisation. Evaluation is utilized by:

- Evaluation as built in & interrelated component of program evaluation. Evaluation is ongoing & continuous.
- Both formative & summative evaluation need to be conducted by "insiders" as well as outsiders.
- Evaluation efforts should not interfere with the operations of an ongoing program. Finally, we do not maintain that every program should necessarily be evaluated. An evaluation should only be undertaken if it is expected to be worth the cost.

Criteria for Good Evaluation

Criteria such as usefulness, impartiality and independence, credibility and participation of partner countries should be satisfied in order to provide appropriate information worth being utilized, all of these are important for conducting a good evaluation.

- Usefulness: Evaluation results should be clear and useful in order to be utilized in the decision making of the organisation. The objectives of the evaluation should be made clear and for feedback to be effective, it is desirable that the evaluation should reflect the need of envisioned users.
- Impartiality and Independence: Evaluation should be impartially conducted in a neutral setting, for assuring the credibility of the evaluation information. It is indispensable to assure impartiality in providing standardized analysis of evaluation results.
- Credibility: For credible evaluation information, it is essential for evaluates to have specialized knowledge of the target fields and schemes (types of project) and also to be well informed in the scientific research methods. Such an evaluator is capable of producing credible information that is the result of an objective analysis of those factors indicating success or failure. Besides, it is important to share the evaluation process itself among stakeholders of the project, because it assures transparency. In the process, it is important to include different opinions proposed regarding lessons learned and recommendations in the report and leave it to a public verdict. Transparency is indispensable for increasing credibility with the public and it also has no small effect on how much the evaluation information is utilized.
- Participation of Partner Countries: Lessons learned and recommendations obtained by the experiences of project management are used as feedback for the development of partner countries and lead to reexamination of the project. It is necessary for evaluators to communicate with the stakeholders of both donor and recipient sides during each stage of the evaluation.

UNIDO Guidelines

United Nation Industrial Development Organisation (UNIDO) evaluation policy derives from a decision of the UNIDO industrial development board, which recognized the importance of an efficient and comprehensive evaluation system, aligned with international policies, standards and practices, for measuring the 'impact of UNIDO Work' at field level. The UNIDO Evaluation Policy complies with the norms and standards for evaluation in the UN system.

The policy has been formulated in conformity with the corporate strategy of UNIDO, the rules and regulations of the organization and its internal guidelines, in particular the technical corporate guidelines. Implementation of the UNIDO evaluation policy is effected by tools, guidelines and methodologies that are updated as appropriate. The UNIDO evaluation policy as laid down in the present document has been approved by the Director General and Executive Board of UNIDO. Evaluation is an assessment, a systematic and impartial as possible of a project, programme or entire strand of activities under a single thematic or institutional heading. Its aim at determining the relevance, impact, effectiveness, efficiency and sustainability of the interventions of UNIDO. They focus on the analysis of expected and achieved accomplishments, examining the results chain, processes, contextual factors and casualty, in order to ascertain the degree of achievement or the lack thereof.

- Evaluation serves three main purposes. It assures accountability, supports management and drives learning and innovation. It assure accountability by reporting on UNIDO activities to the governing bodies of UNIDO and the other stakeholders of UNIDO.

- Joint evaluations involving UNIDO, other UN and Multilateral organization and bilateral donors are gaining in importance as means of assessing the effectiveness of the UN system at country level.
- Project and programme evaluations are part of project cycle management as defined in the UNIDO guidelines. Through their higher more aggregate analytical content, thematic, evaluations inform UNIDO management at both the policy making and organizational effectiveness level.

Thematic evaluation provide strategic information to UNIDO management on policy making and organisational effectiveness. Thematic evaluation may cover regional, corporate or organisational issues. It is carried out at the request of UNIDO management and governing bodies. The industrial development board (IDB) is one of the Principal Policy Making organs of UNIDO. It reviews the implementation of the work programme, the regular and operational budgets and may submit recommendations to the general conference on policy matters. The director-general and the executive board of UNIDO enable the UNIDO Evaluation Group to operate effectively and with due independence.

The UNIDO Evaluation Group is responsible of or the independent evaluation function of UNIDO. It carries out different kinds of independent evaluations within UNIDO and monitors the management response to such evaluations. EVA ensures also the effective dissemination throughout UNIDO of lessons learned and the UNIDO evaluation Group is part of the Bureau for organizational strategy and learning (OSL). Its location is independent of any line management functions in the divisions involved with project/programme development and implementation. EVA staff members should not perform financial transaction outside EVA, nor should they be decision makers or chair of a decision making or appeals committee.

The UNIDO appraisal and approval bodies, ensure that programmes and project comply with established quality criteria. To this end they take prior evaluation findings and recommendations into consideration when reviewing new programmes and projects. EVA representatives advise the UNIDO appraisal and approval bodies in these matters. Project managers and team leaders contribute to due preparation, execution and follow up of evaluation and provide the evaluators with a complete information in advance of the evaluation and project manages ensures that the necessary evaluation funds are properly allocated in the project budget during the formulation phase.

The evaluation group is responsible for the independent evaluation function of UNIDO in support of lesson learning and accountability and provides a continuous feedback of insights gained from evaluation into the strategic decision making process. Evaluation is an assessment, as systematic and impartial as possible, of a programme, a project or a theme. Independent evaluation provides evidence based information that is credible, reliable and useful enabling the timely incorporation of findings, recommendations and lessons learned into the decision making processes at organisation wide programme and project level. The evaluation group cooperate closely with and supports the work of the bureau for programme design and knowledge management and also supports the implementation of results based management and monitoring in UNIDO.

Functions

- Undertake and manage independent evaluations to determine the relevance, efficiency, effectiveness, sustainability and impact of technical cooperation programmes and projects.

- Undertake and manage independent evaluations of global forum activities to determine their relevance and effectiveness.
- Monitor and track the implementation of recommendation by those in UNIDO who are responsible for the evaluated technical cooperation or global and rum activity.
- Undertake strategic and thematic evaluations on cross-programmatic or institutional issues.
- Promote continuous improvement within the organisation through the application of evaluation findings, lessons learned and recommendations in policy and programme formulation and implementation, in close cooperation with the Bureau for Programme Design and knowledge management.
- Develop evaluation guidelines as well as methodological and training tools to support managers at UNIDO headquarters and in the field with a view to ensuring that establish quality standards are met in the whole technical cooperation cycle, with particular emphasis on evaluation and results management.
- Maintain dialogue with staff at headquarter and in the field as well as stakeholders to strengthen the application of evaluation standards and ensure transparency and stakeholders participation in all stages of the evaluation process.
- Prepare reports on evaluation for submission to the policymaking organs.
- Maintain and develop partnership with UN system organisations within the contest of the United Nation Evaluation Group (UNEG) and with OECD-DAC on evaluation related work to ensure that UNIDO is fully abreast of developments in the evaluation field and able to implement good and best practices in evaluation.
- Support the implementation of a coherent and consistent-system of result based management in UNIDO.
- Support the mainstreaming of gender in technical co-operation, including development of indicators for monitoring.

Comprehensive framework for appraisal of projects and examine their desirability and merit by using different yardsticks in a stepwise manner. The desirability is examined from various angles, such as the impact on:

- Financial profitability of utilization of domestic resources.
- Savings and consumption pattern.
- Income distribution.
- Production of merit and demerit goods.

These different aspects are examined in five stages, each stage leading towards a social benefit cost of the project.

Stage 1: Measures financial profitability from detailed integrated standard analytical tables enumerating various costs and benefits at the market price and examines profit viability from investors' point of view.

Stage 2: Adjusts the financial costs and benefits to various distortions by introduced by market imperfections by valuing cost and benefits or net benefit in terms of economic efficiency or shadow price, for shadow prices, it categorizes project, inputs and outputs into traded tradable and non-tradable, for traded and tradable, the guidelines use the border prices (F.O.B./e.i.f.) as the relevant shadow prices, whereas non traded input and outputs are broken down into their components and each tradable subcomponent is valued at border prices, and so on. The residual non traded components of commodities are valued at domestic willingness to pay criterion and the labour is valued at shadow wage rate.

Stage 3: This stage designed to examine the impact of projects on saving and consumption which are of vital consideration in the choice of alternative investments in labour intensive and capital intensive projects. It saving is assigned great importance, as should be the case in capital scarce countries, this stage recommends the rate for adjustment for saving by which the social value of a respect dollar investment exceeds its consumption value.

Stage 4: This important for these countries that regard income redistribution in favour of weaker sections and backward regions as desirable objectives. The guidelines suggest weighting net benefits to various income groups or regions that reflect the judgment of politicians or the planners.

Stage 5: Finally, in stage five the UNIDO analysis suggests a methodology for necessary adjustment of the deviations in economic and social value of project output, say between good and bad or merit and demerit goods is not designed for Purists in economics who think that economics should be devoid of political or subjective judgment".

Static and Dynamic Gains from Trade

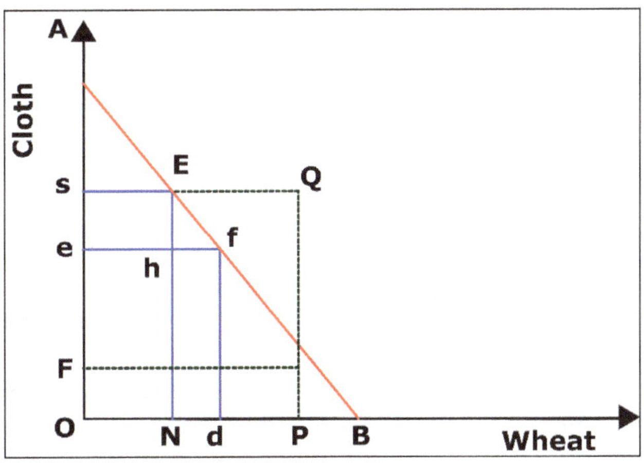

In order to explain this we make some assumptions; resources are fixed, technology is given (there is no change in technology) and nation can produce only two goods. Production possibility curve (frontier) shows all those combinations of two goods which the nation can produce by most efficiently and fully utilizing all its factors of production (resources). The curve shows the frontier beyond which production cannot be carried on with the resources and technology available to the country. Figure shows the production frontier of the nation 1 with the resources available to it, the country can produce OA amount of cloth or OB amount of wheat or it can produce combinations of wheat and cloth if the resources are used for the production of both the goods. Suppose the country choose to produce the combination given by point E then it is producing ON amount of wheat and OS amount of cloth. If it reduces the output of cloth by EL units it can increase the output of wheat by H units. A point R represents a combination of ON units of wheat and OF units of cloth. The nation is not fully utilizing its resources without decreasing the production of wheat and production of cloth can be increased because unutilized resources are available. Similarly without decreasing the production of cloth, production of wheat can be increased. Using the unutilized resources the nation can increase the production of both the goods. Production at point Q cannot take place. If the nation produces OS amount of cloth it can produce only ON amount of wheat with its resources. The production of wheat cannot be increased to OP units when the nation is already producing OS amount of cloth. Resources are not available to produce the combination shown by point Q.

Opportunity Cost

When we move from point E to F on the transformation curve, production of cloth is reduced by EH to increase the production of wheat by HF units. EH amount of cloth is the cost of producing HF amount of additional quantity of wheat. In order to produce an additional unit of wheat the nation will have to reduce the production of cloth by such an amount so that resources become available in sufficient quantity to produce an additional unit of wheat. This cost of producing an additional unit of wheat is written as Δ quantity of cloth/ Δ quantity of wheat.

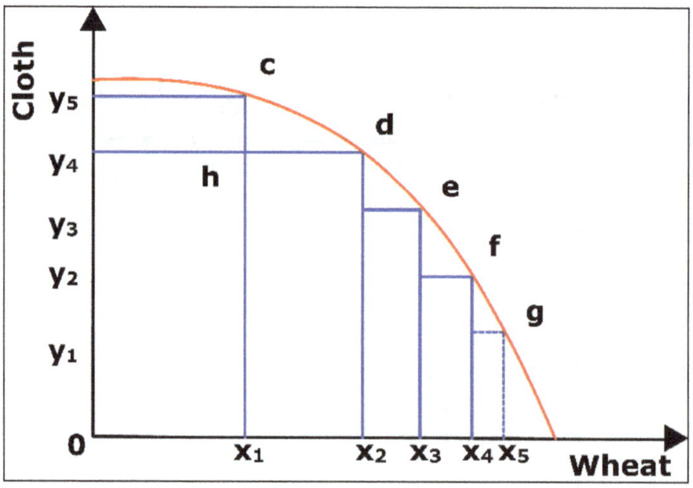

In the figure, cloth is measured on the Y axis and wheat is measured on X axis. This can be written as $\Delta Y/\Delta X$. If the increase in wheat is 1 unit then $\Delta Y/\Delta X = \Delta Y$. This ΔY is the opportunity cost of producing one unit of wheat. The opportunity cost of wheat is expressed in terms of cloth. The inverse of this ratio $\Delta Y/\Delta X$ is $1/\Delta Y/\Delta X = \Delta X/\Delta Y$ which is the opportunity cost of cloth expressed in terms of wheat. If the opportunity cost of wheat increases then the opportunity cost of cloth decreases and vice versa. In the figure production possibility frontier is a straight line $\Delta Y/\Delta X$ is the constant everywhere on this line. ($\Delta Y/\Delta X$ is also the slope of the production possibility frontier).

The slope of a straight line is constant therefore opportunity cost is constant. In order to produce an additional unit of X, ΔY unit of cloth are required to be reduced. This ratio $\Delta Y/\Delta X$ is also called the marginal rate of transformation (MRT_{XY}). Since the slope of production possibility frontier is constant, the curve shows constant opportunity cost. In real life the nations are facing increasing opportunity cost. This means the country must give more and more of one commodity to release enough resources to produce each additional unit of the commodity. Increasing opportunity cost gives us a production possibility curve which is concave to the origin. If figure the production possibility curve is AB. Suppose the economy is producing OA units of Y and zero amounts of good X. If the economy changes production from point A to point C it gives up AY_5 amount of Y and the production of X increases by OX_i. If the economy decides to produce at point D, the production of Y is decreased by Y_4 Y_5 (which is equal to Ay_5 but the of X increases only hd only. Hd is less than Y_5C. Although the nation has reduced the output of Y by the same amount as was done earlier the output of X has increased by a smaller amount. This means larger and larger quantity of good Y is required to be reduced to produce an additional unit of X. This is shown by the points d,e,f, and g on the production possibility curve. The curve shows that if the nation decreases the output of Y by the same amount every time the output of X increases at a decreasing rate (in other words output of X increases by smaller and smaller amount). In other worlds larger and larger quantity of Y is to be reduced to produce each additional unit of X. This means the opportunity cost of X is increasing. When opportunity cost of X is increasing then the opportunity cost of Y is decreasing and vice versa. This can be easily proved if our initial production point B where we are producing OB is zero amount of X and the zero amount of Y. When the economy starts increasing the output of Y the opportunity cost of Y goes on increasing (opportunity cost of X is decreasing).

The slope of production possibility curve shows the marginal rate of transformation (MRT) = $\Delta Y/\Delta X$ which shows the amount of one commodity that must be reduced so that an additional unit of other commodity can be produced. As we move from point A to point B along the production possibility curve the slope of the curve is increasing which shows the increasing cost of X. If we draw tangents at different points on the PPC curve the tangents becomes steeper and steeper (MRT is increasing). If the nation moves from point B towards point A along the curves the tangents are becoming flatter and flatter (slope is decreasing) implying that the opportunity cost of Y in terms of X is increasing. There are many reasons for increasing opportunity cost (or increasing MRT):

- Factors of production are not homogenous. All units of a factors are not identical or of some quality. Some units of labour are more efficient in the production of commodity X then in the production of commodity Y.
- Resources are not used in the same proportion in both the goods. As a result nation has to give up more of one commodity to produce an additional unit of the other good.
- The quantity of some resources may be fixed in each sectors (e.g. quantity of capital), this results in decreasing returns to the variable factor.
- There may be decreasing returns to scale in one or both sectors.

Relative Commodity Prices

The other concept that needs explanations is relative price. Relative price means rate of exchange between two goods. P_X/P_Y is the ratio of price of X and price of Y. If the price of X is \$ 10 per kg and price of Y is \$ 20 per unit then $P_X/P_Y = 10/20 = ½$. This means ½ unit of Y is equal to 1 unit of X. In other words 1 unit of X will exchange for ½ unit of Y, in the market P_X/P_Y gives the relative price of X in terms of units of Y. On the other hand $1/P_X/P_Y = P_Y/P_X$ is the relative price of Y in terms of units of X. According to our example 2 units of X will exchange for 1 unit of Y. Note that under condition of constant cost the price ratio in the nation is determined exclusively by the production or supply conditions in the nation. Demand condition does not enter into the determination of price ratio. If the nation is experiencing increasing opportunity cost of producing the goods then the price ratio is determined by demand conditions in the country. The relative price of the commodity will be higher for which demand is high. The relative price of the commodity can be shown by the figure.

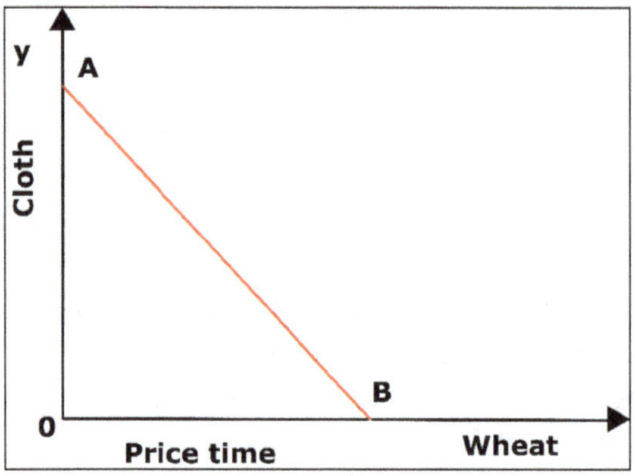

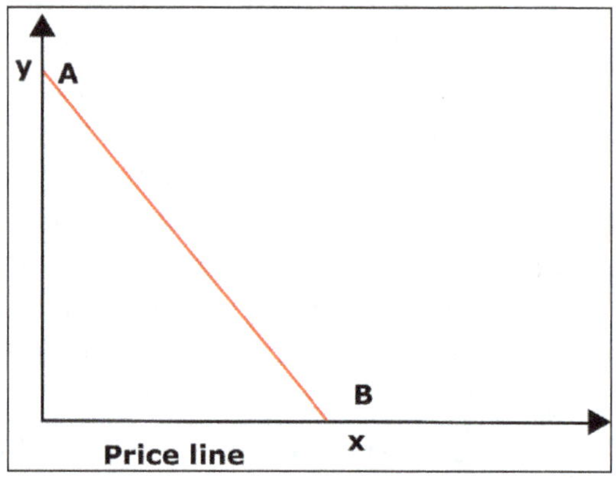

The slope of line AB in shows the relative price of X. Line AB in figure shows a lower relative price of X. When comparing the relative price of a commodity in two countries, the country in which the relative price of a commodity is lower, the lower relative price depict the comparative advantage of the country in the production of that commodity. There is another way of interpreting and finding the importance of relative price. The slope of the line AB (which can be treated as budget line or price line) shows the relative price of X when there is perfect competition in the domestic market and firms maximizes their profit, the economy will maximize its national product measured in real terms, and production will be determined uniquely by the relative prices. Let us choose a set of price arbitrarily and show how these determine the output of each commodity.

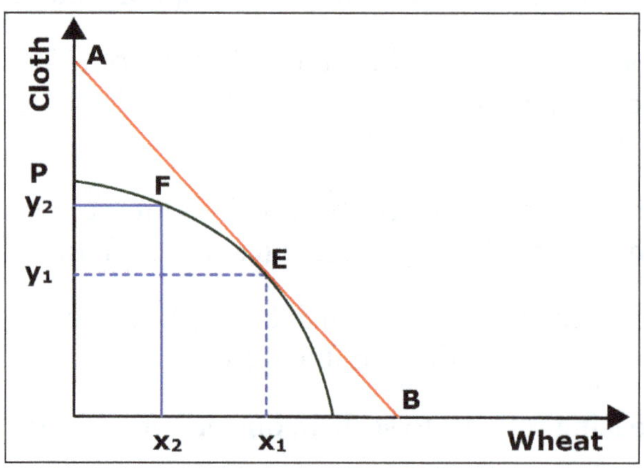

In figure we have the production possibility curve of the country PP and the price line AB. The slope of AB shows the relative price of X. The slope of price line PX/PY and slope of production possibility curve PP are equal at point E (P_X/P_Y= MRT= $\Delta Y/\Delta X$). A competitive economy will produce at point E and by doing this it will maximize its national product. We can show that distance OB (or OA) measures the national product in real terms and production at point E maximizes the national product to show this value of national product= $Q_XP_X+Q_YP_Y$

Where Q_X= quantity of X, Q_Y= quantity of Y, P_X= price of X and P_Y= price of Y. Divide both sides of equation $Q_XP_X+Q_YP_Y$ by P_Y.

Value of national product/ $P_Y = Q_X P_X/P_Y + Q_Y$.

Or national product measure in terms of Y= $Q_Y+Q_X P_X/P_Y$.

Output of Y+ output of X multiplied by relative price of X. Relative price of x is expressed in terms of units of Y. It shows the number of units of Y which are needed to purchase one unit of X. In the figure relative price of X be the slope of line AB Relative price of X= OA/OB, but in figure OA/OB= AY_1/OX_1.

When production is at point E, output of Y is equal to OY and output of X is OX1. Therefore national product measured in terms of,

$Y = OY_1+OX_1 (AY_1/OX_1) = OY_1+AY_1= OA$

Similarly, we can show that national product measured in quantity of X is equal to OB. In order to show that production at E maximizes the national product. Suppose the production takes place at point f and not at point e. The transformation curve is PP and the price line is AB. Since production takes place at point f, we draw a line parallel to AB through point f. This line is CD. If the economy produces at f then it is not maximizing national product since OD<OB (and OC<OA). At point f the slope of line CD (or relative price of X) is steeper than the slope of transformation curve. At point f the opportunity cost of X is lower than the relative price of X. It will be profitable for firms to increase the production of X and reduce the production of Y. By doing so the economy eventually reaches point E where the relative price of X is equal to the opportunity cost of X. The national product will be equal to OA. The national product is maximum when $P_X/P_Y= \Delta Y/\Delta X= MRT_{XY}$. Price line when it is tangent to production possibility curve can also be interpreted as the budget line of the nation.

Demand

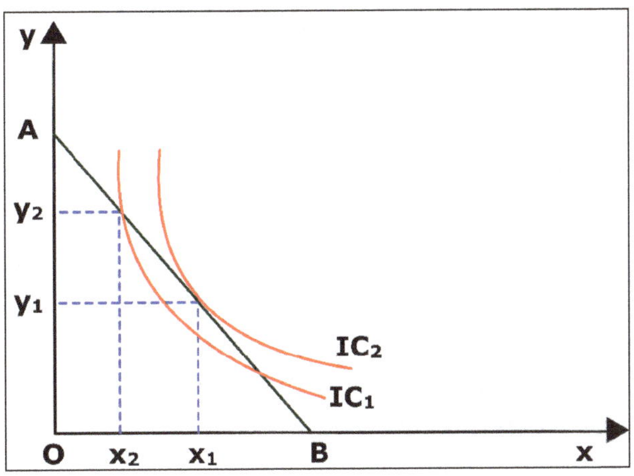

Another concept that needs discussion is demand conditions. Demand in a country consuming two goods can be described with the help of community indifference curves. Indifference curves are built from individual's indifference maps to show how individuals rank various collections of goods. To derive community indifference maps a number of assumptions are made. Without discussing them we assume that they are met. In the figure community has OB of real income measured in terms of X and the relative price of X is measured by the slope of AB.

Consumers can buy any combination of X and Y lying on ABC. Consumers will choose point in E on the indifference curve IC_2. It lies on the highest indifference curve when the constraint is depicted by line AB. The line AB shows two constraints:

- The income that consumers can spend.
- Prices at which they can buy the two goods.

Therefore, we can say that demand for two commodities is shown by point E at which $MRS_{XY} = P_X/P_Y$.

Production and Consumption Equilibrium

In a closed economy the equilibrium occurs when the two markets clear. It is at point E in the figure. In figue we have PP curve as the production possibility frontier, AB the price line and IC as the community indifference curve. At point E the slope of production possibility frontier is equal to the slope of price line (the relative price of X). When this condition is met then the national product in terms of X- output is OB. It is equal to national product in an economy where there are no indirect taxes and depreciation. The value of goods produced at point E must be equal to sum of wages, interest and profit paid to factors of production. Therefore, the line AB is the budget line. The economy will be in equilibrium at point E where the IC is tangent to the budget line. The demand for X will be OX, and equal to supply of X. The demand for Y is OY_1 and it is equal to supply of Y. There are two features of equilibrium which need attention:

- Point E can be located without knowing relative price of X in the case of a closed economy. When firms are maximizing profit and consumers are maximizing satisfaction equilibrium is established at a point where production possibility curve and indifference curves is tangent to each other. At this point MRS_{XY} is equal to MRT_{XY}. Equilibrium requires that this would happen when P_X/P_Y adjust accordingly. This is a point where demand and supply of every commodity is equal to its supply. We can infer the relative price of X (P_X/P_Y) from the slopes of two curves (PPC and price line) at the point of tangency. We can draw AB after we have found E.
- When one market clears other must also clear. When we have found the relative price that clears market for X, we have also of Y. There is only one independent market in a two goods case.

Gains from Trade

International trade leads to realization of two gains, gains from exchange and gains from specialization after the introduction of trade welfare of the economy increases due to more favourable terms of trade and because of greater specialization. This can be shown by figure given below. AB is the production possibility curve of the country. In the pre-trade situation country's output of two goods X and Y is determined at point E. The terms of trade corresponding to this situation is shown by the line P_0P_0. Here the supply of each good is equal to its demand. Demand for the two goods is determined at a point where the slope of indifference curve is equal to the price line (as terms of trade line). In other words MRSXY= P_X/P_Y.

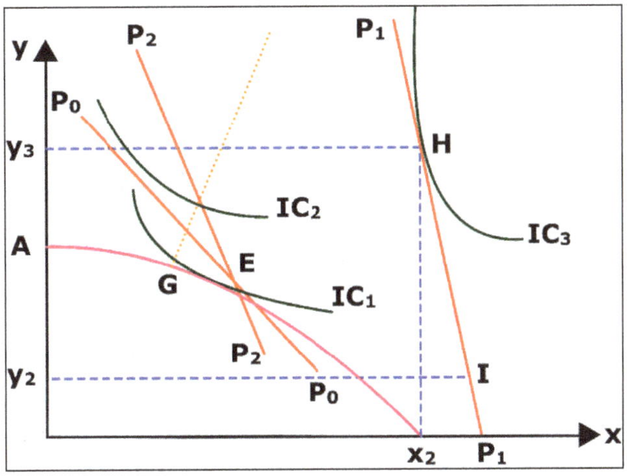

The supply of two goods is determined at a point where the opportunity cost of X expressed in terms of Y is equal to the relative price of X. In other words producers will be in equilibrium where the marginal rate of transformation of X and Y is equal to price ratio. $MRT_{XY} = P_X/P_Y$ or $\Delta Y/\Delta X = P_X/P_Y$ MRT (marginal rate of transformation) quantity of output of Y which should be reduced so that an additional unit of X can be produced. This is $\Delta Y/\Delta X$= opportunity cost of X P_X/P_Y = price of X expressed in Y. When the two are equal the producers cannot increase their profit by moving away from this point. This point determines the supply of X and Y combining producer's equilibrium and consumers equilibrium we get,

$$MRS_{XY} = (=\Delta Y/\Delta X) = P_X/P_Y = MRT(\Delta Y/\Delta X).$$

Demand and supply of both goods are equal at point E. Suppose trade opens and World terms of trade (P_X/P_Y) are given by line P_1P_1. The international price ratio is equal to the slope of line P_1P_1. This is steeper than the pre trade price line P_0P_0. The world price line is tangent to the country's production possibility curve at point J. This means the country will produce quantities of X and Y depicted by point J. In the post-trade

situation the country produces a larger amount of good X because its relative price has gone up, and smaller amount of Y. The community indifference curve IC_3 is tangent to the new price line at point H. The country's consumption of two goods (demand of two goods) is shown by combination of two goods at point H on price line P_1P_1. The consumers are demanding (buying) more of good Y than is being produced in the country. The domestic demand for commodity X is less than domestic production of X. After trade the country consumes Y shown at point H (OY_3). Although the country produces Y equal to OY_1. It consumes OX_1 of X though the domestic production is OX_2. The country exports RJ quantity of X and imports HR and Y. Demand for Y which is in excess of domestic production is met by exporting RJ of X in exchange for HR amount of Y. The satisfaction or welfare of the community is shown by indifference curve IC_3 which lies to the right of IC_1 which was the relevant curve in the pre-trade situation. This means the level of welfare of the economy has increased due to trade. We now show the gains from trade are partly due to exchange effect and partly due specialization.

Suppose after opening of economy the production in the domestic economy remains at point E. We draw a straight line parallel to P_1P_1 passing through point E. This line intersects the production possibility curve at point E. The line is P_2P_2 and its slope is equal to P_1P_1. The terms of trade are same on P_1P_1 and P_2P_2. With no change in the taste of the community there is no change in the indifference map of the community. IC_2 is tangent to P_2P_2 at point F. The economy consumes larger amount of Y and smaller amount of X compared to what it was consuming in the pre-trade situation. The economy imports FG amount of Y and exports GE amount of X. The welfare of the economy has increased because IC_2 lies to the right of IC_1. The movement of equilibrium from point E to F is due to exchange effect. The consumers are able to consume more of Y because it is cheaper to procure it from abroad. This increases this satisfaction (welfare). The country also benefits because it is able to sell X at a higher price (in terms of Y) abroad.

Production in the domestic economy will not remain at E after the trade starts; the reason is that price line (relative price of X) has changed. Relative price of X has increased (relative price of Y has fallen). At point E firms find that opportunity cost of X is less than the relative price of X. Symbolically at point E $\Delta Y/\Delta X< P_X/P_Y$. The firms increases the production of X and reduces the production of Y to maximize their profit. Increase in production of X will lead to increase in opportunity cost of X (because of the prevalence of increasing opportunity cost) and eventually it will become equal to price ratio. Firms equilibrium occurs at the point J where $\Delta Y/\Delta X= P_X/P_Y$.

The country produces OX_2 of X and OY_2 of Y. The consumer's equilibrium occurs at point H. The country imports HR amount of Y and exports RJ amount of X. The movement from point E to point J is specialization effect. The country shifts products from E to J which reflects efficient utilization of resources. In terms of welfare, the movement from point E to point F is due to exchange effect and movement from point F to point H is specialization effect. The gains from trade became available in two steps where both the steps lead to achievement of higher level of welfare by the country. The gains from exchange occur immediately after the opening of economy. The specialization effect will occur after a time gap. How long will the time lag be? It depends on many factors. It depends upon the type of goods involved, the degree of factors mobility and the type of technology used in various goods. It will also depend on stability of terms of trade.

Gains from trade are reaped by a country in the form of increase in welfare. Trade benefits both the trading partners. Trade leads to increase in relative price of the good which is low in each country. Suppose there are two countries A and B and the two countries produce two goods X and Y. Country A is more efficient in the production of X and country B is more efficient in the production of Y. This is due to resource endowments (or in other words due to comparative advantage). Prior to trade relative price of X will be low in country A (relative price of Y will be high). In country B relative price of Y is low (and relative price of X is high). After trade there is change in relative prices. Post trade relative price of X is more than the relative price of X prevailing in country A in the pre-trade situation. Similarly for country B after the starting of trade X becomes relatively cheaper. A similar argument also can be made about the relative price of Y in both the countries. Both countries reap gains from exchange and specialization.

As the countries participate in trade their relative prices change. The world relative price of a commodity will stabilize at the level when the quantity of X which the country A wishes to export is just equal to quantity of X which country B wishes to import. Similarly quantity of Y which country B wishes to export is just equal to quantity which country A wishes to import. The trade is balanced. At any other relative price there will be excess demand for one good and excess supply of the other good. This will result in change in prices of the goods. Price of one goods will increase and the price of other will fall till the equilibrium level is reached when demand for each good is equal to its supply. The relative price of a good is determined by total demand and supply of each good in the international market. Two points can be emphasized:

- Trade will take place only if the pre-trade relative prices in the two countries are different.
- After trade, incomplete specialization will occur because of increasing opportunity cost. In the post trade period also the countries will continue to produce both goods.

Gains from trade accrue to both the countries participating in trade. When the trade takes place each country specializes in the commodity which it can produce at lower opportunity cost. This means after trade resources are utilized more efficiently due to reallocation of resources guided by the needs of trade. The benefits of trade also occur due to the fact that now the country can utilize idle resources to meet the requirements of the foreigners. These changes lead to increase in the National Income, of the country. Question arises that is this growth for all or will go on in future also. If we look at the comparative advantage theory of trade we find that most of the classical economist explain the direct effect (or static gains) of trade. This means that once the economy has started participating in trade, national income will increase due to optimal allocation of resources.

Once the resources have been reallocated and the gains from trade have been realized then no more gains will occur. In this sense the comparative advantage theory of trade explains only the static gains of trade. Question arises can foreign trade have a propelling role in the development of the country? The answer is yes. Trade propels rate of economic growth directly and indirectly. There are indirect benefits of trade which continuously influence the economic growth of the country. These indirect gains are the dynamic gains of trade. These gains are significant in an economy. They affect the economy through increased utilization of plant capacity, economies of scale and export of labour intensive product. There is a multiplier effect of these developments which gives rise to increased demand for intermediate goods and increased demand for consumer goods. All these developments lead to increase in productivity in the export sector and other sectors which are directly and indirectly linked to it. Trade creates intersectoral beneficial external economies.

The gain of trade is that it leads widening of market. In most of the less developed countries the size of market is small as a result there is no incentive to investment. Trade widens the market. Plants producing for exports can be utilized to the full capacity as a result the sectors supplying inputs to export industry also benefit. There is overall improvement in economic activity. Indirectly there is a possibility of increase in saving and investment due to rise in income. Trade also provides beneficial external economies. The growth of export sector due to the widening of the market helps the country to increase the size of plant and use better technology. The new equipment may be procured from foreign countries which can be paid by using the earnings due to increase in volume of exports. The growing export sector creates beneficial external economies for other sector. There is increase in demand for inputs in the export sector, and also due to increase in national income.

Other sectors also experience increase in demand for goods needed for domestic consumption. Due to all these there is expansion of market, institutional development, organizational changes which promote economic development.

Trade provides capital goods, machinery and raw material essential for economic development. Developing countries draw lot of benefits from technical progress in developed countries through import of machines, transport equipment, equipment for power generation, machines for road building and development of railway system, medicine and chemicals. All these things play an important role in economic development of the countries. The composition of exports of developed countries has changed from textiles and light consumer goods to capital goods in the last half century. These changes are benefiting the less developed countries.

Developing countries are importing technical knowledge, capital goods, skills, managerial talent and entrepreneurship. These are important factors in economic development of a country. In the absence of trade it is not possible to get these or even know about the existence and importance of these determinants of economic development. The developing countries can profit from superior technology and managerial know-how of more advanced countries. The late comers entering the development process have always had greater advantage that they could learn from the experiences, from the success and mistakes of the forerunners. In the 20th century Japan has proved to be an expert learner. Adaptation is easier than first creation. Trade is most important vehicle for transmission of technical know-how. There is much more competition in this field than in the past. Now industrialized countries of East Asia are also experiencing this fact.

Trade acts as transmission belt for capital. Due to trade less developed countries can get capital which plays a significant role in economic development. Investment by foreigners in underdeveloped countries depends upon the willingness of foreigners. This is influenced by the policies followed in under developed countries. Larger the volume of trade, larger will be capital imports from abroad. If the volume of trade is large, transfer of interest and repayments became easier. It is much easier to get foreign direct investment for export industries with built in solution for retransfer of interest and principal. Once the process of foreign investment starts in exports sector the opportunities in other sector will also start appearing and attract foreign direct investment. Trade makes it possible for the country to borrow from abroad for capital formation. Larger the volume of trade larger will be the bargaining power of the country. Country will be able to borrow at easier terms and finance its capital formation.

Staple Theory

The staple theory of economic growth is most closely linked with the name of Harold Innis (1894–1952), a University of Toronto economist who argued that current theories failed to explain the economic evolution of countries such as Canada, which has a relative abundance of land and other natural resources. Innis's staple theory narrative, fleshed out in the 1930s and 1940s, is deeply imbedded in a detailed discourse of Canadian economic history, wherein Canadian economic evolution and development is explained through highly detailed historical analyses of the development of key commodities such as cod, furs, timber, and the transportation infrastructure which allowed for and facilitated the export of such products. The staple theory is now closely linked to export-led theories of economic growth wherein exports determine the growth process irrespective of whether these exports are raw materials or manufactured goods or services.

The staple theory has been used in efforts to explain the path and pattern of economic evolution of, for example, pre- and post confederation Canada, colonial and postcolonial United States, Australia, New Zealand, and Argentina. The staple thesis has also been applied to analyses of economies that rely on raw material exports such as cotton, cocoa, wood, oil, and sugar to drive their development process. The evidence as to whether staple exports has played and continues to play a critical and positive role in the development process is mixed. Canada, the United States, Australia, and New Zealand are nations where staples appear to have played a positive role in fostering economic development. Argentina is a classic example where staple exports have failed to foster sustained economic development. Although critics of the staple theory argue that failure of a staple economy is proof of failure of the staple theory, the staple theory was not designed to predict a particular successful course of development for regions where staple exports are important. Rather, the staple theory was developed as an analytical framework to help explain the economic evolution of economies where exports of raw materials or their processed by-products have been of some consequence, and to determine the conditions under which staple-related economic activity positively contributes to economic development.

Early Staple Theory

The staple theory was first articulated prior in 1923 by Queen's University (Canada) economist W. A. Mackintosh, who argued that explaining a nation's economic evolution requires incorporating economic and geographical factors into one's analysis, going beyond a narrative which relies largely upon individuals and politics as the main or only causal variables. Mackintosh maintained that critical to the economic development of Canada and the United States in the nineteenth and early twentieth centuries were markets for staple products and the ability of people to overcome or take advantage of geographical factors to bring the staples to these markets competitively. Staple exports drove the development process by spurring investments and consumption in other domains, outside of the staple sectors. This raises the notion of linkages, largely overlooked by Innis, but critical to later refinements of staple theory. Mackintosh acknowledges the influence of the work of U.S. scholar Guy Callender, who posits a clear connection between staples and U.S. economic development.

A critical underlying assumption of the staple theory, as articulated by Innis and Mackintosh, is that not all output is created equal with regards to their productivity-generating capacities. Exporting staple products, products that can be produced in surplus or excess relative to domestic demand potentially yields a higher per person level of output than focusing on a less export-oriented process and treating staple products like any other product. Another critical attribute of Innis's staple theory is that a region endowed with staples does not depend for its economic development upon the demand side alone that is, upon the existence of ever-growing markets for its staple products. Rather, given the demand for its staple products, the ability of a region to engage in staple exports depends upon its capacity to reduce the unit costs of its staples. This supply-side issue resides in the hands of the staple producers, and Innis pays particular attention to transportation costs as an important cost variable which staple producers can significantly affect to make their staples cost competitive, thus spurring a region's capacity to develop through staple exports. Thus, whether or not economic development is fostered by the presence of staple products depends not simply on the demand side, over which the staple producers have little effect, but also by staple producers' ability to reduce their relative production costs.

Much confusion surrounding the staple theory relates directly to the view that it is a demand-side theory wherein staple-rich regions can do little to affect their economic destinies and are largely subject to the ebbs and flows of variables over which they have little control. When staple exports depend on both the demand and supply sides, staple theory suggests that the path of economic evolution taken by a region is very much contingent upon the supply-side initiatives taken by individuals in staple-rich regions. Both the supply and the demand sides are important to an understanding of the economic evolution of staple-producing economies, with the supply side playing a preeminent role given that staple economies have the most direct control or influence over the supply side.

Recent Developments in Staple Theory

This early emphasis on the supply side, all too often ignored by critics of staple and export-led theories of economic growth and development, was reiterated and elaborated upon by Douglass North in his articulation of models of economic development and of U.S. economic history. Focusing upon the demand side paints a distorted picture of the growth process and distorts the analyses of the role, which exports play in this process. More recently Irving Kravis argued that domestic supply-side variables were of overriding importance in the determination of export-led growth in the nineteenth and twentieth centuries. The heart and soul of economic growth are internal to the economy (supply side) and relate to how the economy and its endowments are managed economically, socially, and politically. Thus, exports and trade expansion are the "handmaidens" of growth, not the true engines of the export-led growth process. Most recent empirical work reiterates the importance of the supply side to the export-led growth process causality runs from supply-side improvement to exports, not vice versa.

Of the various extensions and amendments to the staple theory, of particular importance has been the explicit introduction of linkages into analytical framework. Albert Hirschman introduced the notion of backward, forward, demand, and fiscal linkages. Backward and forward linkages relate to economic activities or industries associated with the production and servicing of the staple and to the further processing of the staple, respectively. Backward linkages refer not simply to activities related to the immediate production of the staple product, but also to the production of the infrastructure, such as transportation, necessary to make staple production economically viable. Demand linkages refer to the manner in which staple-related income is distributed and spent and how this affects the economy. Fiscal linkages relate to how government income accruing from staple production is spent. Melvin Watkins argued that key to staple theory is the extent to which staple production links positively with the rest of the economy. In other words, the extent and strength of spread effects is critically important in determining the ultimate effect of staple exports upon per-person output growth.

Douglass North pays particular heed to demand linkages with respect to what he refers to as residentiary industries in the secondary or tertiary sectors of the economy, which develop to meet the needs of the local staple-producing population. Such staple-related industries can generate cost savings or economies to other unrelated industries in the region, thereby fostering the growth of these industries and attracting new industries to the region. These non-staple industries can, in time, become export oriented given their low production costs, which are partially attributed to the development of the staple-related residentiary industries. North also finds that staple production and the economic linkages that they generate can give rise to the growth of nodal centers that are home to staple and related industries. These nodal centers can themselves become export centers not simply or even largely of staples, but of nonstaple outputs, wherein the latter's base is the staple sector. In time, a vibrant nonstaple sector may become delinked from the staple sector, fostering economic growth on its own. Thus, North further emphasizes the significance of linkages and related spread effects as critical dimension of staple theory and staple growth.

This discourse on linkages speaks directly to one of the basic critiques of staple theory, that staple exports or their growth appear to be of little or diminishing importance to so-called staple regions as a percentage of exports, output (GDP), employment, or the growth in these variables. But, as North points out, even if staple production does not dominate an economy directly, this does not mean that staple production is not the dominant force in the economy by way of its complex linkages with the rest of economy. Staple exports can be important to the growth process through their direct and indirect (linkage) effects on the economy, even if staple exports themselves constitute a small percentage of GDP.

Staple theorists including Innis have long recognized that staple economies need not prosper, and might even fall into what has been dubbed as a "staple trap." The staple trap is largely a product of economies failing to develop the potential linkages embedded in the production of staple products. This can be related to the underdevelopment of requisite economic, social, and political infrastructure. And this can be associated with a very unequal distribution of income, which biases the structure of production towards luxuries or relatively low-productivity growth industries. Thus, economic performance can be affected by forms of labor organization adopted in the staple economy for example, free labor versus slavery or serfdom, or unionized labor versus nonunionized labor. For this reason, it is possible for a staple economy to evolve into a relatively low per-capita income economy. Moreover, narrow staple economies that fail to develop linked and related residentiary industries become subject to relatively substantial and independently determined volatility determined by the ebbs and flows of the demand for staple products. But the staple trap is not an inevitable by-product of staple production; rather, it is largely a function of supply-side decisions made by decision makers within the erstwhile staple economy.

A more fundamental critique of staple theory was one put forth in the mid-1960s by Edward Chambers and Donald Gordon. It focuses on the case of Canadian growth during its wheat boom of 1896 to 1913, an era said to exemplify successful staple-led economic development and proof of the success of staple theory. Chambers and Gordon challenged the received view that staple exports played an important role in Canadian economic development. They argued that the evidence suggests that it would have made little difference to Canada's economic performance had it been completely unable to produce wheat.

Chambers's and Gordon's results were entirely assumption-driven because they measured the effect of staple exports within the framework of what they referred to as conventional economic theory. They assumed as nonexistent each and every causal connection that staple theorists either implicitly or explicitly assumed to be important. For example, staple exports are said to have no differential effect on the rate of technological change, unit production costs in other industries (related to economies of scale), or in attracting higher-productivity industries to the country. They argued that such assumptions should be applied to the analyses of any staple economy. However, the evidence suggests that linkages assumed to be nonexistent were, indeed, of considerable importance in Canada and in other successful staple economies.

To determine the importance of staples to the per-person growth process, one cannot simply assume away linkage or spread effects. Rather, determining the veracity of the causal assumptions made by staple theorists is at the heart of any determination of the role played by staple exports in the development or growth process. Moreover, proof of the analytical value of the staple theory is unrelated to the successful staple-related development. Staple theory is meant to facilitate an explanation of successful and failed staple-related development by determining the extent to which staple exports were able realize their growth potential for an economy. Success and failure are equally possible according to staple theory. However, success requires that important supply-side decisions are made within staple economies such that linkages at every level are maximized, a point made some time ago by Innis, Mackintosh, and North. Staple economies are in no way largely dependent upon the wiles of the market for their economic development. Instead, staple theory underlies the importance of human agency in the development process through the supply side, given the demand for staples and related products.

References

- Developing-country-status-in-wto: drishtiias.com, Retrieved 18, July 2020
- Wto-and-developing-countries: fpif.org, Retrieved 07, March 2020
- Dual-gap-analysis-and-foreign-exchange-economics-30268: economicsdiscussion.net, Retrieved 11, June 2020

Permissions

All chapters in this book are published with permission under the Creative Commons Attribution Share Alike License or equivalent. Every chapter published in this book has been scrutinized by our experts. Their significance has been extensively debated. The topics covered herein carry significant information for a comprehensive understanding. They may even be implemented as practical applications or may be referred to as a beginning point for further studies.

We would like to thank the editorial team for lending their expertise to make the book truly unique. They have played a crucial role in the development of this book. Without their invaluable contributions this book wouldn't have been possible. They have made vital efforts to compile up to date information on the varied aspects of this subject to make this book a valuable addition to the collection of many professionals and students.

This book was conceptualized with the vision of imparting up-to-date and integrated information in this field. To ensure the same, a matchless editorial board was set up. Every individual on the board went through rigorous rounds of assessment to prove their worth. After which they invested a large part of their time researching and compiling the most relevant data for our readers.

The editorial board has been involved in producing this book since its inception. They have spent rigorous hours researching and exploring the diverse topics which have resulted in the successful publishing of this book. They have passed on their knowledge of decades through this book. To expedite this challenging task, the publisher supported the team at every step. A small team of assistant editors was also appointed to further simplify the editing procedure and attain best results for the readers.

Apart from the editorial board, the designing team has also invested a significant amount of their time in understanding the subject and creating the most relevant covers. They scrutinized every image to scout for the most suitable representation of the subject and create an appropriate cover for the book.

The publishing team has been an ardent support to the editorial, designing and production team. Their endless efforts to recruit the best for this project, has resulted in the accomplishment of this book. They are a veteran in the field of academics and their pool of knowledge is as vast as their experience in printing. Their expertise and guidance has proved useful at every step. Their uncompromising quality standards have made this book an exceptional effort. Their encouragement from time to time has been an inspiration for everyone.

The publisher and the editorial board hope that this book will prove to be a valuable piece of knowledge for students, practitioners and scholars across the globe.

Index

A

Agricultural Production, 4, 110, 183-184

Average Product, 29-31, 110, 113

B

Balance Of Payments, 5, 137, 188, 190-191, 193, 210-211

Big Push Theory, 72, 147, 150

C

Capital Accumulation, 3-4, 17, 21-22, 52-53, 68, 74, 76, 82-88, 90, 99, 101-105, 109, 111-114, 120, 125-126, 128, 130, 141, 155-156, 161

Capital Goods, 4, 13, 17, 40-44, 66, 107, 125, 151, 153, 172, 208-212, 230

Capital Intensive Technology, 101, 104-105, 107

Capital Investment, 18, 130

Circular Causation, 16, 132

Commodity, 17, 27, 102, 129, 146, 178, 187, 190, 192, 223-224, 226-227, 229

Constant Capital, 97-98, 103, 107-108

Corruption, 7

D

Demand, 4, 7-17, 21, 25, 41, 47, 88-89, 101-102, 104, 109, 112-115, 117, 124-125, 127-128, 130-136, 139, 144-151, 154-157, 159, 165, 169-174, 178, 184-193, 224-227, 234

Depression, 7, 16, 22, 25-26, 108, 117-118

Disequilibrium, 22, 24-25, 46, 90, 137, 143, 188, 191

Dual Gap Analysis, 169, 207,209, 211

Dualism, 17, 127, 143, 145-147

E

Economic Development, 1-2, 6-7, 15, 17-18, 83-89, 101-102, 105-106, 110, 112, 116, 118, 122, 126-127, 131, 136, 139, 147, 158, 163, 165, 167, 172, 194, 198, 202, 207, 230

Economic Evolution, 230-232

Employment Growth, 23, 64, 155, 178

Entrepreneur, 84-85, 89, 99, 115-117, 119, 122-123, 142, 151

External Economies, 16, 138, 147-149, 151, 153, 229

F

Final Goods Production, 171

G

Globalisation, 175, 177-178

Growth Agents, 142

H

Homogeneous, 6, 61, 146

Human Capital, 3, 72, 74-79, 81-82, 90-92, 95-96, 129

Human Resources, 6, 201, 206

I

Incentives, 91, 140-142, 144, 150, 163, 184-185

Income Elasticity, 187-192

Input Combination, 27, 33

Intermediate Goods, 151, 169, 171, 173-175, 208, 210, 213, 229

Internal Migration, 163

International Trade, 88, 124, 127, 132, 134, 137, 151, 153, 187-188, 195, 198, 211, 226

Isoquant, 28, 161

K

Keynesian Theory, 7, 9

L

Labour Power, 6, 102-103, 114

Liberalization, 170, 174-176, 178, 199-202

M

Manufactured Goods, 5, 115, 188, 190-192, 231

Marginal Product, 17, 29-32, 35, 41-43, 48, 69-70, 72, 110, 113, 159-162

Marxian Theory, 83, 96, 100, 106

N

National Income, 2, 14-16, 21, 85, 108, 125, 140-141, 143, 150, 152, 208, 210, 229

O

Opportunity Cost, 77, 96, 164, 222-225, 227-229

P

Per-capita Savings, 50-51

Perfect Competition, 46, 89, 109, 156, 169, 224

Population Growth, 3-4, 53-54, 68, 70, 72, 74, 86, 108, 124-127, 137, 141-143, 158, 165-166, 186, 191

Production Function, 6, 18-19, 21, 27-29, 32-33, 40, 42-43, 45, 47-48, 50-51, 55, 61-62, 71-72, 74, 76, 78, 82, 90, 110-111, 120, 135, 148-149, 155

Production Possibility Curve, 223, 225-228

Profit Rate, 60, 99, 112

Project Evaluation, 215-216

Proletariat, 104
Public Investment, 175, 178
Public Utilities, 135, 138, 149

R
Recession, 7-8, 26, 100, 118, 178
Relative Price, 178, 188, 224-229

S
Separation Theorem, 92, 95
Slope, 43-44, 50-51, 60, 62, 73-74, 223-228
Smart' Cities, 203, 206
Social Climate, 121-122, 124
Social Organisation, 6
Social Overhead Capital, 130, 134-135, 138, 148-149, 151, 153
Social Welfare, 147, 157, 203
Sociological, 92, 145
Staple Economies, 232-234
Staple Theory, 230-234
Stationary State, 112-114, 128-129
Stimulants, 139-141
Supply Curve, 113, 144, 156, 159, 162, 189
Surplus Value, 97-98, 100-107

T
Technical Cooperation, 195-197, 219-220
Technical Indivisibilities, 148, 153
Technological Changes, 4, 112
The Basic Model, 40, 42, 68, 92, 164
Total Income, 12, 55, 101, 103, 107
Total Output, 41, 97-99, 104, 106-107, 111, 113, 156-157, 161, 180
Total Physical Product, 29
Total Product, 29-31, 112, 161

V
Variable Capital, 97-98, 103, 107

W
Wage Bill, 97, 106-107, 112, 121, 161-162
Wage Fund, 110, 112-113, 128

www.ingramcontent.com/pod-product-compliance
Lightning Source LLC
LaVergne TN
LVHW080738210926
848485LV00003B/575
* 9 7 8 1 6 3 9 8 9 1 6 4 1 *